HALVOR MOXNES is Professor of New Testament Studies at the University of Oslo and a member of the Norwegian Academy of Sciences and Letters. His previous books include *Constructing Early Christian Families* (1997) and *Putting Jesus in his Place: A Radical Vision of Household and Kingdom* (2003).

'In a work of stunning originality and insight, Halvor Moxnes has combined the widest learning and the deepest research to illuminate how the growth of lives of Jesus in the nineteenth century influenced and was influenced by the assertion and development of European national identities. His book is remarkably revealing on how understandings of the Holy Land featured in this process. For anyone interested in the social, economic and religious factors affecting the rise of European nationalisms, or the way in which biblical interpreters are creatures of their times and contexts, *Jesus and the Rise of Nationalism* makes compulsory and compelling reading.'

Philip F. Esler,
Principal and Professor of Biblical Interpretation,
St Mary's University College, Twickenham

'Interpreting the biblical accounts of Jesus of Nazareth always demands from the reader a number of complex analogical strategies. Our present imagination is needed in order to decode the ancient story. Hence, any vision of who Jesus was and what he proclaimed bears too the marks of our attitudes to our own world, of our ways of making sense of ourselves, of our communities, and of our universe. Halvor Moxnes critically unravels the intimate relationship between an emerging national imagination and the development of new biographical accounts of Jesus during the nineteenth century. This fascinating examination of the fusion of horizons of classical German, French and British theological appropriations of Jesus and their respective social-political hermeneutics not only offers new insights into the development of biblical studies; it also challenges contemporary interpreters of Jesus to face up to their own particular contextual premises and subjective imagination and to explore their own hidden collective agendas and projections.'

Werner G. Jeanrond,
Professor of Divinity,
University of Glasgow

'In *Jesus and the Rise of Nationalism* Halvor Moxnes has written a very welcome contribution, which reminds us that unless we take the hermeneutical context of the interpreters seriously as a first priority we miss seeing the way in which interpretative preferences have continued to influence the pictures of Jesus that emerge.'

Christopher Rowland,
Dean Ireland's Professor of the Exegesis of Holy Scripture,
University of Oxford

JESUS
AND THE RISE *of*
NATIONALISM

A New Quest for the
Nineteenth-Century
Historical Jesus

HALVOR MOXNES

I.B. TAURIS

LONDON · NEW YORK

BT
301.9
. M69
2012

Published in 2012 by I.B.Tauris & Co Ltd
6 Salem Road, London W2 4BU
175 Fifth Avenue, New York NY 10010
www.ibtauris.com

Distributed in the United States and Canada Exclusively by Palgrave Macmillan
175 Fifth Avenue, New York NY 10010

Copyright © 2012 Halvor Moxnes

The right of Halvor Moxnes to be identified as the author of this work has been asserted by him in accordance with the Copyright, Designs and Patent Act 1988.

All rights reserved. Except for brief quotations in a review, this book, or any part thereof, may not be reproduced, stored in or introduced into a retrieval system, or transmitted, in any form or by any means, electronic, mechanical, photocopying, recording or otherwise, without the prior written permission of the publisher.

ISBN: 978 1 84885 080 4

A full CIP record for this book is available from the British Library
A full CIP record is available from the Library of Congress

Library of Congress Catalog Card Number: available

Typeset in Adobe Garamond Pro by Progressus Consultant AB, Karlstad, SE
Printed and bound by CPI Group (UK) Ltd, Croydon, CRO 4YY
from camera-ready copy edited and supplied by the author

MIX
Paper from
responsible sources
FSC
www.fsc.org   FSC® C013604

In memory of Marianne Gullestad

Contents

Acknowledgements

What are the links between ideologies of nation and national movements and the nineteenth-century pictures of the historical Jesus? It has taken a long time to develop vague ideas about possible connections into a research strategy that could result in what I hope is a convincing presentation of interconnections and mutual influences.

The process that led to this book started with my previous work *Putting Jesus in His Place* (2003), which was an attempt to see Jesus in his places, namely his home and village society in Galilee, that both shaped him and that he also influenced. It was Leif Vaage of Emmanuel College at the University of Toronto who suggested that I follow up my first-century study by exploring how nineteenth-century scholars had portrayed Galilee. I realized that their descriptions of Galilee were shaped by nationalism and colonialism, and I became intrigued to see if this was also the case with the presentations of the historical Jesus. I therefore decided to study the pictures of Jesus, placed in Galilee, by four different scholars, from three different European countries.

Early inspirations for my study also came from Susannah Heschel and Shawn Kelly and their work in the area of race and anti-Judaism in nineteenth-century and early twentieth-century studies of Jesus and early Christianity. The research project 'Jesus in Cultural Complexity', supported by the Norwegian Research Council and located at the Faculty of Theology at the University of Oslo, has been most congenial. In addition to my collaborator in the project, Marianne Bjelland Kartzow, and my Oslo colleagues Oddbjørn Leirvik and Dag Thorkildsen, the project has brought together for seminars, discussions and great fun a group of younger scholars from several universities in the UK, Canada and the USA: William Arnal, Ward Blanton, Denise Buell, James Crossley, Jennifer Glancey; graduate students such as Rene Berger and Jonathan Birch; and a wider group, including some of our own Oslo master students.

This book has taken me into uncharted waters, from the New Testament and early Christianity to the nineteenth century with all its complex intellectual, political and social patterns, and with great diversity between Germany, France and England, the nations under study in this book. I could not become an expert in these areas, but my travels have taken me to universities and libraries that have facilitated this study. Friends and colleagues have shown their usual hospitality, that is to say, an extraordinary hospitality, and great interest in my topic, and they have brought together scholars from a wide range of fields for seminars and discussions of papers that I have been invited to give. Therefore, it is with a great sense of gratitude that

I mention the names of friends and institutions that have made my research possible: John Barclay and Durham University; Philip Esler and the University of St Andrews; Alan Segal and Columbia University; Birgitte Kahl, Davina Lopez and Union Theological Seminary; Wilhelm Gräb at Humboldt Universität; and Ward Blanton, Heather Walton, Werner Jeanrond, Yvonne Sherwood and Jonathan Birch and the University of Glasgow.

Finally, once more to bring a book project to completion, I ended up at Emmanuel College in Toronto, a home away from home, at the invitation of Principal Mark Toulouse. Here I enjoyed the extraordinary hospitality of Leif Vaage, both in terms of the physical space of his home and office, and even more in terms of a mental and social space with conversations about the nineteenth century, Norway and Canada, and life in general.

These acknowledgements suggest I have been like a medieval wandering student among universities, a privilege of academic life, but I have always had a home base at the Faculty of Theology at the University of Oslo, with support from colleagues and students in New Testament Studies. I am also grateful to the Faculty for granting me sabbaticals to finish the manuscript.

The libraries and librarians at the Faculty of Theology, University of Oslo and all the other institutions I have visited have been invaluable resources. Even in the age of the Internet nothing can substitute for a library where you can browse the shelves and find books that make your heart jump. Many of the chapters in this book had their beginnings as papers at meetings of societies such as the British New Testament Society, the Society of Biblical Literature (SBL), SBL international, the European Association of Biblical Studies, or as lectures at universities or seminaries such as Copenhagen, Columbia, Union, Emmanuel, Durham (UK), Humboldt, Sheffield and St Andrews.

I am especially grateful to several experts, whose works on the nineteenth-century theologians under discussion have greatly influenced this study, and who have been willing to read chapters of the book and give valuable comments (unfortunately, I have not been able to follow up on all of them): Ward Blanton, Friedrich Wilhelm Graf, Werner Jeanrond and Matthias Wolfes. It is not possible to express my gratitude to my friend and colleague Leif Vaage who in the last stages of the production of the manuscript used all the time he had (and much that he did not have) to read and reread the whole manuscript with a view to content, language and style.

Alex Wright at I.B.Tauris was the first editor to believe in the value of this project, and has supported it with insight, valuable criticism and friendship. I hope that he will be proven right in his trust in me. I am also grateful for the efficient and friendly assistance from the staff at I.B.Tauris, the copy-editor Sara Millington, and I am especially grateful to Christer Hellholm, who with great expertise produced the camera-ready copy and the indices.

A major inspiration for this study was the personal and intellectual influence of the Norwegian social anthropologist Marianne Gullestad. She brought a moral urgency to academic studies of issues such as race, ethnicity and nation. In her last works she focused especially on the hidden prejudices that spring from everyday life and influence discourses about nation and race. She died all to early in 2008. As a small token of thanks for a long friendship this book is dedicated to the memory of Marianne Gullestad.

Finally, thanks to Arnfinn J. Andersen who has lived with this book for ten years. More than that, he has kept it on track, always with insights and challenges when it was tempting to do something else, and with steady support in the emotional and physical ups and downs that have also been part of these years.

Smaller parts of Chapter V on Renan, and Chapter VI on Smith, have appeared previously as 'Renan's *Vie de Jésus* as Representation of the Orient' in Hayim Lapin and Dale B. Martin (eds), *Jews, Antiquity, and the Nineteenth-Century Imagination* and 'George Adam Smith and the Moral Geography of Galilee' in Zuleika Rodgers, Margaret Daly-Denton and Anne Fitzpatrick McKinley (eds), *A Wandering Galilean: Essays in Honour of Seán Freyne* (see Bibliography for full details). These are used by permission.

Introduction

Jesus and Modern Identities

Recently I was co-teaching a course entitled 'Jesus, Muhammad and Modern Identities'. The purpose of the course was to explore how historical presentations of the founder figures of Christianity and Islam are used to express meaning and identities in the present. The hypothesis was that historical questions like 'Who was Jesus/Muhammad?' always are related to the question 'Who am I/who are we?' Moreover, this question concerns not only religious but also social, political and national identities. When Jesus and Muhammad serve as identification figures for groups in today's societies, the way they are portrayed is of significance for contemporary issues. For instance, the question of the integration of Muslims into European societies, or the perception of and politics between the USA and Western Europe, on the one hand, and Middle Eastern countries on the other.

Jesus has often been associated with the West and identified with a Western 'we' that often is perceived to be in conflict with the 'others' – previously often identified with 'the Jews', but now increasingly with 'the Muslims'. This raises the question of the roots of this association and the nature of the larger cultural context and history of which it is a part. The roots of a Western Jesus go back to the Middle Ages, when Europe became the centre of Christianity. However, I will take up the specific configuration that this association acquired in the nineteenth century, through the confluence of two modernizing processes that started in that century: the rise of nationalism in Europe and the beginnings of historical Jesus studies.

The confluence of these two processes meant that Jesus (and Christianity) became identified with national identities and with Western colonialism and imperialism; a legacy with which we are still confronted constantly.

The Rise of Nationalism and the Historical Jesus

Nineteenth-century nationalism and the historical Jesus

The French Revolution is often taken as the starting point for political nationalism in Europe. It was indeed an earth-shaking event, evoking fears among the autocratic monarchs and their bureaucracies in the rest of the continent. But apart from the French Revolution there were other, internal, forces at work in many European states. Early nationalism represented a modernization of known forms of authority and politics, in that it aimed to transfer power from the monarchs and their bureaucracies to the people inhabiting a certain territory. These political reforms were based on philosophical discussions of the relationship between a sovereign and its people and citizenship, and on notions of peoples and their unique cultures as manifested in language, art and folklore.

Many of the most important issues of the nineteenth century converge around the ideas and politics of nations and nationalism. Politically this was a period characterized by the establishment and development of nation states combined with and supported by the expansion of colonialism and imperialism. Socially and economically the period was characterized by the Industrial Revolution and dramatic changes in the areas of work, social distinctions, families and gender. The stability of these relationships in traditional societies was shattered; discussions of the role of citizens, the relations between social classes and the structures of family, gender and public morality became issues of the character and identity of the emerging nation states.

The churches uniformly resisted these changes through their organizational structures that were part of the state apparatus, and through their teachings. Religious language is always political language, and the teaching of Christ as ruler of the church and as a model for kings and emperors in their rule of the world played a central role in supporting the status quo.

It is against this context that the beginning of historical Jesus studies – that is, the writing of the life of Jesus as a historical human being – took on a political role. By placing the historical person of Jesus in focus, such studies took away authority from the dogmatic teaching about Christ in the church and challenged the Christological legitimatization of the political authority of monarchs and rulers.

The impact of these early nineteenth-century works, which might be collectively referred to as the 'Lives of Jesus', was very much a result of their form, being both foreign and familiar. They were written in the genre of biography, which was foreign to traditional dogmatic writings on the Christology of the church but familiar in that it described Jesus as a human person in social contexts with which readers could identify. Moreover, the Lives of Jesus placed him in a geographical location, Palestine, which was described in terms of a country and a people that made up a nation – that is, in terms of categories that were part of the ongoing discussion about nations and nationalism. Thus, presentations of the historical Jesus and his relations with his household and family, with the Jewish people, with the political powers in Roman Palestine and his proclamation of the Kingdom of God brought up for discussion key social and political issues of nineteenth-century societies.

Furthermore, the quest for the historical Jesus was part of the nineteenth-century search for *origins*, not just of Darwin's species but of European societies; for the beginnings of that process of development represented by these societies, which was the sign of God's providence in history. Despite growing criticism of religion, religious beliefs were still important, and the human Jesus was presented as a model for humanity, as the providential beginning of history.

It is here that I see intersections between the ideas and ideologies of nations and presentations of the historical Jesus. The goal of this book is therefore to explore how nineteenth-century constructions of the historical Jesus contributed to national projects at different stages of development and in different geographical locations. I am looking primarily at the *cultural meaning* that is created through these texts about Jesus; I am not exploring the social and political practices that the books generated or in which their authors participated.

This study of the role of the historical Jesus in national imaginaries of the nineteenth century is not undertaken merely out of historical curiosity. It is also an investigation into the religious roots of ideas about the nation and nationalism that continue to exert strong influence in contemporary politics. They are part of a heritage where the nation state as a model for sovereignty is presented as a 'natural' fact and taken for granted as being the way the world has always been. But this is a problematic heritage. In many areas, nationalism has been a success story of freedom and democracy, but it has also been a story of conflicts, wars and ethnic cleansing. Furthermore, a world divided into nation states has been singularly unable to deal with the global challenges of today.

The nineteenth-century studies of the historical Jesus take us back to a period when statehood based on the idea of the nation was not a given fact, but something still under discussion. Present studies of the historical Jesus do not seem to be aware of their relevance for ideas of nationhood and nationality. Nineteenth-century pictures of Jesus are therefore of particular interest because they represent the imaginations of societies under construction. I find their national imaginaries partly outdated, but not the act of imagining itself as an action for creating a possible future. The nineteenth-century studies of the historical Jesus challenge today's scholars to become aware of the political implications of our constructions of Jesus and Jesus' Palestine. In light of the present situation of the world, I also think that in our constructions we are challenged to move beyond the imagination of the nation, to a post-national world order.

The Lives of Jesus in national contexts

This book is an exploratory study, not an attempt to write a full history of the nineteenth-century Lives of Jesus. My goal is to take exemplary cases that together will reveal how national imaginaries were expressed through narratives of Jesus, which allows for an interaction with various forms and stages of nationalism in Europe at that time. For this purpose, I have chosen works on the historical Jesus by four scholars from different parts of Europe who between them represent the beginning, the middle and the last period of the nineteenth century.

My first examples are taken from the region that in the course of the nineteenth century became the German Empire under the leadership of Prussia. Germany is a special case since in contrast to France and England it did not exist as a unified state at the beginning of the nineteenth century; therefore the intellectual discussion about a nation preceded unification into one state. With his lectures on *The Life of Jesus* (1819–32),[1] Friedrich Schleiermacher represents the early phase of this intellectual discussion of German nationalism. *The Life of Jesus, Critically Examined* (1835–6)[2] by David Friedrich Strauss influenced an early phase of popular nationalism in Germany, while his later book, *The Life of Jesus for the German People* (1864),[3] reflects the influence of state nationalism in a later phase leading up to Bismarck's Germany.

The third example is Ernest Renan's famous (or infamous) *Life of Jesus* from 1863.[4] Written from a French perspective, Renan's book expresses nationalism in the context of empire and Orientalism; the construction of the Orient as the 'Other' serves as a negative mirror image of the nation.

Finally, towards the end of the nineteenth century George Adam Smith's portrayal of Jesus in Galilee in his *Historical Geography of the Holy Land* (1894)[5] interacts with ideals of family, class and masculinity as expressions of 'national character' in Victorian Britain, an empire with great social conflicts at home.

These four authors represent three diverse political, cultural and religious contexts within Europe in the nineteenth century. The varieties of nationalism they represent have had significant influences on the development of national identities and ideologies in Europe in the late nineteenth century and throughout the twentieth century. Their patterns of constructing Jesus in relation to people, land and gender roles have been accepted as 'natural' structures wherever Jesus and early Christianity have served as models for society.

Beyond Schweitzer's Account of the Quest for the Historical Jesus

Re-reading Schweitzer

This book suggests a new way to look at historical Jesus studies from the nineteenth century by considering them in their cultural and political contexts of developing nations, instead of viewing them within the confines of the development of a literary–historical discipline, the so-called 'Quest for the historical Jesus'.

Most references to nineteenth-century Jesus studies build on Albert Schweitzer's review of these studies in his *The Quest of the Historical Jesus* from 1906/1913.[6] Schweitzer's criticism of the Jesus scholarship of liberal theology labelled its picture of Jesus a mirror image of its own society, and claimed that it therefore did not have any historical value. In contrast Schweitzer presented his picture of an apocalyptic Jesus, reflecting Jewish expectations of the time and utterly foreign to the modern world. Schweitzer's *The Quest of the Historical Jesus* has had an enormous influence on later studies of the historical Jesus. Among the received truths of New Testament scholarship is that it closed an era of historical Jesus scholarship, the so-called 'First Quest', and that it set the stage for Jesus scholarship in the twentieth century with historical objectivity as its unquestioned goal. Schweitzer's verdict on Jesus scholarship of the nineteenth century was generally accepted. In consequence, these studies were no longer read and, more importantly, Schweitzer's own presuppositions for his judgements were not questioned.

It is surprising that there has been relatively little discussion of Schweitzer and his own cultural and philosophical presuppositions when he gave such critical evaluations of the presuppositions of earlier generations. Recently, however, Ward Blanton has given an incisive critical reading of Schweitzer's *Quest of the Historical Jesus* in light of his works on cultural philosophy with their criticism of the modern worldview as a moral failure.[7] In *Quest of the Historical Jesus* this worldview is represented by the failure of liberal scholarship on the historical Jesus. In designing his history of this scholarship Schweitzer had to find an organizing principle that could help him to 'bring order into chaos'. Not surprisingly, the principle he introduces as the underlying 'logical question' is their position in variation to his own answer to that question, namely, the eschatological approach to the historical Jesus. Blanton finds that Schweitzer establishes eschatology as a model by which, retroactively, all the former answers are evaluated. Thus, Schweitzer's history of nineteenth-century scholarship amounts to a deconstruction of the legitimacy of that history.

Schweitzer's criticism of Schleiermacher's *Life of Jesus* is an example of how Schweitzer works from the viewpoint of a later position in order to deconstruct a previous work.[8] Schweitzer poses his criterion as 'either-or'; for instance, Jesus' miracles are either historical or supernatural. Measured against such a position, Schleiermacher's dialectics, deliberating between these two extreme positions, is faulted as showing that Schleiermacher had an unhistorical mind. Measured by another 'either-or', this time the Synoptic Gospels or John's Gospel as the primary source for a life of Jesus, Schleiermacher's choice of John is criticized on the basis of the later work of Strauss, which destroyed the Johannine hypothesis.

Strauss is the first hero of Schweitzer's history,[9] representing much of the critical historical acumen that Schweitzer shared. Schweitzer has high praise for Strauss' *Life of Jesus* which 'solved' the problem of the historicity of Jesus' miracles (which had been the main historical problem before Strauss) by assigning these stories to myth. However, Schweitzer was much more reserved towards Strauss' later *Life of Jesus for the German People*,[10] seeing it as retreating from many of the critical positions of his first *Life of Jesus*. Moreover, it was not written in an engaging style that could catch the attention of a popular readership.

Schweitzer accords praise to Renan's *Life of Jesus* for being written in an engaging literary style, although that was the end of his praise in what otherwise amounts to a literary execution of a work and its author. Renan's book was one of the few studies written by a non-German author that Schweitzer included in his review.[11] Schweitzer describes it as a work of literary kitsch, full of bad taste,[12] claiming it was written not as a serious history but as a theatrical play in three acts. His most serious criticism is a direct attack upon Renan as a person, that he lacks conscience and that his work is one of insincerity.

Schweitzer does not relate his criticism of the works of Schleiermacher, Strauss and Renan to the question of the nation of their day. Nevertheless, in another sense Schweitzer does place historical Jesus scholarship in a national context.[13] In the very first paragraph of *The Quest of the Historical Jesus* he states that the critical investigation of the life of Jesus is the greatest achievement of German theology; it is a result of the 'German temperament'. It is only here one can find the combination 'of philosophical thought, critical acumen, historical insight, and religious feeling'.[14] Schweitzer's statement is one more example of a long tradition of ascribing typical characteristics to nations,[15] but is more than that; it makes the critical investigation of the life of Jesus a special responsibility for Germans. In the end, Schweitzer finds that even in its failure the result of German research into the life of Jesus is 'a uniquely great expression of truthfulness'. This becomes evident when he compares the works of the German modern liberal scholars with 'the literature and social culture of the Latin nations'.[16]

Therefore, the fact that the history of this investigation in the nineteenth century ended in failure is also a failure of the national project. That Schweitzer's own answer, the eschatological Jesus of Jewish apocalypticism, was in a sense also a failure has escaped the attention of his followers who over more than a hundred years have hailed it as *the* solution. But an eschatological historical Jesus who is so foreign to this world that he returns to his own time represents a collapse of Schweitzer's own project, since it cannot respond to the enduring need for a Jesus who can give meaning to the world.[17]

This is a situation Schweitzer cannot live with. Here Schweitzer as a historical scholar is confronted by his own moral imperatives; the collapse of the liberal Jesus scholarship is part of a larger collapse of modernity as a moral culture. In a criticism of Germany that Schweitzer later made much more explicit as a criticism of nationalistic ideologies, he states: 'Our religion no longer has as its great aim the final moral consummation of all mankind, and is hemmed in by its preoccupation with national and confessional ideas instead of directing its gaze outwards on the world.'[18] The way to regain a moral culture is via 'a living relationship with Jesus', which consists in thinking 'ethically and eschatologically', dominated by Jesus' conceptions of the kingdom of God.[19]

This is not the historical Jesus, however; for Schweitzer there is no way to proceed from the historical eschatological Jesus to the present. For Schweitzer the only Jesus that exists in the present is not the historical Jesus, but intuitively the Jesus of the Gospels. His authority is transmitted not by 'understanding' or by 'historical observation', but by becoming 'united with Jesus in a mystical relationship'.[20] An irrelevant historical Jesus and the moral authority of a Jesus encountered in a mystical relationship seems to be a very different heritage to the one traditionally passed on in the name of Schweitzer as the triumph of objective historical Jesus scholarship versus the subjective pictures of Jesus held by liberal nineteenth-century scholars.

New readings of the historical Jesus

To see that Schweitzer has left behind an example of a struggle more than a solution to the quest for the historical Jesus (i.e. an unsatisfactory attempt at a response to a question that remains urgent) may be his most important legacy. This result should also make us more intrigued by the question of the nineteenth-century scholars: what was required for writing a life of Jesus that would make sense in the modern world?

There are now many studies of the historical Jesus that engage with contemporary questions of identities in terms of race, gender and specific social locations. Being conscious of the role that the placement of a reading plays, this study shares approaches with recent contextual studies of Jesus, for example the African Jesus, the Asian faces of Jesus, and the images of a Latin-American Jesus.[21] These studies are contextual in that they explicitly place presentations of Jesus in a specific geographical and social location, and in their interpretation they interact with contemporary issues of identity, tradition and culture.[22] In this way they represent a critical 'talking back' to Jesus studies written from the often taken-for-granted hegemonic positions of white male Europeans and North-Americans.

Feminist studies likewise combine a critical perspective on mainstream and male Jesus studies with a constructive interaction with contemporary theories of gender and identities. In *Jesus and the Politics of Interpretation*[23] Elisabeth Schüssler Fiorenza shows how many male images of the historical Jesus are constructed on the bases of contemporary models of anthropology and sociology that present, for instance, patriarchal household structures as historical 'facts'. Schüssler Fiorenza suggests the possibility of other structures with the help of models of egalitarian communities *and* social movements of change. An important side result of the studies by Schüssler Fiorenza and other feminist scholars is that they make clear that *all* presentations of the historical Jesus are based on modern theories of human identities, social relations, locality and society.[24]

An engagement with the philosophical and ideological contexts of nineteenth-century European presentations of Jesus and the beginnings of Christianity represents a similar trend; these were historical studies but with an eye to the contemporary relevance of such studies. With *Racializing Jesus*,[25] Shawn Kelley has investigated how nineteenth-century ideas of race have influenced the structure of thought in biblical scholarship, despite its rejection of racism at a conscious and political level. Related to the ideology of race, Susannah Heschel has traced the nineteenth-century ideological roots of anti-Semitism in her thorough research of Jesus studies in Nazi Germany, in *The Aryan Jesus*.[26] Ward Blanton's *Displacing Christian Origins*[27] brings to life the largely forgotten discussion between philosophers and theologians about the role of Christian origins in understanding contemporary society through an interaction with modern philosophers concerned with similar issues. The present book will supplement these studies with an exploration of nineteenth-century Jesus studies and their interaction with the growth of nationalism and expressions of national identity in European societies, aiming to raise awareness of nationalism as a basic presupposition underlying modern Jesus studies.

The Historical Jesus and Discourses of Nationalism

When I started reading the historical Jesus books of the nineteenth century I was struck by how they were presented as *biographies*, and how that choice of genre obviously was of great importance to the authors. Biographies usually place the individual in a social context, and my interest was in how these biographies imagined nation and national identities as the context for Jesus.

Since the concept of 'nation' is highly contested, it is necessary to discuss how I will use it in this book, as well as to describe the three main components that are central to the construction of a nation. These components are, first, the idea that a nation is made up of *a people*; second, that is has a fixed *territory*; and third, that national identities are associated with a set of values and social mores, especially expressed through ideals of *family, sexuality and gender roles*.

What is it to write a biography?

It was Schleiermacher who introduced the term 'biography' to characterize his lectures on the historical Jesus, and questions about the form and functions of biographies bring us into the larger social context of presentations of the historical Jesus in nineteenth-century Europe. First, since a biography was of a genre used to describe human beings, a biography of Jesus was viewed as a break with dogmatic Christology. The shift from dogmatic presentations of Christ to a biography of the historical, human Jesus was a seismic shift in religious and political symbolism; from Christ as a celestial symbol of the church and the monarch to Jesus as a critical symbol of individuals and a people.

By choosing biography as a medium to present Jesus, the nineteenth-century authors chose a popular genre that aimed not just to entertain, but also to provide life models for its readers: 'In this genre the individual came to be presented as a morally autonomous subject capable of shaping himself (rarely herself) and the world.'[28] Most readers belonged to the bourgeoisie and recognized the biography as a distinctive bourgeois practice. Biographies did not just report on a life; they presented an argument for seeing this life in certain way.[29] For instance, the way they praised the virtues of the emerging middle class challenged those that were associated with the more traditional structures of privilege, and thus they claimed for the bourgeoisie a recognized place in society. In this way biographies participated in claiming and creating a place in the nation for individual citizens.

There was one particular sub-genre of biography that provided a model for the Lives of Jesus and that was the biography of 'the great man'. This was a model with its roots in biographies from Antiquity; but the concept of the 'great man' or 'hero' was central to nineteenth-century ideas of progress and the role of significant individuals in shaping history. Thus, the genre of biography made it possible to write of Jesus as a human being, but at the same to assign to him a special role in history, especially in the history of nations.

What is a nation?

The nationalist discourse has been so successful at imposing itself that it has suppressed alternative forms of political thinking and it presents itself as the 'natural' way of doing politics and of understanding the world.[30] Therefore 'nation' and 'nation states' are so easily taken for granted, being presumed as something everybody knows. That makes it easy to think that it must always have been like that; nations must surely have always been part of how the world has been organized. However, most likely this is not the case. Many historians will argue that even if states have existed for a long time, they were not built on the self-understanding of being nations. In this view, nations are a much more recent development. These two positions cannot easily be reconciled, and therefore there is a wide and sometimes confrontational discussion of what constitutes nations and nationalism.

In the texts from the nineteenth century that form the basis for this book there are no fixed or absolute definitions of what a nation 'is'; rather, there are ideas, imaginations and discussions. (A central text is the famous address by Renan from 1882, 'What is a nation?'[31]) Therefore, for the purpose of this study, I do not consider nation and nationalism to be 'natural' categories. The history of nationalism is, on the one hand, a history of social and political movements and practices to create or reform nation states. The history of Europe in the nineteenth century can to a large extent be written from this perspective. This is not the interest of this book, even if I do attempt to locate the authors I discuss within their political context.

The other side of the terms 'nation' and 'nationalism' is their cultural meanings, their roots in tradition and how they are expressed as identity categories through normative forms of social roles, values, gender roles, education and so on. It is with an interest in how these cultural meanings are shaped, upheld and challenged that I will look for intersections between them and nineteenth-century Jesus studies.

My perspective on nation is inspired by recent studies by John Breuilly and Benedict Anderson on the cultural meaning of nationalism, which emphasize its character as constructed or 'imagined'.[32] This perspective is linked to the means that are used to construct or imagine nations. In this study, the focus will be upon the role of discourse and texts. In these texts, 'nationalism' is a fluid rather than a fixed concept; it is always determined by its context and its relations.

It may be too rigid to assert that 'Nationalism is a doctrine invented in Europe at the beginning of the nineteenth century.'[33] 'Invented' may suggest a sudden invention, rather than a process of evolution, and the fixation in time may overlook aspects of growth and possible roots. But the suggestion indicates that nationalism was a movement arising in a particular time, when specific situations and political and social problems demanded new solutions.[34] Rather than focusing on specific events, such as the American and French revolutions, Breuilly sees nationalism arising in times with a heavy rate of modernization that demanded new solutions where 'appeals to tradition no longer carried conviction and one had to construct images of the future which were not forward projections of one's understanding of the past.' These changes made it impossible to continue to 'appeal to religious or dynastic or customary justification for authority'.[35] New social imaginaries were called for in such situations.

In most instances, political changes are prepared through new ideas and thoughts, often starting with the intellectual elite in the form of a new *discourse*.[36] Germany serves as an example of how the cultural elite (as distinct from the political elite) had a significant place within nationalism, especially in the initial phase. Friedrich Schleiermacher represents this early stage of nationalism. However, in Germany, in a relatively short period of time (from the beginning of the nineteenth century to the middle and later third of the same century), national imagery was accepted by the majority and arrived at the centre of political discussion. Finally it became the basis of the state as a 'nation state', and the political authorities made use of the idea of nationalism to legitimize its power and to defend the nation state against internal and external threats.[37] In the course of his career, with his various studies of Jesus, David Friedrich Strauss spanned all the stages of German nationalism. He starts out at the end of the early stage, and with his last books prefigures Bismarck's authoritarian nation state.

England and France, on the other hand, were 'state nations' in the sense that the state was established before the rise of nationalism. In Britain the nineteenth century was the period when a common, national identity was forged (although this process had started already in the eighteenth century). In France, the French Revolution was the starting point for understanding the state as a nation. Ernest Renan was an important participant in discussions of the principles of defining a nation, explicitly voicing a French position based on a common history and a commitment to a common future, *vis-à-vis* a German position based on race and descent. In Britain, the question of national identity seemed to be most explicitly associated with the question of national 'character', which in George Adam Smith's writings was expressed in terms of a moral, manly character.

Although the ideas and understandings of nation clearly varied in different European countries, there were some basic components: a nation comprised of a people, based in a territory and with a number of shared institutions and values. Nevertheless in these areas, too, there were no fixed meanings.

What is a people?

Today, ethno-nationalism is the dominant ideology of the state; it builds on the idea that a people is defined by ethnicity, and that a coherent ethnic group makes up a nation. Moreover, it is often taken for granted that every nation should have its own state. This understanding is so commonly accepted that it is not easy to argue that it is an example of ideological construction.

The relationship between 'nation' and 'people' has always been complex. A couple of examples may show the fluidity of the concepts at the beginning of the nineteenth century. Back in the eighteenth century, various languages had words that were similar to the modern term 'people', for example *Volk, peuple, popolo*. However, they were used in a pejorative sense with the meaning of 'the great mass of the population' or 'common people'.[38] Two instances illustrate how this meaning could be changed in distinctively different ways in France and in Germany, with a lasting influence on the understanding of politics and nation.

In the events leading up to the French Revolution in 1789, a young priest, Emmanuel Sieyès, wrote a pamphlet titled 'The Third Estate, What is that?'[39] Here he argued that it was the Third Estate, the non-noble part of the population, which constituted French society; the First and Second estate (the clergy and nobility) did not form part of the French population but lived off the people. When Louis XVI dissolved a gathering of the Three Estates that had been assembled for the first time in 150 years to discuss the economic crisis of France, the Third Estate refused to leave. Instead, it took the name *Assemblée nationale* so that in its battle with the King it used the word 'nation' for the Third Estate. In this way 'nation' became defined as consisting of citizens who made up a people in contrast to their former status as subjects under a monarch.

The idea of a nation made up of free citizens was developed in the famous lecture by Ernest Renan from 1882, 'What is a nation?'[40] Renan is generally taken to represent a French way of speaking about a nation, linked to a common political history and loyalty to the constitution, and he himself presents his views in clear distinction from what he sees as a German position, based on a common language and even race.

At about the same time as Sieyès in the late eighteenth century, J. G. Herder redefined the meaning of the German *Volk* from 'common people' to a community of people that was constituted through a common language and culture with its roots in the folklore, traditions and customs of the lower classes.[41] This made up the national identity that was unique for each nation and defined through its difference from other nations. In a lecture pointedly called 'What is a people?',[42] Jürgen Habermas analyses how German scholars in the humanities in an assembly in 1846 discussed this question.[43] They were inspired by the universalizing principles of popular sovereignty from the French Revolution in 1789 but they struggled with how these could find a form 'in a political environment defined by "the nation" as the expression of a people with a pre-political, organic form of shared identity rooted in place, descent and language'; that is, in an understanding inspired by Herder.[44]

It is within these discussions of 'people' and 'nations' that our authors of the Lives of Jesus present Jesus in his context of a Jewish people and Palestine; we shall therefore expect to find the differing positions reflected in their presentations.

Localised identities and national territories

Studies of the historical Jesus and of nationalism are held together by the importance of place or locality. This perspective has not been given sufficient attention in earlier studies of individual identities. Most studies have discussed personal identity in terms of time and social context, but the significance of place has only recently come into view. In one sense we may speak of a recurrence of interest, because in the nineteenth century the relationship between place in terms of geography, nature and human beings was a topic of great interest. Therefore the question of the place of Jesus was significant for the specific character that was attributed to Jesus in the biographies of Jesus under study in this book.

In the Lives of Jesus the geographical places in Palestine, and Jesus' location at home, in a village or Galilee, were considered important; they were part of his identity and mission. Moreover, they presented similarities to the readers' own locations and made possible identification with Jesus both on a local and on a national level.

The importance of place for identity on an individual level corresponds to the importance of territory for the identity of nations. Territory makes the nation seem 'natural'.[45] In the Napoleonic period, the German elite combined their struggle for constitutionalism with the more ancient idea of the *national territory*: 'The national territory (i.e. territory of the nation) became the "natural" as well as institutionalized space within which the constitutional project could be realized.'[46] In addition, since territory was an important part of the definition of nation, borders and boundaries served to create distinctions, to distinguish both geographically and socially between 'us' and 'others'. Finally, the importance of landscape as bearer of memory is still another aspect of the grounding of the nation in territory.[47]

Territory and landscape as integral to the idea of nation takes on special significance in the presentations of Jesus in Galilee and Palestine. In *Putting Jesus in His Place*[48] I investigated the importance of place to a discussion of Jesus and his identity. I found that with the so-called Third Quest Galilee and its relationship to Jerusalem and Judea have returned as a hotly debated issue in contemporary Jesus scholarship with political implications for national identities.[49] It was these discussions that brought me back to the beginnings of historical Jesus scholarship to trace the role of Galilee in that period and how it has been constructed by subsequent scholars.[50]

The material under discussion from nineteenth-century Jesus scholars is primarily drawn from their presentation of Jesus' situation in Galilee, both in the context of his family and hometown of Nazareth and in the larger region of Galilee and its relations to Judea and Jerusalem. The description of Jesus in a specific geographical territory with a history of differing political structures within the larger area of Palestine suggested parallels with the situation in Europe.

Sexuality and gender as national identity markers

From a European perspective one of the differences between Europe and the USA is the role that family values, sexuality and in particular homosexuality plays in discussions of American national values. However, the difference may be more in the intensity with which these issues are discussed, and the explicitly national nature of the discussions, which brings out into the open issues that traditionally have been associated with national identities.

There is more to national identity than people and territory. It is often the content of this 'more' that is in the focus of discussions about what it is it to be British, or French, for example. What exactly '*this*' is mostly belongs to category of that which is taken for granted in a culture; perceptions that do not need to be discussed, only stated. These are views that may be shared by many people, sometimes discussed by scholars of the period, but not necessarily under a rubric of 'nation' or 'nationalism'. It is mostly from the outside, at a distance, that texts can be read with 'hidden' references to nation and national characteristics. In the area of behaviour, morals and manners such taken-for-granted assumptions may be expressed, for instance, by terms such as 'nice', 'proper', or 'respectable'. In an innovative study of nineteenth-century culture, *Nationalism and Sexuality*,[51] George Mosse traces the relationship between nationalism and the notion of respectability in relation to sexuality and gender.

Since nationality is a relational term based upon systems of difference and hierarchies, other identities that likewise are associated with differences and hierarchies are used to express ideas about nation; especially family, sexuality, gender and race.[52]

This is a point where the genre of the Lives as Jesus, as biographies of 'the great man', and his perceived place in a national context come together in the issue of the masculinity of Jesus. Feminist and post-colonial criticism of nineteenth-century Jesus studies point out that these studies are all written from a male perspective to support European male hegemony over women and over the colonized parts of empires. Therefore, one of the questions to raise is how Jesus as a national character embodies masculinity, or rather, what type of masculinity he embodies. The nineteenth century saw many changes in masculinities, and competing interpretations of masculinity within nations, related to conflicting positions on issues of national politics like citizenship and authority.[53]

How to Read this Book

The first two chapters of this book introduce the methods and main topics that serve to bind together the studies that follow. The common genre of biography and the significance of 'holy land' and 'homeland' as places for national identities present the main questions that are discussed in Chapters III–VI.

Chapter I uses Schleiermacher's question 'What is it to write a biography?' to explore the wider context of historical Jesus studies in biographical writings of the nineteenth century. It traces the underlying anthropological model for the presentation of Jesus in the popular genre of biographies of 'great men' and the discussions of the role of individuals in shaping history and influencing nations.

Chapter II explores the fascination with 'the Holy Land' in the nineteenth century and its significance as the land of Jesus. By combining the concept of Holy Land with 'homeland' I try to trace the special character of the relation between the two 'lands' that seems to suggest an identification between the two and a blurring of conceptual boundaries. The Holy Land was not a stable category, however; at the same time as it was identified as homeland, there were experiences of foreignness and distance. The discussion of Jesus' relationship to places, especially Galilee and Jerusalem, provides an entry point to the following chapters, which study how the various authors work out the parallels between the Holy Land and their own homelands.

The purpose of the chapters that follow is to study the discourses about the historical Jesus in the different writings with respect to how they portray Jesus as a 'national figure', and how Palestine and Galilee are used as localized metaphors for contemporary issues of nation and national identities. In some instances, especially with Schleiermacher and Strauss, source criticism of the Gospels play a part in their constructions of a biography of Jesus and his national context.

Schleiermacher's lectures on the historical Jesus (Chapter III) present an imagination of 'the Jewish land' as a nation, parallel to the political situation of his time, with many small principalities but no German state corresponding to the idea of a German nation. He is the only one of our authors who does not place Jesus in Galilee; he uses John's Gospel as his source, which shows Jesus travelling around the country. However, Schleiermacher's main reason appears to emanate from national concerns; Jesus' mission was directed at 'all the people' and 'all the land'. Two main models underlie the picture of Jesus: namely, the king not being distant from but in a relationship with his people, and the teacher as an important figure in the democratic national movement in Germany.

David Friedrich Strauss and his various theologically and politically different presentations of Jesus from 1835–6 to 1872 (Chapter IV) reflect the fortunes of nationalism in Germany, from the early democratic movement to its cooptation by Prussia under Bismarck and the establishment of a Prussian German Empire after the Prussian–French war. Strauss' radical criticism of the possibility of writing a Life of Jesus in his first *Life of Jesus Critically Examined* (1835–6), placing the divine incarnation in humanity, was widely read as a radical and democratic criticism of the state. But his theological radicalism was not matched with corresponding political views. He presented a more conservative view on the possibility of writing a Life of Jesus in the third edition of the book, before he finally returned to his radical position in the fourth edition. He criticized Schleiermacher's biography for not being critical enough, but wrote himself a rather traditional book, *Life of Jesus for the German People* (1864), which presented the search for the historical Jesus as a contribution to the unification of Germany (that is, a smaller union without Austria). His Jesus was an apolitical Messiah in the shadow of the Empire (Roman and German). Building on Matthew's Gospel as his main source, the contrast between Galilee and Jerusalem in their attitudes to Jesus was reflected in the contrast Strauss saw between Protestant Northern Germany and the Catholic South, and this became a paradigmatic pattern in later interpretations.

Ernest Renan admired and learned from the critical German work of Strauss, but did not go into detailed criticism of biblical texts in his *Life of Jesus* (1864) (Chapter V). Stylistically this work combines biography with travel writing (based on Renan's travels in Syria/Palestine); his is the first of the Lives of Jesus to use the landscape as a main source. His book is an expression of *Orientalism*, where the contrast between the West and the Orient is played out in topographical space. Galilee as a space that inspired visions of the Kingdom of God is an ideal representation of, but also a criticism of, the West; Jerusalem and Judea represent the fanatical Orient, the home of Muslims and Jews. The identity of Jesus, described as being of 'non-race' as the initiator of a new humanity, reflects the importance of race in the discussion of national identities in Europe, in particular in the conflict between France and Germany. In this way Renan's picture of Jesus and the new humanity anticipates Renan's famous address on 'What is a nation?' with its ideal of a humanity not based on racial distinctions.

Finally, Chapter VI studies the picture of Jesus in Galilee within the *Historical Geography of the Holy Land* (1894) by George Adam Smith, who shared with Renan a direct knowledge of Palestine. Smith was not concerned with national unification, as Schleiermacher or Strauss were, nor with the race of the inhabitants, as Renan. Instead Smith partakes in a British discourse discussing political and social conflicts in moral terms, concerned with the character of the individual. Smith's Galilee is described in terms of *moral geography*, and the conflicts that Jesus encountered in Galilee are described in light of pressing social issues in Victorian Britain – to such a degree that it is tempting to call it a picture of 'Galilee as Glasgow'. Likewise, the portrait of Jesus as a young man reflects the particular pressures and ideals of young men in Britain in Smith's time, described in a way that attempts to include working-class men in an essentially middle-class discourse. In a time of social conflicts, Smith's picture of Jesus represents an effort to create national unity in terms of a moral character.

In the last chapter I will attempt to go beyond the nineteenth century to reflect on the challenges for a political interpretation of the historical Jesus today in a post-national world. I will argue that instead of viewing the historical Jesus through today's dominant lenses of ethno-nationalism, we should see him in categories that are more inclusive and global. Moreover, I will try to establish a dialogue between the historical sources on Jesus and contemporary philosophers, especially Habermas, to imagine a 'domestic world community' where solidarity is extended beyond household and nation to a global world.

CHAPTER I

WRITING A BIOGRAPHY OF JESUS
IN AN AGE OF NATIONALISM

What is it to write a biography? With this question Friedrich Schleiermacher started the very first lecture series ever to be given on the topic of the historical Jesus.[1] The year was 1819, and the venue was the recently opened University of Berlin where Schleiermacher was an influential professor who lectured in nearly all disciplines within theological studies. He started as follows:

> In connection with the subject with which we are to concern ourselves in these lectures there are certain important preliminary matters to be dealt with before we proceed to the study itself. The first will be that we must agree on *what we actually mean by biography, for that is what we wish to provide for the person of Christ*.[2]

A New Form of Writing about Jesus

Jesus as a human being

With his question Schleiermacher introduced a very controversial issue; he proposed a new picture of Jesus, breaking with the image of a supranatural Christ and presenting the life of Jesus as the biography of a human being. To choose the form of biography was a dramatic way of signalling this shift from writing about the divine Christ to the human Jesus. Therefore it is worthwhile noticing how carefully Schleiermacher phrases his proposal: there are 'certain important preliminary matters' that are necessary to discuss before 'the thing itself'.[3] His first question is, 'What do we mean by biography?', but that leads to further questions, such as: 'What is history?'; 'How can an author grasp the true "self" of a person?'; 'What are the relations between the external activities and the inner unity of a person?'; 'How much does an individual influence his surroundings, and how much is he determined by his context?'

We can all understand that these are important questions; they deal with the deepest concerns of what it is to be human, how we can understand the interactions between an individual and society, and how we can describe the past, either of a collectivity (history) or of an individual (biography). So to write a biography of Jesus was not something that could be undertaken easily; it was a matter of bringing together all the various disciplines that studied human life. Schleiermacher was in many ways almost a renaissance scholar in his command of a wide range of areas, and he felt at home in many of them. With the development of academic disciplines and specialization, these are issues that are dealt with variously in history, philosophy and a number of forms of the human sciences such as psychology, sociology and social anthropology.

Why did Schleiermacher start this discussion? In modern studies of the historical Jesus one finds at most some discussion of the source material but very little of the larger issues that Schleiermacher raised. We may say that Schleiermacher was in a special situation. He was the first to give a lecture series on the historical Jesus, and one might think that he therefore felt it necessary to clarify what he was doing, to explain this quite new undertaking in theological education. But it was also a way to base his lectures on Jesus in history, to emphasize the importance of Jesus as a historical person for theology. This emphasis was one of the lasting influences of Schleiermacher for theology in the nineteenth century. Therefore we may read these lectures not only as Schleiermacher's introduction to his own project of a biography of Jesus, but also as introducing biography as a new genre of writing about Jesus in the nineteenth century.[4]

A generation later, in his introduction to *A New Life of Jesus*, D. F. Strauss starts with a discussion of why the genre of biography being applied to Jesus was so controversial, and in the process he offers a very critical view of Schleiermacher's lectures.[5] Strauss writes from a perspective where he can look back upon the history of biographies about Jesus, as well as reflect upon the effects of his own *Life of Jesus Critically Examined* from 1835. Strauss was well prepared to start his book with a discussion of the genre of biography. Between 1842 and 1864 he did not write theological works but many successful biographies, for instance on Ulrich von Hutton as an example for German nationalism from the reformation period.[6]

When Strauss explains what characterizes biography as a genre in contrast to doctrinal teaching, he emphasizes that biography is a *modern* idea. Therefore it could not have been used in the pre-modern period. Although the term 'life of Jesus' is old, it now has a totally different meaning to the ancient understanding of it. The Christology of the churches had two main doctrines, the person of Christ (as the incarnate Son of God), and his works 'for us', especially as redeemer. Within this theological context, presentations of Jesus' life were merely paraphrases of Scripture that illustrated this dogma, not 'what we now understand by a life or history of Jesus'.[7]

Over and against this Strauss places the modern understanding of biography, in which 'the hero of a biography should be entirely and clearly human'. A biography must present a person not as half human, half divine, but with everything that belongs to a human person, with both natural and spiritual aspects. That implies, for instance, struggles between these aspects, hesitation and failure; sinlessness is therefore excluded and this dogma about Christ cannot be included in a biography. A human person is always influenced by his surroundings, his family, age and nation – in contrast to a divinely begotten Son of God, who is not under such restrictions. Therefore the hero of a biography is a finite individual, influenced and limited by his surroundings, 'acting according to natural laws'. Strauss holds that the proper subject of history is to study the interaction between these forces, and that causality is the fundamental law in history.[8]

Strauss concludes that the church's conception of Christ is in fundamental conflict with this understanding of history and biography. It is impossible to reconcile the content of that belief with the form of a biography. To make the Christ of the church a subject for biography is self-contradictory. Thus Strauss from his point of view explained why so many in the church reacted strongly against the Lives of the human Jesus.

The politics of Jesus' biographies

Why did the biographies of Jesus as a human person meet with such extreme outbreaks of criticism, not just from within church bodies, but also from state and university authorities? The authors of the two most influential and popular books on Jesus in the nineteenth century both suffered censorship. D. F. Strauss published his *The Life of Jesus, Critically Examined* in 1835 and lost his teaching position in Zurich as a result. Ernest Renan, in the inaugural lecture for his chair in Hebrew at the College de France in 1862, spoke of Jesus as 'an incomparable man whom some call God'. Four days later, the Emperor Napoleon III himself suspended Renan's lectures, and later Renan was dismissed from his position.[9]

From a distance of 200 years and after a process of secularization and the marginalization of religious symbols and the Bible in European societies, it is difficult to imagine the significance of the symbols attached to Christ in pre-nineteenth century Europe. The images of Christ were part of the religious models that helped to represent monarchic power in early modern Europe. From Christian antiquity and onwards the iconography of Christ as the heavenly ruler, portrayed as an emperor on his throne, provided support for the idea of the king ruling over his subjects in analogy with Christ.[10]

Whereas the dogmatic picture of the divine Christ supported the authorities in society as well as in the church, the picture of the human Jesus often played a role in popular movements that were both religiously and socially radical. From the pre-modern period we may think of St Francis, who through his life and words revived the image of the poor, human Jesus that attracted many people but also caused great anxiety for the power holders in both church and society.

In early modernity, there were movements and individuals that presented portraits of the historical Jesus in criticism of the church.[11] However, these came from the outside, from autodidacts or men who were not part of church or academic institutions. Therefore they could cause a stir and gain popular hearing, but they did not represent a serious challenge to the authority of church and state. The case of Reimarus, who kept his radical studies of the historical Jesus secret so that they were not published until after his death, suggests the strength of the powers of censorship and public social control.

It is against this background that we can realize the importance of the nineteenth-century studies of the historical Jesus, and since they were presented by respected university professors, how they represented a much more formidable challenge to the authority structures and powers of European society. The impact of the biographies of Jesus as a human person must be seen in light of the larger political and mental or ideological shifts occurring from the late eighteenth century onwards. These shifts were influenced by philosophical criticism of religion, but they were also initiated or strengthened by the American and French revolutions and their repercussions throughout the nineteenth century. John Horne describes this in the following way:

> The American and French revolution lay at the heart of a process extending to our own day that transformed politics by taking real and symbolic power from monarchic and religious models of fatherhood and reinvesting it in citizenship and the nation.[12]

To undercut such authoritative images of Christ could therefore be seen as a political act, withdrawing legitimacy from the symbols of monarchic and ecclesiastical power. Horne's observations of the transformation of politics by reinvesting the symbolic power of religious models in citizenship and the nation provide a context for understanding what was at stake when Jesus was portrayed in biographies as a human person. The shock of having the dogma of Christ challenged and substituted by a human Jesus was felt far beyond theological circles and church communities; a human Jesus represented a totally different model of reality within the larger symbolic systems of society and politics. While Christ had been a symbol that in many instances served to keep the masses positioned as obedient subjects, the human Jesus became a symbol that helped to give people a new place and invested them with the dignity of citizenship. The human Jesus was thus not just a symbol; he became the subject of biography, where his life was presented as that of an exemplary human person.

Biography as history and philosophy

The effect of Schleiermacher's question 'What do we mean by biography?' was to place his lectures within a known genre of writing, and to use known procedures and models in the presentation of Jesus. His lectures were not going to be about revelation, but about biography. It was an approach that corresponded to Schleiermacher's main hermeneutical project: to shift from a theological to a general hermeneutics.

Schleiermacher raised three major questions about writing a biography. The first concerned the requirements for biography as a way of writing history. The next question was how to understand a person in her/his context: should a person be understood as a singular individual, or as part of and dependant upon a wider community? Finally, was it possible within a human biography to speak of Jesus as a special or unique person? These questions brought up issues that were vigorously discussed within the fields of history, philosophy and theology of the time; Schleiermacher could not just refer to commonly accepted meanings, but had to take a position that represented what *he* meant by biography.

The first question concerned the meaning of history. Schleiermacher's lectures stand within the process of establishing history as a distinct discipline with discussions of methods and philosophy.[13] At the University of Berlin, where he was teaching, there was a conflict between philosophical schools, centred on Hegel, and a historical school, which among others included von Ranke, von Humboldt and Schleiermacher. Hegel maintained that behind the diversity in the world there was a rational principle, while the historical school held that the diversity of the world could not be reduced to a conceptual scheme.[14] Therefore, for the historical school the form of history became the *narrative*.[15] Both groups held, however, that there was a metaphysical reality behind historical phenomena, and that the task of history was to grasp this reality.

In his introduction to the lectures on the *Life of Jesus* Schleiermacher voices these concerns. Schleiermacher starts by distinguishing his project of writing *history* from that of a *chronicle*.[16] According to Schleiermacher, a chronicle is simpler and more primitive than history. Human life consists of a series of separate moments, and chronicles do not do more than list them as they were perceived, as temporal phenomena. But such a chronicle does not present a *history*. The task of history is to grasp the meaning behind the individual events, the reality that shapes them. Schleiermacher sets up a series of contrasts between chronicle and history. A *chronicle* deals with what is particular, and which therefore can be separated out, whereas *history* aims to grasp a unity that is indivisible. A chronicle reports what can be perceived externally, but history will grasp something inward, which is not perceptible but 'can be grasped only in another way'.[17] When this distinction is applied to biography, the task of a biographer is to find the inward element, the unity of a life 'by which this individual in all his varied appearances is distinguished from every other individual'.[18]

Schleiermacher's discussion of history was not just a way to deal with the methodology of his study of the Life of Jesus; it was a fundamental issue in his way of doing theology. At the crux of his method was his conviction that Christianity must fundamentally be understood historically.[19] He started not from the revelation of Scripture, but from a combination of individual experience with the historical experience of Jesus as the redeemer. In this way, history and especially the history of Jesus and of the early forms of Christianity, was of ultimate importance for the present church and society.

The question of how to write history and to establish an inner meaning for events placed nineteenth-century historians at the centre of the political issues of the day.[20] The metanarrative of history that was established in the nineteenth century was seen as 'progress', and many of the presentations of Jesus presented him and Christianity as examples of progress. Jesus was viewed as the new man who represented the future. This idea of progress was associated with the development of nationalism. The process of progress needed a form; it needed to take place somewhere. Just as progress represented a modernization *vis-à-vis* a previous state of inertia, so the idea of nations represented modernization *vis-à-vis* previous forms of state rules and static social structures. This was the intellectual climate for presentations of the historical Jesus at this time, and we shall see how the question of the historical Jesus was also a question of how he represented forces of progress in history that pointed towards modernizing movements in the present.

Writing a biography also brought up issues discussed in philosophy. Schleiermacher points to such issues when he sums up his first lecture by repeating his initial question: 'What is the actual task of a biography which is to correspond wholly to the idea of a description of a life?'[21] How do you describe a life? Obviously, such a description cannot proceed in just any way; it has to be based on the idea of a life. Here Schleiermacher opens up the really big questions that link biography to philosophy and religion: What is a life? What is it to be a human being?

In this discussion of Schleiermacher's second major question he stands at the transition from the Enlightenment to Romanticism. How to understand the human being was a much discussed and unresolved question in that period, as it continues to be today. Where the philosophers of the Enlightenment emphasized the independence of the individual, the Romanticists emphasized interdependence.[22] At the very beginning of his summary of his second lecture, Schleiermacher offers in one sentence his position. A human being does not exist in isolation, but in a specific context: 'No individual can be torn loose from his time, age and people (*Zeit, Alter und Volk*)'. In Schleiermacher's idea of the authentic person, there was a mutual reinforcement between the description of human existence as both an expression of individuality and of collective influence.[23] In addition to a person's place in time, Schleiermacher emphasizes his place in 'the people', and thereby points to his own focus on nation as the context for Jesus. This focus on Jesus in the context of nation becomes second nature to the biographies, as we shall see.

Was Jesus a unique person?

The third question Schleiermacher raised was whether it was possible within a human biography to speak of Jesus as a special or unique person. Here he addresses an issue that was of immense theological interest. Schleiermacher refers to the criticism he encountered from other theologians that to speak of Jesus as a human being meant to take away the uniqueness attributed to the divine Christ.[24] In line with Schleiermacher's hermeneutics, he responds to that question within the structure of a common human anthropology, where the individual person stands in a double relationship to the common life. It consists in the influence of the community upon the individual, but also of the individual upon the community. This situation is true for all persons, Schleiermacher argues, but the relationship varies, according to the power and influence held by the individual. It is possible to think of Christ as having an influence 'which extends over all peoples and over all ages'.[25] This does not make Jesus into a supranatural figure; Schleiermacher points to an analogy with the concept of 'the great man' who has an extraordinary influence on society, state or church. What gave Jesus such power, and which made him unique, Schleiermacher argues, was his consciousness of God.

With his questions about what it is to write a biography of a person, Schleiermacher raised a thoroughly 'modern' question about what it is to be human, and how one can grasp a person in his or her unity and totality. Thus, Jesus was an example of authentic existence, at the same time that he was a part of a community. Thus for Schleiermacher, what was unique about Jesus is found within that which is completely human, at the same time that he was an archetype for human relations to God. [26]

It is at this point that Strauss, in his 1864 book *A New Life of Jesus*, criticized Schleiermacher for preserving a divine element in Jesus and claimed that therefore he did not fulfil the requirements of biography for writing about a human figure.[27] Schleiermacher's lectures on *The Life of Jesus* had finally been published, more than thirty years after the last time he gave them at the University of Berlin. By beginning his book with a discussion of biography in the same way as Schleiermacher, Strauss could distance himself from Schleiermacher and his pervasive influence on German theology in this period.[28]

Strauss sees the question of a biography of Jesus as having gone through three phases: a pre-modern phase, an age of transition, and finally the present age, represented by Strauss himself.[29] As outlined above, Strauss presents biography as a *modern* idea that therefore could not have been used in the pre-modern period of the dogmatic Christ. The transition period began with rationalism in the eighteenth century, with its attempt to combine dogma and history. In Strauss' criticism of this age of transition, Schleiermacher played a central part. Strauss' criticism is that Schleiermacher has only gone halfway. Schleiermacher followed modern intellectual reasoning about a human being, but he combined that with the image that was required by traditional piety of Jesus as the divine redeemer and of Jesus as being without sin. Thus, Strauss argues, Schleiermacher takes a middle position between faith and science.[30]

It was this criticism of Schleiermacher for not having a sense of history that Schweitzer appears to have adopted from Strauss.[31] Strauss' criticism seems partly justified; Schleiermacher's acceptance of John's Gospel as the best source leads him to include John's theological perspectives on Jesus as historical. However, that does not mean that Schleiermacher lacked a sense for history. His reflections on a biography of Jesus as a form of writing history belong within a tradition of making sense of historical events by finding their centre of meaning; his goal was to keep empirical events and ideas together.[32]

After this 'age of transition' follows the third stage, that of critical and secular interpretation, i.e. Strauss himself. Strauss contends that when the biography of Jesus was taken seriously, it meant the end to traditional theology. The only way that Christ could be made intelligible to the modern world was by treating his life in the same way as that of 'other illustrious men'. The previous attempts to write a biography of Jesus were based on the belief that the Gospels presented a historical picture of the human Jesus. But the real problem arose with the realization that the Gospels presented a picture that was not historical, but theological and dogmatic, and therefore incompatible with the demands of biography.

Therefore the Gospels must be exposed to a 'full and unsparing investigation' of their credibility as historical sources.

It was such an investigation that Strauss had undertaken with his *Life of Jesus Critically Examined.* His conclusion regarding the prospect of a biography of Jesus is rather pessimistic: 'the Gospel materials, when critically tested, dwindled – to a faint and hesitating outline'.[33] That was the outcome of his first *Life of Jesus*, and it distinguished his position from that of Schleiermacher. However, despite his deconstruction of biography as a possibility for writing about Jesus in his first *Life of Jesus*, almost thirty years later in *A New Life of Jesus* Strauss returned to a more conventional biographical mode.

The Function of Biography

Schleiermacher initiated questions that placed his Jesus biography in the middle of the intellectual discussions of his time. They show Schleiermacher's concern for hermeneutics and his participation in a broad range of intellectual and academic discussions, far beyond the narrow niches of biblical and theological studies. If we look at historical Jesus studies today, most of them have retreated into those niches. Many of them have a discussion of the sources for the historical Jesus and their credibility, but the authors rarely present their own views regarding, for example, the self, human agency, and the relations between an individual and his or her community. As a result, current scholars' presuppositions about human life and society remain unexamined, and many studies of Jesus are historiographically and hermeneutically naive.[34]

How can we read the biographies of Jesus by Schleiermacher and other nineteenth-century authors in a way that makes it possible to understand their project and to interact critically with them? I will try to look at them from the perspective of modern discussions of biography. Susan Tridgell points out that biographies are not neutral; they are 'an argument for seeing a self in a certain way'.[35] A biographer's view is always seen through a particular pair of eyes, and therefore a biography argues for a particular way to see and to make sense of the life of its subject. This particularity is also its strength; subsequent biographers can always challenge this view. Therefore persons who have made an impact upon a society or a nation frequently have several biographies, in which different authors view them from different locations or ideological positions.[36]

To see Schleiermacher's and others' biographies of Jesus as *arguments* raises the question of what they are arguments for. I contend that Schleiermacher's question 'What do we mean by biography?' must be followed up by the question, 'What does a biography *do*?' What is the relationship between the form of a biography and its functions?

I will therefore look at Schleiermacher's questions from the perspective of the twenty-first century and discuss the relationship between the form of a biography and its cultural and political functions. I will raise several questions. What does the designation of biographies of Jesus as expressions of a 'modern' genre say about their place within the modernization that was occurring in Europe with new communication and technology structures? In what ways did the relations between an individual and the community discussed in biographies reflect social and political changes in European societies? How did this community come to be understood as 'nation', and what role did that understanding play in biographies of Jesus? Who were the ideal figures that provided models for the presentations of Jesus as a 'special' person who shaped history? And finally, what were the shifting models of masculinity that informed the picture of Jesus?

Writing the bourgeois subject into Europe

By choosing biography as the form for his *Life of Jesus*, Schleiermacher turned to a literary form that was popular in the nineteenth century, especially in England and also in Germany and France.[37] In this section, German biographies will serve as an illustration of the general trend.[38]

One reason for the popularity of biographies was that the emerging culture of a bourgeois elite required institutional contexts and technological means that could provide expressions of their ideas. The central group that participated in these reform movements was the intellectuals among the bourgeoisie. They created discussion groups, wrote, printed and distributed publications such as books, journals and newspapers, and participated in new institutions like academies and universities. In addition, there was the public forum of preaching that played a role also in issues related to politics, war and peace.[39]

In his discussion of some of the same nineteenth-century studies on Christian origins that form the focus of this book, Ward Blanton focuses on the importance of forms of communication with new technologies that could spread and share ideas and how these new forms were situated in social contexts.[40] This was not just a technical matter, but an aspect of modernity that was integral to the intellectual process and its contents. As part of this technological and intellectual culture, biographies became an important medium to shape identities among the bourgeoisie.[41]

Biographies placed the individual within a larger history. The biographies and autobiographies of German intellectuals and the bourgeoisie in the eighteenth and nineteenth centuries served to establish ideal lifestyles and presented the bourgeoisie as ideal figures, individuals incorporating individual and civic values that were of importance for society:

In this genre the individual came to be presented as a morally autonomous subject capable of shaping himself (rarely herself) and the world; Christianity was rendered increasingly undogmatic and ecumenical, subsumed within a catalogue of bourgeois virtues of duty, work, non-sexual love, merit, peace and Bildung.[42]

By presenting this 'new' subject, biographies mediated this subjectivity to its readers. Biographies of bourgeois leaders at the time of Schleiermacher served both to establish ideals and to present arguments that the bourgeois should have more influential roles in society and within the state. These bourgeois virtues challenged those associated with the traditional structures of privilege of the aristocracy and thereby signalled some of the important changes in European political life in the late eighteenth and the nineteenth centuries. Biographies became a mirror for the bourgeoisie of its growing importance; they served as documentation for its success. Biographies were mainly a male domain, but not exclusively; some, although fewer in number, served to integrate women and even traditional outsiders such as Catholics and Jews.

It is also worth noticing the important role of religion, with an emphasis on its ethical aspects, in this transformation of values. This influence was mediated especially through the influence of Pietism and of Protestant pastors. In the same manner teachers increased their reputation, since they provided the basis for that formation (*Bildung*) that could give respect and recognition. Thus, the new growing elite that established itself against the old, landed aristocracy consisted of a combination of the economic bourgeoisie, intellectuals and state employees: bureaucrats, professors, pastors and teachers. Even if they only made up a small percentage of the population, they were able to establish a 'bourgeois hegemonic culture'.[43]

Against this general background of the function of biographies it is possible to distinguish between various sub-groups of biographies, each with its own specific characteristics.[44] The biography of 'the great man', typically a king or ruler, was a well-known form from Antiquity and the Middle Ages, with Plutarch's *Lives* of famous Greeks and Romans being a well-known example. In the eighteenth century, biographies of kings and their rule was a common form. These biographies were mostly laudatory, often being a product of the court. More critical biographies might place the subject in a broader context by discussing forms of rule, the ethos of the ruler and political issues that found a solution through this rule (e.g. the relationship between king and his subjects).

The most popular form was the equivalent of the literary biography of our time, the biographies of 'learned men', professors and other scholars in various scholastic areas, especially in theology, law and medicine. Reflecting the self-confidence of these groups, biographies presented them as rising above their estates or their own narrow group; instead they belonged to society at large, even to humanity. They represented education as the universality of culture (*Bildung*), and thereby pointed towards the future development of society. The self-consciousness and claim to respect that these biographies represented made them attractive for self-identification by broader groups in society.

Finally, another type of biography, which might include aspects of the afore-mentioned ones also, gained popularity, namely the religious biographies that served as examples and to build character. Not being hagiographies of saints, but biographies of ordinary people, they presented their exemplary moral life and their faith and spirituality. The religious sentiment of pietism inspired these types of biographies and autobiographies that had their focus on the introspection of the soul, the fight for faith and insight, growth in illumination and divine guidance. Major goals of such biographies were to legitimate the subjects' lives and to establish authoritative examples to be followed.

Placing the individual in the nation

By choosing the form of a biography for his presentation of Jesus, Schleier-macher employed a genre that was closely associated with the bourgeoisie and its ambitions of full citizenship. But he also placed his biography within a line of biographies linked to the idea of a nation.[45] This connection is brought out in his discussion of the second question of what it means to write a biography: How should one understand a person in his social context?

Schleiermacher starts his summary of his second lecture with a statement emphasizing the interdependence between a person and his environment:

> However, one cannot think of an individual without at the same time thinking of him in connection with the general conditions that determine his existence ... The individual comes into being only in and through the common life, and that is a fixed and unalterable relation, and every individual in his development is at the same time a result of a common life.[46]

Schleiermacher goes on to elaborate 'general conditions' and 'a common life' in ways that locate the individual in a specific context. He sums up his view in a short sentence: 'No individual can be torn loose from his time, age and *people*'.[47] The significant term here is the word used for the common life: 'people' – in German: *Volk* – that can also have the meaning of 'nation'. At a distance of almost 200 years, in the present situation where the nation and its people as a political and geographical entity is taken for granted as the 'natural' socio-political structure, it is difficult to understand the significance of Schleiermacher's statement about *Volk*. It must be understood, however, not from our present situation, but in its own historical context.

Nineteenth-century Europe saw transitions in the ways in which such common life could be envisaged. In addition to household and family, an individual's sense of loyalty and identity had primarily been to a village or town or maybe a larger region, all of which could be included in terms like 'home' (in German: *Heimat*). These names for places were ways of expressing communal identities that reflected the predominant importance of the immediate locality. The larger political entities were often of a fragmentary and shifting nature and were therefore not bases for personal or communal identities.

In the late eighteenth and early nineteenth century, however, writers started making use of the term *Heimat* to link the local communities to the central state, and to associate *Heimat* with terms like *Volk* and 'Nation'.[48] With his use of *Volk* Schleiermacher stands within this transition from understanding communal identities within a local place towards a larger entity. The changes in the meaning of the word *Volk* in the last part of the eighteenth century made it useful to express the transition of identity from the local region to a larger entity. Previously, the term *Volk* had been used of the lower classes, or 'the common people' in a pejorative sense. It was J. G. Herder who first redefined the word to include a community of people constituted through a common language, so that it was transformed from a class term to an 'ethnic' term for *a people* together with a 'nation'.[49] It is this meaning of the term that is implied by Schleiermacher: in other instances, he combines *Volk* with or uses as alternatives *nation* ('Nation') and *country* ('Land'). Here we see the idea of nationalism at work in Schleiermacher's discourse; it is a way of constructing the self in a new and larger context, that of people and nation.

By placing Jesus as a subject for a biography in a national context, Schleiermacher's biography takes its place among other German biographies during this particular period. In the first part of the nineteenth century, before the unification of Germany in 1870, biographies illustrated and influenced national moral values. They spoke for a German nation that had not yet come into political being but which, as Herder and the early nationalists argued, shared a linguistic and historical heritage. Biographies of 'famous men' could therefore represent these national values and political aspirations. Furthermore, there was a shared awareness that an individual was a visible representative of the moral and historical forces of an age. Thus, 'the German biographical tradition might appear to be the product of national liberalism, its function to annex the lives of the great for the sake of overarching cultural and political ends'.[50] Schleiermacher's presentation of Jesus as part of a Jewish people serves as an analogy for a German people; the biography thus establishes an 'imagined community'.

To characterize Schleiermacher's project as 'imagining a community' is of course a play on the title of Benedict Anderson influential book, *Imagined Communities*.[51] But it is more than a play on words; Anderson's book actually provides a larger context for Schleiermacher's biography of Jesus as an argument for a nation. He suggests that there is a link between the origin of nationalism in the eighteenth century and the rise of two types of media, the novel and the newspaper, that made it possible to imagine communities. He argues that nationalism is primarily a cultural system that superseded systems that preceded it, above all the religious and the dynastic. Both these realms were hierarchical and had a legitimacy that was taken for granted. The religious realm was supported by a sacred language, the dynastic by a genealogy; but both lost power and legitimacy during the eighteenth century. The result was that the structures that had created a meaningful universe collapsed. It is in this situation that Anderson sees an important role for new structures that could shape an 'imagined community'.

Anderson speaks of *novels* and *newspapers*, two types of media that flowered in Europe in the eighteenth and nineteenth centuries.[52] It may seem strange to combine the fiction of the novel with what we often consider the facts of the newspaper, but Anderson argues that the newspaper is characterized also by its 'profound fictiveness'.[53] Both the novel and the newspaper 'provided the technical means for re-presenting the *kind* of imagined community that is the nation'.[54] It was this 'print-capitalism', as Anderson terms it, 'which made it possible for rapidly growing numbers of people to think about themselves, and to relate themselves to others, in profoundly new ways'.[55] This print-capitalism provided a basis for national consciousness in terms of languages. The power of printed languages took precedence over vernacular languages that did not become printed languages.

The biographies of the eighteenth and nineteenth centuries shared many of the characteristics of the novel. In particular, there were close similarities between the biography and the *Bildungsroman*, a typical and popular form of novel in the eighteenth and nineteenth centuries.[56] They both had a moral purpose, to assist in understanding and shaping human character. The most important novel of this type, Goethe's *Wilhelm Meister*, showed the close link between biography and the *Bildungsroman*.[57] In a later essay, Goethe discusses human development and the artist's description of it in terms of a movement from 'within outwards'.[58] This corresponds to Schleiermacher's position on the task of a biographer: it is to find the inward element, the unity of a life 'by which this individual in all his varied appearances is distinguished from every other individual'.[59] It was this expression of the individual's inner life that was the goal of the novel as well as the biography.

Anderson's interest is not so much in the novel as a description of the inner life of an individual, as he is in the function of the novel *vis-à-vis* the reader. He sees the novel as a new form of literature with regard to time, in that it describes parallel events as happening simultaneously. He uses examples of early novels from Mexico and the Philippines that were associated with nationalist movements. Anderson finds a characteristic element in the way the novel combines the life of the hero and the social environment of the reading public. This makes it possible to 'see the "national imagination" at work in the movement of a solitary hero through a sociological landscape of a fixity that fuses the world inside the novel with the world outside.'[60]

Here Anderson combines two aspects that were central to nineteenth-century ideas about history and nation. Since history was determined by the influence of 'great men' or heroes, they were also the protagonists of national movements and the founders of nations. Moreover, landscape, not only in a sociological sense but also as a topographical and geographical entity, was central to the formation of national character. These aspects were also central elements in biographies of Jesus; he was portrayed as a hero walking through a landscape of topographical and symbolic importance.

Jesus as a National Hero

There is a tension between Anderson's portrayal of the 'solitary hero' as central to the national imagination in nineteenth-century novels, and Horne's description of the same period as a process of transferral of real and symbolic power from monarch and church to citizenship and nation. Anderson lifts up the image of the 'solitary hero' whereas Horne speaks in much more democratic terms of citizenship. Even when we consider that citizenship was not egalitarian (it was an idea primarily for and of the bourgeoisie), the tension remains between the image of the hero who shapes history, and that of the participation of 'the people' or influential sectors of the people. This is a tension not just in modern presentations of the nineteenth century; it reflects real tensions in the politics as well as in the intellectual discourse of the nineteenth century.

These tensions provide the context for the last question that Schleiermacher brings up in his introduction, whether one in a human biography can speak of Jesus as a special or unique person. From today's perspective it seems strange that even when insisting that they were writing about the historical Jesus as a human and not a divine figure, the nineteenth-century authors continued to speak of him in the highest terms as a model for society and an ideal for humanity. They shared the view that Jesus was a unique person who represented a divine presence in history; even more, Jesus was considered to represent the movement towards modern (i.e. Western) European society. Thus, although the historical Jesus' studies were regarded as extremely dangerous for traditional Christianity, they presented Jesus and other figures from the history of early Christianity as models for European societies.

The 'Great Man' of history

The authors of biographies of Jesus had to find a model for their presentations that corresponded to this view of Jesus as an exceptional human being. They found such a model in biographies of heroes or 'great men'. 'Biographies of great men' as a literary and historiographical genre were very popular in Europe in the nineteenth century. Together with a growing interest in Antiquity and antique societies such as Greece, Rome, Egypt, Palestine, and so on, there was also a great interest in the major figures from the classical period.[61] Biographies of 'great men', for example of Greek philosophers, functioned as ideals within a social environment.

In his book on how the biographies of Abraham Lincoln were shaped by national memory,[62] Barry Schwartz describes the type of social environment that made images of Lincoln into models for character-building. Schwartz argues that the eighteenth and nineteenth centuries represented a hierarchical world order that was characterized by a 'culture of deference':

> Cultures of deference exist when role relations and social classes are demarcated and vertical mobility is limited … In this quintessentially hierarchical world, history, in Thomas Carlyle's words, appears as 'a succession of biographies of great men', and we socialize children by teaching them about the feats and characters of such men.'[63]

This culture of deference stands in contrast to cultures of equality where role relations and class distinctions are unclear. Within this type of culture, history is described as a result of collective rather than of individual achievements. In his observations on American society in the first part of the eighteenth century, Alexis de Tocqueville concludes that with the rise of democracy traditional character models lose their impact.[64] He contrasts the situation in America with that of Europe, still dominated by the aristocracy and elites.

In the concept of 'the great man', biography and history were united. It was a widely shared presupposition in nineteenth-century Europe that history was made and shaped by heroic individuals. This view was most clearly expressed in the writings of the Scottish essayist, historian and critic Thomas Carlyle (1795–1881). Carlyle now comes across as an almost stereotypical representative of hero worship in the Victorian period. This found its most characteristic expression in his *On Heroes, Hero-Worship, and the Heroic in History*.[65] The book was based on a series of popular public lectures that dealt with six categories of heroes: the hero as divinity, as prophet, as poet, as priest, as a man of letters and as king. Carlyle starts by stating his conviction that 'as I take it, Universal History … is at bottom the history of the great men who have worked here'.[66] He even speaks of the great man as saviour: 'In all epochs of the world's history we shall find the Great Man to have been the indispensable saviour of his epoch.'[67] Carlyle links the 'great men' to the fate of the nation. Although Carlyle had lost his Christian faith, he had preserved many Calvinist values from his upbringing. He describes the Great Men as those who 'made moral character the final criterion of the greatness of the nation'.[68]

Ernest Renan, who spoke of Jesus together with Paul and John as 'extraordinary men',[69] also links the great men to the formation and the grandeur of the nation. In his famous lecture from 1882, 'What is a nation?', Renan speaks of the nation as 'a soul, a spiritual principle', and continues by saying that 'The nation, like the individual, is the culmination of a long past of endeavours, sacrifice and devotion. Of all cults, that of the ancestors is the most legitimate, for the ancestors have made us what we are.' Renan considers these 'ancestors' as 'great men', and he concludes with a bombastic statement: 'A heroic past, great men, glory (by which I understand genuine glory), this is the social capital upon which one bases a national idea.[70]

This emphasis on the unique and elite role of the 'great man' in world history met with criticism from early sociologists. They attributed change more to the laws of physical and social evolution, and emphasized collaborative efforts.[71] Only a few months after Renan's lecture on the nation, the sociologist Emile Durkheim used his address to students at Lycée de Lyon to attack Renan for the way he distinguished the 'great men' from ordinary citizens. Durkheim was concerned about the relations between individual and society, and held that the justification for an elite was not in its exclusion from the larger society, but its contribution to move humanity forward. Thus, the elite ought to serve as benefactors for humanity.[72] Here Durkheim is almost echoing Schleiermacher sixty years earlier in his Academy lectures on Fredrick the Great of Prussia as 'a great man'.[73]

Before we can discuss these lectures and their possible impact upon Schleiermacher's biography of Jesus, however, we must consider the nineteenth-century ideologies of heroes and great men in light of a decidedly modern perspective, *viz.* that of gender and masculinity studies.

Masculinities and nation

Schleiermacher started his lectures on *The Life of Jesus* by addressing his students as 'Gentlemen'. In itself, this greeting only reflected the obvious fact that the student body at the University of Berlin in his time was all male. But just because it was so 'natural', Schleiermacher's address signals the general context of historical Jesus studies in the nineteenth century. This was an all-male enterprise, and it has been criticized (and ridiculed) for being part of a male, European attempt to secure its position in a changing world, on a par with colonialism and imperialism. The interest in Jesus and the portrayal of him in first century Palestine as a figure of identification has been very much a male prerogative.

Writing a biography of Jesus in the nineteenth century meant writing within a gendered system where men and women were shaped in different ways.[74] The nation was also gendered, predominantly as masculine. But 'masculine' was not a fixed category; it was constructed in different ways that reflected the conflicts over the formation or identity of the nation. Typically in societies with criticism of traditional political authorities, as in the German states, or with new challenges, as in Britain with the expansion of the Empire and social conflicts at home, challenges to the dominant masculinity was one of the forms of such conflict.

Another term for dominant masculinity is 'hegemonic masculinity', understood as 'the masculine norms and practices which are most valued by the politically dominant class and which help to maintain its authority'.[75] The usage of the term 'hegemony' goes back to the Italian Marxist theorist Antonio Gramsci in the 1930s. He used it to refer to a domination that no longer needed to use force or legal power because it had become part of culture; it was generally accepted and kept in place by popular culture and everyday morality. John Tosh sums up the close connection between nation and hegemonic masculinity in this way: 'In periods of emerging national identity or of national resistance, this dominant masculinity is likely to become a metaphor for the political community as a whole and to be expressed in highly idealized forms.'[76] The term 'hegemonic' implies, however, that it is not absolute; it invites challenges and contestations from other forms of masculinity. We cannot therefore speak of a singular masculinity, but must speak of *masculinities* in the plural.

The presentations of Jesus as a human being by Schleiermacher, Strauss, Renan and Smith all present him as male and in terms of male metaphors as a matter of course.[77] There are few examples of explicit discussions of the masculinity of Jesus, but the presentations of him obviously take place within cultural and political contexts that reflect the changing forms of masculinity in Europe in the nineteenth century. Therefore it is against the background of these changes in masculinities that we can identify the discourses of masculinity and nationality in which our Jesus scholars participate.

Several of these discourses are discussed in the essays in *Masculinities in Politics and War*, which provides an excellent introduction to a study of the relations between different positions on nation and male citizenship.[78] Three of the examples from this book are especially helpful for identifying discourses of masculinity in the Lives of Jesus: first, conflicting masculinities in the Prussian–French war in 1813;[79] second, the masculine myths of heroism and their imagination of the nation;[80] and third, hegemonic masculinity and the formations of national character.[81]

The first example illustrates how Schleiermacher was part of a conflict that forms the background for the way he imagines the role of Jesus (and the king of Prussia). As part of the war efforts against Napoleon in 1813 and 1814, the Prussian state introduced universal conscription, whereby the total male population was integrated into the military. Schleiermacher took an active part in the war efforts in Prussia, both by writing and as a pastor and preacher. Together with other intellectuals, he argued for a people's defence against Napoleon's forces, organized in militias, that is, civil forms of military organization, and not as part of the state military. Moreover, he called for an extension of civic and political rights for the men who participated in the militias. Behind this argument, we may identify a form of masculinity that can be characterized as 'a valorous, civic masculinity that was located in the nation *and* demanded to be represented in the state'.[82]

Within the hierarchical system of Prussia, however, the autocratic rulers rejected any civic rights for the conscripted men; they remained 'duty-bound subjects of the King'. Instead of introducing citizenship into the idea of the nation, as called for by Schleiermacher and his colleagues, the term 'nation' was employed by the authorities and shaped in their image. The result was that 'a masculinity of duty, loyal service and sacrifice helped to articulate and shape this vision of a monarchical nation, ultimately embodied by the King'.[83] In this case the idea of the nation was brought back solidly into the monarchic realm and stripped of all links to citizenship. It is against this context that we can read Schleiermacher's reformulations of the ideal figure of the king and of Jesus as 'great men' in an interdependent relationship with their people, as an alternative to the hegemonic masculinity embodied by the Prussian king.

An essay on heroism points to an ambiguity in the ways nations were imagined in the nineteenth century.[84] The nation encompassed society, and included women and children, since the family was regarded as the primary cell of society. However, when ideas of nation were formulated or presented in images, they were very often expressed in male roles and expressions of masculinity; the famous image of France as Marianne is an obvious exception, but she is also portrayed in a masculine, fighting role.[85]

An ideal that was particularly strong in times of war was that of the soldier, especially in the form of the volunteer, who was ready to die in defence of the fatherland. The central element of this and other myths was heroism, which found its male expression in valour and the sacrifice of one's life for the fatherland. Karen Hagemann points out how the call to show patriotism and willingness to die for the fatherland combined personal interests with those of the state: it was expressed in terms of the trio of family, home and fatherland. This myth and cult of the heroic was used to construct Prussia as a 'manly nation',[86] which is rather similar to Renan's use of male-gendered terms such as 'a heroic past, great men, glory' to describe the nation. [87]

Sacrifice and the willingness to give one's life for others were central Christian ideals, found in the stories of many saints (also female saints), but first and foremost in the history of Jesus. Therefore, there was ample room for interaction between images of Jesus' sacrifice and images of masculine sacrifice as an ideal of the nation. In Victorian Britain, however, 'sacrifice' had taken on the meaning of a feminine, domestic value, so G. A. Smith must struggle to reclaim it as part of Jesus' masculine character.

Building and upholding a national character was a third area of interrelation between masculinity and nation, being especially important in periods when national identities were emerging or were under pressure. In several studies, George L. Mosse has shown how the construction of modern masculinities took place in concert with the rise of a new national consciousness.[88] Mosse points out, for instance, how in France the ideals of the heroes of the Revolution were used to support patriotism, and how the male German sports associations were put to use to build national unity.[89] Public morals played an important part in the building of nationalism, and Mosse explores how 'respectability' with an emphasis on manliness and family was an important factor. In England this respectability took the form of 'building character' in young men, especially through the public school system.[90] G. A. Smith's portrayal of Jesus as a young man, set in Galilee, presents a striking example of this contemporary national discourse.

Thus, the different portraits of the masculinity of Jesus were expressed 'in highly idealized forms', and through the form of biography they addressed national issues as 'a metaphor for the political community as a whole'.[91] In the following chapters we will see in more detail how these pictures of Jesus participated in discussions about masculinities, attempting to contribute to the establishment of a dominant masculinity. Schleiermacher's Jesus transformed the picture of the authoritarian king into one who was more influenced by the citizens; and Jesus' role as teacher served to emphasize the significance of teachers for the formation of the nation. In George Adam Smith's presentation of Jesus as a young man resisting temptation there was an obvious attempt to shape an ideal male character, applicable both to the working and to the middle classes. It is indicative of the place of the authors within their societies that they envisaged Jesus as a role model for ideal masculinities. Even Renan, who portrayed Jesus in part as an 'ideal primitive' of the Orient, and possibly with more feminine characteristics,[92] saw him as a positive challenge to modern societies. It was only Strauss, in the last phase when he had despaired of making Jesus into a model for modern society, who depicted him in an unmanly role as an 'enthusiast', a suitable figure for a 'degenerate race'.

Conclusion

Schleiermacher's question: 'What do we mean by biography?' took us into a little explored context of historical Jesus studies, that of the place of biographies in the culture of the nineteenth century, and especially their forms and functions in building national consciousness. Schleiermacher, Strauss and Renan had an awareness that writing about Jesus in the form of a biography was controversial; Strauss especially seemed to have relished the opportunity to write about Jesus in a form that represented a 'modern' criticism of the Gospels and the church. But even if biography was a form for writing about humans and not divinities, it was obvious that they did not consider Jesus an 'ordinary' human being. It was here that the popular genre of biographies of 'great men' and 'heroes' provided a model that could combine the human side of Jesus with his extraordinary influence in shaping a people or initiating a new humanity. And the form of biography presented Jesus in a way that made it possible for readers to identify with him. Moreover, placing him in the social and geographical setting of Galilee and Palestine made it possible to see that identification also in terms of a people, country and nation.

Within these common approaches to writing a biography of Jesus we will notice in the following chapters distinctive differences among the authors. Schleiermacher's approach in the way that he places an individual (Jesus) in a social context is one that points towards the future of biographical writing, even anticipating some of the discussions of the so-called New Biography or social biography. It is not the single individual but rather a person as part of a community that is Schleiermacher's model for portraying Jesus, pointing towards future studies of the sociology of the Jesus movement. Strauss' critical examination of the life of Jesus effectively deconstructs Jesus as a subject for biography, but his later *Life of Jesus for the German People* returns to a more conventional biographical form with autobiographical similarities in the description of a quietistic Jesus within a powerful empire. Renan's *Life of Jesus* is much more of a psychological portrait or *Bildungsroman*. Where Schleiermacher and Strauss might discuss differences in Jesus' positions, for instance on the Kingdom of God, in terms of source criticism, Renan ascribes them to the development of his personal character confronted with adversity. Finally, Smith, in his descriptions of Jesus in various locations in Galilee, gives 'snapshots' of Jesus as a young man facing the same temptations as young men in Britain 1800 years later.

CHAPTER II

HOLY LAND AS HOMELAND

The Nineteenth-Century Landscape of Jesus

Introduction

In *Imagined Communities*, Benedict Anderson reminds us that people and nations are made up not only of social entities, but also of territories and landscapes. He points to how nineteenth-century novels allow us to 'see the national imagination' at work in the movement of a solitary hero through a sociological landscape of a fixity that fuses the world inside the novel with the world outside.[1] This is also what the biographies of Jesus make us see. Jesus was placed not only in a social context, but in a particular landscape and topography. In this chapter, I will look at Palestine, the landscape where the hero, Jesus, was placed, and how religious and national consciousness fused it with the world of the readers, i.e. one or another European nation. Images of home, home place and nation were some of the ways used to describe Palestine as the 'Holy Land', which was also conceived of as 'homeland'. These imaginations of the Holy Land were part of the religious and political context for writers and readers of the Lives of Jesus, in particular in the last half of the nineteenth century.

The schoolhouse of my childhood in the 1950s had three maps. It had one map of Norway and another of Palestine at the time of Jesus. The third one was a map of the world; if I remember correctly, it was a political map, with large parts coloured pink, indicating the British Empire. These maps show how we were brought up to see the world; namely, a world still dominated by empires or the heritage of empires, with the map of our homeland situated beside a map of a land that was almost as familiar to us, the land of Jesus. To bring home that last message, these two maps were the same size, creating the impression that Palestine was the size of Norway. These maps, and a school curriculum with a strong dose of biblical narratives, made the transition between the homeland and the Holy Land almost seamless, under the gaze of the world map of the British Empire.

I have another experience with the Holy Land fifty years later that has also influenced my reading of nineteenth-century texts about the Holy Land and Jesus. That experience was a visit to Galilee in 2000, travelling by bus from Tel Aviv via Nazareth to Tiberias. The bus trip was an encounter with distance, or rather, of surprise at the short distances. The Holy Land of my childhood was, in fact, nothing like the land of Norway; it could be tucked away in a small corner of Norway, and Galilee was only a small part of that again. And even if it was so small that many of the places that were mentioned in the stories of Jesus were covered in short trips, it still did not seem to be the Galilee of Jesus that my memories led me to expect. 'My' Galilee was a Galilee fully influenced by Jesus, but in modern Galilee the traces of him seemed scattered and insignificant.

It was the same on a large map of Galilee I saw at a tourist centre. That map was dominated by references to sites of ancient synagogues from Roman and Hellenistic times, but it did not indicate ancient churches from the same period. Obviously it was a map from a specific perspective. The land that became visible through maps and signs and excavations was based on a different memory than the memories I carried.

These encounters between memories and experiences of places illustrate the difficulties in reading lands and landscapes. They show how much landscapes are the works of memories or constructions, based either on lived experiences or images, maps and literature, which create identification and identity. Moreover, my confrontation with 'reality', with Galilee today, could not be explained as encountering a place that was 'real' compared to my memories; what I encountered was a place that was also constructed, but based on different kinds of memories. What Galilee was 'really' like was impossible to say; instead, I ended up with constructions, ambiguities, and expressions of changing power relations and hegemonies.

Between Homeland and Holy Land

The power of seeing

It is with these experiences of memory, identification and a sense of foreignness that I approach the presentations of Palestine in travel writings, scholarly explorations and map-making of the nineteenth century. This double set of experiences and reflections has influenced my reading strategy for nineteenth-century discourses and literature on Palestine, as implied in the title of this chapter, 'Holy Land as homeland'. It is based on a triangular model, with 'Empire' at the top and 'homeland' and 'Holy Land' in each of the bottom corners.

The position of empire is the dominant one and represents the 'power of seeing'. This is a term used by the geographers James Duncan and David Ley to illustrate the unequal relations implied in the process of seeing.[2] They use a drawing by Joanne Sharp that is titled *Topographical Survey* to illustrate their point. The drawing shows a large eye looking down on a mapped world. Topography and mapmaking claim to be an objective science but, in fact, they constitute a 'science of domination', which creates and confirms boundaries and naturalizes social conventions.[3] And as Duncan and Ley remark, 'it is usually a white, male elite, Euro-centric observer who orders the world he looks upon, one whose observations and classifications provides the rules of representation, of inclusion and exclusion, of precedent and antecedent, of inferior and superior'.[4]

This is a perspective inspired by Foucault and, in particular, by Edward Said's description of modern Orientalism, beginning in the late eighteenth and nine-teenth century: 'Orientalism was ultimately a political vision of reality, whose structure promoted the difference between the familiar (European, the West, us) and the strange (the Orient, the East, "other")'.[5] This is a perspective that has been very influential and fruitful, not only in studies of the Orient, but in post-colonial studies of all parts of the world. Nevertheless it is also a perspective that has been rightly criticized as too monolithic.[6] My experience of the schoolhouse maps sug-gests that a simplistic understanding of Orientalism is too one-sided to explain the multifaceted relationship between European societies and Palestine in the nine-teenth century. For Christian Europeans, Palestine was above all the 'Holy Land', so that there was a special relationship between Holy Land and homeland, with a reciprocal exchange. The Holy Land was appropriated into the familiar, into homeland, but in a similar way the 'homeland' nation shaped the understanding of the Holy Land. Placing Holy Land together with homeland suggests a complex relationship between orientalism and nationalism.

This complex relationship is elaborated in an illuminating study of the images of the Holy Land, primarily in Victorian England, by Eitan Bar-Yosef, *The Holy Land in English Culture 1799–1917*. It is the conception of the Holy Land as a land that already prior to the political domination beginning in 1917 belonged emotionally to the English nation, and the pervasive use made of biblical imagery to create 'Jerusalem' in England, that makes Bar-Yosef reject the binary logic of Said's Orientalism. In his study, Bar-Yosef combines two fields of historical in-quiry that had been separated: on the one hand, the role of biblical vocabulary in the emergence of the British working class and in forming the modern British state; on the other, imperial history and its study of British political interests in Palestine. He sees the relations to the Holy Land as part of the national project of establishing England as a nation and as centre of an empire. His main thesis, however, is that the Protestant Bible's vocabulary evoked 'a unique sense of am-bivalence towards the imperial desire to possess the land'.[7]

I find Bar-Yosef's perspective convincing, but I think that he underestimates the power of possession implied in biblical and religious vocabulary. Bar-Yosef understands expressions of religious identification with the Holy Land as blurring Said's oppositions between East/West, self/ other, with their emphasis on conquest and domination. But I do not think the example he uses supports his point. Bar-Yosef quotes two statements from a speech by the president of the Palestine Exploration Fund (PEF), the Archbishop of York, to a meeting of that society: 'This country of Palestine belongs to *you* and *me*, it is essentially ours'; that makes it like 'this dear old England'.[8] For me, it is difficult to see that the language of religious identification, set in the context of PEF (see below), is not at the same time making claims of constructing Palestine in a certain way, and that such cultural claims supported activities of imperial domination structurally.[9]

However, Bar-Yosef rightly emphasizes the independent role that the vocabulary of the Bible and Protestant faith had in making the Holy Land into a 'homeland'. By combining the concept of Holy Land with 'homeland', I attempt in this chapter to trace in nineteenth-century travel literature the special character of the relations between the two 'lands' that seems to suggest an identification between the two and a blurring of conceptual boundaries. It should be kept in mind that the Holy Land was not a stable category, however; at the same time as it was identified as homeland, there were also experiences of foreignness and distance.

These categories are used to establish distinctions; 'home' and 'foreign' are central to definitions of nations and national identity in contrast to 'the other'. Therefore, we should explore the ways in which writings of the experiences of the Holy Land as 'home' and 'foreign' might serve as a paradigm for nineteenth-century discourses about nations and national identities. This chapter will prepare the ground for the studies that follow of individual authors and how their picture of Jesus in the Holy Land contributes to the way they imagine nation and national identity.[10]

Homeland as nation

In the travel literature and geographical descriptions of Palestine, there are frequent comparisons with 'home' and 'homeland'. We therefore need to look at the meanings carried by this terminology. 'Home' and 'homeland' became increasingly important and frequent terms in the English language in the nineteenth century, and they were associated with nation and nationality. 'Home' was imagined not only as the local area, the village/ town or region, but was also identified with a nation. This process that had started previously became one of the strongest ideological and political movements in the nineteenth century. As the understanding of the state moved from conceptions of rule by an absolute monarch to ideas of a nation, images of home, the home place and homeland became increasingly important to express the link between people and nation. Notions of home and home place were associated with the rural character of England. In the nineteenth century the relationship between land and nation was discussed in terms of political reforms of the land question, for example with issues like allotments to land labourers and smallholdings to develop a class of small farmers. The political discussions of these issues were conducted in a language of patriotism, in terms of the importance of rural land and of a self-reliant livelihood for English national character.[11]

A similar development took place in the German language where the term *Heimat* had covered a great many meanings, shifting from the local home place to the region and eventually the nation.[12] A significant change in its meaning was introduced by the early Romantic writers at the end of the eighteenth century when *Heimat* became part of the vocabulary of the German language and people, pointing towards a German nation. It was taken up as political vocabulary when the different German states were disintegrating under the power of Napoleon and political reformers attempted to integrate local communities in a central structure. *Heimat* became part of this modernizing process in common with words like nation, state, people (*Nation, Staat, Volk*). This started a process that made it possible to combine localized traditions with the ideal of one transcendent nationality. In the end, 'Heimat was both the beloved local places and the beloved nation; it was a comfortably flexible and inclusive homeland, embracing all localities alike.'[13] This *Heimat* was perceived as being in contrast to that which was foreign (*Fremde*) and distant (*Ferne*), for instance in descriptions of adventurers to strange lands, 'It was the place to which one finally returned: the homeland.'[14]

Home away from home

What happens when you travel, when you leave your familiar homeland and go to a far-off, foreign land? And what happens when you write about your travels? What actually are travel narratives doing? Such questions underlie all attempts to read and make sense of travel narratives or other descriptions of foreign places.

These are some of the questions Lisa Lowe discusses in her book on writings by French and British authors on travels to the Orient.[15] She does not turn Orientalism into a stable, fixed category, but she points to some attitudes that may be shared tropes in travel writings: descriptions of the oriental world as exotic and uncivilized had as their counter-discourse the European world as stable and knowing (personified by the traveller/author), but also as facing internal social difficulties, changes and instability. In this way the geographical expansion implied by the travel narrative addressed national anxieties about maintaining order, an anxiety that was solved by ascribing these challenges to the 'others' in a foreign land.

If these are common issues in travel writings about the Orient, there was an added dimension to the writings of nineteenth-century European travellers to Palestine. Palestine was not just foreign and oriental. It had a unique symbolic and religious significance because of its links to Europe, through the history of Judaism, as the birthplace of Christianity and as the place of the Crusades. For Protestants, moreover, it was above all the land of the Bible and of Jesus, and it was this that made Palestine into 'the Holy Land', 'waiting to be reclaimed both spiritually and physically'.[16] It was this expectation that the 'Holy Land' could be *reclaimed* that made travels there so different from travels to other places in the

Orient; the 'Holy Land' represented something that was *known* and also something to which the traveller had a claim of *ownership*. This attitude seems to have been a cultural assumption underlying not just individual travels but also national and imperial politics; the spiritual and physical in the desire to reclaim the Holy Land were closely intertwined.

Modern travellers (including myself, in my wish to find the unchanged Galilee of Jesus) can recognize the 'fervent wish' of nineteenth-century travellers 'to traverse an unchanged landscape where biblical journeys could be endlessly reenacted'.[17] It was this combination of 'landscape and memory' that shaped the reading of the landscape in travel writings; nature was primarily characterized by the biblical references it evoked, and therefore it had an immediate rapport with the traveller. He or she could immediately identify with the biblical figures associated with each place, and the present inhabitants had little relevance for this process of memory and identification.

These seem to be some of the common factors that give travel writings on 'the Holy Land' their special character. For travel writers who felt identification with the Holy Land, it seemed 'natural' to express that identification in terms of their feelings towards home, home place and homeland. Thus in this literature the Western authoritative view, 'the power of the gaze', is combined, almost seamlessly, with an identification with the Holy Land as homeland.

Imperial Gazes at the Holy Land

The Holy Land after Napoleon

Napoleon's military expedition and brief occupation of Egypt and Palestine (1798–1801) opened up the Orient in a new way to European imperialism, scholarly investigation and popular travel.[18] This included the Holy Land to an extent earlier unknown. This does not mean that the Holy Land did not have an important place on the European map before that, but direct access and information were much more restricted.

The origin of the term 'Holy Land' goes back to late Jewish prophets and other literature from the Hellenistic period, and it was an expression used of the land that had been promised to Abraham.[19] It was not a term in common use by the early Christians; the first Christian usage of it was by Justin Martin in the mid-second century CE. It is only in the fifth century that it begins to occur more regularly in Christian texts, primarily those by monks and bishops who lived in Palestine. The term 'Holy Land' in Christian usage may have developed from the interest in holy places and pilgrimage.

In earliest Christianity, there seems to have been little interest in holy places. The statement by Jesus in John 4:24 that true worship was not to be located in any one place but 'in truth and spirit' sums up this position. The beginning of the links between memory traditions about Jesus and their locations as central aspects of Christianity goes back to the fourth century. That was when the cult of the 'holy places' was introduced through the churches built by Constantine and his mother Helena in places associated with the life, death and burial of Jesus in Palestine. As churches and monasteries were built, these holy places became centres of Christian worship and pilgrimage, with a large presence of Christians in what then became identified as a Christian 'Holy Land'.

This development fundamentally determined the later history of Christianity.[20] The notion of the Holy Land was of importance for medieval spirituality, for pilgrimages and for the Crusades. However, after the fall of the Christian crusader states, until the beginning of the nineteenth century, for most Christians the Holy Land was a presence mentally, in faith, and in ideological or physical representations in their home countries.[21] The changes that turned the Holy Land into a place that could actually be experienced by many came as a result of larger political, technological and cultural changes in the relations between Europe and the Orient.

The modern, i.e. European, 'seeing of the Orient' started with Napoleon and his enormous influence upon the history of Europe and the Orient. His military expeditions and politics provoked changes in Europe and the Orient in many areas. The reactions against Napoleon's 'colonization' of many German principalities were important for the early period of nationalism in Germany. Napoleon's military expedition to Egypt and Palestine in 1798–1801 established a new basis for the cultural and political relationship between the West and the Orient.[22]

Napoleon's expedition brought the competition for political influence in the Ottoman Empire to a new level. There was competition among the major European powers, especially England, France, Russia, Austria and Prussia, with eventually the USA also playing a role. Apart from their political relations to Constantinople, the European powers also had a special relationship to Jerusalem and Palestine through the Christian holy places.[23] Part of this competition was played out in their roles as protectors of these places and of the Christians in the Holy Land. France held the role as protector of the Roman Catholics, Russia of the Greek Orthodox, and later England and Prussia established their protection of Protestant Christians.

The influence of Napoleon on scholarly activities in the Orient was equally important.[24] His military expedition was accompanied by a large group of scholars and artists who eventually produced the enormous work *Description de l'Egypte*,[25] which provided a basis for Western views of Egypt and the Orient. The nineteenth century saw a period of development in biblical studies with a combination of philological and historical studies, so there was a great interest in studying the

lands, places and peoples of the biblical narratives. Many biblical scholars therefore made the journey from Egypt via Sinai to Palestine, to trace the route of the
Israelites from Egypt to Canaan and to identify the most important places along
the route. These journeys resulted in a large number of scholarly and popular
travel books about the Holy Land and its historical geography.[26]

The nineteenth century also heralded important changes in the possibilities for
travel to the Holy Land. Throughout the Middle Ages and early modern times,
there had always been pilgrims travelling to the Holy Land.[27] However, due to
high costs and the risks of travelling, the numbers had been small, with most
of the pilgrims coming from the Catholic countries in Western Europe, such as
France, Spain and Italy. With the opening up of the Orient after Napoleon, the
'Grand tour of Europe' for many young members of the elite was extended from
Italy and Greece to the Levant and Egypt. With the Egyptian annexation of Palestine in 1833, access to Jerusalem was made easier. Moreover, with modern technologies, new and larger ships for example, and with a growing affluent class the
numbers of pilgrim-tourists increased greatly. Palestine became the destination for
a large number of visitors, scholars, missionaries and modern-day pilgrims. Most
significantly, the number of Protestants from Northern Europe and America rose
sharply.[28] It is some of these Protestants travellers, who travelled with the Bible in
their hands, and their views of the Holy Land that I will follow.[29]

Seeing the Holy Land with English eyes

Among the many books written by European scholars and travellers, I have chosen
one that in an exemplary fashion presents these experiences and this gaze, this
'seeing'. In the introduction to his influential book, *Sinai and Palestine in Connection with their History*, A. P. Stanley represents the authoritative gaze of the
topographical surveyor in the way he combines the perspectives and language of
empire, nation and home. The book was based on his travels in Sinai and Palestine
in 1852–3, was first published in 1864 and became an authoritative handbook for
British travellers.[30] Stanley was an influential churchman in nineteenth-century
England;[31] he was a professor of Ecclesiastical History at Oxford and Dean of
Westminster Abbey and one of the founders of the PEF. His discussions of the
Holy Land and homeland illustrate my earlier point about the three maps in my
own childhood classroom – that the maps of Palestine and the 'home country'
were placed together under the dominant influence of the map of the world em-
pires.[32]

Stanley's main interest in his book is to discuss the relationship between the
'sacred geography' and 'sacred History', the latter being identified with the Scriptures (the Bible). He employs the terminology of 'seeing' when he says that his
task is to:

point out how much or how little the Bible gains by *being seen*, so to speak, *through the eyes of the country*, or the country by *being seen through the eyes of the Bible* – to exhibit the effect of the 'Holy Land' on the course of 'the Holy History'.[33]

But *who* does the seeing? Stanley speaks of the country or the Bible as 'seeing', but it is obvious that the country or the Bible can only see through the eyes of Stanley himself, when he brings 'the recollections of my own journey to bear on this question'.[34] Thus, it is he who has the surveyor's eye on the issues that he brings to his readers, under the (pious) disguise of objectivity.

Stanley starts by presenting the special case of the sacred geography of Palestine and the sacred history of Israel as an illustration of a general situation. This refers to the widespread idea of the time that geography and landscape influence and shape the character of the people who inhabit the area. Given those common presuppositions, it is Stanley's terminology that catches my eye. The ancient Israelites who lived in this area are identified as 'a nation' and the area as a 'home'. Stanley speaks of the relation between the geographical features of the country and 'the *nation* to which it has furnished a *home*', and how this has shaped 'the national character.'

The idea of a nation and the geographical area as 'home' are introduced in a matter-of-fact way and ready to be employed as definitions. Stanley's terminology illustrates one of the main points in Keith Whitelam's *The Invention of Israel*, viz. that ancient Israel was described in terms of nineteenth-century European ideas of a nation state.[35] Through the categories of 'nation' and 'home' the Holy Land and its ancient, historic people are brought closer to the self-understanding of English readers, in the very way that these images were internalized in English consciousness.[36]

Stanley emphasizes the special character of this people: they make up 'the most remarkable nation which has appeared on earth'. It came into being through a divine process that is presented as a progress from Sinai as a birthplace for 'the infant nation' to Palestine as 'a natural home for the chosen people'.[37] What Stanley presents as the 'seeing' of the country and the Bible, and what he wants his readers to see, is the Holy Land as the homeland of the Israelites as a nation, as the Chosen people. It is a language that prefigures that of the Balfour declaration some fifty years later, speaking of 'the establishment in Palestine of a national home for the Jewish people'.[38]

If this was the result of looking back upon the history of Israel, the meaning of 'sacred geography' provides another possibility when looking at the present situation. Stanley uses the terminology of something that cannot be overlooked, and that he is able to see, since it is 'brought home with especial force to the Eastern traveller', so that he can now convey it to his readers. The 'prospects and scenes of the Holy Land' have 'poetical and moral associations', for instance, the events associated with the passing of the Red Sea, Mount Sinai and the Lake of Gennesareth, to name only a few. Stanley presupposes that these 'local features of the Holy Land' are well known among his readers, since they have 'naturally become the household imagery of Christendom'. It is this *naturally* that betrays how the images of landscapes have become a link between the Holy Land and the English people.[39]

The term 'naturally' evokes something that can be taken for granted and goes without saying. Since Stanley uses the term, however, it might suggest that the role of biblical imagery could not be taken for granted, that it was contested. Thus, this seemingly innocent term may point to a cultural conflict in mid-nineteenth century England as the context for Stanley's book. Instead of particular places, it was the *landscape* itself that was regarded as having preserved the sacred character of the Holy Land. This corresponds to the importance of nature for nineteenth-century national identity, not least represented by paintings, music and poetry. Central to the imaginations of a nation were descriptions of the landscape and the history associated with that landscape.

For Protestant travellers to the Holy Land the landscape was shaped by the close relationship between the geography of Palestine and the biblical text; it was a specific version of Simon Schama's *Landscape and Memory*[40] where the memory was filled with narratives from the Bible. They have been characterized as representing 'polemical Scriptural Geographies' engaged in a controversy over the culture and character of Victorian society.[41] Stanley's presentation of the Holy Land, his 'seeing', was therefore also part of a struggle for how to define the modern British nation.

Stanley's map of the Holy Land is also placed securely within the context of the map of the British Empire. He introduces the journey he has taken from Sinai to Palestine 'as it is usually taken by modern travellers' as unique. Stanley writes that the successive scenes of his journey 'faithfully reflected the dramatic unity and progress which so remarkably characterizes the Sacred history'. 'Progress' was a typical word in the nineteenth century to characterize the superiority of the Western world over the static timelessness of the colonized world. This progress was not only present in the history of the Bible and in the geography of Sinai and Palestine. It continued in time and space – via Early Christianity in the cities of the Church councils in Asia Minor until it was fulfilled in Europe: 'the life of European scenery and of Western Christendom completes by its contrast what Egypt and the East had begun'. The statement is that beginnings in the East are recognized, but they belong to the past; history and Christendom have made progress, and are now located in Europe.[42]

For the English and other Westerners, the Holy Land is presented as homeland, but at the same time the progress that started in the Holy Land has now been completed in Europe and in Western Christendom. There is a direct link between the nation of ancient Israel and the nations of modern Europe; they are configured in the same way. This is, on the one hand, to define ancient Israel and the Holy Land by categories of nation; on the other it brings them 'back home', both as a sense of 'home' and also as a political argument.

Within a context where Biblical imagery and Englishness seemed still secure, the link between the two could become so strong that the Holy Land became homeland. At a meeting of the PEF its president, the Archbishop of York William Thompson, declared that the Fund's object was

> to know Palestine through and through; and our reason for turning to Palestine is that Palestine is our country ... We mean to walk through Palestine in the length and the breadth of it because that land has been given unto us ... it is the land to which we may look with as much patriotism as we do to this dear old England, which we love so much.[43]

In this terminology the spiritual and physical sides of reclaiming the Holy Land are intertwined. The terminology of walking through the land 'in the length and the breadth of it' is a direct reference to God's promise to Abraham in Genesis 13, and presents the English as a 'Chosen people' whose task it was to fulfil a biblical promise by exploring and surveying Palestine. To speak of Palestine as 'our country' and as an object of patriotism may be hyperbolic language, but at the same meeting other comments pointed to the colonial importance of Palestine to England, and to rivalry with the French with regard to Palestine and the Orient. Thus, the relationship between England and Palestine as English homeland was linked to issues of national identity and politics.

At about the same time, an American Methodist bishop speaks in terms of home when he describes his experience of a visit to Palestine: 'This is the first country where I have felt at home.' The reasons for his feeling at home are the awakened memories of childhood: 'I find myself at my mother's side and my early childhood renewed. Now I see why this strange country seems so natural.' Although similar in content, the terminology and tone is very different. Here the idyllic notions of mother and child and the myth of 'home and hearth' are combined, so that the holy also becomes homey. This is a domesticated description that makes the Holy Land seem 'natural'.[44]

A domesticated Holy Land

In the nineteenth century writing about Jesus in Palestine was an activity dominated exclusively by men. In that sense, it resembles Orientalism: colonization of
the dominated regions and peoples was considered structurally parallel to patriar-
chalism and domination over women in the West. And in Edward Said's construction and critique, Orientalism is a male activity; women are written out of it. This
is now in the process of being rectified through many studies that present *Women's
Orients*,[45] making the picture of the Orient much more heterogeneous and fluid.

In a study of English women's descriptions of the Middle East, Billie Melman
discusses writings of evangelical women in nineteenth-century Palestine.[46] The
high percentage of English women who spent time in Jerusalem is striking; of the
small group of English subjects who made up the colony about half were women,
most of them were single, and many working class. The women who were writers,
travellers or amateurs engaged in archaeology and ethnography were mostly middle class. Some of them wrote travel narratives that were full of information on
history and archaeology, speaking as it were 'in a male voice'.[47]

Many women were involved in mission societies and in education for girls
and women, primarily in Jerusalem. This opened up for them an opportunity for
contact with local women that was closed for European men, and made it possible to produce travel writings and novels like *Domestic Life in Palestine*.[48] They
shared many presuppositions with male writers; since their primary interest was
the relationship between the Bible and the land, they tended to overlook Muslim
Arabs. Instead they focused on Jewish and Christian women, whom they saw as
descendants of biblical women. However, they found a stark discrepancy between
the role of the biblical women, made into ideals of Christian femininity, and the
low status of the women in contemporary Palestine. Their poverty and sufferings
were described in terms similar to those used by philanthropists about poverty
in the slums of industrial cities in Britain. The English women described their
relationship to the Christian and Jewish women they encountered in familial (and
hierarchical) terms, with themselves mostly in the role of 'mothers', the others as
'daughters'.

The landscape was also domesticated.[49] In European travel literature and novels, the Orient was made exotic and erotic; even the geography was eroticized.
Evangelical Christians divested the landscape of this sexuality by placing landscapes and people in conceptual frameworks with which they were familiar. This
was done, for instance, by evoking the biblical narratives about places and persons,
to be interpreted as changeless morals or religious truth. In that way, 'the sights
of historic places visually evoke "types" or examples of truly Christian feminine
life'.[50] That also made it possible for the women writers to identify with biblical
women and to place themselves in their history. The result was that although the

patterns of interpretation and identification were the same as those employed by men, the examples were different. Where men, like Stanley, saw in geographical places the events that prefigured political history, women saw them as domesticated landscapes with female figures that exemplified virtues like motherhood, humility and repentance.

Mapping the Holy Land

The image of the gaze of the surveyor provides a useful perspective on yet another aspect of the role of Western powers *vis-à-vis* Palestine. One of the ways in which this power manifested itself was by making maps. In *Imagined Communities* Benedict Anderson explains how new institutions in the nineteenth century changed the ways in which the colonial powers imagined the dominated regions.[51] Anderson brings together the *census*, the *map* and the *museum* as activities and institutions that were especially important for the relation between the colonial powers and their subject areas. Making maps of an area and drawing boundaries created an 'imagined nation'. His examples are from the Far East, but his suggestions have validity also for the European powers in their relationship to Palestine as a part of the Ottoman Empire.

Palestine was under the rule of the ever-weakening Ottoman Empire, and the nineteenth century saw constant competition among the major European powers for influence and eventual control over Palestine. For good reasons, the European powers could not conduct censuses within the Ottoman Empire, but they were engaged in the other two areas, namely, surveying and producing maps, as well as collecting *objets d'art* and archaeological artefacts for museums.

The Palestine Exploration Fund is an example of such imperial activity. The PEF was an institution that combined its religious interests in the Holy Land with an obligation to conduct scholarly surveys in collaboration with the English military in its mission for British imperial politics.[52] As one of the founders of the PEF, A. P. Stanley was involved in many of its activities. In his introduction to a publication of excavations in Jerusalem undertaken by the PEF in 1871, he made the remark that 'The Ordnance Survey of Palestine was so obvious a duty for the English nation to undertake, that it is needless to dwell on its importance.'[53] This comment can be read as an illustration of familiarity with Palestine in England, of how the interest in the Bible and Palestine as the Holy Land had made it into an English homeland. Maps and descriptions of Palestine made it a familiar place for the English; they had, so to speak, naturalized it as an English place.

Another perspective is also possible, and that is to read the statement as an example of the surveyor's imperial gaze on Palestine. In that perspective, the survey represents a 'national territorialization of space',[54] whereby Palestine is territorialized as a national space for Britain. In his history of the PEF, John James Moscrop supports this last view. He writes of the survey of Western Palestine that 'It came of an idealistic imperial religious wish to possess the land for the British Empire, to symbolize the achievements of the world's greatest Protestant Christian empire.'[55] The mixture of Protestant religion and the politics of nation and empire can hardly be described more vividly than by the expression 'an idealistic imperial religious wish'.

The PEF was established in 1865, 'during a period when Britain was struggling to define its imperial purpose and to secure its imperial frontiers'.[56] The surveys of Palestine conducted by the PEF beginning in 1871 were part of concerted efforts by official British interests in the mapmaking of Palestine. It had started with surveys by the Royal Engineers in 1841; in 1864–5 the Royal Engineers conducted a survey of Jerusalem. Officers of the Royal Engineers also participated in the large survey of Palestine undertaken by the PEF from 1871 onwards. Through this and many other forms of support from the military, the PEF was very dependant upon the War Office (now the Ministry of Defence) for its existence.[57] In the same period, the British Admiralty mapped the coasts of the Red Sea and the Mediterranean.[58] These efforts were a British follow-up to the maps made by the French surveyors in the expedition of Napoleon in Palestine in 1799, and were part of efforts to control the sea routes to India.

There is another aspect of the surveying of Palestine that is easily overlooked at a distance of 150 years, and with sixty years of existence of the state of Israel. In the nineteenth century, there was no entity called Palestine with clearly defined boundaries.[59] The area was made up of various administrative districts of the Ottoman Empire. This represented a traditional, pre-modern model where dynastic or tribal authorities ruled over territories that could be organized into various forms of administrative units, and where boundaries were fluid. When the PEF set out to make its survey of Western Palestine, they defined their task as to map 'the country ... bounded by the Jordan, and the sea, and (which) extends from Dan to Beersheba'.[60] The expression 'from Dan to Beersheba' refers to the biblical description of the extent of the area, from north to south, ruled over by King Solomon (1 Kings 4:25). The terminology of the PEF represented an 'imagined Palestine', the ancient Holy Land, which was to receive a scientific foundation through this survey. The result was a 'modern', nation-like mapping with boundaries that actually became the borders for the territory approved by the League of Nations as the Mandate for Palestine.

This survey of Palestine was not only a result of imperial politics; it was also part of a nineteenth-century attempt to establish a scientific study of religion. Establishing a territory with clearly drawn boundaries created a 'biblical land' within this region of the Ottoman Empire, so that the Holy Land was configured clearly. In defining such a territory, the survey also followed up a Protestant focus on the landscape versus the architecture of holy places, as the basis for the holiness of the land. Thus the religiously based criticism of holy places by Protestant travellers was now put on a scientific foundation.

Surveying and mapmaking went hand in hand with collecting antiquities and establishing museums as efforts at making 'holy lands' into homelands. Here we must speak of 'holy lands' in a broader sense, because the interest was not primarily in the Holy Land in a narrow sense, but also in the great 'nations' of Antiquity: Greece, Egypt, Babylon, etc. The collecting of Greek and Near Eastern antiquities occurred alongside the establishment of major museums in European capitals where the antiquities were displayed proudly as symbols of their continuity with the great nations of the past.[61]

Ernest Renan's visit to Galilee that inspired him to write his *Life of Jesus* illustrates this interplay between diverse interests. He had secured the support of Emperor Napoleon III for his journey to Syria with the purpose of collecting artefacts for the Louvre museum, and he asked for protection by the French navy stationed along the coast of Syria when his situation became problematic.[62] Thus, the idyllic presentation of sun-filled Galilee in his *Life of Jesus* was only one part of the picture; the presence of empire was not far off.

Another aspect of the close relationship between mapmaking and empire is represented by George Adam Smith and his *Historical Geography of the Holy Land* at the end of the century.[63] In his presentation of Palestine, Smith took special interest in mapping the ancient road system, to show that Jesus lived in an area with easy communication to the rest of the world. In a later edition of *Historical Geography of the Holy Land* Smith says that he was encouraged by thanks from Field-Marshall Allenby for 'the usefulness of my volume in framing the strategy and tactics of their campaign', i.e. the war in Palestine in 1917.[64] The book with its maps of Palestine was also used in Versailles in 1919 to determine the boundaries for the British mandate of Palestine.[65]

What the imperial gaze did not see

What does the imperial gaze see, and what does it not see? Stanley's description of the land, of what could be seen when geography and history looked at each other, was a correspondence between the ancient nation of Israel and the modern nation of England and Western Christendom. The scene of the Holy Land was a witness to the past that also pointed forward to modern Europe. In one sense, it was the European 'homelands' that fulfilled the aspirations of the Holy Land. Holiness was transferred from its geographical beginnings to be expressed in the progress identified with modern European nations.

This was only one aspect of the relationship between Holy Land and homeland, however. In his discussion of biblical history and geography, Stanley described the ancient Israelites as a 'nation' and spoke of Palestine as their 'homeland'. This way of writing about the history of Palestine was well received by small but very active groups of evangelical Protestants in Britain and the USA engaged in a movement for 'The restoration of the Jews to the Holy Land'.[66] The idea of the return of the Jews to Israel was part of the chiliastic concept of the fulfilment of the prophecies of the end time. The return of the Jews and their conversion to Christ became the goal for English evangelicals as well as American millenarians, and resulted in many mostly unfruitful attempts at mission among Jews.

However, the notion that Palestine was the God-given homeland for the Jews became widespread. Among the participants in the PEF it found great acceptance and was the basis for suggestions for policies that combined English imperial ambitions with Jewish colonization in Palestine. Eventually the ambitions of the restorationists became identical with those of the Zionist movement, and they also influenced the British government in the Balfour declaration of 1917.[67]

The PEF's map of Western Palestine is an example of an imagined map that eventually resulted in 'facts on the ground'. But Stanley's focus on the geography of Palestine as home of the ancient Israelites was typical of many travellers' writings. It was the relationship between the geography and the people and heroes of the Bible that was their main interest. Their descriptions of the Holy Land took notice only to a small extent of contemporary Palestine and its inhabitants, consisting largely of Muslim and Christian Arabs, with a small number of mostly European Jews.[68] From the point of view of European scholars and travellers, the contemporary local inhabitants were dislocated from the Holy Land.[69] Although evangelical travellers and missionaries took some interest in Christian Arabs and Jews, most writers showed an 'amazing ability to discover the land without discovering the people'.[70] When mentioned at all, the local population was regularly described in negative terms, as lazy, poor, and fanatical.[71] They could at most be used as illustrations of how little change there had been since biblical times.

The nineteenth-century travellers as well as recent students of this literature have not been interested in what the local Muslim Arabs thought about Palestine as a Holy Land. So can the subaltern speak back? Is it possible to retrieve the gaze from the 'people on the ground'? The difficulty in part is that history is shaped by recent developments and this history determines the gaze of modern historians.[72] The early Zionist movement was based on the idea that the Jews throughout the world made up one single nation.[73] It adopted the views of nineteenth-century nationalism that a 'normal' nation had its own national territory, and the most suitable was its ancient homeland, Palestine. The movement's arguments for political claims to Palestine as a 'homeland' for Jews and eventually as a nation state were accepted by the British government in the Balfour declaration,[74] and eventually by the other Western powers in 1922.

In the carving up of the Ottoman Empire into new states, Syria, Jordan, Lebanon and Iraq were recognized as state territories and their populations were regarded as 'nations'. However, the mandate for Palestine did not grant this recognition, so the Palestinians were not recognized as a nation with a territory, but were left with an ambiguous status within the Palestine mandate area.[75] This recent history has shaped the construction of the past, and it has often been claimed that Palestinian national identity was a recent phenomenon, only created in response to Zionism.

One way to trace a national identity in analogy with the Christian and Jewish Holy Land traditions is to look for similar Arab ideas. Here one can find literature from the Middle Ages, especially after the crusades, which praised Jerusalem and other parts of Palestine as a Holy Land. But modern Palestinian national consciousness was also shaped by events in the nineteenth century.[76] European activities in the Holy Land heightened a sense of community and belonging together among the people living in Palestine, and reinforced a consciousness of Palestine as a Holy Land.[77] This illustrates the insight from post-colonial studies that the colonized subjects can subvert and exploit the power and ideology of the colonizers.

Thus, European interests in the boundaries of the Holy Land 'from Dan to Beersheba' played a role in creating a geographical sense of the land for the local inhabitants also. The churches of the Christian Arabs, even if their hierarchy was mostly European, played a similar role. The boundaries of the Greek Orthodox and the Latin (Roman Catholic) patriarchates as well as the Protestant diocese included Palestine in this sense, although it was not yet a political entity.

The European mapmaking of Palestine may even have influenced the Ottoman administration. Under Ottoman rule at the beginning of the nineteenth century there were three different districts, Jerusalem, Nablus and Acre, within a larger province, either Sidon or Syria.[78] But about the same time as the PEF drew the boundaries of Western Palestine in its survey maps, the Ottomans in 1874 elevated the Jerusalem *sancak* (district) into a separate administrative unit, directly under Constantinople, encompassing all the Palestinian districts. The establishment of this administrative entity contributed to the ideological creation of national entity. Moreover, there was also a strong sense of 'home' in attachment to the local place, village and town. This deep sense of rootedness was supplemented gradually by a sense of belonging to a larger entity, to Palestine. Thus there seems to have been a confluence of local experiences, of Islamic notions of holy places, and adaptations of Western, Christian ideas of Holy Land, that resulted in a gradual heightened awareness of a Palestinian identity among the Arab inhabitants in the land.

A Protestant Holy Land

The Holy Land as foreign

To dislocate the Arab inhabitants, even if only mentally, was one way of making the Holy Land conform to the biblical images and expectations of finding a homeland for European travellers. But it was impossible to avoid other encounters with experiences of foreignness. A common theme for many travel narratives from the Holy Land was the disillusion felt when the travellers experienced a contrast between their imagined 'Holy Land' and the real land, with its barrenness, poverty and squalor.

There was also another, maybe more unexpected, experience of the Holy Land being foreign, which many travellers encountered. Most of the nineteenth-century travel writings, both by professional Bible scholars and by missionaries and pious tourists, were written by Protestants, and therefore they present Western Protestant constructions of the Holy Land. One common thread through these books is the negative and sceptical descriptions of the sites guarded by Greek Orthodox or Roman Catholic priests and monks and their liturgies.[79] The American biblical scholar Edward Robinson finds the priests of the Holy Sepulchre Church in Jerusalem 'ignorant and often illiterate men, chiefly from Spain', and sums up his description by saying, 'The whole scene indeed was, to a Protestant, painful and revolting.'[80] The scene is clearly described as 'other'; priests and monks were 'orientalized', since Spain as a Catholic country was on the verge of becoming like the Orient.

These negative experiences affected the Protestants' view of the sacred places themselves. Biblical scholars and historians expressed strong doubt about the historicity of these places; their arguments were partly that the holy sites could not be identified in the Bible, partly on a Protestant conviction that it was not the place that was important, but the worship of God 'in truth and spirit'.[81] Also some of the early visitors to Palestine in the Middle Ages held that spiritual contemplation was more important than seeing the places themselves.[82] But it was Protestant travellers who developed the critical discussion that shifted the understanding of holiness from holy places to the land itself. Thus the Holy Land became a much more ambiguous place than it had been before their direct encounter with it. It became partly homeland, as a land to identify with and where it was possible to recognize features of one's own homeland, but it was also partly a foreign land, inhabited by foreigners and 'others'. How could a Holy Land be secured in the midst of such ambiguities?

The Holy Land as text

Instead of particular places, it was the *landscape* itself that was regarded as having preserved the sacred character of the Holy Land. This corresponded to the importance of nature for national identity, not least as represented by nineteenth-century paintings, music and poetry. Central to the imaginations of a nation were descriptions of the landscape and the history associated with that landscape.

For Protestant travellers to the Holy Land, the landscape was shaped by the close relationship between the geography of Palestine and the biblical texts. Again, it was a specific version of Simon Schama's *Landscape and Memory*,[83] where the landscape was filled with narratives from the Bible. A well-known example is *The Land and the Book* by the American missionary W. M. Thomson.[84] It is remarkable that within a tradition that so much emphasized the Bible as sole authority the land was recognized as a source of revelation. The reason Thomson gives is Christological. The Land was the land of Jesus: 'The land where the Word made-flesh dwelt with men, is, and must ever be, an integral part of Divine revelation … In a word, Palestine is one vast tablet whereupon God's messages to men have been drawn.'[85] In another instance, Thomson makes the parallel between the landscape and the biblical text explicit: 'The Land and the Book constitute the entire and perfect text, and should be studied together.'[86]

At about the same time, Ernest Renan starts his *Life of Jesus* by raising the question of the relationship between the landscape and the text of the Bible. Like Thomson (but less dogmatic) Renan said that, 'the striking agreement of the text with the places, the marvellous harmony of the Gospel ideal with the country which served it as a framework, were like a revelation to me.' The result was that, 'I had before my eyes a fifth Gospel.'[87] But in light of the state of the country when he visited it, which he found desolate and disappointing, he describes it as a gospel that is 'torn, but still legible'. That makes his own role as an observer (or surveyor) more important; in much the same way as Stanley, Renan presents himself as a person with the authority to see and to read the landscape.

A divided Holy Land

For many visitors, it was first and foremost in Galilee that the parallels between the biblical texts and the landscape became visibly present. The special place that Galilee held in the Holy Land in the nineteenth century was well summed up by the British cartographer Captain Wilson: 'With the exception of Jerusalem, there is no place in Palestine which excites deeper interest than the lake district in which our Lord passed so large a proportion of the last three years of his life, and in which he performed so many of his mighty works.'[88] This observation shows that what first caught the interest of the visitors to this region was the relationship between the geography of Galilee and Jesus, his life and activities. The statement expresses a religious sentiment of identification with the lake region of Galilee as the 'home place' of Jesus.

However, there is more to this statement when it is placed in its context. Wilson was not just any visitor.[89] He was an officer with the Royal Engineers, appointed to the War Office, and served as a liaison between the British government and the PEF. He participated in the PEF survey task force that made the first 'scientific' maps of Palestine after 1871, and the cited observation was part of his introduction to the survey of the Sea of Galilee. Thus his remarks should be placed within the broader cultural and political context of nineteenth-century Europe.

Wilson's comments show how religious images are intertwined with imperial politics. They also indicate the place Galilee acquired as the primary location of Jesus in popular consciousness as well as in scholarly studies of the historical Jesus in the nineteenth century. In this interest in Galilee, common ideas about landscape and topography were important factors. The role of the natural landscape in shaping the social landscape and also individuals was part of the construction of national identities. It is this larger context, with the importance of nature and landscape for human character and social structures, that helps us to understand the role that Galilee played in the presentations of Jesus.

Besides the Lake region, it was particularly Nazareth as the home place of Jesus that interested travellers. In attempts to read the nature of his home place for clues to the character of Jesus, the wide view from the hilltop at the edge of the town became the favourite starting point for visitors.[90] This view has been read in surprisingly similar ways by many visitors, and these interpretations indicate how landscape is shaped by cultural memories. Renan describes how the mountains form an 'enchanted circle', to which he ascribes the (gospel) meaning of 'the cradle of the kingdom of God' in contrast to the 'dreariness of Judea'.[91] Here the differences in landscape are seen as reflections of religious attitudes. George Adam Smith in his *Historical Geography of the Holy Land* has many examples of this; he climbed the same mountain and used observations from nature to fill out 'the silence of the Gospels'. Looking south to all the other mountain ranges, all with their stories, Smith concludes: 'It is a map of Old Testament history.'[92]

The underlying assumptions of these nineteenth-century readings are brought into the open in an early twentieth-century version by the popular British travel writer H. V. Morton in his *In the Steps of the Master*. He reads the view towards the south, towards ancient Samaria and Judea, as expressions of the Old Testament. When one turns north, however, one looks towards Galilee and the New Testament. These two directions signal two different attitudes: 'in the New Testament we seem to have emerged from a dark, fierce Eastern world into a clear light that is almost European'.[93] Not many decades ago, these descriptions were fully acceptable as 'natural' expressions of a European power to define the world; now they read as confirmations of Said's *Orientalism*.

No doubt it was for these writers the historic presence of Jesus in Galilee that was the source of Galilee's holiness; it had, so to speak, a relational holiness. This was made visible through the Galilean landscape and especially the Lake region of which Wilson spoke so highly, which appealed so much to European visitors and provided a familiar sense of 'homeland'. Thus this landscape with its difference from the mountains of Judea appeared to support a distinction between two parts of the Holy Land that corresponded to the division between the New and the Old Testaments.

Moreover, this division was replicated in the immediate identification with the geographical land and the figures of the biblical past that the European visitors imagined; their experience of the Holy Land as 'our country' made them citizens of that country, much more than the local Arab Muslims. The focus on Jesus as the source of the holiness of the landscape dislocated the Muslim population even more. The contrast between the negative stereotyping of the Arabs as 'others' and the positive image of 'us' Europeans (partly including European Jews) found a structural parallel in studies of the historical Jesus and their descriptions of Jerusalem and Judea in contrast to Galilee. By the mid-nineteenth century, the Synoptic Gospels became preferred (over John's Gospel) as the primary historical sources for Jesus. As a result their pattern of a division between Galilee and Jerusalem became an overarching paradigm of interpretation. Most explicitly in Mark's Gospel this pattern showed acceptance of Jesus in Galilee versus his rejection and crucifixion in Jerusalem. When this structural pattern was applied to human agents it resulted in very different presentations: a positive one of the inhabitants in Galilee, and a negative one of those in Jerusalem.

Here we can see the beginning of a hermeneutical paradigm that has had widespread influence. It combined landscape and human character with the question of Christian identity, and thus was ideally placed to make distinctions between 'us' and 'others'. We might say that biblical interpretation and identity formation applied a well-known paradigm that attributed characteristics to nations and other groups; the result was that patterns of biblical interpretation supported potentially damaging labelling.

Conclusion

One of the women travellers to the Orient, Frances Power Cobbe, gives an apt illustration of the sort of imagination that made the world of Jesus in Palestine in the first century fuse with the world of European homelands in the nineteenth century (to refer back to the reference to imagination from Benedict Anderson at the start of this chapter). Cobbe sees travel as the only means to comprehend and to identify with Christian history since travel diminishes the two hindrances to an understanding of authentic Christianity: geographical distance and the distance in time. Travel gives the possibility of 'familiarizing to ourselves the actual scene of the Bible story', and thereby one realizes 'how much this familiarity with sacred localities will effect towards bringing us closer to the great souls who once inhabited them'.[94]

Travelling and reading travel writings from the Holy Land as an 'armchair traveller' represented a simple hermeneutics of familiarity that summed up one aspect of the combination of Holy Land and homeland. It represented a way to come closer to the 'great souls', including Jesus, who inhabited the Holy Land. This familiarity also meant that they were brought closer to the homeland.

Cobbe here does not use the other language of homeland, that of the Holy Land as a country, to be made familiar in categories of nation and chosen people, and as a land to possess, not only religiously but also physically and politically. From European perspectives, the Holy Land was also part of national politics and the ambitions of empire, colonization and competition. The 'power of seeing' was always present in the images of the Holy Land, even when it was combined with a sense of familiarity.

It was the unfamiliarity, however, that caused the greatest challenge and that made a single view of the Holy Land impossible; it did not fit completely into 'us', but it was not totally 'other' either. Bar-Yosef has borrowed a term that he describes as the 'slippery dynamic' of 'this/that/the other' to indicate the fluidity of characterizations. The perceptions of Palestine in the nineteenth century may be characterized as exotic but also as strangely familiar, 'terrifying' but yet 'manageable', and as a result, Palestine occupies 'that ambiguous space between "this" and "the other"'.[95]

I suggest that we also see attempts to manage these ambiguities by making distinctions inside the Holy Land. The dislocation of the people actually living in the land in contrast to the everlasting presence of ideal persons of biblical history is one example of this strategy, as are the divisions between (suspect) holy places and Holy Landscapes, between Galilee that can be identified with 'us' and Judea that is characterized as 'the other'. What is at work here may be what Lowe described as a transfer of problems to the foreign place that goes on in travel writings; national anxieties about internal social difficulties, changes and instability at home are ascribed to 'the other' in a foreign place. Thus there is also a negative transfer in play between homeland and Holy Land.

CHAPTER III

IMAGINING A NATION

Schleiermacher's Jesus as Teacher to the Nation

Introduction

Much seemed to be in flux at the time Schleiermacher gave his first lectures on the historical Jesus at the University of Berlin in 1819. He framed them explicitly as biography, with the purpose of writing the life of Jesus as the life of a human person. The goal for Schleiermacher was to place Jesus in interaction with 'his time, age and people'; that is, as an individual in relationship to his people in a specific period. This was no purely historical undertaking; Schleiermacher emphasized that the lectures must also be relevant for his own time: 'If therefore we cannot extract Christ from his historical setting and in order to think of him within that of our people and our age, it follows again that the knowledge of him has no practical value, for he ceases to have exemplary character.' [1]

A biography of Jesus was therefore both of historical and of hermeneutical importance; for Schleiermacher, history was not disinterested but always undertaken in dialogue with the present situation.[2] It is this interaction between the image of Jesus and the contemporary context that is the main interest in my discussion of Schleiermacher's lectures. This contemporary context is understood in a comprehensive way; it includes Schleiermacher's development as a religious thinker, the social and political situation in Prussia at the time, and also his own situation as a university professor under suspicion from the state bureaucracy.

With his collection of speeches *On Religion* from 1799 Schleiermacher established the modern, religious subject who found religion in the experience of utter dependency and not in supernatural revelation.[3] This book and Schleiermacher's follow-up on its perspectives, especially in his *Christian Faith*,[4] represented one of the most important transformations in the history of theology. He shifted the ground from the institutional authority of the church with its dogmas to the human subject in his or her experience of the divine. It was a religious equivalent of the political transformation represented by the American and French revolutions, taking symbolic power from the monarchy and reinvesting it in citizenship and the nation.

Both of these transformations represented a greater focus on the individual subject, at first located primarily among the intellectuals and the elites, but eventually spreading widely across different social classes. The quest for the self and for authenticity was not only a philosophical and intellectual undertaking; inspired by pietism and revival movements, it was also part of being a 'true' Christian. Similarly, the political transformation of power towards citizenship and nations provided new contexts and new horizons for the individual and his/her identity.

How could such new individual self-consciousness be formed, and how could this new individual be integrated into, and even take responsibility for, new collectivities like the nation? What was the relationship between the individual and the nation in a period when neither of them was clearly established or settled? These were matters of great concern for Schleiermacher, as reflected in many of his writings and activities, and he always emphasized that the individual was part of a community, be it a household, the church or the state.

In this chapter I suggest that these are some of the underlying issues for Schleiermacher's lectures on the *Life of Jesus*, and that they are influenced by the particular situation in which they were given. Schleiermacher was actively engaged in the 'national cause' against Napoleon's warfare in the German states and had strong views on the questions of citizenship and state authority. In the period of restoration after Napoleon's defeat in 1815 these ideas were not popular with the state authorities. Schleiermacher did not, like Strauss and Renan, face censure and loss of position because of his lectures on Jesus. However, in 1817 and for several years afterwards Schleiermacher was under investigation by the Prussian state bureaucracy for views expressed in his lectures on the state, for his support of the student movements of radical nationalism, and for his sermons, for suspicion that they contained hidden political exhortations.[5] In his lectures on the historical Jesus it is possible to find implicit references to all these issues. Schleiermacher's lectures on Jesus, explicitly placing him in relation to 'his time, age and people', must therefore necessarily participate also in the political discourse of their time.

Schleiermacher and His Biography of Jesus

Reading Life of Jesus *as a biography*

Reading Schleiermacher's *Life of Jesus* as a biography means to read it from a different perspective than from within the history of New Testament research, which has a primary interest in the evaluation of sources, the question of their historicity and the development of analytical methods. Reading Schleiermacher's *Life of Jesus* as a biography is also different from undertaking a theological interpretation of the lectures in light of Schleiermacher's Christology as he developed it in *The*

Christian Faith.[6] My focus will be on the lectures as a biography in the context of Schleiermacher's engagement in the struggle for a German nation.

In Chapter I the contribution of Schleiermacher in raising the question of what it means to write about Jesus in the form of a biography was discussed. The main questions concerned biography as a form of writing history, the relationship between the individual and the 'common life', and Jesus as a 'special' or 'unique' person. In this chapter we will explore how Schleiermacher develops these general issues in specific areas of the life of Jesus. My perspective is that of Susan Tridgell, that a biography is 'an argument for seeing a self in a certain way',[7] and I am therefore interested in what Schleiermacher seems to be arguing for in his *Life of Jesus*.

The question of sources is important in writing history, so Schleiermacher discusses and defends his choice of John's Gospel as his primary source. Since the presentation of an individual subject always takes place in a social context, the question of the location of Jesus' activities was important in all nineteenth-century biographies. Schleiermacher gave his lectures before the full impact of the travel narratives to Palestine had occurred, but he does have his own version of the relation between Holy Land and homeland. These questions concerning the *content* of Schleiermacher's picture of Jesus are illuminated through the biographical *form* he uses. Schleiermacher uses the different types of biography that were popular in the nineteenth century, namely those of the 'great man', of the 'learned man' and the religious ideal, to present a Jesus who is of practical value and has exemplary character for the religious and political situation of Schleiermacher's own time.

Schleiermacher's lectures therefore included an act of *memory*, of bringing to awareness a history of Jesus that by a hermeneutical act of imagination became relevant for the present.

The place of the biographer: Schleiermacher and German nationalism

In order to understand a biographer's perspective, it is necessary to know the place from which he or she is speaking. The first task is therefore to turn to Schleiermacher as biographer and to turn his own definition of the biographer's task around and apply it to him as a historical subject: how can we understand Schleiermacher within his own time, age and people?

In much of the history of the reception and use of Schleiermacher within theology and philosophy, his place within politics and the national movement has not been an important question. Also, in the recent renewal of interest in Schleiermacher his legacy has been primarily that of an initiator of modern Protestant theology. In addition, he became the founder of modern hermeneutics, started sociological investigations of the church, and remained an interpreter of the New Testament, a pastor and a preacher in addition to being a professor. And even these activities made up only a part of his very active life. His restless activity as a writer, essayist and polemicist, together with his work to establish the University of Berlin and influence education policies, formed another part. In the international theological discussions of Schleiermacher there have been few attempts to see the links between these different sides of him,[8] and his political activity has for the most part not been much discussed.

In Germany, however, the situation is different. Beginning with Wilhelm Dilthey, Schleiermacher's biographer in the nineteenth century, there was great interest in Schleiermacher as one of the founding figures in the history of German nationalism.[9] But what form of nationalism did he represent? There has been a long tradition of interpreting Schleiermacher as a German patriotic nationalist. The basis for this tradition is Prussian history writing, where the purpose was to see history as leading up to the establishment of a German empire in 1871. In the historical continuity that was created, the 'wars of liberation' from Napoleon in the early nineteenth century played an important part. The picture of Schleiermacher as nationalist patriot was based above all on his sermons from this period. He was portrayed as the ideal type of patriotic preacher, and seen as a protagonist for a view that combined the new Prussia with the task of creating national unity. This was a picture of Schleiermacher perpetuated into the early part of the twentieth century.

There were also attempts to exploit Schleiermacher to support the type of nationalism that reached prominence leading up to the Third Reich. Understandably after the Second World War, with the total questioning of this form of German nationalism among German historians, this image of Schleiermacher also became problematic.

Schleiermacher's political role has been discussed anew following the publication of his lectures on the theory of the state.[10] In a large study of these lectures and of his political activities, Matthias Wolfes challenges the traditional interpretation of Schleiermacher and charges that this picture is a result of a politically motivated reception history.[11] Instead Wolfes finds in Schleiermacher's political theory and activity a focus on civil society, free speech and citizens' participation in political life.

From this perspective the formative political events of Schleiermacher's time were the French Revolution and the Napoleonic Wars in Europe and their effect upon Prussia and the other German lands. The French Revolution made a great impression on Schleiermacher and enduringly influenced his political thoughts. It incorporated many of the ideas of enlightenment that were popular also among the German intellectual elite; it represented a democratization of power and administration, and the establishment of a modern legal corpus. The idea of freedom in contrast to the tyranny of *l'ancien régime* was at the centre of Schleiermacher's interpretation of the French Revolution, and remained an important part of his theory of the state. He was, however, critical of the terror regime and the execution of the king.[12] Due to the different socio-political situation, he did not think that a similar revolution would occur in German states, and he saw possible political transformation more in terms of reform than revolution.

The reign of Napoleon and the Napoleonic Wars (1806–15) transformed Europe and had a direct impact on the rise of nationalism in Germany.[13] The way in which Napoleon had run over most of the German principalities inspired ideas that went beyond a traditional patriotism within each principality to imagine a German nation. These military events also influenced Schleiermacher and led to his engagement on behalf of the war against Napoleon. When Napoleon closed the university in Halle, where Schleiermacher was teaching, he moved to Berlin. He was active there as a preacher, essayist and publicist during the years of the war.[14]

Schleiermacher's engagement in defence of Prussia and his sermons were expressions of a Prussian patriotism, but it was a patriotism that was combined with a spirited defence of the right to free speech.[15] And in his lectures on the theory of the state in 1817, he argued for citizenship rights for the young men who had fought against Napoleon in militias, several of whom had become his students. It was within the context of Prussia that Schleiermacher developed his political ideas, but he developed perspectives that went beyond Prussia, and that included a larger Germany.

The final result of the wars with the defeat of Napoleon in 1813 and the subsequent Congress in Vienna was a victory for the old dynastic powers. The main purpose of the Congress was to restore the old structures, based on the idea of the territorial rights and authority of the princes, not on ideas of a German nation being politically influenced by its citizens. Within this climate, Schleiermacher was looked upon with suspicion by the government. Once again he was under surveillance professionally, with demands from the government that university professors should not be 'political' in their teachings.[16] It appears that it was only with Schleiermacher's direct appeal to Frederick Wilhelm III that he avoided being removed from his position. However, he continued to be a strong critic of the king and the way in which the king, without consultation with the churches, established the unified Protestant church in Prussia (containing the Reformed and the Lutheran churches) and also introduced a new liturgy. But despite these conflicts Schleiermacher was regarded highly, even also by the king, eventually.

Berlin at the time was where much of the discussion of a German nation took place within the public institutions for debate, in publishing and preaching as well as in art and architecture.[17] One set of ideas from Herder and other Romantics was based on common language, culture and even descent. With some antecedents in the eighteenth century, modern nationalism was exemplified by Johann

Gottlieb Fichte in his *Address to the German Nation* in 1808, where the unity of Germany and civil liberty anchored in law belonged together.[18]

It is within the context of this last type of discourse, Wolfes argues, that Schleiermacher belongs, and in certain ways transcends it. Not a revolutionary, Schleiermacher joined those who suggested reforms in the form of *constitutionalism*. This approach provided a way to set up rules for popular sovereignty where subjects also had a role, and for relations between the state and society. Schleiermacher's main focus in his lectures and in his frequent criticisms of the political system in Prussia was recognition of the right to political participation and expression – for instance, through free speech and writing. These issues were directly related to the role and authority of the monarch, which Schleiermacher accepted, but not the authoritarian monarchic system. He was concerned to reinterpret the relation between the monarch and the people, so that, for example, the population as a whole should participate in the process of making laws.

Wolfes also points to other aspects of Schleiermacher's teaching that place him within the history of democratic thinking in Germany. After the Napoleonic wars, Schleiermacher reoriented his thinking away from the nation state and attached greater importance to the internationalization of politics, such as with principles for an international system of peace. In his lectures from the 1820s the universal aspect of the state became important, in the form that the protection of the earth could not be undertaken by any state in its particularity, for example. He asserted that it was the cultural sectors beyond the state, such as religion and science, which could best express these universal tendencies. In Wolfes' view, Schleiermacher comes across as a theoretician of state and society who inspired a model of liberal civil society.[19]

I find that Wolfes has argued well for his reading of Schleiermacher, focusing on the progressive and democratic motives in his works without hiding aspects that run counter to that tendency.[20] It is an example of a reading oriented by contemporary interests but evaluating Schleiermacher against the context of his own 'time, age and people'.

In contrast, studies by modern liberation or post-colonial theologians like Frederick Herzog[21] and Joerg Rieger[22] seem to evaluate Schleiermacher primarily against the values of their own context. They portray Schleiermacher's theology as representing his social class and privileged position in Prussian society, or simply as reflecting colonialism. It seems to me that this strategy of reading and interpretation is reductionist. They do not see the principles involved in Schleiermacher's arguments in relation to his own time, and therefore they also do not recognize their potential for discussions of democracy and the relations between the individual and the state today.

Schleiermacher's sources: John as a national Gospel

When the lectures on *The Life of Jesus* at long last appeared in book form in 1864, Schleiermacher was criticized for his reliance upon John's Gospel as the main source for Jesus' life. By that time, there was much more of an agreement in New Testament scholarship that the Synoptic Gospels were historically more trustworthy. But Schleiermacher's position appears to be based not only on New Testament criticism but also on an evaluation of the Gospels in light of his criteria for history. His evaluation of the Synoptic Gospels was that they correspond to what Schleiermacher in the introduction had described as 'chronicle', that is, a collection of separate events.[23]

In contrast, history was concerned with the inner meaning of events that combined them in a unity. This was what Schleiermacher found in John's Gospel; individual events were held together in such a way that the unity and underlying meaning became visible. With a term that pointed forward to a later stage of literary criticism in Gospel studies, Schleiermacher spoke of the 'unifying tendency' in John's Gospel, which he presents in two central passages of his lectures. The first is in one of the early lectures, discussing the beginning of Jesus' public ministry. In contrast to the unconnected collection of material in the Synoptic Gospels, in John's Gospel

> everything is set forth in order to give a clear picture, in the first place of the actual nature of Christ's activity, and in the second place of the development of *his relationship to the people* and to the authorities among the people.[24]

In the second instance Schleiermacher introduces the final conflict in Jerusalem, and again finds John superior to the Synoptic Gospels:

> *Concerning the development of Christ's relationship with the nation.* In this respect the Gospel of John must again be our main source of information. The other Gospels have so little interest in the conditions of the time that they are of little use in determining an intensification (of Christ's relationship with the nation).[25]

For Schleiermacher, it was obvious that the true character of Jesus and his activity could only be understood when seen together with his relationship to the people and to the nation. It is only from this perspective that one can write a history of Jesus; without this tendency, a life of Jesus disintegrates into unconnected events. The Gospel of John was concerned to make this connection understandable, and therefore the question of how to understand the inner nature of Jesus and his relation to the nation became one and the same question.

Schleiermacher's thesis about a biography, that it must see a person within 'his time, age and people', which sounds rather general, becomes quite specific when read in light of his choice of John's Gospel as a primary source; to reach a picture of Jesus' 'inner character' one must see him in relation to the (Jewish) nation.

Even if Schleiermacher considered John's Gospel to be the superior historical source, it does not provide a full historical narrative of Jesus' life. The difficulty of filling in the gaps could only partly be bridged, Schleiermacher suggests, by drawing inferences from the picture of the character of Jesus already established, and to some extent by building on the customs at the time of Jesus.[26] In other instances, Schleiermacher takes recourse to analogies, based on common knowledge or generally accepted views. These examples clearly reflect the situation in Germany at the time of Schleiermacher or present his view of what ought to be generally accepted; that is, they function not only as descriptions but also as prescriptions. It is especially in these analogies that Schleiermacher's perspective on his society becomes visible, and we can see how he makes his picture of Jesus relevant for his own day.

How does Schleiermacher follow up his argument that in order to understand the self of Jesus, one must understand him in relation to 'his time, age and people'? In Chapter I we saw how the figure of 'the great man' was commonly used as an archetype for the special character of Jesus and his relationship to people and history. In what follows, I will explore first how Schleiermacher's 'great man' figure is based explicitly on King Frederick II of Prussia and how his relationship to the people is described according to Schleiermacher's theories of an ideal relationship between king and people. With this as an underlying presupposition for the biography, we can move on to the actual description of Jesus' relationship to his people in terms of location, which Schleiermacher portrays as 'the totality of the Jewish land'.

When Schleiermacher has established that it is the Jewish people and nation to whom Jesus relates, the next question is what social role he attributes to Jesus to express that relationship. The role that returns again and again, described with analogies to the ambitions of German teachers as national leaders, is that of a teacher. Jesus' teaching was about the Kingdom of God. The term 'kingdom' belongs to the vocabulary of state and rule, so this raises the question of how Schleiermacher saw the relationship between the Kingdom of God and the politics of nation and state. Finally, with Schleiermacher's starting point that Jesus must be understood in relation to his people, what happened when this was the *Jewish* people? In conclusion, we shall see how Schleiermacher has drawn on various types of biographical models of Jesus to present a picture of the nation that goes beyond the history of Jesus and points towards a German future.

The Great Man and His People

Schleiermacher's presentation of Jesus was part of Schleiermacher's ongoing attempt to form a new subjectivity, to provide an image of Jesus as a human person, as a model to be imitated. The challenge that Schleiermacher faced was to explain how a person who belonged to 'his time, age and people' could have exemplary character, so that the knowledge of Jesus in his historical setting could be of practical value in the present.[27]

Jesus and Frederick the Great of Prussia

It is here that Schleiermacher uses the example of the Great Man and his relation to the people.[28] In his lectures on Jesus he does not use the terminology of the 'great man' but speaks of the individual and the common life.[29] He uses the same example as Carlyle, of the individual and his influence upon history. In one sense, Schleiermacher appears to say the same thing, that there would be no historical progress were it not for the individual, so that 'the whole stands under the power of the individual life'. And he speaks of the individual having 'a directing influence on the common life'.[30] To speak of a directing influence and a power under which others stand is to describe masculine power; the terms seem to express a specific form of hegemonic masculinity that found expression in Carlyle's and later in Renan's writings.

This is only the one side of the relationship between the individual and the common life, however. Schleiermacher sees it as a double relationship, consisting of the influence of the individual upon the community, but also of the community upon the individual. Schleiermacher balances the roles of the great men and that of ordinary people. He proposes that life must be seen in terms of continuous progress, where both 'the individuals' and 'the common life' stand in a necessary relation to one another, but in which they have different tasks. That the individual with a stronger directing influence always stands at the same time under the power of the common life is an extremely important point for Schleiermacher, which he repeats five times in slightly different forms. Schleiermacher concludes by saying that Jesus 'could not have been directing if he had not borne in himself the age and life of his people'.[31] The most significant expression of this influence from the people was *language*, which gave Jesus the concepts he had to use. Here we meet the idea, brought into prominence by Herder, of language as the expression of the identity of a people, as one of the main elements that made it a nation.

In this way, Schleiermacher has explained what it is that is special about Jesus without employing specifically theological arguments.[32] He argues on the basis of analogy with the relationship between the 'individual' and the 'common life' in the progress of history. Schleiermacher draws on the model of the great man, but modifies it in a significant way by expressing the interdependence between individual and common life. The individual – and therefore also Jesus – is inextricably bound to the common life and dependent upon it, as most powerfully expressed by the language of the people. Thus Schleiermacher's Jesus represents a transformation of the metaphor of the great man, a metaphor that must now be expressed as the 'great man in community', and which therefore gives greater dignity to the community.

This emphasis on interdependence between Jesus and the people corresponds to Schleiermacher's presentation of the relationship between the king and the people in his memorial lectures on Frederick the Great of Prussia (1712–86). Schleiermacher gave two such lectures on Frederick's birthday. The first was in 1817,[33] two years before Schleiermacher started his lectures on Jesus, and the other was in 1826, explicitly titled 'On the concept of the Great man'.[34] The lectures are divided into two parts. First, there is a discussion of what made the king a great man in his own time; and, second, how he was a continuing influence in the present time.

These lectures read as a reshaping of the collective memory of the King to serve as arguments for Schleiermacher's position on the relationship between king and people in his own days. Schleiermacher walked a fine line between the necessary acceptance of the king and his authority and a protest against the authoritarian rule of Frederick Wilhelm III, who never kept his promise of giving Prussia a constitution. Schleiermacher argued for stronger influence from the people, rights of participation and of free expression in speech and writing, with a corresponding limitation of the king's power.[35] He lectured extensively on the theory of the state and treated there this issue. His memorial lectures on Frederick II parallel the theoretical discussions in the form of eulogies and recreations of memory.

Schleiermacher emphasizes the interdependence between king and people: 'We cannot imagine a man who is separated from his time and his world.'[36] A king who shall be a 'great man' must 'carry the life of the people in himself'; he must be 'the living soul of his people'.[37] The great man's life is a result of the combination of his specific powers and the influences from surrounding forces. This is the same point and even the same terminology that Schleiermacher used in his introduction to the Jesus biography: 'No individual can be torn loose from his time, age and people'.

In his 1826 lecture 'On the concept of the Great man', Schleiermacher describes the form of the relationship between the 'great man' and the larger population (*die Masse*) in a way similar to his discussion of Jesus' relationship to his people; in both instances the latter expression probably also includes the large mass of uneducated people among the peasant population. The 'great man' inspires the population so that it ceases to be just a mass of people and gains self-confidence so that it can be formed as a community with a common life. It is this creative quality that is the criterion for a 'great man'.[38] Schleiermacher here presents a position that points forward to Durkheim's position in his criticism of Renan sixty years later.[39] Schleiermacher preached regularly to poor people in his parish; indeed, for his funeral such large masses of poor people turned up that the authorities feared an uprising.

A major issue in the memorial lectures was how the 'great man' could possibly inspire people in the present time. Here Schleiermacher makes a distinction between the outer side of the great man's activities as king, and the inner side, that is, his personality and the essence of his life. It is this inner side that can be made present for new generations, enabling Schleiermacher to conclude his lecture on Frederick II from 1826 thus: 'So his memory is part of our self-consciousness.'[40] The memory of the great man was not an external knowledge; it was so integrated into the life of the community that it became part of its self-consciousness. Schleiermacher reaches a similar conclusion in a discussion of the consequences of the influence of Jesus: 'Consequently, without overlooking the fact that there had to be a definite relation of Christ to his people and age, we can nevertheless think of an influence of his activity which extends *over all peoples and over all ages.*'[41]

Schleiermacher's Academy lectures on Frederick II present a transformation of the ideal of a king from absolute ruler to a king in relation to his people – *viz.* a constitutional monarchy. Moreover, the people are transformed from 'a mass' into a community with rights and influence. In a similar manner, Schleiermacher's discussion of what Jesus would look like within the literary genre of biography breaks with the dogmatic picture of a divine Christ who was above people and not influenced by them. Even if Schleiermacher preserves the idea of Jesus having a special influence, the emphasis on how Jesus was influenced by his setting among a specific people represents a transformation of the concept of a people from subject to agent. The Academy lectures and the discussion of biography in *The Life of Jesus* are parallel to one another and provide interrelated examples of a process whereby symbolic power was taken away from monarchic and religious models of authority and transferred to citizens, the nation and the church community.

Galilee versus 'the totality of the Jewish land'

The great man – Jesus – could inspire, even create a people. But who and where was this people? Where did Jesus come from? What was his home? This is always a significant question in biographies; and the setting of a person in a home place and environment is central to the description of him or her. Often the author's description of a subject's relation to the home place signifies important aspects of the subject's relation to self. So what does Schleiermacher have to say about the home place for Jesus?

Galilee as the home for Jesus was an important topic in nineteenth-century Jesus studies and popular imagination, as we have seen in Chapter I. This was due both to readings of the Synoptic Gospels, which place most of Jesus' activities in Galilee, and to the fascination with Galilee evidenced in travel reports and geographical surveys of Palestine. From the mid-nineteenth century on the Synoptic Gospels were regarded as the most reliable sources for the life of Jesus, and that consensus served to locate him securely in Galilee. Therefore Galilee took on an increasingly important role as a place with positive connotations in the descriptions of Jesus. The books by Ernest Renan and D. F. Strauss from 1863 and 1864 respectively presented Jesus as located in Galilee in a way that made it easy for European readers to identify with him. In both works, Galilee served as a positive point of identification for Jesus, and Galilee was presented as an ideal compared to the negative images of Judea and Jerusalem.

These meanings ascribed to Galilee as the home place for Jesus in later periods of the nineteenth century present a stark contrast to Schleiermacher's focus on Galilee as a *problem* in his presentation of Jesus. The question of the geographical location of Jesus' ministry comes up in his discussion of the most reliable sources for a historical reconstruction of the life of Jesus. One of the most important differences that Schleiermacher sees between the Synoptic Gospels and John's Gospel concerns the way in which they locate Jesus differently.[42] In the Synoptics Jesus' main location is in Galilee and he goes to Jerusalem only once, at the end of his career. In John's Gospel, however, Judea is the site of Jesus' public ministry. John brings Jesus frequently to Jerusalem, but he always gives a special explanation when Jesus occasionally goes to Galilee. From a historical point of view, Schleiermacher notes, it is of vital interest to be able to place activities in time and place, so these conflicting positions on Galilee are embarrassing.

However, the Gospel of John also records that Jesus was named 'a Galilean', so Schleiermacher must resort to a strained argumentation for how this false attribution could have entered into the Gospel.[43] The decisive argument for Schleiermacher appears to come from his view that to write a biography is to find the inner meaning of a life. A historical view of Jesus is meant to grasp the internal aspect of his life, his spiritual activity – that is, Jesus' preaching and creating a community of followers. It is this that is provided by John's Gospel; it shows that the true character of Jesus and his activity can only be understood when his relation to the people and to the nation is seen together with his activity. Consequently, this relationship between Jesus and the nation must also find a spatial expression.

Schleiermacher's arguments about Galilee can be illuminated by considering two different views of space and their consequences. David Harvey's discussion of space as a 'key word' is helpful to grasp the meaning of Schleiermacher's argument.[44] Harvey suggests that various perspectives on space illustrate different ways of using and speaking of space. The first is *absolute space*. In this perspective, space is fixed and we record or place events within its framework. This has been a common way to see space in geographical science. In this view people are placed in space or in a location. In the nineteenth century this view of the relation between location and people was widespread, together with popular ideas that geography and nature influenced people and also determined their character, as we will see especially in the studies by Renan and G. A. Smith.

For Schleiermacher such a view of space was unsatisfactory; that would make the external, such as localities, function as boundary markers that put limits on the inner side of Jesus' life, that is, his teaching activity.[45] Schleiermacher therefore holds that in order to give a satisfactory account of Jesus' life, the inner side and the external side must be viewed in connection with one another.[46] Schleiermacher here applies the perspective of *relational space*. In this perspective, space does not exist in isolation; there is no such thing as space or time outside of the processes that define them. Thus, the locality is not absolute in itself; as a relational space it is defined by the processes that take place *vis-à-vis* the area. We might say that Schleiermacher here represents a more modern view on space; this perspective comes close to what Jonathan Z. Smith has argued in *To Take Place*: 'People are not placed, they put place into being.'[47]

Schleiermacher's view appears to be that by placing Jesus in Galilee, one turns Galilee into a *limitation* for Jesus' activities. He concludes his discussion of Galilee with a section that summarizes why it was unsatisfactory to 'place' Christ in that locality. It is a dense text that is worth quoting extensively:

> If we now take a look at all the local relationships and ask *how the public life of Jesus was related to the totality of the Jewish land*[48] since he himself considered his vocation as limited to the Jewish land[49] this is the way things appear:
> At the time Judea was a Roman province and the other parts of the country were sometimes under various members of the Herodian family and sometimes united, but the terms that were in common use were Judea, Galilee, Samaria and Perea. If we now have to say that Christ thought of himself as *called to proclaim the Kingdom of God and establish it among his people by that proclamation*, this fact explains why he put himself as much as possible into contact with them.
> That could happen only in two ways. One method would be to stay continually in Jerusalem, for that city was the center of the land, partly because great crowds from all parts of the country came there at the time of the festivals …
> The other method would have been a constant journeying in order to visit all parts of the country. We find that Christ combined both methods.
> … We see then that *Christ neglected no part of the Jewish land* and excluded no part of it from the scene of his personal ministry.[50]

The physical or topographical geography that became so popular in later Lives of Jesus, inspired by travel writings and geographical descriptions, is of no interest to Schleiermacher. Instead, in this description he works with three different kinds of space related to geography. The first is political geography; he outlines the administrative and political divisions that indicate forms of government at the time of Jesus. Schleiermacher characterizes this as 'the dominant division', that is, determined by Rome where, as Schleiermacher observes, regions could be put under separate rule or combined under one vassal prince or the other at will. This description reflects the situation after the death of Herod the Great; the political and administrative entities were under personal, autocratic rule. [51]

In contrast to these forms of political division, Schleiermacher introduces a different division. It is indicated by 'the terms that predominated in common life', that is, those that were recognized by people and part of popular tradition.[52] This division represents regions or 'landscapes', a term that was much used in pre- and early modern times to designate territories of individual and collective attachment and which expressed identity, a feeling of 'home'.[53] Schleiernacher names 'Judea, Galilee, Samaria and Perea'; he also includes Samaria in this list, but later he describes the Samaritans as 'not members in the same way of the Jewish people'. But he does not mention areas that were under the political rule of Herodians without being Jewish, like Idumea and Trachonitis Batanea. Schleiermacher moves here from something that is very specific in terms of boundaries, areas of rule, to areas that are recognized in 'common life' as regions with some accepted characteristics, but without necessarily being administrative units.

Finally, there is a third category that apparently is of the greatest importance to Schleiermacher and represents a kind of 'imagined geography'.[54] Jesus' ministry is defined by its relation to 'his people', being linked with a geographical space called 'the Jewish land'. For Schleiermacher, it was important to emphasize Jesus' ministry to the 'totality of the Jewish land'. Jesus' goal was the proclamation of the Kingdom of God for his people, and therefore he neglected 'no part of the Jewish land'.

This 'Jewish land' represented the limits of his vocation to his people, but the limits are not defined clearly in terms of territorial boundaries. The administrative units that Schleiermacher speaks of go beyond the regions he mentions as parts of 'the Jewish land'. Furthermore, since there was a diaspora of Jews outside Palestine, Jewish land and Jewish people are not identical or mutually inclusive terms. Thus, 'the totality of the land' cannot be identified as a unit that consists of a fixed population in a definable space determined by borders. It becomes apparent that the terms 'people' (*Volk*) and 'land' (*Land*) are part of Schleiermacher's imagination; they are arguments and not necessarily categories that point to fixed entities.

When Renan and Strauss presented Jesus as a Galilean it was, so to speak, in a *passive* relationship to Galilee; he was shaped and influenced by its nature or the people and their views and perspectives. Schleiermacher attributes to Jesus a much more active role with regard to place and location. Jesus was influenced by 'his time, age and people', but he was also showing 'a directing influence'. Jesus' desire to communicate with 'his people' found also a spatial expression; therefore he could not be limited to Galilee. In Schleiermacher's view the 'Jewish land' becomes a *relational space*; it is shaped by the connections between the land and Jesus' communication of himself. Moreover, it is this Jewish land that Schleiermacher will make his hearers and readers imagine; it overrides the dominating image of political rule or the popular image of local regions. Schleiermacher brings the land into existence, making it the basis for Jesus' activity; and then he sets about transforming it with the overlay of another spatial image, that of Jesus' message of the Kingdom of God.

The 'Jewish land' and Germany

The terms that Schleiermacher employs in his discussion of Jesus' ministry, 'people' (*Volk*) and 'land' (*Land*), are part of the terminology of nationalism. Schleiermacher did not speak of 'nation' (*Nation*) in the long paragraph quoted in the previous section, but he uses the term frequently in other passages of the *Life of Jesus*. He speaks, for instance, of the schools of the Pharisees and the Sadducees as national institutions or forms of instruction, and the goal of the common teaching was to impart a national spirit.[55] The 'Jewish land' is the main term that Schleiermacher uses to describe the area for Jesus' public ministry in its special character as Jewish. The combination of ethnicity, religion and land in the German term gets lost in the English translation of the *Life of Jesus*, which instead frequently uses the geographic term Palestine as a translation of 'das jüdische Land'.[56] In Schleiermacher's lectures there is an immediate link between the people and a territory, with both characterized as 'Jewish'.

These images of a people and a land in their undefined totality suggest that Schleiermacher in his description draws on a context that is closer at hand than Palestine. Schleiermacher's description of the landscape of Jesus in his *Life of Jesus* shows strong structural similarities to his imagination of a German national landscape in a well-known letter from 1813 to his old friend Frederick Schlegel.[57] Politically, 1813 was a decisive year in German history. In that year Napoleon suffered a crushing defeat in Russia, and after a period of indecisiveness most of the German states united in a front against him. In his letter, Schleiermacher addresses both the existing political divisions, as well as his long-term perspective on political development after the end of the French occupation.

Schleiermacher is struggling with the German map of his time and describes it in categories that later he would use of the 'Jewish land'. First he speaks of 'tribes', like Saxons, Brandenburgers, Austrians and Bavarians. Second, these had political forms, but since they were based on dynastic policies, the territories of these principalities did not always correspond to the various regions with their specific tribes. He recognized the strength of the characteristics of these various units and envisaged that they should have a large degree of internal liberty in a new political system after the liberation. But beyond these divisions, Schleiermacher holds out something different: 'a greater National Unity', based on the idea of a German people (*Volk*) and land (*Land*) *in its totality*, which in its external relations should be represented by the emperor. Within the political context of his day, he spoke of this leadership in a noteworthy way. The emperor is described not as a ruler by divine authority, but as representing the totality of the land and of the people.[58]

Schleiermacher here combines a practical suggestion for political realignment after the end of the French occupation and domination, with a vision of a state organization of the German *Volk* and *Land* that went beyond the individual tribes and small states. They should be united in a political entity, with a national unity (*NationalEinheit*) that should be more than a loose confederacy. Here we find the concepts of the German *Volk*, *Land* and *Nation* that express the hopes of a new future after the liberation from the French, and a new organization of the political landscape. Thus, the terms referred not so much to existing realities as they were but expressions of hope and the vision of a new form of collective identity. In subsequent sections of the letter Schleiermacher is, correctly as it turned out, sceptical that his vision will come true.

Nevertheless, he returns to a similar vision in his address for Frederick II's birthday in 1826.[59] Here Schleiermacher's imagination of the nation is expressed in his attempt to shape a memory of the king that would be relevant both for the present and for the future. Schleiermacher argues that the influence of the memory or the spirit of Frederick the Great was not limited to his own state, Prussia. Instead, Schleiermacher speaks of how Frederick inspired a Germany that was *not* to be understood as a geographical category, but associated with the North, and manifested in language, art and science. This 'Germany' that Schleiermacher spoke of could not be identified with existing state territories, and it did not exist as a unified state; it was a Germany that was still an imagined state, but with the cultural institutions of a nation in place (language, art, sciences). It was Schleiermacher's vision of a future German state, invoked as part of the (constructed) memory of Frederick the Great as the one who inspired and organized it.[60]

In his discussion of Jesus' relation to Galilee versus 'the totality of the Land' and 'people', Schleiermacher has given a narrative example of what it means to say that a biography must see a person in the context of his people. The picture is an imagined reality, not a strictly geographical one. In this way Schleiermacher reflects the engagement of his own time, the post-Napoleonic period with Romantic nationalism and a more democratic and political nationalism, in the German question. In a book on *Volk, Nation, Vaterland*, Ulrich Herrmann has pointed out how these terms did not refer to a concrete reality; rather, they were expressions of a political desire and a hope, and therefore their meanings and internal relations were not clearly defined.[61] In Schleiermacher, likewise, it is difficult to give fixed meanings to the terms that he is using.

If we go back to his first lectures on biography, however, where he starts by saying that nobody can be torn loose from his people, we can get an impression of how Schleiermacher imagines this people.[62] He uses different terms, the English translations of which do not always adequately render their full meaning. Schleiermacher says that an individual stands in a relationship to the 'common life' to which he belongs; the German term '*Gesammtleben*' expresses more of a collectivity. Next, Schleiermacher presents Jesus with his 'setting in the life of his people', an expression that does not capture the nuances of the German '*Volksthümlichkeit*'. This term is derived from *Volkstum*, a term coined by Frederick Jahn (1778–1852, the founder of the sport association as national movement), in his *Deutsches Volkstum* (1806). The word *Volkstum* in an idealistic sense expresses the essential quality in a people (*Volk*), the spiritual principle behind its concrete manifestation. It can therefore be translated as nation-ness, nationhood, or national identity.[63] Jesus' *Volksthümlichkeit* therefore implies more than a spatial location; it expresses his deep identification with the character of his people. This identity was above all expressed through language. Even if Jesus' knowledge of God was uniquely his, in terms of expressing it he stood within the power of his *Volksthümlichkeit* and its expression in a common language. This language also belonged to the essential character of nationhood; Schleiermacher describes it as the language 'into which he (Christ) had been born and in which he was reared and on which his fellowship with other men depended'.[64]

The various terms that Schleiermacher uses combine to express an ideal identity, based on a collective life and a sense of nationhood, expressed in a language that one is born into and that signified the bonds of communication with others in the national group. Here are the elements of an idea of nation as a 'total community' based on language and descent, which corresponds to 'the totality of the Jewish land' and to the larger 'National Unity' in Schleiermacher's vision of a future German state.

The discussion of Galilee and the Jewish land participates in and makes a clear argument in the discourse of German nationalism at the beginning of the nineteenth century. In *Intellectuals and the German Nation* Bernhard Giesen has identified various stages of the national movement, in the period from the late eighteenth century through to state nationalism with the establishment of the German Reich in 1870 based in Prussia.[65] These stages have various forms of discourse or 'codes' for describing the nation. The Romantic intellectuals of an early stage saw the nation as a cultural identity in a transcendental realm, standing in an antithesis to the visible and limited present of the German territories in their political impotence.[66] Thus they saw a parallel between the present situation of Germany and their own, being politically and socially marginal but also carriers of the national ideas that pointed towards the future.

There are some similarities between this position of the Romanticists and the movement and tension represented by Schleiermacher's liberation of Jesus from the political boundaries of principalities and local communities and his identification with an abstract land and people. But both in his discussion of Jesus and in his memorial address for Frederick II there is not the type of resignation that Giesen attributes to the Romanticist intellectuals; Schleiermacher may point towards the next stage, which Giesen speaks of as 'the democratic code'.[67] Characteristic of this stage is an expansion of the social strata engaged in the construction of a national consciousness, and the development of new forms of communication that brought larger groups of people together, in social and sports organizations, in arts, song and rituals. We have already seen how Schleiermacher was part of this expansion of communications, with his preaching, addresses, pamphlets and journals.

The 'code' changed from the antithesis between the transcendental and the present, to a division in time with the goal of a future unity that could be realized through human action. It appears that with his image of Jesus who was influencing the people in analogy with the 'great man' Schleiermacher imagines that history can be changed, that the future can be influenced by the present. Schleiermacher also, through his university position, stood in direct relationship to a group that Giesen identifies as especially important in this democratic stage, namely, the German teachers. Due to educational reforms there emerged a large group of teachers at various levels of education from seminaries and universities, and a large percentage of these had studied theology. Many of them were liberal or radical, inspired by modern ideas of education, and were engaged in bourgeois forms of communications, such as social and gymnastic associations, etc. They were receptive to radical democratic ideas and became, in Giesen's words, 'carriers of a *democratic concept of the people*'.[68]

I suggest that this environment and, specifically, the teachers' important role in the democratic national movement, as well as Schleiermacher's own commitment to the extension of political participation and his role as teacher, provide the context for his presentation of Jesus as a 'teacher to the nation'.

Jesus as Teacher to the Nation

In all biographies, the occupation or the work of the subject plays an important part; the professional career is often where a person expresses much of her or his personality and character. That Jesus was teaching is an observation that is gained easily from reading the Gospel stories. Thus it is not surprising that Schleiermacher presents Jesus as teacher, but he puts extraordinary emphasis upon that role, and he is concerned to draw parallels between Jesus as teacher and the role that teachers played in Germany.

For Schleiermacher, Jesus' teaching was an expression of his 'inner' character; his activity as teacher was the main expression of the subjectivity of Jesus in his relation to the collectivity, defined as nation. This is an example of how the image of Christ was relocated from a domain which was otherwise unobtainable for ordinary humans, i.e. the divine, to become an exemplary figure, Jesus, within the range of human experience.[69]

The education of Jesus

Following a traditional form in biographies, the first section of Schleiermacher's *Life of Jesus* deals with Jesus' life before he started his public activity.[70] In order for Jesus to be truly human, Schleiermacher contended, he must have experienced a development in consciousness from childhood through to adulthood. This point corresponded to presentations in the *Bildungsroman* or the exemplary religious biography; they were concerned with the development and the shaping of human character. Education was part of that development and Schleiermacher discusses what education Jesus might have received.[71] The problem Schleiermacher encountered was that there were no sources on that question and therefore, Schleiermacher says, he must resort to *analogies*. These analogies refer to Schleiermacher's own time, to what could be taken for granted by himself and his audience; these analogies therefore point us towards questions of the social role and status of teachers and their place in the national project.

The first problem that Schleiermacher sees with regard to Jesus' role as a teacher lies in the social distance between that role and Jesus' original social location. There seems to be no connection between his situation as a child in the home of Mary and Joseph, who was a carpenter, and his later appearance as a teacher:

> In the Jewish national development of the day there were two completely different stages of existence. Christ appears in his childhood in the house of Mary and Joseph, and, since Joseph bears the title of *tekton*, he was therefore one who followed several trades. Christ appears later as a teacher. That is quite a different stage, and with reference to the way and manner that he passed from the one to the other we have absolutely no information. What I have said is not to be un-

derstood as implying that among the Jewish people there was an order of castes. The only caste was the priestly caste, but the function of the teacher was not associated with this ... But the scribes formed the distinguished part of the nation, naturally, because they represented its historical relationship, for informed in the law and informed in history were one and the same, and for this very reason the scribes enjoyed the highest esteem.[72]

Schleiermacher here describes the social situation in Jewish society at the time of Jesus with the help of categories that are recognizable to his audience, and therefore the distinctions Schleiermacher establishes are more characteristic of Prussia in the early nineteenth century than of Palestine in the first century. That 'a man of many trades', i.e. a craftsman, and a teacher represented 'two completely different stages of existence' was true within the Prussian hierarchical system of estates with its divisions between various social classes such as the aristocracy, the townspeople or burghers, and the peasantry. Handworkers, together with people working in other small trades or services, belonged to the rural proletariat[73] and might even be considered to be outside the estates altogether.[74] Therefore, even if they received some education to rise to become a teacher it would have been an exception in a socially static society. However, with educational reform, education had become more accessible, so more teachers came from a peasant or proletarian background.[75]

In Jewish society, teachers, or scribes, had an important place; Schleiermacher says that they formed 'the distinguished part of the nation'. The teachers took a place of national importance that went beyond that of other occupations; they represented the link to the history of the nation. Their training combined history, and the interpretation of the law, as well the study of the language of sacred scriptures.[76]

This combination of expertise in national law, history and language in one group of scholars corresponds to the annual conferences of the 'Germanisten' from 1822–47, an association of university teachers of German law, German history and the German language. Their goal was to contribute to national unity, and also to represent a wider mission to humanity on the basis of the divine Logos that was revealed in their respective subject.[77] The activities of this association reflected the growing consciousness of teachers, at a university level but also at lower levels, of their role in society, and shows how they saw themselves as making an important contribution to its development. The description of Jewish teachers as highly respected, but not to be placed within an estate or caste system, reflects the developing role of intellectuals and also of teachers in the gradual transformations of German society, along with their attachment to the bourgeoisie and its growing importance.

But how could Jesus realize the transition from being a child of a carpenter to becoming recognized as a teacher? In the Jewish educational system, Schleiermacher holds, every boy was educated in the law with the purpose to implant in him the' national spirit'.[78] For further education and training to become a teacher, there were schools of scribes. It was a popular theory of the time that Jesus had secret relations with the Essenes.[79] But Schleiermacher refutes the hypothesis that Jesus was educated in a school run by the Essenes. The exclusive and enclosed character of the Essene community showed that they lacked an engagement in public life and since teachers had a public and national role, Jesus could not have been trained in an Essene institution.[80] That left only the possibility that he could have entered one of the schools of the Pharisees or Sadducees. Schleiermacher does not exclude the possibility that Jesus could have gone to such a school, and argues that it does not impair the dignity of Christ to have attended such 'national institutes'.[81] However, it is more plausible that he did not attend such schools, Schleiermacher argues. Since Jesus was in conflict with the Pharisees and the Sadducees, and they did not accuse him of being a renegade – that is, somebody who has turned against his earlier views – most likely he had not attended their schools. Therefore, in terms of formal education Jesus probably received only the standard synagogue education common to all Jewish boys.

There is a tension in Schleiermacher's discussion of Jesus' education, however. He gives a positive evaluation of the schools as national institutions and of the public role of teaching. Schleiermacher also has a positive evaluation of Jewish laws as expressions of national customs, included in the elementary teaching that Jesus received in common with all other Jewish boys. Likewise, Schleiermacher's high regard for the philological and historical knowledge of the Pharisees and Sadducees corresponds to his view of the German teachers and their national role. Thus on the level of a national education with the teachers as a national elite, the Jewish system was an ideal. However, it was the content of the teaching that, he asserts, represented a 'one-sided and erroneous view'.[82]

Jesus as a public teacher

When it comes to Jesus' own function as a teacher, Schleiermacher emphasizes the public role of his teaching as corresponding to the role and self-consciousness of teachers in Germany at the time. This determines Schleiermacher's interpretation of the sources in sometimes unexpected ways. Jesus' public role as teacher provides the key to a question to which Schleiermacher returns several times: Did Jesus on a regular basis spend time with his group of disciples to instruct them and to give them a special teaching? This would seem to be such an obvious conclusion from a reading of the Gospels, in particular John's Gospel, that it is surprising that Schleiermacher rejects this idea on the basis of lack of evidence. He evidently makes his judgment according to the public character of Jesus' teaching. Schleiermacher therefore rejects that Jesus was teaching the disciples something different from what he taught the crowds, or that Jesus gave them 'esoteric teaching'.[83]

According to Schleiermacher, since the idea of the Kingdom of God was central in all his public preaching Jesus did not teach anything else to his disciples; it was all public teaching. 'Public preaching' was also typical of Schleiermacher's own role as a preacher and publicist in Berlin. His rejection of the Essenes as a secret group may have been a way of distancing himself from the secret societies of a political nature that had been established in Berlin. The result was a democratization among the addressees for Jesus' teaching. The apostles did not any longer hold a privileged position in terms of knowledge of Jesus' teaching.[84] Schleiermacher's conclusion is that 'Christ sets forth his teaching of the absolute equality of all members of his community.'[85]

Another example where the public right to speech plays a role is found in Schleiermacher's re-telling of the Passion story. Here he follows closely John's Gospel, with fewer observations of a general nature or analogies than in other sections of the book. It is therefore remarkable when, in the account of Jesus' cleansing of the temple, Schleiermacher repeats the same analogy several times.[86] Schleiermacher does not ascribe great importance to this episode, which often is used as a significant example of Jesus' Messianic self-consciousness. Quite the contrary, Schleiermacher argues; such a protest against improper actions on the temple grounds was something that everybody who was a teacher had the right to do. He repeats this no less than four times and concludes: 'Christ can only have cleared the temple of merchants by virtue of his office as a public teacher.'[87] He does not produce any historical evidence for this quite remarkable suggestion, but the purpose seems clear. He wants to find a basis for Jesus' acts not in a special Messianic consciousness, but in analogy with ordinary human practice. The analogy he finds is that of a teacher, using a general right of protest for Jesus' specific purpose of teaching. This seems to be an example of how Schleiermacher presents Jesus as making use of a common right to public speech or protest – thereby using Jesus to support his arguments for the right to public utterances and criticism of Prussian authorities in speech and print.

The social location of Jesus as a teacher

The social location of teachers in German society provided an important analogy for Schleiermacher when he tried to explain (or explain away) sayings in the Gospels that appeared to locate Jesus in a marginal position in his society. Schleiermacher presupposes that

we know in general that the profession of scribes and of those who were entitled
to engage in public teaching was a highly honored one and that everyone made
a point of showing courtesy to anyone who belonged to it. Because he had no
special means of subsistence, the support of a person of this profession was often
dependant upon the respect in which his profession was held and the hospitality
extended to him as a member of it.[88]

This respect and honour in which teachers were held provides Schleiermacher with
a response to suggestions in the Gospels that Jesus was poor and homeless. Faced
with the statement in Luke's Gospel that the Son of Man has nowhere to lay his
head, Schleiermacher suggests:

> If Christ was recognized as a public teacher, we cannot think of him as poor.
> Teachers were the object of respect and the recipients of hospitality. We have
> every reason to believe that this was so to a high degree at all times and in all
> places.[89]

On the face of it, Schleiermacher appears to draw on an existing situation for
German teachers to explain the role of Jesus as a teacher in Jewish society. The
public role of teaching and the importance of education as a means of attaining
to a national spirit both point to a high degree of self-esteem for teachers. But the
statement can also be read in a different way, as drawing on Jesus as an example
or prototype in an attempt to create respect for teachers, to point out their value
for the nation and to enhance their status. Such a perspective corresponds well
with Schleiermacher's concern for the role of teaching and education to promote
a national spirit. Since many teachers were educated as pastors, they would be
among Schleiermacher's students; he might also have them in mind.[90] And the
role of teachers and their function as educators of the coming national elite might
have been in need of support in this particular period.

Giesen has pointed out how the teachers as a large and growing group suffered
from an inconsistency of status between their own self-regard and view of their
important national task and their poor salaries and unclear social situation.[91] In
Bishop Eylert's report to King Frederick Wilhelm III in 1819, Eylert singled out
teachers as a group for strong criticism because of their perceived threat to the
conservative structures of learning and authority.[92] Thus, Schleiermacher's picture
of Jesus as a teacher who brought a new message but who was still accorded the
respect and remuneration that were due to teachers in a society might serve as
support for a group under suspicion.

There is another aspect to Schleiermacher's picture of Jesus as teacher that is
suggestive of the social location of teachers in Schleiermacher's time. Jesus' role as
teacher made it possible for Schleiermacher to integrate him within a social struc-

ture even though Jesus did not have his own household. According to Schleiermacher, Jesus did not have a permanent home, but was attached to the households of the disciples, especially that of Peter.[93] Here Schleiermacher presents Jesus in the position of a house teacher, a role that Schleiermacher knew from not-so-pleasant experiences in his own life.[94] The position as house teacher to provide private teaching for children of the nobility was a common first step in a career mostly towards a position as pastor. It was often a difficult position within a large aristocratic and autocratic household, and not highly regarded. For Schleiermacher, it ended with probably his own decision to leave, maybe over differences in views on the French Revolution. Thus, the position of house teacher provided a certain analogy to Jesus' own social location – for instance, that as a resident house teacher Jesus was at the same time inside society and at the margins of household and family life.

The Kingdom of God and the Nation

After Schleiermacher created the new space of the nation as the scene for Jesus' proclamation and presented Jesus as a teacher to the nation, Schleiermacher's next move was to present Jesus' message to the nation: the Kingdom of God. Schleiermacher is credited with being the first to have emphasized the central role of the Kingdom of God in Jesus' preaching and activity in the Gospels.[95] The meaning of the Kingdom of God in Jesus' proclamation has always been a contentious issue among biblical scholars. Frequently, it has been discussed in categories of time: 'When will the Kingdom of God come?' Reimarus, in his Fragments published by G. E. Lessing after Reimarus' death due to his fear of the controversy his views might cause, suggested that the Kingdom of God should be understood in a political sense.[96] He argued that Jesus wanted to be the king of an earthly kingdom, that is, a Messiah (anointed leader) in the line of David. Also other biblical scholars at the time of Schleiermacher held that Jesus' original view of himself was as a political leader over the people.[97]

The kingdom as transformation of the state

Schleiermacher rejects the idea of Jesus as a political leader, but he does it in a much more original way than later scholars who have spiritualized the concept of the Kingdom. Instead, Schleiermacher identifies Jesus with the Kingdom. The content of the Kingdom is not something different than Jesus himself, but a 'self-communicating power' whereby Jesus imparts the Kingdom: 'So Christ's impartation of his unique life to men and his foundation of a Kingdom of God as a life together is one and the same thing.'[98] Therefore this Kingdom is a community, both between Jesus and the individual who receives him, and among all who receive him. Jesus' activity as a teacher is not only to teach, but also to establish a community through his communication of himself. Therefore it was also formed not just around him, but inspired by him, similar to the way Schleiermacher spoke of the 'great man' as a king who inspired his people. This was a community that was established in a different way from that of a political Messiah with a king's power, and therefore it was totally different in character. In that sense, it was not political; it was not structured along the lines of a state. The Kingdom represented human society viewed from another perspective.

Schleiermacher's presentation of Jesus' communication of himself, which inspired and thereby became fused with the collectivity of the Kingdom, shows similarities to typical expressions of nationality in Romanticism.[99] According to Giesen, in Romanticism 'a further possibility consisted in translating the idea of individuality to collectives, in particular that of the nation'.[100] This combination of the individual and the collective identity of the nation resulted in a 'radical tension between culture and politics ... the identity of the nation was of the beyond, infinite and sublime. The present world of the state, on the contrary, was of this world, finite and contingent.' Giesen concludes: 'State and nation, society and community henceforth stood in a contradiction that reserved history for one, identity for the other.'[101]

Schleiermacher cannot be identified with Romanticism totally: he did not reject the state. On the contrary, he developed a theory of the state that showed his concern with practical politics.[102] But there are enough similarities between his identification of Jesus with Kingdom and the translating of individuality to the nation in Romanticism that Schleiermacher's ideas would be understandable within that context. To speak of culture, nation and community instead of politics, state and society meant viewing the world in a totally different way; it represented a transformation of the world 'as it was'.

This contrast between state politics on the one hand and the nation as community on the other becomes visible when Schleiermacher presents the Kingdom in Jesus' teaching as a totally different relationship between God and people than that found in the Old Testament. This contrast between Jesus and the Old Testament is a central element in Schleiermacher's theology. Within his theological system, the Old Testament was on a lower level than the New Testament; it did not have the same authority in the Christian church.[103] Moreover, the implication of this view was that Judaism as a religion was surpassed by Jesus and Christianity. This position influenced later Protestant theologians, and has continued to dominate later historical Jesus studies, even if there are now contrary voices that place Jesus within Judaism, and not in conflict with it.

I think a criticism of Schleiermacher and his continuing influence on this point is necessary,[104] but my point in the present study is a different one. I will

look at the contrast between Jesus' Kingdom and the Old Testament in Schleiermacher's presentation from the perspective of the social and political structures
they represent. Schleiermacher says that Jesus spoke of God as father, whereas in
the Old Testament the dominant idea was that of the 'theocratic nature of the
Lord'. Therefore, Schleiermacher characterizes Jesus' statement as anti-Jewish, for
in this statement 'the order of the household' takes the place of the 'order of the
state'.[105] This brief passage from Schleiermacher's own summary is first followed
up in the lecture by an explanation of what was implied in the Jewish use of the
term 'theocracy': 'their prevailing idea of God was by far that of an overlord, a
lawgiver and a regent' – i.e. an absolute monarch.[106] Consequently, when Jesus
speaks of his relation to God as father and of the disciples as children of God,
Schleiermacher finds that this had 'a decisive influence on the presentation of the
whole relationship between God and men'. What Schleiermacher finds original
in Jesus is that Jesus combines his own consciousness of God with the thought
that others can have the same relationship to God. Jesus' use of the term 'Father'
represented a tendency to 'transform and modify the idea of the relationship of
God to the people who stand in an association with Christ'.[107]

We recognize here the idea of the unity of the individual and the collectivity
within a community in relation to God, but it is of a totally different character
than that represented by the Old Testament. Schleiermacher uses terms like 'transform' and 'modify' with regard to the character of this new relationship to God[108]
and he speaks of the structure of the household which takes the place of the state.
Here he uses a similar type of language to that of Horne in the quote that I have
used several times to suggest larger mental and ideological moves in the period
when the Jesus biographies were written. Horne speaks of 'a process extending to
our own day that transformed politics by taking real and symbolic power from
monarchic and religious models of fatherhood and reinvesting it in citizenship
and the nation'.[109]

Schleiermacher uses fatherhood in a more positive sense than Horne, but the
shift is the same. The social organization of society that Schleiermacher identifies
with the Old Testament was the monarchic state with God described as an autocratic monarch: 'overlord, a lawgiver and a regent'. This was an image of the state
ruled by a king with absolute powers, while 'overlord' indicated a relationship
between someone 'over' and 'under'. In Schleiermacher's lectures on the theory
of the state, he indicated that a state was characterized by the contrast between
overlords and subjects.[110] The description of the relationship between God and
people in the Old Testament therefore made for an easy parallel to the relations in
contemporary European states between monarchs and the great masses of people.

Schleiermacher spoke of a transformation through what he describes as a radical change in the model for the relationship between God and humans in Jesus'

Kingdom, the idea of household with God as Father so that all who belonged had the same relationship to God as Jesus. It is the contrast between the structure of the household and the structure of the state that suggests that this statement had contemporary political relevance. The household represented for Schleiermacher a different form of human sociability; one that, for Schleiermacher, was more fundamental than the state. He regarded marriage and family as the basic forms of human community,[111] and combined with his emphasis on the individual, they were the place where the process of expressive individual subjectivity happened. The national unity was created when a great mass of families were united through a common language, and other social and cultural bonds, which represented a unity before the state was established. Starting from the household, Schleiermacher presented a view of human society as culture and community, in contrast to state and politics. For Schleiermacher, it was important that the household represented a private sphere that should be protected from invasion by the state.[112]

Consequently, the concept of household as an expression for the relationship between God and the community of Jesus and those associated with him provided a possibility for imagining human society as different from that of the static 'over' and 'under' relationship that was the state. Schleiermacher's lectures on the conflict between Old Testament theocracy and Jesus' Kingdom resonate with concepts and ideas about people, society, state and household that were part of the political discussions of the day. Why, then, did Schleiermacher emphasize that these notions in the teaching of Jesus were not political?

An unpolitical Kingdom?

One of the difficulties in discussing Schleiermacher's arguments about 'political' and 'unpolitical' is that the concept of politics has so many different meanings which also have shifted over time. In Germany in the eighteenth and early nineteenth century, the term 'politics' was used in a variety of ways – for instance, of an academic discipline, of inter-state relations, or of a specific social sphere. The definition given by a contemporary of Schleiermacher, Wilhelm von Humboldt, that the ultimate purpose of politics was the purpose and limits of the state,[113] may help us to understand Schleiermacher's use of the term when he discusses the difference between the Old Testament theocracy, which had an 'essentially political character', and the Kingdom of God, which was essentially unpolitical.[114] Schleiermacher outlines two different relations between nation and state: one unacceptable to Jesus, and the other he might accept as a 'preliminary stage'. It was unacceptable if obedience to God's laws was regarded as 'the means of maintaining the political existence of the people'.[115]

Here we see clearly that, for Schleiermacher, politics and the political were linked to the foundation and purpose of the state. However, it was another case if the political existence of the people was a means to *a larger end, viz.* that through them other people would be blessed by knowing God. Here the political form (as a state) is accidental, and the people are viewed from another perspective, namely, characterized by knowledge of God that can be transmitted to other peoples. Consequently, when Schleiermacher holds that the Kingdom was 'unpolitical' it was so *vis-à-vis* the political organization of a state, and not because it did not have any relation to a people or nation.

In another instance, Schleiermacher outlines his ideal relationship between the Christian community and the state: 'Since the Christian community has no political character, it is *eo ispo* neutral with respect to all political orders and must be able to be compatible with all'. But Schleiermacher could not be completely neutral. When he speaks of the way in which Jesus differed from the 'religious conditions that were part of the theocratic structure', it was in the form of 'the absolute equality of all members of his community'. The theocracy of Israel was based on the distinction between priest and people, and between teacher and student. The distinction between priest and people had fallen away with the fall of the temple, and that between teacher and student with Jesus' saying: 'None of you is to be called master with respect to the others'. The two characteristics of the Christian community in contrast to a theocracy, according to Schleiermacher, were that it had no political tendency, and its members had 'an absolute equality'. To a modern mind, however, to proclaim absolute equality within a society with great inequalities necessarily had at least potential political consequences.[116]

Schleiermacher's usage of the term 'political' seems restricted compared to our contemporary use of the term over a much wider field of activities and societal policies. Therefore, as long as we know that we are raising these questions from our own perspectives, it is possible and relevant to ask if Jesus' communication of the Kingdom could have political consequences. Schleiermacher's 'Great Man' address on Frederick the Great provides an example. Schleiermacher outlined how it was a quality of the Great Man to inspire the masses so that they could gain self-confidence and become a community. At this point in his lecture Schleiermacher brings in a comparison with 'one unnamed', obviously Christ, who can awaken new life in the totality of human society in all zones and at all times.[117] Schleiermacher comments that he will just mention this example to his audience, but leaves it without consideration, since it goes beyond what is humanly possible. Thus, Schleiermacher brings in Christ and his community-shaping activity as an analogy for the relationship between king and people; but then he makes a disclaimer as to its relevance. This seems like a rhetorical strategy for bringing in Christ and his community as a metaphor for the political community, whilst claiming that it is apolitical.

Jesus and the Jewish nation

From a present-day perspective Schleiermacher's theological position *vis-à-vis* Judaism is problematic, even unacceptable.[118] He put up a total opposition between the God of the Old Testament and Jesus' teaching on God, thereby opening the way for a rejection of Judaism as religion. Although Schleiermacher took a more positive position with regard to political rights for Jews in Prussia, distinctions between theology and politics were easily broken down. In the early national movement there were also examples of anti-Jewish attitudes and acts.[119]

Nevertheless Schleiermacher's views are complex, and in his *Life of Jesus* he seems to continue to describe Jesus' relation to the Jewish people in positive terms despite his rejection of Jewish theocracy. He makes a distinction between people and nation as social and cultural forms and the state as a political form. This position becomes clear when the narrative enters into its last phase, with the final conflict ending in the death of Jesus in Jerusalem. Here Schleiermacher elaborates his central argument, that the true character of Jesus' activity becomes visible in his relation to the people, the nation.[120]

Since Jesus' activity consisted of teaching and attracting followers, Schleiermacher asks why he did not create a community around him in his lifetime. One possible reason might be that this would have hastened the catastrophe at the end of his life. But Schleiermacher finds another possibility more plausible, that it was out of his concern for the people.[121] Schleiermacher here refers to Jesus' prophecy of 'the destruction of the political order as it then existed and of the temple' (Matt 23:37–9), a prophecy that in the Gospels is presented in the last period after Jesus' entry into Jerusalem. Schleiermacher finds that this prophecy reflects Jesus' 'great interest in the national situation', which made him realize that a conflict between the Jews and the Romans would soon emerge. He asserts that it was Jesus' concern not 'to give occasion for the outbreak of that conflict' which kept him from forming a separate community of his followers. Schleiermacher finds evidence in John's Gospel for his hypothesis in the statement of the high priest that unrest among the Jewish people would lead to Roman destruction of the Jewish nation (John 11:50). Thus, it was concern about a possible 'national catastrophe' that made Jesus not want to establish a closed community of followers, which was left to the apostles after his death. Here Jesus' concern for the preservation of the Jewish people is paramount.

However, as so often with Schleiermacher, he complicates the picture by raising a new question.[122] He engages in counterfactual thinking: *if* Jesus had decided to establish a community, 'what would he have done?', and would this community have been different from the organization of the Church as it was later established? More especially: would this form of the Kingdom of God have become something political? In this hypothetical discussion Schleiermacher argues that Jesus would not have undertaken any 'revolutionary change' in the law or in temple worship, seeing the law and the temple as national institutions.[123] But how can Schleiermacher imagine that Jesus would have established a community with the Jewish temple, cult and priesthood intact? The short answer is that he would have left them as national institutions but no longer as religious institutions. In that case, the followers of Jesus could not have attached themselves to the temple. The only alternative would have been the synagogue, whereby they would obtain an organization and 'at the same time spread among the Jewish people'.[124] Thus, even in this hypothetical argument, Schleiermacher keeps the same focus on mission to the Jewish people as in his description of Jesus' activity.

This counterfactual argumentation is revealing regarding how Schleiermacher sees the importance of the unpolitical Christ community for the nation and the Jewish people. The reasoning behind why Jesus did not found a community in his own days was based on concern for the Jewish people and the nation in a very positive sense. Schleiermacher's hypothetical imagination of the possible effect upon the Jewish institutions left in place by Jesus is an attack upon the Jewish theocracy and its combination of religion and politics. But Schleiermacher appears to be undercutting theocracy from another side *vis-à-vis* the previous discussion of the dangers of religious supremacy. Now Schleiermacher argues that when true religion, 'the actual spirit', is dislocated from the theocratic system, religious institutions and rituals become an empty shell and only 'a purely national matter'.[125] Here 'national' clearly is used in a negative sense.

However, to look upon Jewish institutions merely as national institutions, not attributing any religious value to them, may reflect Schleiermacher's position on political rights for Jews in 1812. He saw it as a political question for the king to decide, but he rejected that it should be linked to questions of religious assimilation.[126] It is also possible that Schleiermacher's ideas about a hypothetical Jewish history might be a warning about what could happen to a nation if it loses the spirit of Christ. One possible reference could be to Schleiermacher's criticism of the king's autocratic introduction of a new liturgy for the united Protestant churches in Prussia, instead of it coming from the church community itself.[127] Infringement of true religion did not only happen under Jewish theocracy.

Conclusion: Jesus as Nation

Schleiermacher's starting point for his *Life of Jesus* was to present the topic in terms of a human biography, based on the central idea that 'no person can be cut loose from his time, age and people'. Did he succeed in describing Jesus as a human person in the context of his people and nation, the focus of our study in this chapter?

Schleiermacher's human Jesus shows strong similarities to the Christ of his dogmatic writings[128] (hence the criticism that Schleiermacher drew from Strauss and Schweitzer) but in his *Life of Jesus* Schleiermacher described Jesus in fully human categories and within a historical narrative. However, the sub-structure of the biography is the concept of the 'great man' as the one who determines history and moves it forwards; a very popular model in nineteenth-century history and political philosophy. It could be put to use both in portrayals of Christ in church dogmatics as well as in eulogies of kings. But whereas this often would result in an image of the solitary hero versus the masses, in Schleiermacher's anthropology the individual is always part of a community and thus stands in a mutual relationship of interdependence with it.

Schleiermacher describes this community with a cluster of terms that belong to an early nineteenth-century discourse about people (*Volk*), nation (*Nation*) and national identity or characteristics (*Volksthümlichkeit*). It was a discourse that did not yet have a German state as its concrete point of reference; there were only various ideas about a German nation and what would characterize this nation, among them a sense of belonging together and language. For Schleiermacher language was of significant importance in Jesus' relation to his people, since Jesus must express his knowledge of God, the basis for his existence, in the common language.

However, it is what Jesus had to say about God that represents his 'directing' influence upon the people. And it is in Schleiermacher's description of Jesus' directing influence that he presents his vision of how Jesus defines the people and influences the idea of the nation. This influence was expressed above all through Jesus' mission, his communication of himself to the people. Here Schleiermacher moves his readers beyond divisions according to small political entities and tribal regions to a notion of the totality of the land and the totality of the people. In analogy with Schleiermacher's view of the divisions of Germany in his time, this was not a state that yet existed; his imagination is of a nation that Jesus brings into being with his mission, so to speak.

This ideal nation, moreover, is not imagined as a state. Schleiermacher's presentation of Jesus' preaching of the Kingdom of God places it in strong contrast to the Jewish theocracy. In that theocracy God was represented as a sort of overlord of a state; that is, in the terms of the autocratic rule of kings and princes of Schleiermacher's own day. By contrast Jesus' Kingdom represents a transition to another type of structure, that of the household, which is described as non-political. Indeed, it is more adequate to speak of it as pre-political; Schleiermacher points thereby to what for him is the fundamental basis for human community: the family and household. This type of community belongs to the given structures of life.

This has two important consequences. First, the people and the nation that Schleiermacher imagines is a cultural entity; it is the idea of a community based on a common language and a sense of communality. It is not a political project of a state. Second, the individual and the community to which he or she belongs, be it household or church, has dignity and independence *vis-à-vis* the state.

Even if Schleiermacher emphasizes that the Kingdom is non-political, the community that Jesus forms represents a challenge to political structures with its non-hierarchical and egalitarian structures. The implicit political criticism in Schleiermacher's lectures becomes visible when he uses an explicit biographical model to describe Jesus as teacher. To explain – or rather, to explain away – features in the Gospels that Schleiermacher found difficult to integrate into Jesus' life, Schleiermacher draws on the analogy of the role of teachers in contemporary Germany. Central to this role of teachers was the respect they enjoyed from people, and the authority they had to speak out against wrongdoings. However, these analogies can also be turned around: based on the example of Jesus, they could be used to defend the authority of teachers in their position as active participants in movements for democratic nationalism.

The role models that Schleiermacher identified as analogous for Jesus are all masculine figures. But instead of criticizing Schleiermacher for supporting male patriarchy from a modern, feminist perspective, I suggest looking at his *Life of Jesus* as raising the question of how to define the masculinity of the nation. With his biography of Jesus, Schleiermacher challenges hegemonic masculinities by introducing new forms of masculinity to represent the nation. John Tosh describes hegemonic masculinity as 'the masculine norms and practices which are most valued by the politically dominant class and which help to maintain its authority.'[129] Schleiermacher transformed the 'great man' figure underlying his pictures both of Jesus and of Frederick the Great from an autocratic, single hero to 'a great man in community', interacting with his people and representing the spirit of the community. Therefore Jesus' 'directing influence' through his proclamation of the Kingdom of God took the form of his communication of himself, so that the Kingdom reflected his character and took the form of a community of equals. Similarly, the image of God as autocratic overlord of a state was transformed to that of a father over a household. Thus, society was not viewed as the state ruled by the king with the authority of God, but as a people and nation made up of households.

To portray Jesus with the explicit use of analogies to contemporary teachers and their important national role presented not only Jesus as a teacher for the nation, but also supported the growing group of German teachers in their function as leaders of a movement towards a democratic nation with the rights of free speech and participation in government of the state. Thus, instead of the hegemonic masculinity of the autocratic 'great man' with the ultimate authority that reduced other men to subjects, Schleiermacher introduces a role for the great man who creates a space for the recognition of other men as citizens in a nation whose ideal is a community of equals. In particular, the growing group of teachers at all levels is lifted up as an important national role model.

Schleiermacher's concern in presenting the biography of Jesus was historical, but also hermeneutical, so that the knowledge of Jesus might have practical value in a contemporary setting. With his portrait of Jesus set explicitly in the context of the totality of the Jewish nation, Schleiermacher has fused the landscape of the Jewish land and people with his imagination of a German land and nation in his own time. Schleiermacher's theology, centred on the experience of the individual and the historical Jesus, here received a narrative form whereby the interrelationship between individual and collectivity was told as the relationship between Jesus and the nation.

CHAPTER IV

A PROTESTANT NATION

D. F. Strauss and Jesus for 'The German People'

Introduction

When the young theologian David Friedrich Strauss published his *The Life of Jesus, Critically Examined* in 1835[1] it caused an immediate uproar. That was not just because it was a radical theological book, its main thesis being that the Gospel stories were not history but myths that originated among the early Christian communities. Indeed, it was this thesis that made the book so significant within the theological profession and turned it into a reference point for modern New Testament studies. But at the time its influence was much wider; it changed the intellectual landscape of Europe with its criticism of religious foundations, and it had strong political repercussions. How could this almost 800-page, very detailed, academically argued book have such an effect, not just in theological and church circles but also in society at large?

Two comments by contemporary authors may help us to grasp the mentality of Europe in the first part of the nineteenth century. A comment by the poet and critic Heinrich Heine one year before Strauss' book was published illuminates the context within which it appeared. He describes the situation as one in which 'Christianity and the old regime formed an absolutely inseparable alliance.' It was this alliance to which Strauss' *Life of Jesus* dealt a deadly blow. Another comment by the renowned theologian F. C. Baur describes how the book created reactions in both areas: '*The Life of Jesus* evoked "panic-stricken terror" in the breasts of the defenders of the political status quo and images of the proximity of Satan in souls of the defenders of Christian orthodoxy.'[2]

The book apparently struck at the intersection between religion and politics; its criticism of the historical Jesus affected both Christology and the monarchy. The reaction to Strauss' *Life of Jesus* illustrates the proposition that religious symbols played an important role in the process of the transformation of politics from monarchy to citizenship and nation.[3] However, this may not have been Strauss' intention. His critical views on the Church's tradition about Jesus did not translate into radical politics on his part; he began as a liberal and became increasingly conservative. Thus, in contrast to Schleiermacher whose words and life appeared to be closely interconnected, Strauss' text may have had a life of its own, independent of its author.

The picture becomes more complicated when we try to follow the development of Strauss' presentations of Jesus. Their character changes over time from a 'democratic' image of Jesus to one that seems to support the power of the state, linking nation and empire. Thus, Strauss is an example of the fact that the historical movement, in this case from authoritarian monarchy to nation, does not always proceed in one direction. Strauss' various images of Jesus show how the democratic impulses in nationalism can be co-opted by an authoritarian state. Therefore, rather than seeking Strauss' intentions behind each text, we will ask what readings the texts themselves opened up in the context of their time.

A 'Modern' Nineteenth-Century Writer

Strauss understood himself to be a modern theologian, representing the ideas of the modern world. He describes explicitly the idea of a biography of Jesus as a modern project, presenting Jesus in categories of a modern human being in contrast to the ancient Christological images. He was engaged in discussions with the scientific advances of the modern world, such as those represented by Darwin, for instance.

Strauss studied theology in Tübingen where he was particularly influenced by reading Hegel and his question of the relationship between the (revelation of the) Spirit and actual history. In was in light of this question that Strauss wrote *The Life of Jesus* in 1835–6. He responded vigorously to the strong criticism he had received in many polemical publications, partly by modifying his views in the third edition of his book and then by returning to his original position in the fourth edition. He continued to write theology, which mostly consisted of attempts to explain the Christian faith in light of the modern world and the advances of the sciences;[4] for many years he also wrote biographies, some of national German heroes and some of European intellectuals like Voltaire. In 1864, thirty years after his first *Life of Jesus*, Strauss published a more popular work on Jesus, addressed to 'the German people' and along the lines of the less radical, third edition of the original work. Strauss' final work, *The Old Faith and New*, from 1872, represented his most radical critique of Christianity, based on a world view influenced strongly by evolutionary thoughts.

Theologically Strauss was a radical who tried to go beyond the liberal adaptation of Christianity that Schleiermacher represented. Politically Strauss started out as a 'left-Hegelian' of (mildly) liberal political views, but in time became increasingly conservative and a defender of bourgeois values.[5] He tried to engage in politics, which turned out to be no great success, but he did remain interested in politics for all his life.[6] In his private life, he was not successful; a brief and unhappy marriage ended in divorce.

One major factor that determined Strauss' life and writing was that, since his *Life of Jesus* made it impossible for him to get a university position, for almost forty years he had to support himself as an independent intellectual through his writings. This meant that he did not have the authority awarded university professors, and that he depended on the reading public as his audience. That was made possible by living in Berlin, where he moved from the small university town of Tübingen after he had completed his *Life of Jesus*. As the capital of Prussia, Berlin was an intellectual and social centre that provided Strauss with many opportunities.As noted earlier, the nineteenth-century German book market was a large institution and important for the intellectual and national formation of the growing middle class.

This observation provides Ward Blanton with a basis for reading Strauss as a public theologian who depended on mass circulation of his publications not just for money but also for his arguments.[7] He depended on his arguments to convince his reading audience, and therefore Blanton sees a link between the medium of the book through mass circulation and Strauss' biblical criticism. Herder had spoken of Luther's translation of the Bible as a '*Volks Buch*' for the German people, a book that installed national consciousness. In order to be a '*Volks Buch*', both mass circulation and an educated public were needed. Strauss saw his critical interpretation of the Gospels in this context, to provide an interpretation for his audience, and thereby to shape a modern German identity. Blanton shows how the very medium of the printing press and mass circulation shaped Strauss' thoughts on biblical criticism as he addressed his audience.

Two other authors also investigate the relationship between Strauss' theology and its socio-political context. In *Christ Unmasked* Marilyn Chapin Massey undertakes an explicitly political reading of Strauss' work.[8] Massey argues for a reading of Strauss' theological texts in light of the cultural idioms of German society in this period, with social and political tensions leading in the period of *Vormärz* ('pre-March') up to the unsuccessful revolution of 1848.[9] In this way she brings Strauss' text out of the traditional theological way of reading it, that is, merely within the development of New Testament literary criticism.

Massey finds that the original, first edition of Strauss' *Life of Jesus* represented a radical democratic politics comparable to that of Marx and Heine.[10] She does not claim that this expressed Strauss' *intentions*, but that the medium he used, theology expressed in the form of irony, created this effect.[11] In several studies Friedrich Wilhelm Graf has also suggested that the theological programme of Strauss 'can be interpreted as an attempt to legitimize the bourgeois claim to socio-political emancipation in the medium of classical theological subjects'.[12] Against criticism that Strauss only espoused a 'negative theology', Graf argues that Strauss was engaged in positive constructions of theological positions.[13]

Blanton, Massey and Graf represent the beginnings of an interpretation of Strauss in a cultural and political context that inspire my reading in this chapter.[14] They each read Strauss' texts expertly in light of contemporary philosophical positions, including those of Hegel, and various groups of the disciples of Hegel, as well as Nietzsche. Drawing on their readings I will apply a more general approach by placing the texts in their cultural context in nineteenth-century Germany.

Jesus of *The Life of Jesus*, Critically Examined

The democratic Christ

After the restoration of monarchic rule following Napoleon's defeat in 1815, the political situation in many of the German states became increasingly repressive.[15] The kings or princes and their bureaucracies were insistent upon restoring their authority and therefore very critical of the various democratic and partly radical nationalist movements that had sprung up at the beginning of the century. As a result many members of the bourgeoisie turned inward and became apolitical. The liberal and radical elements of the intelligentsia took refuge in literature. Intellectual and philosophical discussions might serve as a retreat from politics, but philosophy had political implications, however. Hegel's philosophy of society played an important role as the official philosophy of Prussia.[16] The philosophy of the Right Hegelians supported hereditary monarchy and linked it to true religion, while the Left Hegelians represented a critical attitude.

It was within this atmosphere that Strauss' critics sensed that the *Life of Jesus* had implications that went far beyond an acceptable questioning of Church dogma. Criticism did not come only from inside the theological academia or from the churches; the reaction was swift and critical on a broad front. The most influential literary critic in Germany, Wolfgang Menzel, denounced the book as 'immoral, heretical, cynical, and anti-social'. This was the same terminology that he used of another book that caused public uproar, namely a 'pornographic novel' by a political liberal, a former student of Hegel. So not only books about sex but also those about Jesus could evoke the criticism that they were destructive of morality, religion and the political order.[17]

With his book Strauss not only broke decisively with the orthodox image of Christ that secured the stability of the Church and state, but he also broke with an image of Jesus as the virtuous sage of the Enlightenment or Schleiermacher's sinless ideal 'great man', which was acceptable to the liberal, intellectual establishment.[18] Strauss stood accused that his *Life of Jesus* was not a life of Jesus, but in fact a radical questioning of the possibility of writing a life of Jesus. The structure of the book was quite traditional, following the same model that Schleiermacher used in his lectures.[19] The first part of Strauss' book covered Jesus' birth and childhood, the second his public life, and the third part concerned the Passion, death and resurrection of Jesus. The difference was the way in which Strauss analysed the stories. He started with a long section on myths and placed the Gospels within that context. This perspective was followed up by a detailed analysis of the historical basis for the Gospel stories. The outcome of the analysis was that they were deemed unhistorical; they were explained as myths of the early Christian communities. Thus, not only did the figure of Jesus as a historical and ideal person disappear, what emerged was the central importance of *myth* to create and uphold the figure of Christ.

At the end of his *Life of Jesus* followed a brief exposition of what Strauss had originally planned as the third, major part of the book, drawing the theological conclusions from his analysis. Here Strauss formulated the theological results of this deconstruction of the historical Jesus in terms of the relationship between God and man expressed not through a single figure but through humanity in general.[20] He goes on to suggest how this 'critical and speculative theology' can be related to the church.[21] Read today, his ideas seem to be quite theoretical discussions of how the divine is represented in the world, appearing abstract and not very original.[22]

If read in their historical context, however, it is possible to see the political implications of Strauss' conclusions. Strauss wrote in a situation of monarchic rule that was supported by church dogma and underpinned by philosophy. He argued that the idea of the unity of the divine and the human could not manifest itself, once and for all, in a single individual. Instead he asks, 'Is not the idea of the unity of the divine and the human natures a real one in a far higher sense, when I regard *the whole race of mankind* as its realization, than when I single out one man as such a realization?'[23]

According to Strauss, the realization of the idea of the divine should not be placed in a single individual, i.e. Christ, but in an idea that has an existence in reality in the race – another name for humanity. Finally, Strauss transfers Christological language from Christ as an individual to humanity in general: 'It is Humanity that dies, rises, and ascends to heaven … By faith in this Christ … the individual man participates in the divinely *human life of the species*.'[24]

Graf has pointed out that Strauss here undertakes a significant transfer of the manifestation of the divine from Christology to human identity; it becomes part of the self-understanding of people.[25] In this way the idea of the divine is no longer the unique privilege of one person; the Christ idea is democratized. Christ as the absolute authority figure had been turned into a democratic community.

How then could this theological and philosophical reasoning be read as politi-cally subversive? Strauss' discussion of divine revelation in a single individual or in humanity builds on a point in Hegel's philosophy that argues for the monarchy. Karl Marx's criticism of these Hegelian ideas shows the same structure as Strauss' argument in *Life of Jesus*, and reveals how philosophical discussions may lead not only implicitly but directly to political conclusions. In his *Critique of Hegel's 'Phi-losophy of Right'* Karl Marx critiques the following statement by Hegel:

> Sovereignty, at first only the universal *thought* of this ideality, comes into *exist-ence* only as subjectivity sure of itself … This is the strictly individual aspect of the state, and in virtue of this alone is the state one. The truth of subjectivity, however, is attained only in a subject, and the truth of personality only in a per-son … Hence this absolutely decisive moment of the whole is not individuality in general, but a single individual, the monarch.[26]

Against this Marx argues that Hegel creates a mystification when he turns the sov-ereignty into an idea that can only be expressed in an individual, when in reality he is only a sovereign as long as he represents the unity of the people, as a symbol of the sovereignty of the people. Thus Marx elaborates:

> Sovereignty of the monarch or sovereignty of the people, that is the question … (It is a question of) two completely opposed concepts of sovereignty, one such that it can come to existence in a monarch, the other such that it can come to existence in a people. This is like asking, is God the sovereign or the man?[27]

Hegel's argument about the universal thought of sovereignty and how it can only be represented by an individual, the monarch, has exactly the same structure as the Christological argument of the church that the idea of the unity of the divine and the human can only be fully expressed in an individual, Christ. This was the position against which Strauss was arguing when he said that it was humanity that represented the idea of the divine. Marx's criticism of Hegel follows the same structure when he questions that sovereignty can only be expressed in one indi-vidual, the monarch, and holds that the idea of sovereignty comes to existence in a people.

Bringing these two sets of arguments together makes it possible to see how per-sons with some knowledge of Hegel's thoughts would recognize that the theologi-cal reasoning of Strauss' book was politically subversive. Strauss used religious con-cepts that took on a political meaning.[28] If Jesus was no longer a divine authority, but divinity instead was present as the consciousness of the community, this posi-tion supported a radical democratic politics. The reception of *Life of Jesus* among supporters of radical politics indicated that this destruction of the symbolic power of Christ invested in the monarchy and the attribution of divine representation to the people was quickly taken up. Strauss' *Life of Jesus* became immensely important for the radical national movement in Germany in the *Vormärz* period leading up to the attempted German revolution of 1848. At least intellectual members of the radical nationalist movement could read his suggestion of the creative role of the community as a political statement that was critical of state authorities.[29]

On the other side of the political spectrum critics realized that the implications of the book challenged not only Christian beliefs, but also the very power structures of society and its social and political order; the close links between church and state made any questioning of authority threatening. The book therefore caused a strong reaction from the Prussian conservative establishment. The defence of Jesus as God became also a defence of the absolute authority of the monarchy over the people. It was the text of the *Life of Jesus*, more than any political intention on the part of Strauss, which caused this reaction.

There are also other aspects of Strauss' early work that would become increasingly important in his later works; they concern his view of history and progress. Strauss puts down as insignificant the few healing miracles reported of Jesus in Galilee. Instead he says that one should be interested in 'the miracles of intellectual and moral life belonging to the history of the world – in the increasing, the almost incredible dominion of man over nature – in the *irresistible force* of ideas, to which no unintelligent matter, whatever its magnitude, *can oppose any enduring resistance.*'[30] Strauss sees the movement of history as the progress of a power that crushes all resistance. Here he uses these military metaphors in a description of the history of ideas, but they will reappear in descriptions of world history in his *Life of Jesus for the German People*, and then with heavy overtones of contemporary politics.

The return of the 'aristocratic Christ'

The storm that *The Life of Jesus* created around Europe and all the written responses to it made Strauss publish new editions of the book and write numerous responses.[31] Such strong criticism made an impact on Strauss and he was surprised by the hostility of the attacks. He weakened his criticism in the third edition of the *Life of Jesus* and described Jesus as he is understood along traditional lines as a unique religious hero.[32] The concluding sections are markedly different from those in the first edition, which proclaimed that the religious future lies in the transfer of divinity in one person to its representation by humanity.

With the third edition Strauss returns to a view of history on the basis of 'the great individual', a view that all new periods in history were initiated by exemplary personalities, and so also Christianity. Jesus belonged to the category of highly gifted individuals that were generally named 'geniuses', and Strauss concludes:

He is the one who to this extent remains unique and unequalled in world history, without, however, having to deprive the religious consciousness first achieved by him of purification and further development in details through the progressive formation of the human spirit.[33]

This represented not only a weakening of his position in the first edition, but a total rejection of the whole project of a mythological interpretation and a return to the pre-critical age that Strauss had previously rejected.[34]

This return to a more traditional Christology with a focus on the individual personality of Jesus did not satisfy his conservative theological critics, and the political radicals were disappointed. In his criticism of the third edition, the left-wing Hegelian philosopher Arnold Ruge named it 'aristocratic'.[35] Within a Hegelian view of history there was both a subjective and an objective side, represented by great individuals and by collective forces. The first edition, in which humanity was the representation of the divine, emphasized the role of the collective forces in history and, by implication, the political conflicts of the time. When Strauss in the third edition presented Jesus according to the type of the great individual, it meant that he aligned himself with a view of history and politics that supported the role of the monarch and the aristocracy. The idea of the subjective consciousness of the genius was not just philosophical metaphysics; philosophical positions were evaluated for their political implications. The young intellectuals engaged in politics in the 1830s recognized Strauss' position as a return to a conservative political viewpoint.

Strauss' description of Jesus as a 'genius' took place within the context of an ongoing debate in Germany about the role of the genius, and the relation between use of the term to describe individuals, on the one hand, and the character of the people, on the other.[36] The conservative and aristocratic view was that the king and the nobility represented in themselves, as such, the silent masses. Early Romanticism presented a competing view wherein the king's representative powers were limited to his own age, and that it was the poetic genius that represented humanity in the form of the national character of Germany.

It was this image that Schleiermacher used of Jesus, and also in his memorial addresses on Friedrich II, when Schleiermacher described the king as representing the spirit of the people, and therefore with an influence that was not limited to his age. Thus Schleiermacher used the image of the genius to transform the ideal of a king in a way that from the outside might appear conformist to the political authorities but actually contained subversive elements.

In Strauss' use of the notion of the genius of Jesus, there are no traces of subversion *vis-à-vis* the authoritative ideal. Massey has compared the picture of Jesus in the third edition of *Life of Jesus* with other writings from this period and finds that Strauss places Jesus among geniuses whose focus is 'the harmonious shape of the inner life' and whose lives are 'work(s) of art'.[37] He was not among the geniuses who expressed themselves externally, such as Alexander the Great or Napoleon. Thus Jesus seemed more like a person who would be at home in Strauss' *Biedermeyer* Germany with the educated bourgeoisie. Massey's conclusion to the comparison between the first and the third edition elegantly sums up the political implications of these pictures of Jesus:

> The first edition portrayed the subject as real *only* in the collectivity, in a spiritual democracy; it removed the theological ground from the monarchical theory and from any Hegelian affirmation of throne and altar. The third edition portrayed the subject as real in the individual, in the genius, who stands above others; it provided a ground for the legitimation of status differences between people and thus for an aristocracy and ultimately for a monarchy.[38]

It was the *text* of the first edition that had radical political implications; they were not part of Strauss' intentions as an author. It was therefore not political but theological considerations that made him in 1839–40 publish a fourth edition that was very similar to the first edition. It was this fourth edition that was translated into English by George Eliot,[39] and that brought the controversy over his positions on Jesus into the English-speaking world, not only in academic circles but also among many educated people. With this fourth edition Strauss returned to his intention of changing Christianity into a religion of humanity, but this expressed a religious radicalism that was not followed up by his politics.

The text of the first edition of *Life of Jesus* made possible and even plausible a reading that combined a radical criticism of Christology and of the Bible with a political criticism of authorities and the social order. The text of the third edition, on the other hand, presented a more conservative picture of Jesus, with corresponding political implications of support for a political status quo. Although Strauss in the fourth edition returned to a text with a more radical religious position, his own political position turned increasingly conservative. His critical religious position represented a spiritualized religiosity that adapted easily to reactionary power politics. His last book on Jesus, *The Life of Jesus for the German People*, published in 1864, makes this shift to a politically conservative position explicit, so it will be helpful to place it in the context of the changes in the political situation leading up to the Prussian creation of a German empire.

A German Jesus

German nationalism before Bismarck

In the first part of the nineteenth century Schleiermacher represented a democratic nationalism that met with difficulties and some repression after the restoration of the power of the German monarchies and principalities after the defeat of Napoleon in 1815. Towards the middle of the century, this form of democratic national movement expanded with greater participation of people from outside the group of intellectuals, but eventually it was disappointed and lost much of its force. The events of 1848 were as close as Germany came to a revolution in the nineteenth century.[40] Inspired by the Paris revolution that brought Napoleon III to power in France, the liberal and bourgeois national movements managed to establish a parliament in Frankfurt with representatives from the various German states and principalities with the purpose of writing a constitution for a united German state. Popular unrest and the mobilization of the masses supported this movement and led many of the monarchs to introduce political and social changes.

However, in the end the effort to establish a union on a democratic basis failed. The parliament became factionalized, and it ended in a fiasco. The outcome of the 1848 attempted German revolution was that the autocratic forces, especially in Prussia, found a strategy to exploit the rhetoric of nationalism, and they were able to minimalize the influence of the popular movements. Nevertheless, the question of the unification of Germany remained an important issue in the years that followed. The main conflict was over the issue of whether Prussia or Austria should play the leading role in such a unification. The alternatives were *kleindeutsch*, that is, a smaller union mainly of the Protestant Northern German states with Prussia as the central power, or *grossdeutsch*, a greater union including all German states with Austria as the central power.

The divisions between *kleindeutsch* and *grossdeutsch* were reflected also among the historians, and political conflicts were often argued out in the form of historical debates.[41] In this period historians held the dominant place among intellectuals on the issue of nationalism and German unification.[42] In the first part of the period in question they continued to view history from the perspective of the ideal of the constitutional state with the participation of the bourgeoisie and freedom for the educated masses. In this view, the state must respond to moral goals. The position was that the nation that had existed as a cultural entity must be helped to form a state. The priority was the nation that, by the means of the state, would come into its own.

In the last decades before 1870, Giesen argues, the idea of objective history weakened these moral perspectives and led to historical presentations of the state based solely on its own power.[43] In this view, the only measure of the state's exercise of power was its political success. This resulted in a new perspective for the historians: 'the past is the past of possible state power organizations, and the current historian's mission is to reveal the potential for the possible development of state power that had existed in the past'.[44] Thus, the state was no longer bound to moral obligations, to cultural ideas of a nation as community, or to political participation by the people. As a result the relationship between nation and state was turned on its head. Based on their view of the state as the ultimate power, the Borussian (Prussian-oriented) historians now saw the nation as the means for the state to become established.

For *kleindeutsch* historians this became a programme to study history, as it pointed towards the goal of a unification of Germany under Prussia. In practical politics the result of this was Bismarck's cooptation of the national movement, especially among the intellectuals and the bourgeoisie, in many North German principalities, as legitimation to establish a German Empire on the basis of Prussian power.

Nipperdey sums up the position of these historians, who for the most part were both *kleindeutsch* and *liberal* nationalists:

> This liberalism was 'Protestant', anti-Catholic and anti-clerical, justifying the individualism and the culture of the nineteenth century and the secular state of the Reformation ... These historians were nationalistic, seeking not only the cultural, but the political unification of the nation.[45]

It was this 'state nationalism' based on Prussia as the dominant northern and Protestant state that formed the ideological context within which Strauss published his *Life of Jesus for the German People*.

Jesus 'for the German People'

Strauss' *Life of Jesus for the German People* was a very different book from his first, *The Life of Jesus, Critically Examined*. Within the disciplinary boundaries of New Testament studies, the legacy of Strauss and his *The Life of Jesus, Critically Examined* has been that of a radical questioning of Christology, of introducing the discussion of mythology, and of establishing methods and theories that have influenced all later historical Jesus studies. Strauss' later work, *The Life of Jesus for the German People* has been judged much more harshly. Schweitzer wrote in his criticism of that work that in spite of its title, 'the book did not become a book for the people. It had nothing new to offer' and it was written in a style that 'could not make any impression upon the popular mind.'[46]

Schweitzer was wrong, however. *The Life of Jesus for the German People* was enormously popular and went through many editions in a short time, remaining in print for many years.[47] Therefore, if we move outside of the narrow niche of biblical scholarship and into the late nineteenth-century German culture of communication, publishing and popular exchange, the question of Strauss' influence and legacy looks very different.

The dedication 'to the German people' in Strauss' last *Life of Jesus* has primarily been understood as being 'for the people', i.e. as a popular book, addressed to the laity and not the theologians.[48] This is obviously the idea behind the titles of the English translations, which in fact, have different titles in the first and second edition: *A New Life of Jesus*[49] and *The Life of Jesus: For the People*.[50] The first title makes clear that it is a new book, different from his original *Life of Jesus* not just in its simpler form but also with a broader presentation of the life of Jesus as a historical person. The second title makes clear that it is a popular, non-technical book.

The English titles do not, however, grasp all aspects of the meaning of the German subtitle with its 'for the German people' (*für das deutsche Volk*). The translations do not take into account the ambiguity in the original title with its address to the *German* people. One aspect of the address is that with this book Strauss turns to the people, whom he addresses as 'the thoughtful among the laity', since from experience, he did not expect an 'unprejudiced judgment' from the theologians.[51] He was correct in his expectation; since the book was a popular one, it was regarded by its critics as 'non-scholarly'.[52] So when Strauss speaks of 'the people', here it is in the sense of the reading public, the bourgeoisie. But when Strauss explicitly says that he is dedicating the book to 'the German people', 'people' (*Volk*) must be understood in a broader sense than just the bourgeois reading public.

Strauss refers to the Reformation as the event that defined what it means to be German: 'I look upon the German people [*Volk*] as the people of the Reformation; of the Reformation considered not as a transaction already finished in the past, but as a work to be carried on and progressively accomplished in the future.'[53] Ward Blanton points out that Strauss does not seem to distinguish between the *Volk* and the reading public,[54] but here 'the people' is viewed from a distinctive perspective, as being the German people of the Reformation. Thus, although 'the German people' appears to be an inclusive term, Strauss de facto seems to limit it by characterizing it as a Protestant people.

The Reformation represented in its time, according to Strauss, a true version of Christianity, based on the Bible. Now, however, in Strauss' view, Protestant Christianity had become an outward religion only. Thus, what was needed was a spiritual religion, where 'man' became more conscious of 'his own true nature'.[55] It was only by realizing with Strauss that Jesus was the individual in whom this consciousness became a pervasive influence, that Christianity was truly understood.[56]

Strauss here presents his own critical discussion of Jesus as the fulfilment of the project of the Reformation, and he also makes it a precondition for the political question of the unification of (a *kleindeutsch*) Germany (that is, under Prussia). By addressing his readers as 'people of the Reformation', he is using a well-known phrase with which his readers would identify. However, he explains it in a way that gives a particular meaning to that national identity, combining German unity under Prussia with a non-dogmatic spiritualized understanding of Christianity.[57]

His statement is situated within the context of the role of the Reformation in the politics and ideology of nationalism in nineteenth-century Germany.[58] Already in the first phase of nationalism during the war of Liberation against Napoleon there was recourse to the Reformation as a defining moment in the history of a German nation. Luther played an important part in this history – already Herder had spoken of him as the 'great patriot', and for the student *Burschenschaften* Luther was the great hero.[59] In their search for a specifically German role in Europe, Luther and Germanness were almost synonymous for Protestant. Towards the middle of the century, however, it became clear that these strong ties between Protestantism, nationalism and Germanness primarily characterized liberal Protestants.[60] The growing new orthodoxy among Protestants otherwise supported the bureaucratic state and its laws and protested against what they saw as an idolization of the nation.

Most historians traced the history of German nationalism back to the Reformation. In his influential *History of the Reformation in Germany*, Leopold von Ranke told the story of the Reformation as the unfulfilled business of fusing cultural identity and the German state. The promise of Luther was not fulfilled. The Reformation was met by the counter-organization of the Catholic Church and the Catholic princes 'blocked the fulfilment of reformation as a national task and thereby deprived the Germans of national unification in both a political and religious sense'.[61] As a result the German nation remained internally divided and vulnerable to foreign enemies for 300 years, according to von Ranke. He must have experienced the unification of Germany at the defeat of France as 'putting history right', and in the same manner evaluated Bismarck's *Kulturkampf* against the Catholic Church after the Vatican's decree of papal infallibility in 1870. The pro-Prussian historians created the slogan 'from Luther to Bismarck' to express what they saw as continuity in the history leading up to the declaration of the Prussian Empire.[62] It was in this spirit, but before 1871 (when the task of the Reformation was still unfulfilled as far as the unification of Protestant Germany was concerned), that Strauss wrote the preface to his *Jesus for the German People*.

Strauss presents his point about the unity of the religious task and the political one at the very beginning of the book. He outlines how the national and religious tasks are connected, or, even more, how there is a mutually dependant and reinforcing symbiosis between the two. It is the sixteenth-century Reformation that has this symbiotic relationship with the German nation:

> For as the Reformation, engendered out of the peculiar characteristics of the German nation, has set its stamp upon them for all time, so it is certain that no national enterprise can have a chance of success which is unconnected with the Reformation – which does not essentially grow out of their intellectual and

moral culture. We Germans can be politically free only in proportion as we have made ourselves spiritually, morally and religiously free.[63]

For Strauss, the Reformation was first of all a result of what was most characteristic of the German nation; it was a national project.[64] Consequently, it was only natural that a continuation of the Reformation was necessary to secure the present national enterprise, namely the unification of Germany.

In line with von Ranke's position in *History of the Reformation in Germany*, Strauss holds that it was the religious division caused by the halt of the Reformation that was the main source of division between the North and the South that prevented 'the efforts of our people to effect a united Germany'.[65] This was a goal that Strauss supported strongly and which would be effected shortly after he wrote this book, although not by the people but by Bismarck. Strauss indicates the way towards a union that overcomes the confessional divisions, consisting in a third and higher position elevated above the two rival parties.

Strauss speaks of how politics and religion cannot be separated: 'This higher position the *German nation* can never reach until it is initiated into the *eternal essence* of religion, and emancipated from the *external accessories* which form the root of confessional distinctions.' And therefore this religious task is a task for the German people: 'To effect this separation is now the proper task of Protestantism, and of the German people as leaders and pioneers of Protestantism.'[66] The superstition that needs to be rooted out is both supernatural religion with its miracles as well as priests and their authority, and Strauss once more emphasizes the political importance of this task: 'In calling upon the German nation to enter upon this enterprise, I by no means withdraw them from politics, but only indicate the safest and most effectual way of solving the political problem (i.e. the unification of Germany).'[67]

To Strauss, this theological project was a prerequisite for a solution to the main political problem of the day, the unification of Germany. Therefore it was only to be expected that Strauss' book should be *German* in character. In the preface, Strauss also praises Renan's *Life of Jesus* that had appeared the previous year. He concludes by wishing that he had written 'a book as suitable for Germany as Renan's is for France'.[68] Thus, the two lives of Jesus are inscribed not just in personal but in national characteristics.

Strauss has explicitly invited a reading of his revised *Life of Jesus* in light of its subtitle: *For the German People*. A political reading is therefore not a subversive reading of the text, but a reading demanded by the text. The German nation is characterized by the Reformation; for Strauss, that is shorthand for what he himself represents, the search for the 'inner essence' of religion, quite similar to the position of Schleiermacher. However, Strauss' arguments show that he cannot take this focus on the Reformation for granted, although he wishes this to be the case and attempts to have the German nation accept this characteristic. That the 'German nation' is an illusive concept becomes obvious when Strauss speaks of the divisions between North and South, a division that 'violently arrested' the progress of the Reformation.

Implicitly Strauss says that the Catholic South did not share in the Reformation and therefore neither did it have the national characteristics of the German nation (although he speaks in a conciliatory tone of the possibility of a third position, a higher one). So the Germanness of Strauss is an ambiguous proposition; it reflects his support for a smaller German union under Prussia. Prussia is the power that lies beneath much of his discourse. It is this 'natural' development towards increased power for Prussia and the division between the North and the South that thus provides the model for his description of Galilee and Palestine at the time of Jesus.

Jesus and a split nation

Strauss' position on the political and religious divisions in Germany is reflected in his presentation of Jesus' location in Palestine. Schleiermacher's goal had been a union of the 'totality' of the German nation and therefore he presented Jesus' mission as uniting the Jewish people and the Jewish land. As a result, for the sake of this unity he downplayed the role of Galilee. Strauss also wished for German unity, but he saw it within the context of the political and religious divisions between a Protestant North and a Catholic South. Therefore he gave priority to a *kleindeutsch* union under Prussia. Similarly, in his description of the location of Jesus, Strauss sees a contrast between Galilee in the North and Judea and Jerusalem in the South.

Strauss follows the synoptic Gospels, with priority given to Matthew,[69] in placing Jesus' ministry primarily in Galilee. In a chapter on 'Theatre and the duration of the public ministry of Jesus' Strauss outlined how the Synoptic Gospels present the locations of Jesus' ministry:

> from the time of his return after the baptism by John until his last journey to Jerusalem, he never passes the borders of Northern Palestine, but travels around in the countries west and east of the sea of Galilee and of the upper Jordan, where Antipas and Philip, the sons of Herod, were governing as Roman vassal princes, without ever touching Samaria to the South, and Judea and Jerusalem further in the same direction, or generally the territory that was immediately subject to the dominion of the Romans. And again within these boundaries it is more immediately the country west of the Jordan and of the sea of Tiberias, consequently Gallilee, into which the ministry of Jesus principally falls.[70]

Strauss here employs the language of *physical and political geography*. This is not a geography of 'the Jewish Land' that Schleiermacher talked about, nor is it 'the Holy Land' that became a common terminology not only among theologians but also among scholars in history and geography. Strauss employs the term 'Palestine', which was a name introduced by the Roman administration in the second century. It was also in use in the West in the nineteenth century, for example by the Palestine Exploration Fund and other scholarly groups.[71] The boundaries and the location of each area are explained in relation to geographical features like Jordan and the Sea of Galilee (Tiberias), but there are no descriptions of the topography or the landscape which are such significant features in the studies by Renan and G. A. Smith.

The other important factor is Strauss' focus on political geography; the geographical areas are described also in terms of political rule. Strauss is interested in the political structure of the area. In particular, he emphasizes the presence of the Roman Empire: Antipas and Phillip are Roman vassal princes and Jerusalem and Judea, the area that Jesus avoids, is under the direct rule of the Romans. Instead of Schleiermacher's picture of national unity with little emphasis on various types of rule, Strauss presents the scene as one of a marked contrast between Galilee and Jerusalem, with the presence of the Roman Empire constantly in view.

Which of these two dimensions in Strauss' picture has the greatest significance? First, concerning the contrast between Galilee and Jerusalem, Strauss criticizes the Gospel of John by suggesting that its use of geographical space is theologically motivated. John wanted to exalt Jesus as much as possible; therefore he brought him out of a corner of Galilee and into the more appropriate scene offered by the capital. Schleiermacher, who followed the Gospel of John, employed a spatial model based on totality versus the parts. Jesus' wish to reach the totality of the Jewish people put him in Jerusalem as the most central place for that purpose. Strauss' model, however, is equally theologically motivated: it is not based on *totality* versus *parts*, but on *good* versus *evil*. Galilee represents that which is good and positive, Jerusalem that which is bad and negative.

Strauss draws comparisons between the characteristics of Jesus and Galilee and those of Jerusalem. This comes out in his description of Jesus' education received by growing up in Galilee.[72] Jesus was characterized by the originality, freshness and lack of pedantry in his speech. This suggested that he had not received an education in any of the schools of the Pharisees, Sadducees or Essenes. These schools are not presented as national institutions and in a certain way as positive examples, as Schleiermacher did; they are described only with negative characteristics. Before he faced the negative response awaiting him in Jerusalem, Strauss contends, Jesus needed a preparation in regions 'where men's minds were more open to his teaching'. In Galilee, he met with a positive response and also gathered a circle of disciples. In contrast, the relationship between Jesus and Jerusalem was one of conflict. Jerusalem is portrayed in negative terms, with statements about its religion similar to stereotypes about the Catholic South. Jersualem represented the opposite of Galilee: 'there the Pharisaic party ruled over a population readily excitable to fanaticism, there the spirit of formalism in religion, the attachments to sacrifices and purification, had its hold in the numerous priesthood, the splendid temple and its solemn services.'[73]

What could account for the more positive attitudes among the Galileans? This was obviously a question Schleiermacher, with his position on Galilee, did not need to answer. In all studies that have taken Galilee as Jesus' home and location for his activities, however, the characteristics of Galilee and how they influenced Jesus have been of primary interest. The presupposition, which we shall see explicated by Renan (see Chapter V) and Smith (see Chapter VI), was that the locality influenced the inhabitants living there. But whereas Renan and Smith placed emphasis on the topography of Galilee, Strauss finds the explanation in ethnic mixture, geographical separation and social reaction:

> We know of this region that its population, especially in the northern parts, was much mixed with Gentiles, and on this account this division of it was even called Galilee of the Gentiles; and as besides this the province was separated by the intervening Samaria from that of Judea, so proud of its faith, the Galileans were contemptuously despised and not considered as entitled to the full privileges of the Jews; and even these circumstances might aid in the development of a more liberal religious tendency.[74]

It was this combination of location, its closeness to gentiles and rejection by the Judeans, that Strauss suggests might lead to a more 'liberal religious tendency'. Here the idea of a mixed population enters. Strauss is not interested in the racial aspect in itself, but in the distinction it represents in that Galileans were not regarded as full Jews.[75] From the point of view of the Jews in Judea, Strauss presents this as a flaw; but with regard to his own ideal of a liberal religious attitude, it was a favourable condition. Thus the openness of the Galileans is contrasted with the pride, exclusiveness and stiffness of the Judeans, represented above all by the inhabitants of Jerusalem and their leaders, the Pharisees and the Sadducees. That the population of Galilee was mixed had to do with the location of Galilee; it was in the border areas that the population was most mixed and in which Jesus must have come into contact with Gentiles.

That mixture in nations was an advantage was a point Strauss developed in his last book, *The Old Faith and the New*,[76] where he speaks of 'mixed races'. Racial mixture was characteristic of the large nations in Europe. In France and England, the old elements of the Celtic and Teutonic tribes had become blended and had ended by 'assimilating and crystallizing ... into a new formation – that of the present nationality of those peoples'.[77] A possible source of influence for Strauss on this point was Darwin.[78] Strauss attempted to build his new world view, which was becoming increasingly conservative, on natural science and biological progress, but he also argued that the influence could go the other way, so that Darwin applied social theories to nature. This seems to be the case when Darwin 'argued that, in the struggle of human groups for domination over their environment – embodied during his own time by European colonial expansion throughout the world – "hybrid vigour", not racial purity was the key to success'.[79] Strauss speaks of how the great cosmopolitan Germans, Schiller and Goethe, always combined their cosmopolitanism with patriotism.

In contrast to Schleiermacher's vision of 'the totality of the land', Strauss' picture is that of a *split nation*. The distinction between Galilee and Jerusalem, characterized as good versus bad, reflects a moral geography based on the character of the population, not on topography. The Jesus story in the Synoptic Gospels provided material on Galilee and Jerusalem, but it was interpretation in terms of a common pattern of ascribing distinctive characteristics to different tribes and peoples that gave this difference a paradigmatic force.

The contrast between Galilee and Jerusalem was part of Strauss' argument in favour of Matthew and the Synoptics as more reliable historical sources than John's Gospel. Their description of Jesus' ministry in Galilee as preparation for his journey to Jerusalem and a final confrontation with the Pharisaic party was more plausible historically than John's picture of several stays in Jerusalem without serious problems. Strauss regarded a long preparation period in Galilee as indispensable for Jesus' wish to do more than just start another Jewish sect; what he wanted was 'to give a different form to the whole religious system of his people'.[80]

Thus, Galilee was necessary for Jesus' project of a new religious form; in fact, it prefigured Christianity. It was this aspect that gave Galilee its metaphoric importance, and that likewise turned Jerusalem into a negative metaphor. The synoptic problem and the historical value of John's Gospel were matters of intense discussion among German Protestant biblical scholars over much of the nineteenth century.[81] These discussions were also part of larger cultural trends; critical investigations were a sign of the independence of the universities, and of a liberal search for the universal truth of Christianity. Since these goals were regarded as German values, source criticism could even be regarded as a contribution to national glory for Germany, in the same way that Strauss considered his critical search for the historical Jesus to be in continuity with the Reformation.

Thus, literary source criticism was not an innocent activity. As part of philological science in the nineteenth century, it was also part of a political quest, with its search for the origins of the Gospels and of early Christianity.[82] Since Jesus' founding of Christianity was prepared through his ministry in Galilee, Galilee necessarily took on symbolic significance. With the acceptance of the Synoptic Gospels as primary sources for the historical Jesus, this division between Galilee and Jerusalem became *the* dominant model in scholarship on Jesus and the Gospels until the beginning of the twenty-first century, with far-reaching religious and political consequences.

Galilee and Jerusalem have become metaphors for 'good' and 'bad' that could be historicized and applied to contemporary conflicts. Most seriously, it has presented Jesus and subsequent Christianity as good versus the Pharisees and subsequent Judaism as bad.[83] The metonymic use of Galilee and Jerusalem has also been transferred to other types of conflicts or divisions. For instance, in Protestant biblical studies it could be used for comparisons between Protestant and Catholic positions. One example of this is the negative term used for later New Testament writings as representing 'Early Catholicism' (*Früh-Katolizismus*).[84] In Strauss' text, it has a parallel in his description of the religious splits in Germany corresponding to the political splits between the Protestant North and Roman Catholic South. It was this parallelism that made Strauss' argument plausible, that a religious solution to the split between Protestants and Catholics was necessary for a political solution to the question of unification.

A spiritual Jesus for the Roman Empire

In *Jesus for the German People* Jesus is an ideal figure; Strauss has returned to the position of the third edition of *Life of Jesus, Critically Examined*. The main question was therefore: what type of ideal was Jesus? This question came to the fore in the discussion of whether Jesus saw himself as a political Messiah or not. For Schleiermacher the meaning of Jesus' Kingdom as 'apolitical' was put over against the Old Testament theocracy as the form of the state; Jesus' kingdom should not create a state, but it should reach out to a people and influence a nation.

Strauss agreed that Jesus was an apolitical Messiah, but Strauss places his discussion in a very different context. He sets out his view on politics, nations and empires in an introductory chapter on the development of Greco-Roman culture.[85] Strauss asks what the Romans did to prepare the way for Christianity. His first point is that the Roman Empire created a unity which included all the known nations of the ancient world. Strauss sees this as a prerequisite for 'cosmopolitanism', the view that regards humans as simply humans and no longer as belonging to a specific people like Greek or Jews. It was only within this empire that the separate divinities of various tribes and nations could mix and unite, and evolve into 'the one supreme and only God, the religion of the nations into a religion of the world'.[86]

Strauss' main point is that with this unity the spiritualization of religion must follow. Christianity provided such spiritualization and it could spread freely because of the unity created by the Roman Empire. Thus the Roman Empire appears as a good thing. Strauss does notice also, however, the reverse side of empire. This manifested itself in the destruction of the happiness associated with the former independence of these various peoples, and in the pressure and injustice that they now experienced and which embittered their lives. Nonetheless, the result of this is presented as not altogether negative. When they had despaired of resisting Roman oppression they directed their hopes towards the next world, represented by the idea of the Jewish Messiah and the spiritual promise of Christianity.

Strauss presents the pressures and use of power by the large empires of the world as the given facts of a situation where Jesus had to choose between two components of the Old Testament prophecies about the Messiah, one that was religious–political and one that was religious–moral. The political element of Messianic prophesies had a destructive effect, so that when the Jewish people had followed the religious–political path it had always led to destruction.

Over and against this political–religious Messianism Strauss places the religious–moral Messianism of Jesus. Jesus did not share the idea that God would invert the social relations of the world by making the Jews into rulers and their former rulers into subjects. The content of his religious–moral Messianism was that

> in that spiritual and moral elevation, that new relation to God, no longer that of slaves to a master, but of children to a father, they would have a happiness desirable in itself, but including at the same time the natural germs of external and material amendment.[87]

In this Messianism piety and morality were not just preconditions for salvation, but salvation itself. The situation of the believers corresponded to that of Jesus; they shared his religious consciousness, which Strauss described as 'in so far as Jesus … felt himself one with his heavenly Father, there hence arose for him an inward blessedness, compared with which all external joys and sorrows lost their importance'.[88] Thus, the goal was a 'spiritual and moral elevation' and an 'inward blessedness' – a share, so to speak, in the religious consciousness of Jesus himself.

When Strauss in his *Life of Jesus for the German People* brought Jesus back as a historical figure, it was as a 'religious Genius', representing a strong authority.[89] Moreover, Strauss' ideal was an inner religion that supported a distinction between social and material situations and the spiritual elevation that he saw as the goal of religion. However, the non-political, religious–moral Messianism Strauss set up as the ideal went well together with an acceptance of empire and of the right of the stronger power to rule. The solution that Strauss proposed, a fulfilment of the spiritual and religious freedom of the Reformation, turned out to be based on a spiritualized understanding of religion that leaves the political power free to fulfil its ambitions. Thus, it appears that an apolitical religion was the necessary foundation for a solution to the political dilemma of Germany as a split nation. How can such an abdication to the political and military power be explained?

Last Stage: Jesus as 'Enthusiast'

Jesus for a 'degenerate people'

The Old Faith and the New of 1872 was Strauss' last book and his farewell to Christianity in favour of a world view based on natural science and ideas of evolution.[90] His conservative political views were deplored by many of his friends, but among the German bourgeoisie the book was an enormous success; its views appeared to vindicate German culture as the main force behind the Prussian victory over France in 1870. It was exactly its enormous success among the German bourgeoisie that made Nietzsche attack it so vehemently. It was not so much Strauss as a person whom Nietzsche was attacking as the book that through its popularity had become a symbol of what Nietzsche called the German 'philistine culture'.[91]

This book puts Strauss' view on the rule of the Roman Empire in Palestine in *The Life of Jesus for the German People* into a broader political perspective. Here Strauss comes back to the state of the Jewish people at the time of Jesus under the Roman Empire. He compares their situation to that of the Poles under the Russians. Strauss describes their loss of independence and their misery, which attempts at rebellion and conspiracy could only plunge into more misery. Other attempts at reform were stopped and therefore turned into fanaticism. In this situation there was even less prospect for a higher culture through science and art, which for Strauss appears to be the most significant measure in ranking a nation.

In this regard the Jews were inferior not only to the Greeks and Romans, but also to 'many other oriental nations'. It is a very dark picture Strauss paints of the Jews, focusing explicitly on Galilee, in a scene that does not go logically well together with the portrait in his *Life of Jesus for the German People*:

> It is impossible to realize to the full the squalor and penury which were rife at that time in the villages and small towns of Galilee ... In a word, the world and existence therein had grown to be so unbearable to the *oppressed and degenerate race* which then dragged on its days by the banks of Jordan and the Sea of Tiberias.[92]

This is such a vivid description that one wonders where he got it from, and whether it had any historical basis. But more disconcerting is the fact that Strauss did not use this portrait of suffering to criticize the Roman Empire or at the very least to show empathy for the suffering. Quite the contrary: he praises 'the noblest and loftiest spirits' who did not want to have anything to do with this sordid situation, who did not try to improve it, but who turned to hope of deliverance from heaven. It follows that attempts to protest or to change one's situation were not only futile but destructive.[93]

In Strauss' argument the Roman Empire was associated with progress from divisions among nations and religions to a stage set for the unity of humanity and a more spiritual concept of God and salvation. The prerogative of progress towards these goals is clearly taken for granted, therefore negative elements like loss of independence and the associated pressures are accepted as necessary.

Strauss' text may be repulsive to twenty-first century social thought, but it reflects widespread ideas about progress and race held by the conservative elites of Europe in the nineteenth century. One important source for these ideas is Arthur Gobineau's *Essay on the Inequality of the Human Races*.[94] In this essay, Gobineau argued that the distinction between classes was based on race, of which the highest race was the Aryan, the race of the aristocrats. He put forth that the mixing of races, especially of the Aryan race, led to degeneration. When Strauss described the Galileans as an *oppressed and degenerate race*, the accidental fate of being oppressed was associated with their essential character of being degenerate. The very fact that a race was oppressed, that it lost out in the fight for survival, in itself proved that it was degenerate. Thus, a fate that for at least many present-day readers would seem to be a cause for empathy was instead in Strauss' perspective a fate that was ascribed to the 'fact' that they were degenerate.

Strauss' arguments here should be seen in the light of social Darwinism, which had many proponents among natural and social scientists in Germany in the latter part of the nineteenth century.[95] However, historians, philosophers and theologians like Strauss who had been liberal up until the 1860s also became attracted to social Darwinism. Its ideas of struggle for existence influenced all areas of politics and sciences in Germany, including for instance nationalist militarism, economic competition, and the struggle among individuals, races and nations. Although many of the proponents of social Darwinism had started out as liberals, like Strauss, most became increasingly conservative and ended up supporting Bismarck, the aristocracy and imperial politics.

Strauss was exceptional in that he did not build his views directly on Darwin's theories. Rather, he argued that Darwin applied social theory to nature.[96] Apparently, Strauss had no difficulties in combining positions that, at least to me, are problematic to reconcile, especially how easily he combined his stand on culture and civilization with a positive view of war. It was important for him that modernity represented reason, culture, science, and art (*The Old Faith and the New* concludes with chapters on the great poets and composers of Germany), but at the same time he is totally untroubled by the use of force over 'degenerate races' and viewed war as a progressive force.[97]

Strauss' view on power politics finds its place within the view of many historians of the nation-state in the last period before the founding of the German Empire in 1871, which is characterized by Giesen as 'the code of the *Realpolitik*'.[98] Strauss' presentation of the Roman and other empires was based on the right of power as overriding all other concerns. The Jews in Galilee, who are characterized as an 'oppressed and degenerate race', served only as an example of those peoples and groups who had lost. The attempt to create universal empires caused violent changes in the world and was destructive of much individual happiness, but in Strauss' world it would 'nevertheless serve essentially to promote the progress of the race'.[99] This sentence sums up the idea of 'progress' and its consequences from a social Darwinist perspective: progress meant to conquer local places. The 'race' in Strauss' view here is the race that comes out on top. It is the winning race of empire.

Jesus the 'enthusiast'

It is as one who promised deliverance from above that Strauss introduces Jesus and his proclamation of himself as the Messiah. This context makes his message understandable as it was directed to the wretched people of Galilee, but definitely not to modern, civilized citizens.[100] The chapter on the life of Jesus in *The Old Faith and the New* is placed within the first section of the book: 'Are we still Christians?'[101] The purpose of this section is to show that Jesus, his teachings and what he represented were utterly inadequate as rules or inspiration for life in the modern world. Jesus represented the opposite to everything that had brought the world forward (for instance, love of money) and everything that represented civilization (not only industry and trade, but also art, science, patriotism and civic obligations). In short, Christianity was a principle that was 'directly antagonistic to culture'.[102]

Strauss ascribes this effect to Jesus, whom he calls 'an enthusiast' in the sense of being fanatical or possessed by his convictions.[103] Strauss makes a distinction between 'noble enthusiasts' and others, and it is uncertain where he would place Jesus; but even if an enthusiast can arouse people, he should not be chosen as 'the guide of our life'. His influence must always be subjected to the control of reason, Strauss' 'noble enthusiast' evokes the ethnographic idea of 'the noble primitive'. This is the primitive as an ideal versus 'the dangerous savage' characterized by fanaticisms, who represents the negative side of primitivism *vis-à-vis* civilization. In the next chapter, we will see that this represents a pattern that makes Renan's portrait of Jesus understandable, as the 'noble primitive' in contrast to the fanatical Jewish leaders.

Strauss' picture of Jesus as an enthusiast appears to place him on the fanatical side that must be controlled by (modern) reason. Not surprisingly, it is to Luther that Strauss ascribes the first attempt to curb such fanaticism: 'The Reformation first went to work on a systematic principle, in order to place this ascetic, fanatical side of Christianity under due control of reason.'[104] In a short statement, Strauss sums up his position on Jesus: 'we must acknowledge that the entire activity and aspiration of the civilized nations of our time is based on views of life which run directly counter to those entertained by Christ.'[105]

This is the final stage of Strauss' many positions on Jesus. In the end, Strauss rejected any possibility that Jesus can be an ideal for modern men; the rupture between the primitive, ascetic world of the first century and the civilized, modern world became too drastic. Although this position seems drastic compared to his previous views on Jesus, they were all governed by his confidence in the reasoning of a modern world view based on faith in the progress of civilization, in which he and Germany were placed at the top.

Despite his protestations that true religion was the key to political freedom for Germany, Strauss' religion was so spiritualized and privatized that it had little imaginative power and even less critical power. Giesen's pessimistic evaluation of the nationalist movement after Bismarck's victory can also stand as a description of the lost opportunity of Strauss' *Lives of Jesus*:

> With the realization of the German nation-state coming not through cultural mission or liberal ideas, but through Bismarck's maxim of 'blood and iron', the *Bildungsbürgertum* and the intellectuals lost the chance of constructing cultural identity through the national issue, in opposition to the existing order.[106]

Within this cultural context the claims that the historical Jesus embodied 'Germanness' and that the Jews were a 'degenerate race' represented views that resonated with broader trends in the early period of the German empire. Strauss' position was developed along the lines of a discussion of race in which he did not directly engage. In *The Aryan Jesus*, Susannah Heschel has investigated how 'the story of Jesus, his origins within Judaism, and his emergence as the first Christian, served as a template for racializing religious and cultural analyses'.[107] In the nineteenth century Paul de Lagarde[108] and Houston Stewart Chamberlein[109] especially used racial arguments about Jesus as a Galilean to disassociate him from his Jewish context. This line of interpretation was brought to completion in the Nazi period with Walter Grundmann and the Institute for the Study and Eradication of Jewish Influence on German Church Life.[110]

Conclusion: A Masculine Nation

The discussion in this chapter has focused on the 'Germanness' of Strauss' presentation of Jesus. Less focused in the discussion has been the masculine character of this Germanness, but it is always present in Strauss' texts, combined with an emphasis on the power of empires, the progress of force, and a military vocabulary.

His narrative may be characterized in the way the author Rachael Cusk describes the novel as a male structure: 'The form and structure of the novel, the perceptual framework, the very size and character of the literary sentence; these were tools shaped by men for their own uses.'[111]

In the first edition of *Life of Jesus, Critically Examined* Strauss moves to deconstruct the singular and unique Jesus as the incarnation of the divine idea in a monarchical figure, representing both maleness and hierarchy. Strauss' replacement of the single person with humanity takes away hierarchy, but not masculinity. When Strauss describes the true miracle of humanity, as opposed to Jesus' healings of only a few people, it is with a masculine terminology: he speaks of 'man's dominance over nature', 'the irresistible force of ideas' and 'intellectual and moral life'.[112] In the third edition of his *Life of Jesus*, Strauss returns to Jesus as the traditional nineteenth-century 'great man'. This edition presents a hero image of Jesus, described with terms like genius, unique and unequalled in world history.[113] This is also the picture in *Life of Jesus for the German People*, where Jesus and the Galileans display masculine qualities like originality and open mindedness in contrast to fanaticism and formalism.

In all of these different versions Jesus represented a masculine ideal with whom a 'modern man' could identify. Jesus was spiritual, apolitical and religious–moral in a world full of power, war and oppression. This was the cultured ideal of Strauss, an image of the civilized citizen in a world that otherwise must be ruled by strong power. This latter power embodied 'hegemonic masculinity', i.e. the dominant forms of masculinity that emerged in periods of contestations and conflict.[114] In Prussia and after 1870 in the German Empire hegemonic masculinity was represented by the soldier, or rather by the officer embodying military power. In this context Strauss presented Jesus as an ideal of civilized masculinity at home in a peaceful room filled with books and music, but outside that room another more aggressive and powerful masculinity had the hegemony.

The distance between Jesus of the pre-modern past and Strauss' ideals of a modern masculinity was bridged by attributing to Jesus masculine characteristics well at home in nineteenth-century Germany. But finally Strauss' bridge broke down. In *The Old Faith and the New* the distance between the civilized world of the nineteenth century and Jesus' world in the first century became unbridgeable. Modern society was built on money, family, production, science and art. It had nothing in common with the ascetic lifestyle, and the negation of family and other social responsibilities by Jesus.

After having struggled all his life to make Jesus like 'us', Strauss now presented him as 'the other'. The dominant masculine quality of the modern world was reason, depicted as a truly German attribute introduced by the Reformation and Luther. Jesus, in contrast, was now 'the enthusiast' (*Schwärmer*), a male parallel to the hysterical woman. He was not just distant in time; he was also foreign in character and personality. He was a person who could be a saviour for a 'degenerate people', but not an ideal for modern men.

This paradigm of masculine contrasts was part of a larger cultural system of binary oppositions and hierarchies at work in different ways throughout Strauss' writings. It became visible in the contrast between the Galileans and the Pharisees in the Gospels and in the contrast between the Reformation represented by Protestant northern Germany and the Roman Catholic southern Germany. The idea of the 'split nation' created a pattern of us versus them, of hegemonic masculinity versus negative masculinity. It was a paradigm that was expressed by geography (North versus South), by race (the domineering race versus the degenerate race) and finally by motion (forward progress versus backwards).

These binary and hierarchical structures are obvious in most of Strauss' writings. In themselves, they were not original; they were part of an older tradition of comparison among European nationalities that 'is oppositional in nature and leads to particularism'.[115] It was the same type of structures that Renan developed in philology with the contrast between Indo-European and Semitic languages. The use of these structures in presentations of Jesus was, however, of great significance. Since the Lives of Jesus represented a 'great man' understanding of history and portrayed the ideals and models of a modern Europe, these presentations gave authority to and naturalized these oppositional structures. Jesus became a model, a paradigm, for structures of division and discrimination.

I started by pointing out how the historical Jesus represented a democratic influence by transferring symbolic authority from the monarchy to citizenship and nation. With Strauss' Jesus we see another influence, which gave authority to a nationalism based on distinction from others and a sense of superiority. This is also the fateful heritage of the nineteenth-century Lives of Jesus.

CHAPTER V

'FAMILIAR AND FOREIGN'

Life of Jesus in the Orientalism of Renan

Introduction

Jesus was 'an incomparable man' whom some 'call God'. This statement by Ernest Renan was part of his opening lecture as Professor in Hebrew at the Collège de France on 21 February 1862. Four days later his course was suspended by the Emperor, Napoleon III, and in 1864 Renan was dismissed from his chair.[1] Views of Jesus that threatened his divinity and described him as a human person were controversial, not only in the churches and among theologians, but also within the structures of an empire and among conservative politicians. And this controversy increased when Renan's *Life of Jesus* was published in 1863.[2] The book became an immediate success and a public sensation; it was printed in many editions in its first year and immediately translated into several European languages. It became the first really popular biography of Jesus, written in a literary style of high popularization of an academic work.

In one sense, the book is a period piece of the nineteenth century. This was an age of deconstruction of traditional social, cultural and political forms, as well as one of reconstruction, of finding new means to explain, understand and structure the world. It was a period characterized by a search for the *origins* of the present world order, in which the various scholarly disciplines were searching for the roots of the particular area they were studying, as their way to contribute to that larger search. The most prominent place, of course, was taken by Darwin's *Origin of the Species*;[3] it reflected the central position of biology and the natural sciences in the efforts to understand the world, and such scientific ideals also influenced the social sciences and the humanities.

Within the humanities, philology emerged as a modern form of science. Ideas of nations and nationalism had one of their roots in the search for ancient languages, as Herder's *Origin of Language* made clear.[4] Among these investigations, Renan took his place, most famously with his studies of the origin of languages, playing a central role in the establishing of two main groups of languages, the Indo-European or Aryan and the Semitic.[5] Additionally, he wrote a multi-volume work on the origins of Christianity that shared the same purpose of other studies of origins: namely, to lay a scientific foundation for the history of the present phenomenon. It is as the first volume in this *History of the Origins of Christianity* that Renan's *Life of Jesus* appeared in 1863. This context sets the tone for the book; it places Jesus at the centre of a scientific investigation into the origins of Christianity. In Renan's view of modern religion, the human Jesus was the providential beginning of the history that through progress would lead to its goal, a common humanity.[6]

The Orientalist Location of Renan

A French and Orientalist book

Historical Jesus studies in the nineteenth century were a wholly male, almost wholly German – and, because it involved modern biblical criticism, an almost wholly Protestant – enterprise. Therefore a book by a Frenchman and a Catholic, albeit a liberal one and a lapsed seminarian at that, was a surprise. Renan was well acquainted with German scholarship on the historical Jesus, and he especially admired D. F. Strauss' works and shared many of his critical positions.[7] However, Renan's literary form and style were very different from Strauss' *Life of Jesus* of 1835. In contrast to Strauss' literary critical and philosophical work, Renan's book was biographical and psychological. Moreover, there were also similarities with the genres of historical romance and literary fiction.[8] Thus Renan's *Life of Jesus* was a book of a different character than the German books. Maybe this was what Strauss implied when in his preface to *Life of Jesus for the German People*, which appeared one year after Renan's book, he wished 'to have written a book as suitable for Germany as Renan's is for France'.[9]

For Albert Schweitzer, however, to characterize Renan's *Life of Jesus* as French is no compliment; in Schweitzer's review of nineteenth-century Jesus' studies, he speaks of Renan's book as 'the superficial and frivolous French treatment of the subject'. Although Schweitzer was born and grew up in Alsace-Lorraine, a border region that through history had been switched back and forth between France and Germany, the last time (to Germany) being in 1871 shortly before Schweitzer was born, he took a strong German position. Despite his harsh criticism of Strauss' last book on Jesus, it still belonged within that German tradition of research into the life of Jesus, which Schweitzer described as 'a uniquely great expression of truthfulness' one which had not influenced the Latin nations.[10] In his criticism of Renan, Schweitzer presents the German side of the comparisons between France and Germany that increased after the Franco-Prussian war in 1870–1. That Germany, as one of the Anglo-Saxon nations, represented vigour and seriousness in contrast to the decadence and decay of France, as a Latin nation, belonged to a common style of stereotypical characterizations of nations.[11] Despite the popularity of Renan's *Life of Jesus* among readers, with many reprints of the book into the twentieth century, scholarly opinion has followed Schweitzer's negative verdict, so that it is mostly written off as romantic and of little interest today.

However, Schweitzer has an interesting concluding observation on what it was in Renan's biography of Jesus that would attract a Frenchman:

> the Frenchman discovers in it, behind the familiar form … ideas belonging to a world that is foreign to him, ideas that he can never completely assimilate, but which yet continually attract him. In this double character of the work lies its imperishable charm.'[12]

This combination of the familiar and 'a world that is foreign' points directly to the European fascination with the Orient and especially Palestine, where ideas of 'Holy Land' were combined with familiar notions of homeland. Schweitzer's comment places Renan's *Life of Jesus* within the context of nineteenth-century Orientalism.

In Edward Said's *Orientalism*, Ernest Renan is a central figure in the development of Orientalism.[13] It is primarily Renan's work as a philologist that is at the centre of Said's interest, and Said has paid only scant attention to Renan's most popular and widespread book, *Life of Jesus*.[14] Susannah Heschel gives a brief discussion of Orientalism and racism in Renan's *Life of Jesus*,[15] but the few studies of the book in recent years have read it from other perspectives.[16]

The main suggestion in Edward Said's *Orientalism* is that the picture of the Orient was created by the West as an image of 'the Other' in contrast to one's own 'self'. A passage towards the end of *Life of Jesus* illustrates how Renan creates a negative image of the Orient as the 'Other' at the same time that he presents a 'self' as its positive counter-image:

> One of the principal defects of the Jewish race is its harshness in controversy, and the abusive tone that it always infuses into it. There never were in the world such bitter quarrels as those of the Jews among themselves. It is the faculty of nice discernment that makes the polished and moderate man. Now, the lack of this faculty is one of the most constant features of the Semitic mind.[17]

In this brief passage, Renan first gives a definition of and a judgment on the 'Jewish race' that he then turns it into a general statement about the 'Semitic mind', in both cases speaking as the Orientalist expert. Finally, with the definition of 'discernment' that he interjects into the passage, he distances himself and his readers from this Oriental 'Other', by virtue of the comforting image of the 'polished and moderate man' who, of course, is no other than the European, the Western opposite of the Oriental.

This short excerpt indicates how Renan's *Life of Jesus* can be read fruitfully from a perspective of Orientalism. However, as we found in the discussion of 'Holy land as homeland' in Chapter II, Orientalism is not a strict, unified concept but rather a perspective that also allows for complexities. And what did not come out in the above quotation from Renan is the double character of the Oriental world that the reader encounters in *Life of Jesus*. Said has pointed out that the Orientalists' view of the Orient was characterized by an ambiguity; the Orient represented both something strongly attractive and something repulsive, often at the same time. It is this ambiguity that I wish to explore in a reading of Renan's *Life of Jesus*.

Renan between Orient and Empire

Renan wrote *Life of Jesus* during his expedition to Syria in 1860–1. His travels to Palestine were a by-product of the official purpose of his journey to Syria, which was to study ancient Phoenician inscriptions and sculptures. His task included finding archaeological artefacts and shipping the most valuable of them back to France. His mission was undertaken with the help of the French navy and army, which at the time were stationed in (present-day) Lebanon. Consequently, Renan's travels to the land of the Gospels took place within a context of empire, with a French military and political presence in the area. His journey to the Orient under Napoleon III had overtones of earlier French history in the region, in particular the expedition of Napoleon I in 1799.

The growing French interest in the Eastern Mediterranean and the development of Oriental studies were associated with Napoleon I, and Said argues that the French interest in the Orient was largely cultural.[18] However, the period of Renan's visit was characterized by military and political engagement. In one of his first letters from his stay in Syria, Renan wrote that he planned to make excavations on a large scale 'in company with the army'.[19] The presence of the French military, which made his expedition possible, is rarely mentioned in his letters. In his last letter from the region, however, Renan relates how French authority diminished when France eventually withdrew its military presence.[20] Renan considered it a shame to arrive only to intend to leave. One obvious reason for his criticism was that the withdrawal made his task more difficult. A more profound reason, however, emerges in a comment he made in a letter to his friend Berthelot: 'This country cannot be civilized except by slavery.'[21] Of course, it was France that represented that civilizing mission, the norm against which everything must be measured.

When Renan set out to write his *Life of Jesus* it was within the context of the French empire and its military and political power. Moreover, Renan spoke from the position of French civilization which, he felt, permitted him to pass judgment on peoples of the Orient and to measure their achievements. He places the population in Beirut close to the bottom of societies, as being just above the 'savage state'. Since the Orient represents 'the other' to civilization, a move upwards was possible only by enduring slavery under a civilized nation. Yet there was an ambiguity in the picture. The Orient included 'delightful types' as well as a 'sordid race'.[22] On what basis did Renan make these judgements?

Life of Jesus as travel writing and biography

With his recognized authority as an Orientalist, based on his studies of Semitic philology, Renan's descriptions of the land and the people of Jesus in *Life of Jesus* commanded an authority in themselves and were presented as objective knowledge. Renan has, however, provided other sources that allow us to peer behind the objectivist facade of his book. An important, though little used, source for such a reading of his *Life of Jesus* is the collection of letters he wrote from his expedition to Syria in 1860–1, during which time he visited Palestine and wrote the book in question. In letters to his best friend in Paris, M. Berthelot, Renan gives his observations on Muslim societies at the time.[23] These letters reveal important similarities between Renan's descriptions of nature and valuations of society in his own day and those in the *Life of Jesus*. In his description of contemporary society we encounter the same double character and tension between the familiar and the foreign as in the picture of Palestine at the time of Jesus.

By depicting himself in his letters as a traveller to the Orient, Renan makes himself vulnerable by showing how he became exposed to experiences in the Orient. In his *Life of Jesus* most of Renan's observations take the form of scholarly judgements and definitions; their personal character is mostly hidden. Likewise, the present is mostly hidden, in particular the Arab population. It is in his letters, however, that his personal experiences become visible. In his letters, we catch a glimpse of Renan's social location, and we can follow his observations on two central subjects: the landscape and geography of Palestine, and the character of its inhabitants. The specific form of Renan's Orientalism in *Life of Jesus* is based on a combination of these two, landscape and personal character, and the letters make it possible to see how they are constructed through his own experiences, or rather, his constructions of his experiences.

Renan's *Life of Jesus* combines the two genres that we discussed initially, biography and travel writing on Palestine. Schleiermacher and Strauss discussed at great length the importance of biography for writing of Jesus and they also wrote of Jesus in relation to the land of Palestine and to its different parts. However, they described the land in terms of its political and social structures, for example with divisions according to tribes, and they showed little interest in the topographical or geographical aspects of Palestine – and never travelled to Palestine themselves. In many ways Renan's descriptions represent new advances in travel writing and historical geography.

To Renan, his travels in Galilee and in the rest of Palestine made him see something he had not seen before; it changed not only the character of the land for him,
but also his image of Jesus. Renan followed the common procedure in Lives of
Jesus by starting with a discussion of the sources for a historical Jesus, above all the
four Gospels. He shows a preference for the historical reliability of Matthew and
Mark; he is much more sceptical of Luke and John as historical sources, but nevertheless ends up using all of them, with due historical criticism. However, most importantly, he adds that he has found a new source: 'To the perusal of documentary
evidence I have been able to add an important source of information – *the sight of
the places where the events occurred*'. He says that he has 'traversed, in all directions,
the country of the Gospels … scarcely any important locality of Jesus has escaped
me'. This to Renan was more than a superficial identification of the places 'where
the events occurred'. The experience of the places contributed to his understanding of the events themselves. He speaks of the 'striking agreement of the text with
the places' and of the 'marvellous harmony of the Gospel ideal with the country';
this is a language that turns place and country into text and Gospel.[24]

Renan presents what happened to him in terms of an extraordinary event.
History 'took form', events and scenes appeared 'like a revelation to me', and he
concludes: 'I had before my eyes a fifth Gospel, torn but still legible.' He introduces this gospel as an objective fact that is self-validating and at the same time
places him in a privileged position. After this experience he went to Lebanon for a
short rest and while he was there, he says, 'I fixed in rapid sketches, the images that
had appeared to me, and from them resulted this history.'[25] This is the language
of revelation, of an initial vision, written down in a moment of inspiration, and
therefore the text that resulted was an inspired writing. Renan positions himself as
an inspired writer, as one who has authority.

Thus, again we encounter the authoritative gaze, the power of seeing. But how
did Renan read the text of the landscape; what did he see? Most importantly, the
landscape revealed Jesus to him: 'in place of an abstract being, whose existence
might have been doubted, I saw living and moving an admirable human figure'.[26]
Without the land, Jesus was an abstract being; now, when Matthew and Mark,
Renan's favourite Gospels, were read together with the land, Jesus became a living
figure. It is this revelation that makes it possible for Renan to write a biography
of Jesus as the first volume of his *History of the Origins of Christianity*. Originally
Renan had conceived of this work as a history of doctrine, of the ideas that 'had
grown under his name' and how they covered the world. However, he had learned,
he says, that 'men are more than doctrines'.[27] Therefore, his history of Christianity
becomes the history of Jesus, St Paul and St John.

Not surprisingly, these histories are the biographies of 'great men'. Renan
speaks of 'extraordinary men', 'great souls of the past', and that the purpose of a

biography is to make them 'live again'. To recreate a life is an act of art; it requires what Renan calls 'some share of divination and conjecture'.[28] This element of 'divination' presupposes a form of identification with the subject, and obviously there are elements of autobiography in Renan's portrayal of Jesus.[29] However, I will not explore that perspective here, but will look at what Renan says he is doing when writing a biography.

Renan takes an image from the natural sciences when he says that the author must achieve a vision of life as 'an organic whole' and fit the various small facts of life into a perfect unity. This unity must be expressed through the form of the biography; it must be built up as a 'logical, probable narrative'.[30] Renan's description of the art of biography reflects his general hermeneutics, which is also expressed in his interpretation of languages. In his philological studies, there is a close link between linguistics and biology and anatomy. It is what is organic that is whole and alive, *viz.* the Indo-European languages in contrast to the Semitic languages that were considered to be in-organic.[31] The similarities between Renan's philological system and the biography of Jesus suggest that Jesus is portrayed in Indo-Germanic categories.

Thus I think that Renan's *Life of Jesus* is both an Oriental biography[32] and not an Oriental biography. It is set in the Orient and gives its readers a sense of 'romance and Oriental realism',[33] but Jesus is portrayed as a character that in Renan's sense also is non-Oriental. So what is the reason for this ambiguity and paradox in Renan's biography?

The Two Faces of the Orient

The ambiguity of the Orient

Through the type of philological studies that Renan advanced, Orientalists developed a 'knowing vocabulary' that located the Orient in a comparative framework with the Occident, the West.[34] The Orient and the West were identified as ontologically unequal. Said points out how this ontology produced simultaneously an *over*-valuation and an *under*-valuation of the Orient. The Orient, especially India and the Far East, was sometimes overvalued for its spirituality, its history and its traditions, for example. But such high estimations could be followed by a counter-response of under-valuation, of viewing the Orient as backward and barbaric.

This ambiguity appears to apply to all 'Others'. In a study of European images of non-European peoples, Henri Baudet discusses what he characterizes to be 'a fundamental ambivalence in the European's feeling toward non-Western people'.[35] Europeans killed many wild people in their conquests of the distant parts of the world; at the same time they held ideas that the conquered peoples were noble savages or sages with superior wisdom. In different periods various peoples were identified with such ideals. In the Middle Ages, it was the Negro; in the period of the colonization of the Americas, it was the American Indian; in later periods, the Indians (of India) or the Chinese as the noble Orientals. Such ambivalence towards others may have been grounded in a deep ambivalence towards one's own culture: Baudet argues that this self-doubt is related to the myth of man's fall from paradise, which makes the Europeans look for a 'paradise lost' in distant times and far-off places.

Such ambivalence toward the Other was expressed not only in differing attitudes in successive periods but it could also be held simultaneously. One example is how early American anthropology created the picture of the Indian as an ambivalent Other. The Indian 'was both the romanticized precursor to American Civilization, and a potentially dangerous enemy living within that civilization'.[36]

Renan's special contribution to Orientalism was his philological construction of languages into Indo-European and Semitic families, speaking with biological models about organic and inorganic languages. Models from nature, such as botanical models of 'roots' and 'branches', were used to organize knowledge. There is a danger with such models, however, since 'naturalistic models not only remove the effects of history from language but also makes it possible to stereotype civilizations'.[37] This becomes visible in the way Renan and other Orientalists speak of 'types' and 'characters', be it in languages, cultures or persons. Other peoples are turned into an *essence* that characterizes different groups or races, for instance the Greek, the Syrian or the Turk. Most of Renan's ire was directed against the Muslims as representative examples of the Semitic race: 'The Metualis are a very wicked race, fanatical and deceitful, completely spoiled people.'[38] This corresponds to Renan's view of their religion:

> It is here that one understands what a misfortune Islamism has been, what a leaven of hate and exclusiveness it has sown in the world, how exaggerated monotheism is opposed to all science, to all civil life, to every great idea.[39]

After this harsh denunciation of the people he has encountered, Renan contrasts it with its opposite, represented by nature: 'But nature, here, is always delightful and splendid.'[40] It is as if these two make up the Orient for Renan: the sordid state of the people, who make up the present, and the beauty of its nature, which appears to be timeless, or rather a link to the Orient's past glory. It is this ambivalent picture of the Orient as both the 'ideal primitive' and the 'degenerate savage' that can explain some of the paradoxes in Renan's *Life of Jesus*. I suggest that in the characterizations of Galilee with its nature and people Jesus represents the 'ideal primitive', whereas Jerusalem and Judea represent the 'degenerate' Oriental.

Galilee as the ideal Orient and origin of humanity

Renan's Palestine, and especially Galilee, is one of detailed pictures of houses and villages, of lakeshores with plains and rivers, of landscapes and mountain ranges. It was the vivid representation of Jesus in this locality that caught the attention of so many readers.[41] It was more than a recreation of a historical setting in 'Oriental realism', more than a parallel to historical romances set in ancient France or Scotland, however. One of Schweitzer's criticisms of Renan was the many romantic descriptions of Galilee and Jesus and his happy band of disciples roaming the landscape. Many later readers have also felt this to be too romantic, almost placing Jesus in an eternal version of *The Sound of Music*.

However, what Schweitzer did not see was the role that landscape, topography and nature played in nineteenth-century imagination and scholarship. He therefore missed that Renan's picture of Galilee was part of a complex and ambiguous picture of the Orient: an expression of the interconnection between nature and the character of a people that is also found in other presentations of Galilee from this period.[42] Philology shared with ethnography, geography and social biology many presuppositions about the interdependence between nature, character and race. It was taken for granted that nature and landscape made an impression upon the character of an individual. Herder, with his emphasis on language to study national character, criticized the position that nature gave access to a primordial, paradisiacal state of man that revealed divine creation and truth.[43] Renan's view appears to be similar to that critiqued by Herder. His descriptions of the nature of Galilee are more than romantic illustrations; nature reveals a truth that is otherwise not visible.

Renan's picture of Nazareth may serve as a representation of the ideal state of nature, and of the relation between nature and its population:

> The environs, moreover, are charming and no place in the world was so well adapted for dreams of perfect happiness. Even in our time Nazareth is still a delightful abode, the only place, perhaps, in Palestine in which the mind feels itself relieved from the burden that oppresses it in this unequalled desolation.[44]

He concludes by drawing the parallels between nature and people: 'The people are amiable and cheerful, the gardens fresh and green.'[45] The gardens of Nazareth represented the idea of paradise and Renan presents it as a place where Jesus could see what the Kingdom of God was like. Renan explains that the word 'paradise' in all Oriental languages is borrowed from Persian, and that it summed up a shared dream. It was a delightful garden where the charming life that was led here below would be continued forever. This image, of course, also evoked the original garden in the East: Eden, where life began.

Not only Nazareth but all of Galilee was such a garden of harmony between nature, a 'terrestrial paradise', and its population, which was 'active, honest, joyous and tender-hearted'. They were fishermen and formed a 'gentle and peaceable society'; the riches of the fisheries provided them with an easy life and left them freedom of imagination.[46] This obviously was a picture of the ideal state of society, an ideal that provided a contrast to and a criticism of modern society. Another aspect of this dream of an ideal society was indifference to comfort, luxury and what in modern society was regarded as the necessities of life. Renan says of life in Galilee that 'the accessories of life are there insignificant compared to the pleasures of living',[47] and he elaborates on this theme in a letter to Berthelot: 'it is only in the East that one can understand the pleasure of living for the sake of living'.[48] This image of Oriental simplicity that inspired Renan's admiration appears to be a stock motif among Western observers of the Orient.[49]

Moreover, when Renan writes that 'nothing of that we call civilization, in the Greek and worldly sense, has reached them',[50] we hear echoes of traditions about ideal rural societies, in contrast to city life, that are well known from Greek moral philosophy. The Galileans were out of reach of modern civilization and could therefore not be measured by its standards. Renan presents them in the position of the 'Other,' since they lacked 'our' Germanic or Celtic earnestness, but it seems in many ways to be an admirable 'otherness'. Another of Renan's letters confirms our suspicion that this character portrait is constructed on the basis of his own observations when he says that 'we may imagine them as somewhat analogous to the better populations of Lebanon, but with the gift, not possessed by the latter, of producing great men'.[51]

In Renan's description, Galilee is not just a historic, geographical place, it is also an ideal place that represents the origin of human culture: 'Galilee has created the most sublime ideal for the popular imagination, for behind its idyll moves the fate of humanity, and the light which illuminates its picture is the sun of the kingdom of God.'[52] Renan says that it is the North, i.e. Galilee, that produced Christianity. In the conclusion to this section on Galilee and Jesus Renan says that it was the landscape of Galilee, with 'the green hills and the clear fountains', that shaped the faith of Jesus and his image of God as the heavenly Father.[53]

Jerusalem as the negative image of the Orient

Renan started his *Life of Jesus* by declaring that the landscape of Palestine itself was a 'fifth Gospel'. However, it has become clear that it was above all the landscape of Galilee that played that role, and Renan had to face the dilemma of the double identity that the Orient possessed for the Westerner. The problem could not be solved merely by a division in time between the glorious past of the Gospel period and the sordid present, since also in the past there were both positive and negative elements. Therefore Renan attempted to solve the dilemma, in a way similar to Strauss, by making a division in space between the two aspects of the Orient. The ideally human, the primitive who represented 'the origins' of humanity, was put over against the unacceptable Other, the sub-human, and the two were placed in two different localities with two different geographies. As we have seen, Galilee with the Galileans and Jesus himself represented the ideal primitive, whom the Orientalist admired and in whom he could see his own origins and a criticism of Western modernity.

Renan introduces the geographical contrast to this ideal with a glimpse of what one can see beyond the limits of Galilee: 'Southward, the more sombre aspects of these Samaritan hills foreshadows the dreariness of Judea beyond, parched by a scorching wind of desolation and death.'[54] Renan, who has described how the Galilean landscape was a delight for Jesus, assumes to read his mind on the area around Jerusalem: 'the parched appearance of Nature must have added to the dislike Jesus had for the place. The valleys are without water, the soil arid and stony.' Since it was common wisdom that nature influenced its people, Renan can safely describe the inhabitants and the character of Jerusalem along the same lines. It was 'a city of pedantry, acrimony, disputes, hatreds, and littleness of mind. Its fanaticism was extreme and religious seditions very frequent.'[55]

Jerusalem, with its inhabitants and leaders among the scribes and the Pharisees, is thus pressed into the role of the savage Other. This negative picture is so violent in its total opposition to the peaceful picture of the Galileans that one wonders what could have caused such a tone of hatred. An incidental comment of Renan's description of Jesus' entry into the city, that 'Jerusalem was then nearly what it is to-day', reveals that the picture is based on his own visit to Jerusalem in 1860–1. Moreover, another comparison indicates the origin of his critical picture of the Pharisees and their study of the Law: 'It was something analogous to the barren doctrine of the Mussulman fakir.' It was thus the stereotypically negative picture of the Muslims that served as a model to describe the ancient Jewish Pharisees in an equally stereotypical fashion.[56]

It was Renan's negative view of the Muslims of his day and their institutions that gave force to the negative image of Jews and Jewish institutions. It was the contemporary Arabs in Palestine who provided material for Renan's stereotypes of Semites as fanatical and lacking in civilization. It was this Oriental fanaticism that had destroyed the country as 'the fifth Gospel' and made it torn and hard to read. Palestine had become like a palimpsest where the original writing had to be recovered from underneath the present text. For instance, when Renan describes Galilee as a 'very green, shady, smiling district', that description does not seem to be based on the land that he saw in reality. He says that 'the horrible state, to which this country is reduced, especially near Lake Tiberias, ought not to deceive us.' Instead, Renan points to ancient narratives about the beauty and the wealth of the area. But why had this beautiful country become 'sad and gloomy'? The culprit in this decline was, of course, 'the ever-impoverishing influence of Islam'.[57]

Renan repeatedly comes back to Islam as the source of destruction, especially around the Sea of Galilee, and in one instance he even attributes the oppressive heat to the sins of the Muslims:

> No doubt there has been here, as in the *campagna* of Rome, a change of climate introduced by historical causes. It is Islamism, and especially the Mussulman reaction against the Crusades, which has withered as if with a blast of death the districts preferred by Jesus.[58]

To modern readers this might seem like an absurd idea, but it was another instance of faith in the close relation between nature and human character, this time with human character influencing nature.[59]

Thus, Galilee as Gospel was torn by Islamic influence, not only in its social and religious life, but in nature as well. Such were Islam's destructive powers. We have noticed how Renan frequently introduces comments that clearly do not come from historical sources, but enter the narrative as explanations or comments of a general nature. Several of them are remarks about Muslims and serve to essentialize them, making them into a character or a topos. As a recognized Orientalist, Renan could make these sweeping statements and expect them to be accepted as self-evident truths, but his letters reveal how they were based on his experiences of being uncomfortable in the Orient of his day.

Statements about Muslims serve two purposes in Renan's *Life of Jesus*. First, they are his interpretation of the foreign culture that he encountered in Lebanon and Palestine. Renan treats these experiences as scientific data and by help of his expertise in philology he organizes them and establishes essential character traits. Second, as the exemplary 'Other', Muslims served as a modern analogy to Jewish groups like the Pharisees and Sadducees. This Renan can do since he has established the essential Oriental character; both the nineteenth-century Muslim and the first-century Jew embody the Orient as fanatical, barbaric and anti-democratic.

Galilee, Kingdom and Nation

A Galilean kingdom?

In Renan's search for origins, Galilee as the 'ideal Orient' represents not just the Other, but also Renan's ideals of humanity, ideals that had been lost in modern societies with all their desires for luxuries and their intellectual earnestness. It is this Galilee that brought Jesus to life for Renan, after his scepticism and doubt had left Jesus as an abstract being of doubtful existence. Therefore, although Renan draws on the Gospels to construct Jesus' life and activities, Renan's main source for Jesus' character is Galilee. There are especially three aspects that shaped his character in Renan's description: his education, his message of the Kingdom of God and the question of his race. These aspects are kept closely tied together with the Kingdom of God as the central concept.

From Renan's perspective the landscape of Galilee was the primary source for Jesus' vision of the Kingdom of God. In his description of Nazareth as the home-place of Jesus, Renan himself as the author of the travel narrative enters into the text, to give an authoritative reading of the landscape, viewed from the hill overlooking the village. He starts from the West, describing 'the fine outlines of Carmel, before *us* are spread out the double summit that towers over Megiddo'. Surveying the surroundings, with references to biblical stories, Renan turns in a circle and ends up facing north and the mountains of Safed. He concludes: 'Such was the horizon of Jesus. This enchanted circle, cradle of the kingdom of God, was for years his world.'[60] This conclusion leads into the opening sentence of the following chapter, on the education of Jesus: 'This aspect of Nature, at once smiling and grand, was the whole education of Jesus.'[61]

Here description and interpretation are mixed. The movement from 'enchant-ed circle' to 'cradle of the kingdom of God' is so swift that it appears natural. In this way, Renan paints the meaning of the scene for his readers with the authority of 'us' who have seen it. He concludes with a reference to Jesus, that this – what Renan saw – was 'his world' as well. Convinced of the correspondence between nature and the character of its inhabitants, Renan establishes a unity between the nature of Galilee, interpreted as 'kingdom of God', and the character of Jesus. Thus, the landscape of Galilee becomes Renan's hermeneutical key; it was this landscape that shaped Jesus as the 'incomparable man'.

Renan ascribes to Jesus three different visions of the kingdom of God, partly consecutive, partly simultaneous. One of them had a specific Galilean character – I suggest that this particular vision of the kingdom of God reflects Renan's central ideas about the future of humanity, ideas that are also reflected in his ideal of a na-tion. In Renan's biography Jesus is not a static personality. He outlines three differ-ent stages in his life, parallel to those in the life of Muhammad.[62] In the beginning Jesus keeps closely to traditional views and practices (as does Muhammad). In the next stage he comes into his own with, in the typical terminology of Renan, 'a calm and poetic eloquence, without controversy, sweet as pure feeling'. In the end the opposition he meets influences him, and he finishes with polemics and strong invectives. Renan's divison of Jesus' vision of the Kingdom of God into three dif-ferent forms seems to correspond to this three-stage model and he discusses the various visions in three different chapters of his *Life of Jesus*.[63]

The main issue appears to be how Jesus' visions of the Kingdom relate to the contemporary situation of Renan's own time. That happens most effortlessly with the idea of the Kingdom as spiritual, as expressed with some of Renan's least elegant phrases: 'the kingdom of the soul founded on liberty and on the filial sentiment which the virtuous man feels when resting on the bosom of his father'.[64] This is a type of masculine spirituality or 'muscular Christianity' that mostly had its home across the Channel among teachers of all boys' public schools and of young men in university colleges. This spiritual kingdom was placed in contrast to the apocalyptic kingdom, which Renan also found in Jesus. The apocalyptic kingdom did not arrive, of course, but its advantage was that it inspired reformers.

It is what I have termed the 'Galilean kingdom' of Jesus that Renan is most enthusiastic about. He refers again to nature when he says that Galilee has created 'the most sublime ideal for popular imagination', and that behind the idyll of nature 'moves the fate of humanity', illuminated by 'the sun of the kingdom of God'.[65] Another description of the Galilean kingdom follows the chapter on the Beatitudes and the Sermon on the Mount; it is the kingdom of the origins of Christianity versus its continuity. Poverty was central to this ideal, original situation. Another characteristic is Jesus' love of the people; with his 'chosen flock' of 'mixed character' he 'traversed Galilee in the midst of a continual feast'. It was a movement of women and children. The idea of a disciple was almost synonymous with that of children, and 'it was infancy ... in its divine spontaneity ... which took possession of the earth.'[66]

This description of the Galilean movement of Jesus is similar to Renan's description of Aryan religion as an 'echo of nature', where in 'imaginative societies' people are childlike.[67] In a perceptive comment regarding how Renan used the correspondence between the lush nature of Galilee and the human nature of Jesus, Susannah Heschel finds that Renan's Jesus was a romantic, feminine figure, similar to Renan's description of his sister who died when she accompanied Renan on his expedition to Syria.[68]

These were the origins and the ideals; they might suit 'a simple sect' but not 'the whole of society'.[69] This becomes clear in Jesus' saying 'Render unto Caesar',[70] creating a space different from politics but at the same time recognizing the legitimacy of power. Renan voices the criticism from those who are concerned with the duties of public life, and who accuse Christianity of weakening the sense of duty of the citizen. He recognizes these criticisms, and also finds that the dreams of Jesus' programme offend principles of positive science. Thus, Jesus' Kingdom cannot be practised in a modern society. However, Renan wants to keep the utopian ideal, the revolutionary ideas of Jesus. He does not want to succumb to the 'inferior minds' who regard the saying 'Behold I make all things new' to be a folly, because when these things actually happen, these critics will be the first to recognize the reasonableness of the new world order.

Kingdom as nation?

Renan makes it clear that the Kingdom of God is not political, that actually it is opposed to the practice and principles of contemporary politics. Nevertheless, the structure of the arguments regarding what the Kingdom represents is similar to Renan's arguments in his famous address on 'What is a nation?' almost twenty years later.[71] In this address he discusses the common responses to that question, with race as the most used, but also language, religion and geography. Renan refutes them all. His alternative response is that a nation is based on solidarity between people who share a past and who consent in the present to live together. Renan's lecture is taken to represent a French position on nationalism, over and against a German position based on 'race'. We shall see how Renan himself spelled out this contrast in his exchange with Strauss over the Franco-Prussian war in 1870. First, however, my main interest is in how he developed his argument along parallel lines with his discussion of the characteristics of the 'Galilean kingdom'.

Renan's main argument in 1882 was that, since a nation is based on solidarity and not on race, language, shared soil, etc., human beings (*l'homme*) are the basis of a people, and the concept of a nation is a spiritual principle. Speaking in a secularist mode, what remains when metaphysical and theological abstractions are driven out of politics are 'humanity (*l'homme*), human desire, human needs'. Nevertheless, runs the counter-argument, to make a system where these 'old organisms' are put at the mercy of unenlightened people will lead to secession and the eventual disintegration of nations. Renan's response is that nothing is eternal, nations will probably be replaced by a European confederation but, at the time, the nations are a guarantee of liberty. Although diverse and often in engaged in conflicts, nations serve 'the common purpose of civilization'; and, using a metaphor from music, Renan says that 'each sounds a note in the great concert of humanity (*l'humanité*), which, finally, is the highest ideal reality (*réalité idéale*) we can attain.'[72] Thus, for Renan humanity represents development and the progress of history, and in many instances when the term is used without further explanation, this idea of the ascent of humanity almost as a divine principle is presupposed.[73]

Humanity as the highest ideal is also what Galilee has provided for Renan in his *Life of Jesus*. In his *Life of Jesus* Renan again speaks of Galilee that it 'has created the most sublime ideal for popular imagination', and that behind the idyll of nature 'moves the fate of humanity', illuminated by 'the sun of the kingdom of God'.[74] In its Galilean version the Kingdom of God does not represent a theological abstraction; as 'the Kingdom of the Spirit' it seems to destroy the political system, but it does so in the interest of human beings. Moreover, it has compensated for this loss by creating 'an immense free association', where minds were freed.[75]

By recognizing the power of rulers, the result of Jesus' saying, 'Render unto Caesar' was that it weakened the sense of duty of the citizen, and delivered the world into 'the absolute power of existing circumstances'. However, Renan responds, there was a critical potential in Jesus' saying because 'in declaring that politics are insignificant, he has revealed to the world this truth, that one's country is not everything, and that man (*l'homme*) is before, and higher than, the citizen'. Renan's Jesus does the same as Renan in his 1882 address, making 'man' (*l'homme*) the centre, not the citizen defined by race or language. Thus Renan also anticipates the criticism from those preoccupied with the duties of public life against those who 'subordinate political to social questions'.[76]

Renan imagines the utopian possibilities of representing 'the Christ of modern conscience' today in relation to those social questions. He suggests that 'we represent a moral liberator breaking without weapons the chains of the negro, ameliorating the condition of the poor and giving liberty to oppressed nations'.[77] Such utopian events certainly exemplify what it means to put 'humanity (*l'homme*), human desire, human needs' at the centre, not only of a nation but of the world. Renan sees the same type of opposition to his idea of a nation based on the rights of people themselves to influence politics as that to the 'making all things new' of Jesus; in both instances they would be characterized as folly or ridiculous. But Renan is convinced that, in the end, these ideas will triumph.

Renan presented Galilee with its nature, landscapes and gardens as paradise, as the garden of Eden and a picture of Indo-European origins. This gave him the possibility to speak of Galilee as an ideal, for those who can see behind its idyll, where the 'fate of humanity moves.'[78] However, the Kingdom of God of Jesus adds something new to the Galilean scene; it is the sun that throws light on the picture. The central issues appear to be how Jesus gives importance to the human being (*l'homme*), which takes precedence over his role as citizen, and how Jesus gives precedence to human needs (i.e. social questions) over political questions. Political power is left dangerously unchecked; the compensation, however, was 'an immense free association'.

It is easy to see how Renan makes the spiritual kingdom central in his interpretation, and he recognizes that the first phase of the kingdom movement in Galilee was possible only for a sect and not for a society. But in his presentation of what I have called the 'Galilean kingdom' Renan argues along lines that are developed within a political context in his address on 'What is a nation?'. They share an emphasis on the precedence of the human being, *l'homme*, and a moral concept of humanity. On that basis, I suggest, the Galilean kingdom is a prototype of Renan's imagination of the nation.

This reading, of course, is only possible with the hindsight of Renan's 1882 address, but I think it reflects continuity in Renan's thoughts. Contemporary readers may possibly have found in the Galilean kingdom a reminder of Renan's views on the origin of Indo-European humanity, as well as a revolutionary criticism of modern society, where Jesus' revolutionary ideals confronted the present world order. But Renan was not a revolutionary; he had to find a way to reconcile his utopia with existing reality. Therefore he poses a contradiction in Jesus, which probably reflects his own ambivalence, between the 'belief in the approaching end of the world' and 'the general moral system of Jesus' that had as its perspective 'a permanent state of humanity'. And Renan finds that it was this contradiction that insured the success of his work, so that 'Christianity united the two conditions of great success in this world, a *revolutionary* starting point and the possibility of *continuous life*.'[79]

If it is an unsatisfactory solution, it is probably because this contradiction between the Kingdom of God and the present situation is a real dilemma, unless one moves the Kingdom out of this world and into some distant future. Schweitzer might have had more sympathy with Renan at this point, since he seemed to struggle with the same problem. In his early work, *The Mystery of the Kingdom of God*, Schweitzer suggests that Jesus imagined that the Kingdom would come through the religious–moral renewal of the believers.[80] Fifty years later, in his last theological book, Schweitzer returns to the theme of the Kingdom and to the idea that the Kingdom and this world are intertwined. He holds that Jesus' ethics were inspired by 'the life- and world-affirming ethics of the prophets'. Even if Jesus had a stronger expectation of the immediate coming of the Kingdom, 'dissociation from the world and active love exist in it side by side'.[81]

The discussion of the 'poetics of the kingdom' by the deconstructionist philosopher John D. Caputo suggests that Renan's dilemma is still with us. He sees the 'logic of the world' and the 'poetics of kingdom' as antagonists; the kingdom contradicts the world of calculus and balanced payments. But, Caputo says, this contrast cannot be solved by placing them in two different 'wheres'; they are two different 'hows', 'whose differences must be negotiated in the one and only world we know'.[82] So the dilemma remains.

The Dilemma of Renan and Race

Galilee – and the non-race of Jesus

In his *Life of Jesus* Renan positions himself and his readers in the privileged position of European civilization over and against the 'fanatical Other' of the Orient. Jesus represents the 'ideal Other' and Renan explicitly places him in the East; he represents ideal aspects of Eastern culture that are a criticism of European modernity.[83] Moreover, he is portrayed with images that in other of Renan's writings are associated with Indo-European origins or ideals. The combination of these elements indicates the complex interrelationship between the Orientalist's construction of the Orient as Other, and the parallel activity of establishing a self-image of the ideal West. Lisa Lowe comments on the complexity of this interrelationship, and says that descriptions of the Oriental world as exotic and uncivilized had as their counter discourse the European world as stable and knowing, as personified by the author. However, this European world was facing internal social difficulties, changes and instability that were written into the travel narrative and ascribed to the 'others' in a foreign land.[84]

Renan as an author with authority in the science of philology personifies this stable and knowing European world. However, there is one issue that seems to destabilize his composure, and that is the issue of race. The term 'race' appears several times in his *Life of Jesus*, but the most interesting passage is one where Renan refuses to use that term. That is a passage where Renan presents Jesus' infancy in Galilee in the context of the mixed background of the Galileans:

> The population of Galilee was very mixed, as the very name of the country indicated. This province counted amongst its inhabitants, in the time of Jesus, many who were not Jews (Phoenicians, Syrians, Arabs, and even Greeks). The conversions to Judaism were not rare in these mixed countries. It is therefore impossible to raise here any question of race, and to seek to ascertain what blood flowed in the veins of him who has contributed most to efface the distinction of blood in humanity.[85]

There is something strange about this passage where Renan rejects 'race' and 'blood' as valid categories to describe the identity of Jesus. Why introduce them in the first place? Renan's position, marked so to speak in shorthand, without giving a full argument, seems to be a response to an ongoing discussion about the validity and relevance of 'race' and 'blood' to express the identity of a community. There seems to be two interrelated contexts for such a discussion. One of them is the discussion of the racial identity of Jesus in relation to his Galilean background. The other, a reference to a 'humanity' not determined by race or blood, links this discussion of the identity of Jesus to contemporary political discussions about the relationship between race and national identity.

We saw in the previous chapter of this book how Strauss in his *Jesus for the German People* presented the Jews as a 'degenerate race', and how that notion with a biological understanding of race became prominent among German theologians and church people.[86] Therefore these persons wanted to distance Jesus – and themselves as Germans – from this Jewish background. The way to distance Jesus from a Jewish descent was to postulate that, by being a Galilean, he was not a Jew by race. What provided some plausibility to such a thesis was the scholarly assumption that the population in Galilee was of mixed origin.[87] It was an accepted hypothesis that after the deportation of parts of the population in 586BCE there had been an influx of other people, which resulted in a mixed population, as Renan mentions, with Phoenicians, Syrians, Arabs, and even Greeks.

It was this long-held view of a historic development that took on a whole new meaning and became a contentious issue when the discussion of the race of Jesus was understood in biological terms. Since the population was mixed, the argument was, Jesus could possibly have descended from a non-Jewish racial background. He could even be portrayed as an Aryan, as Susannah Heschel has pointed out in her study of German interpretations of the historical Jesus in the pre-Nazi and Nazi period.[88] So the 'mixed population' of Galilee was an important part of the argument for a Jesus who was not a Jew, but was of a race with which Germans could identify.

However, that is not the way that Renan understands the importance of a mixed population. In his lecture 'What is a nation?' he discusses the importance of a mixed population in a section where he rejects the idea that a nation should be based on race.[89] He accepts that race is a topic of interest in ethnography, but asserts that it should have no political application. Moreover, Renan claims, ethnography shows that there is no such thing as pure race. And what Renan calls 'the noblest countries' (England, France and Italy) are those that are most mixed, with different tribes joined together throughout history, as for example in France with the Celtic, Iberic and Germanic.

As a result of such mixtures it was not possible to define the proportions of Celtic and German blood in the mix. Since race did not play a role in the formation of European states, Renan contends, it should not play any role in the constitution of modern nations either. Moreover, the concept of race was constantly changing and in flux. Consequently it was totally unreliable and dangerous to base politics on shifting constructions of racial groups. Most importantly, 'human history differs from zoology', and 'beyond anthropological distinctions there is *reason, justice, truth, beauty* that are the *same for everyone*'.[90] This, in the end, is the most important argument for Renan: a nation must be built on a spiritual principle, and on the recognition of the human being or humanity (*l'homme*). When he develops this basis historically, Renan sees the nation as created through a common history and through a commitment to that community in the present as well as into the future.

Renan's address in 1882 represents the culmination of his reflections on what constitutes the basis of a nation, and it throws light on his somewhat cryptic remarks regarding why it is impossible to raise the question of race or to define the type of blood that Jesus had. From Renan's understanding of a mixed population it followed that it was not possible to place Jesus in any of the groups that went into the mix (as the Aryan hypothesis suggested); the population was mixed in such a way that no 'pure' race or blood could be separated out. Therefore Renan refuses to discuss the race of Jesus and its parallel, 'the source of his blood'. Not only are these categories not relevant for Jesus, but Renan presents Jesus as the one 'who has contributed most to efface the distinction of blood in humanity'. Thus he views Jesus as the main influence towards a humanity that was not based on distinctions of blood (or race). This proposition represents the same thought structure as in his discussion of race in relation to nation; race was an inadequate basis to reach the goal of the nation, which was a common humanity.

This presentation of Jesus in a chapter on his infancy and youth anticipates what Renan sees as most important about Jesus and what is to be disclosed through the history of his life.[91] The paradigmatic example of what it means that Jesus broke with 'the distinction of blood in humanity' follows much later, in the period that Renan describes as one of hardening and confrontation with his opponents. This period is introduced as 'First attempts on Jerusalem', and describes Jesus' confrontations in the temple.[92] Here Renan combines his impressions of the Muslim Jerusalem of his day with the picture of a Jewish Jerusalem at the time of Jesus: it 'was then nearly what it is to-day, a city of pedantry, acrimony, disputes, hatred, and littleness of mind'. The temple played a central part in the life of Jerusalem: 'this great space was at once temple, forum, tribunal and university … in a word, all the activity of the nation was concentrated there'.[93] In Renan's description it is not possible to distinguish between nation and religion, although he mostly speaks of 'Jewish religion'.

Renan presents the conflict as one over boundaries. The temple and Jewish religion excluded all except Jews from the temple, from possession of the Law, from the right to be a son of Abraham. But Jesus 'had no sympathy with this'. It is here that the question of race, now stated in terms of 'blood', reappears. Renan presents the Jewish position as one of 'the pride of blood'. Jesus' fight against that position meant that he 'was no longer a Jew'. Renan presents Jesus' revolutionary position in terms of his own vision; Jesus wanted to include 'every well-disposed man', 'all men', as sons of Abraham and children of God. Renan concludes with a series of oppositions between Jesus and the Jews that represents the contrast between ideal humanity and the distinctions of blood: 'He proclaimed the rights of man, not the rights of the Jew; the religion of man, not the religion of the Jew; the deliverance of man, not the deliverance of the Jew.' Renan's triumphant conclusion was that 'the religion of humanity, established, not upon blood, but upon the heart, was founded'. Here Renan's understanding of 'true religion' becomes visible; it is a religion for all of humanity and based on the heart. A religion based on blood, or race, on the other hand, signalled particularity. Probably Renan understands the heart as the centre of emotions and sincerity, but to make an absolute distinction between 'blood' and 'heart' requires an idealization that removes the heart completely from its organic relation precisely to blood. The distinction also appears to break with Renan's paradigm of the Semitic representing the inorganic versus the Indo-European organic.[94]

Renan's distinction between a religion based on race and a 'religion of humanity' reflects a discussion in the nineteenth century about how to make a system for classifying religions. One model was based on the distinction between 'natural religions', representing a lower level of development, and 'high religions', which represented more spiritual values. These higher religions could be further separated into different groups. Some years after Renan's *Life of Jesus*, the American Sanscrit scholar W. D. Whitney took a similar position.[95] He held that there was a decisive division between religions that developed from and were restricted to a race community, like Judaism, and religions that had an individual as founder. In Renan and Whitney we recognize popular conceptions in the nineteenth century; religions were ranked according to their place in a hierarchy of development, and an individual ('great man') was evaluated as being higher than 'the masses'.

Race in European politics

Renan's narrative of the conflict between Jesus and the Jerusalem scribes over race in *Life of Jesus* prefigures a European discussion about whether race should play a role in the definition of a nation, as we saw in Renan's address from 1882. Renan's discussion reflects the conflicting positions of the French and the Germans in this debate.[96] This was not a mere academic debate; it had major political consequences in the controversy over Alsace-Lorraine. After the Franco-Prussian war in 1870–1, Prussia claimed and annexed Alsace-Lorraine on the basis that the population was mostly German-speaking.

Since his youth, Renan had great affinity for German philosophy and literature and admired D. F. Strauss' work on Jesus. He had never met Strauss, but during the war in 1870 he attempted to establish a dialogue with him to find a means of reasonable argument across the divides of conflicting politics and raving patriotism.[97] However, the exchange of letters between the two colleagues did not produce any results; in his response Strauss spoke from the superior position of the power that had won the war and he did not accept that Prussia had any responsibility for starting the war. Against Renan's claim that the smaller southern German states would be in a better position if they were not under the domination of Prussia in the new German Empire, Strauss proclaims that 'the blood of sons of North and South has for all future manifested the unity of Germany'.[98] In his last letter, therefore, Renan did not try to hide his criticism of Strauss' position:

> Our politics is the politics of the rights of nations, yours is the politics of races; we believe that ours is better. The division involved in races, which is most accused by humanity, apart from being a scientific error (since very few countries have a race that is truly pure) cannot but lead to wars of extermination ... That would mean the end to that fruitful mixture, composed of numerous and quite necessary elements that is called humanity.[99]

For Renan it was the very idea of *humanity* that was at stake in the war between Prussia and France. In Renan's opinion, the 'politics of race' upon which Prussia based itself dangerously divided a common humanity. Renan refers to the political use of the idea of a 'pure German race' that legitimated the inclusion of territories with German-speaking populations into a German state[100] – if necessary by force, as in the case of Alsace-Lorraine. In his letter, Renan uses the term race to refer to a linguistic or ethnic group; the German use that he rejects is more totalizing and based on theories of biology. Renan speaks of 'an ethnographic and archaeological *politics*' in Prussia, and thus anticipates an argument later made by Hannah Arendt.[101] It is not scientists who have created racism, Arendt argues; rather, it is the ideology of imperialistic or nationalistic politics that has manufactured racism for its own purpose. Renan's warning that a national politics based on racial thinking is dangerous because it leads to wars of extermination sounds prescient in light of later and even recent European history.

The German discussion of nation had a very different history than the French.[102] Within the older system of many small German principalities, citizenry was regarded as a question of territorial community. The emerging discussion of a German nation, strengthened after the defeat of these principalities by Napoleon, focused on what should be the basis for a German identity. The dominant position was that it was not geographical territory, but the linguistic confines of the German-speaking peoples that defined the nation. This position was inspired by Herder's emphasis on language and culture that made up the spirit of the people, and which distinguished it from other peoples.[103] From this emphasis on the people as a distinct group followed the importance of belonging to this people through descent and linguistic identity. Although this idea of a homogenous nation conformed poorly with the universalist heritage from the Enlightenment and political liberalism,[104] it became the dominant position among both intellectuals and the nationalist movement.

In contrast to the Prussian ethnocultural politics of race and language, Renan poses the French politics of *nation*. The French position was that the nation is a spiritual principle based on a common history and a commitment to live together in the future. Renan argues that only the French definition of a nation furthers progress, whereas the German principle of race does not. In his letter to Strauss, he sets forth the position that he developed more extensively in his lecture on 'What is a nation?' a few years later. In this address, Renan starts by positioning his view of the nation in contrast to what he sees as a dangerous mistake in the present: 'we confuse race with nation, and we attribute to ethnographic, or rather linguistic, groups the sovereignty that properly belongs to truly existing nations.'[105]

Renan's position on a nation based on the will of the people has been described as a 'sublimated expression' of the French position.[106] Although Renan had a great interest in the issue of race, he was determined that it should not play a political role in defining the nation. However, in France also there was an increasing ethnic element in the national self-understanding in the nineteenth century. The heritage from the French Revolution was universalist with rationalist views on nationhood, which resulted, for instance, in politically based support of national movements in Europe. But these movements were also, in part, based on ethnocultural positions. And the Franco-Prussian war led to a new focus on what it meant to be French, partly along ethnocultural lines. Finally, ideas of race that had been associated with social class got nationalist overtones towards the end of the century; from this 'nationalization of race' followed 'a certain racialization or ethnicization of nationhood'.[107] Thus in actual politics the dividing lines between French and German positions was not so clear. The Dreyfus affair was a reminder of the acceptance of racism in a large part of the French establishment.[108] Presently the politics against the Roma population in France is criticized by the EU as one of the ugliest examples of state racism in Europe.[109]

What was Renan's position on race?

What was Renan's own position on race? In particular Renan's lecture, 'What is a nation?', with its rejection of race is regarded as one of the central documents in the development of ideas of nations and nationalism. From this perspective, the lecture points forward to the views that developed after the Second World War, where the rights of nations took preference, leaving behind a politics based on race.[110] However, there are a great deal of disagreements and different interpretations of Renan's statements on race; they probably reflect the fact that his views and stands were manifold and not at all consistent – he changed views over time and in different contexts.[111]

To try to read him over and against a later, more developed and unified idea of race will not do justice to him. A further complicating factor is that there was no unified understanding of the concept of race in the nineteenth century.[112] In the Enlightenment, the term race was used of the 'human race' in contrast to animals. In a later period, it was used in a sense that we now would call social class, being used of the higher strands of society to differentiate them from the lower classes. In the nineteenth century, race became a popular term in discussions of nationhood and national characteristics. Thus, for instance, Renan speaks of Celtic or Etruscan races that correspond to what now would be termed 'tribes'.

The different meanings attributed to race mirror the fact that the term was used to establish identities, and therefore it is to be expected that meanings would change according to periods and contexts. In the nineteenth century, nation and national identity became an important context for the use of 'race'; together with language and territory, it belonged to the most significant markers of nationhood. Increasingly, race began to be understood as a biological category, and there were close links between thinking about languages and race.[113] This is reflected when Renan speaks of the 'Semitic race' for the first time in *Life of Jesus*.[114] He emphasizes that the word race 'means here simply the people who speak or have spoken one of the languages called Semitic'; he admits that the designation is defective, but like other such terms, it must be used in order to make oneself understood.

Nevertheless, Renan's strongest critics, such as Edward Said and Susannah Heschel, will not accept that he speaks only about language and not about race.[115] They argue that the philological system he established, distinguishing between Indo-European languages as 'living' and Semitic languages as 'dead', carried those meanings over onto the human groups who used these languages. Thus, they accuse him of carrying a great deal of responsibility for developing theories of race and making them prominent in later discourse. Heschel holds that it was Renan's works that provided the vocabulary that was indispensable to the racialization of Jesus that occurred at a later stage, especially in Germany. But Heschel also sees the ambiguities in Renan's use of the term race, since he was able to inspire and antagonize opposite positions – for instance, both anti-semitism and defence of the accused in the case against Dreyfus. Thus, Heschel finds that Renan's views could be 'put to political uses never imagined by him'; the most prominent example being the German Nazi theologians and their presentation of Christianity as an Aryan religion that must be purged of Jewish influence.[116]

I will attempt a different reading of the expressions on the race of Jesus in *Life of Jesus* in light of Renan's lecture on 'What is a nation?'. I do not think that the expression 'Jesus was no longer a Jew', which Renan used in describing Jesus' conflict with the Jerusalem scribes,[117] should necessarily be understood in the sense that Renan made him into an Aryan. I suggest that the expression can be read in light of Renan's previous statement, that it was impossible to raise the question of race about Jesus, who effaced 'the distinction of blood in humanity'. It seems more appropriate to say that Renan saw Jesus as embodying non-race, thereby representing Renan's idea of a humanity that was not based on race.

This would be in line with Renan's later discussion of nations as not based on race, language, etc., but on a vision of humanity that included 'all'. Renan made race a category that no longer had a place in Europe, and which was either moved back into history or moved into a different territory. In his lecture on 'What is a nation?', Renan presents his idea of the nation as an example of progress in the modern world, in contrast to 'the ancient world' where race was important, for instance, in ancient Greek city states and Israel. Moreover, Renan adds that it 'still is among Arab tribes',[118] thereby signalling that race as a category characterizes that which belongs to the past, or represents a halted development and therefore belongs, for example, in the Orient. Renan's discussion of what forms the basis for a nation is an example of how problems and difficult issues at home are transferred to the Orient.[119] The conflict between Jesus and the Jerusalem scribes seems therefore to be part of Renan's arguments both for an ideal nation and for an ideal religion. Renan's picture of Jesus as non-racial should provide moral authority for what he saw as a desirable development in France and in Europe: a non-racial national identity.

In this light, we may see in Renan's representation of Jesus' opponents among the Jerusalem scribes a parallel to the Prussian ideology criticized by Renan, that nations be based on race and citizenship established through blood (*jus sanguinis*).[120] The impossibility of engaging Strauss in an exchange on this basis led to Renan's outburst of criticism of the Prussian position on race. So long as the Prussians under Bismarck followed an aggressive national politics based on racial ideology, the question of race could not be removed from the West and comfortably located in the Orient. It appears that there was no unified European 'self' over and against which to pose the Orient. The threat of the Orient lay uncomfortably close to home, across the border in Germany, and maybe even within France itself.

Conclusion: After Whiteness

The above discussion of a broader context for Renan's use of the term race is not meant to take away from the negative picture of the Semitic race in Renan, where the nineteenth-century Muslims blend with the first-century Jew into a common 'Other'.[121] Significantly, in Renan's *Life of Jesus* it is the contrast between Galilee and Jerusalem with their acceptance or rejection of Jesus that provides the historic material for this paradigm of 'us' and the 'other'. That Strauss read the Gospel material in a similar way is no coincidence.[122] Both Strauss and Renan found their main sources in the Logia material (a collection of sayings accredited to Jesus, now called *Q*) and in the narratives of Jesus' life in Mark and Matthew, which made possible a reading of conflict between Galilee and Jerusalem. It was the interest in national identity, with biological race as a central category, that created a paradigm of race and national characteristics for interpretation of these texts. This example shows that source criticism is not an innocent or neutral form of scholarship; rather, it can easily be used for ideological purposes.

Shawn Kelley has explored this paradigm of interpretation and the influence of racial thinking in the nineteenth and parts of the twentieth century.[123] He follows the influence of German philosophers from Herder to Heidegger on biblical scholars, primarily the nineteenth-century Tübingen school and twentieth-century scholars like Bultmann, R. Funk and J. D. Crossan. The racial paradigm can be traced especially through the influence of Heidegger's existentialism. It is possible to see the recurrence of Renan's characterization of Galilee and Jerusalem in stereotypical pictures of the development of early Christianity in these scholars. The character of Jesus showed values associated with the West like individualism, authenticity and creative powers. The decline was represented by inauthenticity, decay and institutionalization associated with the Orient.[124] This was not just a paradigm of historical representation; it is used hermeneutically to express the distinction between 'us' and the 'Others'. This is a paradigm that is closely linked to racism. Its use to structure thoughts and representations does not necessarily express an author's intentions, but shows the pervasiveness of racial thought.

Kelley concludes by suggesting that if his argument is correct, 'it may be necessary to reconceive how it is that the discipline reconstructs the origins of Christianity', and he raises the question: 'Is it possible to rediscover the historical Jesus without indulging in the racialized myth of origins?'[125] Considering that Renan's *Life of Jesus* was the beginning of a *History of the Origins of Christianity*, Kelley's suggestion that we need to reconstruct the origins of Christianity is an appropriate conclusion to a discussion of Renan.[126]

I see Renan's emphasis on the non-race of Jesus as a problem that maybe should concern us more than the possibility that Renan ascribed to Jesus an Aryan identity. To take the latter position makes it easy to reject Renan, to distance him from ourselves and to think that Renan is placed safely in a bygone era. Alternatively if we see him, as I suggest, as struggling to make Jesus into a non-racial ideal for humanity, it is easier to identify with his project and to share his ideals. But, then, we must also realize that the problems involved in Renan's proposition are *our* problems, alive in our best and idealistic attempts to overcome racism.

It is probably obvious to the reader that 'our' and 'us' identify me too as belonging to the white minority that speaks as the dominant 'we'. In his book, *After Whiteness*, Mike Hill deconstructs this position and points to the 'absence of whiteness from discussions of race, its pretence to unmarkedness or purity'.[127] This is a form of blindness that is caused by the hegemonic position of whiteness, which allows whites to position ourselves outside the discussion of race. Race is still something that is ascribed to 'others' and is 'their' problem.

In that sense, Renan's picture of Jesus as non-racial is characteristic of later representations of Jesus. Mass media, especially films, provide good illustrations of cultural presuppositions, and the many popular Jesus movies from the 1920s to Mel Gibson's *The Passion of the Christ* (2004) are pertinent examples. Jesus' opponents, the mob in scenes from the Passion, and even his disciples are played by men from the Middle East or North Africa, but Jesus himself is always played by a white European or North American. It seems that in order to present the story of Jesus as universal, to lift him out of his historical setting in a Middle Eastern context, he has to be made into a white man.

The heritage from the nineteenth century lives on. Renan's claim that the race of Jesus should not be discussed was followed up by the so-called Second Quest of the historical Jesus. The very term 'race' was discredited after the Second World War and the Holocaust, and it disappeared from Jesus studies because of the use of racial categories to make him into an Aryan in Nazi scholarship. So in the Second Quest Jesus was moved into a religious sphere where race also disappeared, together with all the issues that race implies. But race is not an abstract category; those who experience the power of race today are predominantly also those who live in poverty, who suffer illness, who experience discrimination and lack of power. Not to speak of Jesus and race means to lift him up above these structures of inequality, oppression and divisions into 'our' own picture of ourselves. It is this danger of speaking idealistically of a common humanity, of overcoming racism, without seeing how we are part of the problem – not least in our lingering and unfocused usage of the term 'race'[128] – that is the really unsettling heritage of Renan.

CHAPTER VI

THE MANLY NATION

Moral Landscape and National Character in George Adam Smith's
The Historical Geography of the Holy Land

Introduction: Britain as Nation

If the subtext for presentations of Jesus in Galilee for Schleiermacher and Strauss was the building of the German nation state and for Renan it was the ambiguous relations to the Oriental Other, what was it for British pictures of Jesus?

The answer to that question must be sought in the history of England. Different from Germany, where we might say that the idea of a nation came before the creation of a German state, England was a state-nation where the state was established before nationalism, and the legitimacy of the state was based on the monarch.[1] There was a political stability of borders and territories, but it is debatable whether Great Britain should be spoken of as a nation state. Since the beginning of the eighteenth century it was a United Kingdom, but one might say that it consisted of several nations, at least the English, the Scots, the Welsh and the Irish. Moreover, it was also a colonial power, and from the nineteenth century an Empire, which provided a larger context for national identities. Nevertheless, Linda Colley has argued that there developed a common identity as Britons in the latter part of the eighteenth and the beginning of the nineteenth century, an identity which to a large extant was based on Protestantism. This Protestant identity played an important role both in defining Britain *vis-à-vis* external Catholic powers like France and Spain, but also internally against the Stuart dynasty. So Colley concludes that 'Protestantism was the foundation that made the invention of Great Britain possible.'[2]

An identity as British in contrast to the 'Other' was reinforced in the beginning of the nineteenth century through the conflict with Napoleonic France. Later, with industrialization and urbanization, other issues became pressing, notably those related to social change, changes in family and gender roles and the rise of a poor working class. At the same time, the responsibilities and possibilities of the Empire became a determining context for the education and training of large numbers of young men of the upper and middle classes.

The central role of men both in developments at home and within the growing British Empire makes it relevant to focus on the relationship between masculinity and nationalism.[3] In periods when identities were under pressure, they were often reshaped through contestations and discussion of 'hegemonic masculinities', which John Tosh describes as 'the masculine norms and practices which are most valued by the politically dominant class and which help to maintain its authority'.[4]

A central component of such hegemonic masculinity was *respectability*, a norm that was closely related to nationalism, not only with regard to sexual morality but in all areas of social and individual life. Respectability, says George L. Mosse in his study of middle-class morality in Germany and England, 'was thought essential for the maintenance of an ordered society. The bourgeoisie had created the age of commerce and industry – and it feared what it had created'.[5] Thus, respectability became the code word for the morality of the British middle classes. It was an ideal that they also tried to impose on the working classes, and which before long was accepted by large sectors of the working classes. This respectability was a societal responsibility, but it was also expressed in an individualized form, as a question of personal 'character'. Since men had the dominant role in society, we may say justifiably that the issue of how to build a 'male character' was central to the question of British national identity in the last part of the nineteenth century.

With their strong emphasis on ethics Evangelical Protestants, who played important roles in British society in the nineteenth century, strongly supported the building of a national character, which to them was the same as a Christian character.

A Geography of The Holy Land, Nation and Empire

George Adam Smith and Victorian Lives of Jesus

It is within this context of Protestant evangelicalism and the building of a national character that George Adam Smith and his book *The Historical Geography of the Holy Land*[6] belong. Smith himself represented many of these different social and geographical locations already outlined.[7] He was born in India in 1856, was brought up and worked in Scotland, and travelled extensively in the Holy Land. As a professor, he was intellectually and socially part of British society and belonged to the upper middle class. As a clergyman in the Free Kirk of Scotland, he was an evangelical with socialist political views and an intense social practice in work for and with working-class communities, especially women workers, a practice he continued as a professor in Glasgow. Thus, he was centrally located within many of the issues and conflicts of his days.

George Adam Smith was a professor in Old Testament studies and not a historical Jesus scholar, at least not in the same way as the previous authors we have discussed. Nevertheless, Smith had studied with prominent Bible critics in Germany and in this way represented the modern biblical criticism that was considered radical in Britain. His presentation of Jesus is not a Life of Jesus but rather a form of 'life-writing';[8] that is, it presents characteristic aspects of Jesus' life set in Galilee. It also occupies a central section in his *Historical Geography*.

This section of his book has many similarities to the form of Jesus-biography and travel writing in Renan's *Life of Jesus*. First, Smith emphasizes the influence of geography and nature upon personal characteristics. Smith was a recognized geographer and engages more than Renan in theoretical discussions of the relationship between geography and character. Second, and in the words of Anderson, Smith's presentation of Jesus in Galilee 'fuses the world inside (the novel) with the world outside'.[9] In Smith's picture of Galilee there are many references to general conditions in industrialized societies, to the situation of workers in Great Britain and also specifically to Scottish conditions. Finally, Smith's interest in how to shape human character and especially in the development of the young, personified in the young Jesus in Nazareth, shares central aspects of the genre of biography and the *Bildungsroman*.

My own reason for choosing to discuss *The Historical Geography of the Holy Land* by Smith and not some of the English Lives of Jesus is that the latter do not show the same interest in the geographical location of Jesus in Galilee, and therefore do not provide material for a consideration of the territorial aspect of nationalism that otherwise was so important in the European Lives of Jesus.

Moreover, with few exceptions, Great Britain did not have critical, historical Jesus studies of the type found in Continental Europe.[10] The books by Strauss and Renan were translated quickly into English and caused a stir and debate, but mostly provoked protests and attracted few followers among theologians. Most important among the critical studies was John Robert Seeley's *Ecce Homo*,[11] which showed similarities to the historical criticism of the Lives of Jesus by Renan and Strauss but left open the relationship between historical criticism and faith in a way that caused much discussion and perplexity among readers and reviewers.[12] British theologians seemed on the whole to be more conservative and more loyal to the churches' teaching, often combining academic and church positions. Among the books written from a conservative viewpoint, Frederic W. Farrar's *The Life of Christ* was the most popular.[13] Farrar also travelled to the Holy Land and used his encounters with Arabs to describe the society and culture at the time of Jesus, but his description, for instance of Nazareth, has the character of a novel with psychological character sketches.

The book and the Land

Based on several visits to the Middle East as well as on his geographical and biblical studies, Smith published *The Historical Geography of the Holy Land* in 1894.[14]

In this book, Smith was able to unite his studies of the Old Testament and of Palestine landscapes and archaeology with his social commitments. Smith's *The Historical Geography of the Holy Land* takes its place among English travel writings about the Holy Land in the tradition of A. P. Stanley's *Sinai and Palestine in Connection with their History* thirty years earlier.[15] However, Smith's book took travel writing to a new level; it was reprinted forty-five times and remained for fifty years the authoritative study until it was replaced by works of the American biblical scholars and archaeologists Albright and Wright.

The positive reception of *Historical Geography* praised it as an example of modern scholarly approaches. With his combination of results from the latest archaeological expeditions, new biblical criticism and extensive journeys in the region, there is no doubt that Smith represented the most modern approaches in historical geography of his day.[16] At the same time, his much admired style of writing was that of a preacher, and it was noticed that he had an 'essentially evangelical purpose' with his historical presentation.[17]

Smith's *Historical Geography of the Holy Land* shared the nineteenth-century presupposition that there was a correspondence between the nature and landscape of an area and the development of its history and the personal character of its inhabitants. Smith places himself within a tradition that recognizes and works with physical geography, but which also emphasizes the human element. Development cannot be explained simply by physical nature, 'moral and spiritual forces' also played a role, and it is Smith's goal to try to discern the contribution of each part. It is in the unique combination of these two sources – physical nature, and moral and spiritual forces – that Smith finds the 'national character' of Israel. The question of these two sources is central to Smith's discussion throughout the book, and it is his awareness of this theoretical problem that makes his book superior to Renan's more intuitive approach.

The first part of Smith's book (pp.1–124) discusses these theoretical questions, combining history, physical geography and information from the Bible. The second part (pp.125–516) is by far the largest and covers Western Palestine, which was also the area where the Palestine Exploration Fund concentrated most of its efforts, comprising most of present-day Israel and the Palestinian territories. The third part (pp.517–650) covers Eastern Palestine, the land to the east of the Jordan River including the Decapolis. Two chapters on 'Galilee' and 'The Lake of Galilee' form a central section of the second part (pp.413–63), and here Jesus is the main figure.

Jesus plays a role of signal importance beyond the two chapters on Galilee, however. Smith makes this clear in his introduction when he explains why he has undertaken this study of geography: 'For our faith in the Incarnation, therefore, a study of the historical geography of Palestine is a necessary discipline.'[18] This statement signals an important purpose for him,[19] and he follows up with a sentence that reveals one of the main presuppositions of historical geography: 'a vision of the soil and climate in which He [i.e. Christ] grew and laboured is the only means of enforcing the reality of His Manhood.' Here Smith will use the general idea of a correspondence between natural environment and human character to investigate one individual, Jesus of Nazareth, from this perspective. This is similar to Renan's mission thirty years earlier with his *Life of Jesus*.

There is a significant difference between Smith's work and Renan's, however. This was not a portrayal of the historical Jesus that would upset the churches; with the term 'incarnation' Smith employs the vocabulary of the churches' teaching that Jesus Christ took on human nature as Jesus of Nazareth, that 'he became like us' and thereby became a model for humanity. Therefore, the context in which Jesus is placed, the 'soil and the climate', is significant. When Smith places Jesus in Galilee, surrounded by the Greek and Roman world, the relationship between Jesus and these places becomes part of 'the reality of His Manhood'. These Galilean villages are more than distant historical places; they are drawn into the same process of identification with the readers as Jesus himself.

Cracking the code

The imagery and evaluations that Smith uses to describe Galilee reflect discussions of character and the relationship between individual and society occurring in England and Scotland in the late nineteenth century. However, many of the characterizations and references to the contemporary situation in *Historical Geography* are brief; one might almost describe them as coded language. In order to decode them, I shall draw on Smith's other writings, especially sermons and works directly discussing the use of the Bible in 'the modern times', as well as studies of Victorian economy, politics and culture. In this way, I hope to show how Smith's picture of Jesus in Galilee contributed to the discourse of manly character. Smith's combination of a focus on individual character and the larger perspective on land and nation was part of a discourse on the national identity of Britain, but also, in some instances, more particularly of Scotland.

For the analysis in this chapter, I will use the theoretical discussion in Stephen Reicher's and Nick Hopkins' *Self and Nation*,[20] which draws on material from contemporary Scotland to combine studies of social psychology and nationalism. A chapter entitled 'In Quest of National Character'[21] covers with a theoretical overview much of the same ground as the methodological approach in Smith's *Historical Geography*. Among various ways to describe national identity, the authors find that 'character' is the most common. Within a social psychology approach, national identity is not a static concept; it is related to a process of becoming. Moreover, to construct national identities has a purpose; it mobilizes people to participate in the evolution of our social world. Thus, identity construction has a strategic dimension. The content of national identity is constructed with various building blocks, of which many are the same as in historical geography, especially in the connection between environment and national character.

Social psychology provides insights especially into the processes of formation and construction. Reicher and Hopkins are particularly interested in how cultural resources are used in the formation of character, and to what ends. Cultural resources are, for instance, narratives about particular figures, often described as myths that have 'crucial importance in defining the way in which a group understands its own identity'.[22] These perspectives will help us to see Smith engaged in shaping personal and national character in a contested situation, drawing on the Gospel stories about Jesus as his cultural resources.

Holy Land and Empire

There had been a long tradition of English involvement with the Holy Land, as discussed in Chapter II. Smith was part of a group of travellers and writers who described the Holy Land and fused it with images of 'homeland'; he combined historical descriptions with observations from his own travels to the area, where he notices parallels between ancient times and the modern period. Smith's discussion of Syria, the larger area of which Palestine was a part, illustrates this point.[23]

Smith found that Syria had great opportunity above all by virtue of its geographical position. Syria was at the crossroad of three continents – Europe, Asia and Africa – although often this also meant it was in the centre of conflicts and war. That put Syria in a passive state, overrun by Arab tribes, or even more fatal: 'conquered and civilized by the great races of Asia, Africa and Europe'.[24] Here we notice the well-known language of 'great races' that represented 'civilizations'. From Smith's own observations from his travels to the region, it was obvious that European colonization had a privileged position and was justified in two ways. First, the colonizers with their farms brought advantages to the soil, so it was good for the physical geography. But, more importantly, the Western modernization brought back something which had been there earlier, an original 'Western' identity.

In the first six hundred years of the Christian Era, Europe in Palestine was represented by Hellenism and Christianity, then briefly by the Crusader kingdoms, but Smith sees the more recent examples of colonization as significant for what they forebode. Their influences were visible, for example, in the houses of European colonizers, with their sloping roofs instead of the flat roofs of Palestinian houses. To Smith, these roofs indicated 'the truly *Western aspect of nature* in the Holy Land'. These signs of Western nature explained 'how Greeks, Italians, and Franks all colonized, and for centuries were at home in, this province of Asia'.[25]

Thus, the Holy Land was not foreign to Europeans; it was a homeland. Within this Western history, the presence of a local, Arab population for 1300 years disappears under the imperial gaze,[26] which goes from the Bible, via a brief Christian history, directly to the modern Western colonization.

For Smith, the Jews represented a bridge to this Western modernity. Syria had a strategic geographic position with its opening over the sea towards the West. But it was only Israel among the Semitic tribes that followed this route to bring true religion to the world. The route towards the West is identified with modernity; the Israelites 'gather up the experiences of the ancient world, and break with this *into the modern*'. This sudden jump into 'the modern' makes Israel an ideal image for modern nations. [27]

The contrast between ancient and modern is also associated with another contrast, that between parochial and universal. This becomes explicit in Smith's description of Jesus in the context of Syria's 'opportunity Westward'.[28] Since he was placed in Syria, Jesus was at the same time centrally placed in the Empire. And he was not only Messiah to Israel, but 'indispensable to the race' (that is, humanity), i.e. not only to the history of Israel but to the history of all men. Smith's terminology is similar to that of Renan;[29] Jesus preached the spiritual rather than the external, the moral rather than the ceremonial, grace rather than law. Finally, Jesus sent his disciples into the whole world. All aspects of this description are characteristic of what was regarded as 'modern' and 'progressive' in religion. These contrasts served not only to distinguish Jesus from Syria, but they also introduced a distinction within Israel. Jesus represented the modernization of Israel's religion and its development towards an individual relation to God.

Smith and his *Historical Geography of the Holy Land* actually became part of the colonization of Syria. In his campaign in 1914–18, Allenby used the book with its descriptions of ancient roads and battles.[30] Smith also served as an advisor to the British government on the Palestinian issue leading up to the Balfour Declaration in 1917 and the political conflicts that followed.[31] These were later political developments, but the mentality of colonization and empire that justified them was present in Smith's descriptions of ancient Syria and the observations from his travels there in the 1880s.

The Nation as Moral Character

Individualism as national character

Unlike Schleiermacher, Strauss and Renan in their presentations of Jesus in Galilee made Galilee an ideal location for Jesus in contrast to Judea and Jerusalem. Perhaps because Smith was an Old Testament scholar, he was reluctant to make this division so important, even if it occurs in his description of Galilee at the time of

Jesus. But when Smith discusses the religious development of Israel, he establishes a division within the nation based on moral and religious distinctions rather than geographical ones. The contrast is one between 'material' Judaism with a focus on sacrifices, and an ethical religion based on the teachings of the prophets.

The transformation of Israelite religion that Smith sees in the later prophets is a development towards the individual's relation to God. The prophets are portrayed as preachers who confront the social ills in their community, but also with an emphasis on the religion of the individual. It is this development to which Smith also wants to contribute at home in Scotland; he draws an explicit parallel between the situation of Israel at the time of the prophets and the contemporary situation in Britain. First, there is the social and economic development from agriculture to commerce, along with the rise of the city, and social problems similar to 'those still urgent among ourselves'. Therefore, the prophets emphasize not just tenderness and pity, but justice and equity in the treatment of the poor. And when the prophets encourage religious observances and institutions, they do it for social ends and for the interests of 'the poorer classes of community'.[32]

Finally, there is an emancipation of the individual from a 'merely' national religion to a solitary relationship with God in independence from the community. However, this does not result in a withdrawal from society but in a new duty and loyalty to the community, 'the higher sense of individualism resulting in a *truer altruism*'.[33] The prophet Jeremiah is Smith's primary example. Living in a nation that had broken away from God, Jeremiah was tempted to leave the community, but he overcomes the temptation of a 'purely selfish religion'. Instead, he represented an individualism that at the same time had a strong loyalty to the community, one which made 'the community his other self'. This makes Jeremiah a Christ-figure in the Old Testament, for it was in Christ that this individualism reached its height. His was an individualism that was not selfish, but characterized by solidarity and sympathy and, ultimately, 'substitution and sin bearing'.[34]

In this way, Smith undertakes a redefinition of national from 'mere national' to a focus on the individual in his moral role in society. The emphasis is on the individual, but not as an expression of a selfish religion. Instead, it represented altruism, and with a specific emphases on the situation of the poor and on justice and equity. Smith combines a traditional Presbyterian focus on the individual with a commitment to the community. Thus, Smith puts a British discourse on national character in an explicitly Christian and evangelical form.

Altruism in nineteenth-century Britain

The significance of Smith's emphasis on the strong commitment to community in religious individualism becomes clear if we place it in the context of the discussion of the relationship between the self and the social in nineteenth-century Britain.

In a book with the subtitle *The Self and the Social in Nineteenth-Century England*,[35] Patrick Joyce provides a broader context within which to read Smith's text:

> Technologies of the self in the nineteenth century involved 'making the self visible to the self', so that the good life would be shown to be about the exercise of 'character' and the exertion of 'independence'. These were to be found within, in a realm where moral choice and religious duty had to be exercised in order to bring the good, and the good life, into being. But choice and duty were directed outwards in turn to shape contemporary understandings of the social and the political, above all the senses of the demotic and democratic.

For Smith, 'the good life' was given a specifically Christian interpretation, and it was the Old Testament and Jesus that were the sources of moral choice and religious duty. While Joyce is most interested in *how* moral choice and duty are turned outwards into the social and political realms, Smith's concern was probably more focused on how to shape the direction of this move outwards through altruism.

Altruism was a word that had only recently been introduced into English, but it seems to sum up values that became significant in Britain in the latter part of the nineteenth century. Stefan Collini discusses altruism as one of 'the governing values' of political and moral life in the nineteenth century. He sees altruism not on the level of philosophy, but as deep patterns of assumption in the larger public conversation. He describes it as 'a recurring pattern of assumptions about the relations between selfishness, altruism and human motive'.[36]

Collini constructs an 'ideal-type of the notion of morality characteristic of dominant Victorian culture'. The main elements are: 1) morality understood as obligations, therefore the category of 'duty' was important; 2) The alternative to performing one's duty was 'giving in to temptation or being seduced by one's inclinations'; 3) In any given situation there was only one morally right answer; and 4) The others whose welfare was the object of one's duty were humanity as a whole. In discussion of some of the leading figures of political and intellectual life, Collini finds that some of these assumptions are sharpened. Particularly significant were their 'obsessive antipathy to selfishness' and their intense preoccupation with how to raise adequate motivation in the moral agent, seeing emotions or feelings as a stronger source of action than the intellect.[37]

Joyce and Collini have outlined patterns of assumption and central values that characterized public discourse on moral and political issues in nineteenth-century Britain. These patterns of moral discourse present a framework for how British society should be envisaged, and the role of the individual within the construction of that picture. Smith's texts can be read as participating in this discourse, especially with regard to the question of how to shape the individual to become a person that could contribute to the common good. Smith uses the special re-

sources provided by his *Historical Geography of the Holy Land:* a historic land and
a nation as an example upon which to work out his own social ideals with the help
of the figure of Jesus.

In the characteristic morality of Victorian culture, the exercise of character in
fulfilling one's duty of altruism seems to be the primary goal. Therefore, 'giving
in to temptation' was a negative alternative that prevented one from reaching that
goal. We shall see that it is exactly on this point that Smith focuses his presentation, at the moment of temptation. He engages the challenges that might hinder
one in fulfilling one's duties, not so much as character weaknesses as challenges
from outside. It is only by overcoming these temptations that one can develop a
character that makes it possible to reach the goal: to fulfil one's duty and practice
altruism.[38]

Jesus incarnated in temptation

In a section in *Historical Geography* leading up to the central statement about
Incarnation, Smith presents a brief outline of the life and works of Jesus.[39] In this
list he gives a prominent position to temptation by 'some of its strongest political
forces', a temptation which Jesus 'overcame by loyalty to its [i.e. the Holy Land's]
distinctive gospel'. In a footnote, Smith refers his readers to a previous passage
on the development of Israel's religion in which he describes how Jesus came as
the expected Messiah. Again, Jesus is placed in relation to the 'strongest political
forces': 'He was born into the Empire' close to the port that the Romans used to
send soldiers into Palestine, in a period when Herod filled Palestine with Greek
architecture and 'the Hellenic spirit breathed across all the land'.[40]

This scene introduces Smith's interpretation of the temptation story (Matt
4:8–10), which is the key to his picture of Jesus and recurs several times in *Historical Geography*. The 'kingdoms of the world' as shown by the devil to Jesus are
here identified: 'He was tempted, we are told, to employ the marvellous resources
of Greece and Rome.' It was these temptations that Jesus overcame through his
confession of the God of Israel.[41] In Smith's first presentations of Jesus as the
incarnated Christ, his focus is on the temptation story in the context of the great
powers of his day, Greece and Rome. In the course of the later chapters, where
Jesus appears in the contexts of Galilee and the Jordan valley, references to the
temptation story recur. This story has a key function in defining the reality of Jesus'
manhood and thereby also the human existence that he shared. Thus, since Smith
wants his readers to identify with Christ in an understanding of human existence
as constantly being tempted, his focus is on identifying with Christ in withstanding temptation.[42]

In the term *temptation* we recognize the terminology of the central moral challenge of the Victorian age, which was to perform one's duty in the face of tempta-

tions or one's inclinations. This was part of building character. It is easy to see that Smith participates in this type of discourse; but for what position was he arguing?

First, how did Smith understand temptation? In his introduction he focuses on external sources of temptation, identified as the great forces of Greece and Rome. So far, the meaning that Smith attributes to these forces is not yet explicated, but they suggest that the definition of temptations implies taking a stand on society and its social, economic and mental structures. And the emphasis on *withstanding* temptation first implies the question of *how* this is achieved, and how character is built to ensure this result. Withstanding evil temptations obviously also introduces the image of the good, with the vision of a good society and a good life. Whatever the story is, in the various scenes of his life in Galilee Smith invariably portrays Jesus as an ideal for modern readers, as one who suffers temptations but withstands them.

The Moral Landscape of Galilee

From 'pious homes' to 'harlot cities': The dangers of communications

Since Galilee was 'the soil and climate in which He [Jesus] grew and laboured', a description of the relationship between Galilee and Jesus is of central importance for Smith.[43] Smith did not spend much time on the political system of Palestine that was so important in German presentations of Palestine and their discussion of the historical Jesus.[44] Nor did he pay much attention to questions of the race, ethnicity or nationality of the population,[45] questions that were of vital interest to biblical scholars on the continent, and that played a role in the conflicts between Renan and Strauss.

What made Smith's section on the geography of Galilee superior to earlier studies was his description of the road system.[46] He focuses on the roads as communication systems with the surrounding world and their importance for the milieu both of Galileans in general and of Jesus in particular. Smith's concern is for the social and cultural effects of communication, more than its role in political rule. However, there is also an emphasis on communication and warfare, so roads have an ambiguous function in Smith's description.[47] He outlines the three main road systems that crossed Galilee: from Damascus to the coast (the Great West Road); from Damascus via Gaza to Egypt (the Great South Road); and finally the Great East Road from Acca via Betshan to Arabia. These roads brought the entire world through Galilee, complete with commerce, beggars and Roman soldiers.

Thus, the physical and historical geography of Galilee linked it to the larger world beyond it; Smith's purpose is to show that Galilee was 'in no obscure corner'. This put Galilee in an ambiguous position, open to not only peaceful contacts but also colonization and military domination. What was the effect on Jesus of contact with all parts of the civilized world? We may come closer to Smith's views on this point when we read the effect this issue had on Smith himself, when he develops the picture of the roads into an example of his effective preaching style, merging geographical observations and biblical images:

> Of all the things in Galilee it was the sight of these immemorial roads which taught me and moved me most – not because they were trodden by the patriarchs, and some of them must shake to the railway train, not because the chariots of Assyria and Rome have both rolled along them, but because it was up and down these roads that the immortal figures of the Parables passed. By them came the merchantman seeking goodly pearls, the king departing to receive his kingdom, the friend on a journey, the householder arriving suddenly upon his servants, the prodigal son coming back from the far-off country. The far off country! What a meaning has this frequent phrase of Christ's when you stand in Galilee by one of her great roads – roads which so easily carried willing feet from the *pious homes* of Asher and Naphtali to the *harlot cities* of Phoenicia – roads which were in touch with Rome and with Babylon.[48]

In this vivid imagery we notice the preacher's views on the roads and the contacts that they made possible. Communication was also dangerous and a temptation; roads lured people away from 'pious homes' to 'harlot cities'; the juxtaposition of Rome and Babylon had some of the same connotation.

This ambiguity becomes even more obvious when Smith looks at contact with the more immediate surroundings. The roads not only lead to far off countries, but also to the regions surrounding Galilee. In contrast to Judea, which had the desert as its neighbour, Galilee had fertile and cultivated areas: Phoenicia, Hauran and the Decapolis. In a chapter on the Decapolis Smith outlines the influence of the Greek world upon Galilee, and thereby upon Jesus and his disciples.[49] This is a chapter where Smith's explorations of East Palestine (present-day Jordan) with visits to Gerasa (today Jerash) and Gadara pay off splendidly. Their magnificent ruins showed the splendour of Greek civilization; Smith found inscriptions that described political culture, and large aqueducts showed wealth and economic activity.

Smith's conclusion was phrased in no uncertain terms: 'The roads which crossed Galilee from the Decapolis to the coast, the inscriptions upon them, the constant trade between the fishermen and the Greek exporters of fish, the very coins – everywhere thrust Greek upon the Jews.' The result of this Greek presence in and around Galilee was that 'the Kingdom of God came forth *in no obscure corner, but in the very face of the kingdoms of this world*'.[50]

Ancient Greece as model and temptation

Renan spoke of Palestine as 'the fifth Gospel', meaning that the landscape gave in-sights similar to those of the canonical Gospels. Smith does not use this term, but in several instances he proposes that insights from historical geography may cor-rect the picture given by the Gospels. The presence of Greek influence in Galilee is one such example. From the Gospels, one would imagine that Galilee was sur-rounded only by 'desert places haunted by demoniacs', but historical geography presented a totally different picture. Smith says that 'the background and environ-ment of this stage of our Lord's ministry was thronged and very gay[51] – that it was Greek in all that the name can bring up to us of *busy life, imposing art and sensuous religion*. The effect upon the Galilean temperament is obvious.'[52]

Greece and Rome were the main powers and cultures that through the roads and the surrounding Decapolis cities influenced Galilee and Jesus. What did these descriptions mean to contemporary readers? In nineteenth-century England the names Greece and Rome signified the most illustrious ideals from antiquity, but here the names have an ominous ring to them. If we take Greece and Rome, rep-resenting 'powerful forces' in Jesus' Galilee, as Smith's code words for temptation, what were their contemporary representations?

The ideals and models from antiquity, especially from ancient Greece, were everywhere visible in the nineteenth century in England and Scotland: in educa-tion, in art, in architecture, in civic ideals. Latin and Greek were important parts of the public school and university curriculum and represented ideals of learning and morals.[53] The civic spirit of the Greek cities was invoked in the development of the cities as industrialization and commerce created explosive growth and the accumulation of great wealth. Wealthy industrialists and merchants were chal-lenged or encouraged to follow the Greek ideal of combining commerce with art and learning. The result was patronage to establish museums, art and learning institutions, and libraries, and to erect buildings in Greek and Roman styles that put their mark on Victorian cities.[54] Thus, the Greek city states became ideals for the city elites, while Rome became a model for the British Empire. The teaching of Greek was also important for the reading of the New Testament in Greek, and similarities between Greek philosophy and Christianity were emphasized.[55]

However, which Greece was it that represented a model for the modern na-tion?[56] From the eighteenth century to early nineteenth century the classical Greco-Roman model of republicanism was the ideal, with its vision of the citizen and the community as interdependent, based on the male warrior as defender of the polis. Masculinity and austerity were central values of the community, against the threats of luxury and corruption, that is, selfishness. This perspective came under attack in the mid-Victorian period with the growth of industrial modernity, large cities and other economic and social possibilities. The old republican ideal was considered to be too rigid, enforcing stagnation, in a situation where diversity and individualism were needed. Working within the context of classical ideals as models for society, liberals like John Stuart Mill, Matthew Arnold and others presented their image of a different Greece, with the high period of Athenian civilization that represented enlightened rational progressiveness together with freedom and non-conformity. This diversity also opened up expressions of emotions and sexuality that during a regime of civic virtues had been confined to the home or private life. Typical representatives of this change were the Pre-Raphaelites in painting and poetry.[57]

Many Victorians were critical of these changes; they felt that they were signs of a society in decline and compared it to the later periods of antiquity, when the ideals of the classical period were lost. Whereas the classical period had been all male and austere, decadence invoked other images from late antiquity. In a history of ancient Greek literature written at the same time as Smith's book, the classical scholar Gilbert Murray made this comparison between how the Greek was portrayed in the eighteenth century and in his own time: 'The "serene and classical" Greek of Winckelmann and Goethe did good service ... in his day ... He has been succeeded ... by an aesthetic and fleshly Greek in fine raiment.'[58] This was the time of Oscar Wilde, of the covert or not so covert sensuality of homosexuality, and of 'Greek sensuousness'[59] in poetry and paintings. Characteristically, both contemporary and modern critics associate these expressions of late Hellenistic and nineteenth-century decadency with the Orient, and cast it in feminine terms as 'the effeminacy of the east'.[60]

A famous attack on this Hellenistic influence showed how the tide had turned, and how much the old virtues of classical republicanism had lost ground. Robert Buchanan published an attack on Pre-Raphaelite poetry, where he denounced it as 'The Fleshly School of Poetry', but he received little support and sympathy.[61] The Victorian public had come to accept expressions of a wider variety of human life. But this controversy also reflected cultural diversities within Britain: Buchanan came from the Scottish Highlands where the old civic ideals were alive in response to what was regarded as an unacceptable modernity.

It is against this complex situation where different images of Greece were used to argue for national and societal ideals that we may read Smith's versions of what Greece and Rome meant. When he first mentions Greece and Rome, they are described as 'some of the political forces'. In the picture of the Decapolis cities, Smith refers to them as Greek 'in all that the name can bring up to us of *busy life, imposing art and sensuous religion*'.[62] 'Busy life' and 'imposing art' appear to be qualities that British cities were happy to imitate; this combination of business and art was a goal among many in the merchant class. However, 'sensuous religion' strikes a negative note. Smith may here voice a negative attitude towards the image of the later Greek world criticized in similar terms by Murray and Buchanan. Even if Smith was not himself a Scottish highlander, he knew the Scottish intellectual tradition, which was more in line with the earlier, republican Greek ideals, and he was sceptical of Mills' ideas on individualism and economy.[63] Smith's description of Greek 'sensuous religion' picks up on its Oriental connection and points to Syria as its place of origin. Smith argues against the thesis of Renan that the monotonous Syrian desert was a natural place for monotheism to arise. Quite the opposite, Smith says; the Semites had gone beyond the (polytheist) Aryans, 'not only developing a polytheism and mythology of great luxuriance, but proving (sic!) its missionary to the Greeks'.[64] Thus, Greece as a model for modern city life also represented a danger, a religion of Oriental character, a mixing of religion with sensuality.

Thus, Smith set the scene: Jesus' Galilean ministry was surrounded by Greek influence. What would be the effect on 'the Galilean temperament'?

Places of Temptation: Nazareth

Sexual purity

In the Jesus studies of Strauss and Renan, Galilee was presented as an ideal, in contrast to Jerusalem and Judea. The Galileans accepted Jesus, and therefore they became ideals for the Christians and Galilee became a place of positive identification for modern readers. Smith obviously also wanted his readers to place themselves in Galilee, but in order to confront them with the challenges that Galilee faced. This becomes explicit in his description of Nazareth.

Smith sets out to disprove a common picture of Nazareth as a secluded and obscure village.[65] This picture was a result of the silence in the Gospels about Jesus' childhood in Nazareth. But here was another instance where seeing for oneself gave new insight: Smith portrays the Nazareth of Jesus' childhood and youth using observations from historical geography to fill out the 'silence of the Gospels'.[66] First, there was the view from the hill above Nazareth, which Smith must have climbed as Renan did some years earlier.[67] Taking in the views of the Great Plain to the South, the Jordan Valley, and the mountains, all with their stories, Smith concludes: 'It is a map of Old Testament history'.[68] In contrast there was the image of 'present life', drawn from the activities on the major roads that were easily visible from Nazareth. With travellers on these roads came news, stories and gossips from Rome and other places: 'all the rumour of the Empire entered Palestine close to Nazareth'.[69]

In recent discussions of the religious character of Galilee, the focus of the discussion has been on the contrast between the influence of Greek culture and socio-economic structures and the religion of the Jewish communities in Galilee.[70] Those who have held that there was substantial contact have understood such contact, in line with Strauss and Renan, as exerting a positive influence on Galilee and Jesus, promoting more open attitudes in terms of religion, and shaping Jesus' rhetoric and ideas. Those who argue that there was little such influence upon Jewish Galileans substantiate their claims by pointing to signs of observance of Jewish rituals, especially the excavations of a number of ritual baths. It was not along these lines that Smith constructed Galilee, however. The issue of ritual observance and the religious difference between Greek culture and a Jewish Galilee do not play a central role. Galilee is described not in religious, but in moral terms. It was a landscape where communications and views from the hilltop formed a *geography of temptation:*

> Here He grew up and suffered temptation, Who was tempted in all points like as we are, yet without sin. The perfection of His purity and patience was achieved not easily as behind a wide fence which shut the world out, but amid rumour and scandal with every provocation to unlawful curiosity and premature ambition. The pressure and problems of the world outside must have been felt by the youth of Nazareth as by few others; yet the scenes of prophetic missions to it, Elijah's and Elisha's, were also within sight. A vision of the kingdoms of this world was as possible from this village as from the mount of temptation. But the chief lesson which Nazareth teaches is the possibility of *a pure home and a spotless youth in the very face of the evil world.*[71]

To Smith the geography of Galilee with its system of roads and communication with 'all the world' first and foremost represented *temptation*. The element of temptation in Jesus' life as a youth was heightened since Nazareth was not an obscure and isolated place. To preserve purity and patience would have been easy 'behind a wide fence which shut the world out', but Jesus was surrounded by the dangers of the world. Nazareth was *not* a secluded and safe place. Smith describes Jesus' upbringing in Nazareth as another example of the temptation on the Temple Mount: 'A vision of the kingdoms of this world was as possible from this village as from the mount of temptation.'

Thus, physical and political geography filled out the silence of the Gospels to present a totally different picture of Nazareth. In Nazareth, Jesus was exposed to 'rumour and scandal with every provocation to unlawful curiosity and premature ambition', 'pressure and problems of the world outside', 'the kingdoms of this world', and even 'the evil world'. But Jesus did not fall victim to such temptations; he showed the superior qualities of 'moral and spiritual forces', since he reached the goal: 'the perfection of His purity and patience'. The focus of Smith's presentation of the geography of Nazareth with temptation as the hermeneutical key concentrates on the spiritual forces of Jesus that were to be imitated. The conclusion, presenting a 'pure home and spotless youth' as ideals, is a very bare statement. It obviously takes for granted that these phrases were part of a shared moral universe. Jesus is an example of resistance to temptation, but no particular acts are attributed to him.

The economy of this description becomes visible if we compare it to other interpretations of Jesus' childhood and youth in Nazareth. Since there was so little information about these years, speculation abounded in attempts to make them relevant for a picture of the ideal humanity of Jesus. One example is *The Life of Christ* by Frederic W. Farrar, published in 1874.[72] Although a conservative churchman whose perspective was far from the rationalism of Renan, Farrar used a similar scenic and romantic style of argument. He had also travelled to the Holy Land, and returned with deep impressions due to the scenes and 'immemorial customs' of Jesus' home place. Farrar uses a description of a visit to an Arab home in Nazareth to give a picture of Jesus' home, based on the supposed identity between nineteenth-century Arabs and Jews at the time of Jesus.[73] Farrar also draws character portraits of Joseph, Mary and Jesus to describe what their life must have been like: 'we may well believe that it was a home of trustful piety, of angelic purity, of almost perfect peace'.[74] He presents the view from the summit above Nazareth and finds that Jesus must have regarded it as a scene of deep 'significance for the destinies of humanity'.[75]

Farrar also sees these silent years of Jesus' life as important: 'they were the years of sinless childhood, a sinless boyhood, a sinless youth, a sinless manhood'. They are important because they provide 'an eternal example to our entire race'. And they do that because we do not know anything about them! Farrar turns the problem of a lack of knowledge about this period in the life of Jesus into an advantage: precisely because they are so uneventful, they can be a model for human life. It is not possible to imitate Jesus' life during his three-year ministry, Farrar says, 'but the vast majority of us are placed, by God's own appointment, amid those quiet duties of a commonplace and uneventful routine which are most closely analogous to the thirty years of His retirement; it was during these years that His life is for us the main example of how we ought to live'.[76] In Farrar's narrative, Nazareth is an idyllic and serene village; it is the ordinariness of Jesus' life that makes it possible to identify with him. The sinlessness of Jesus is an ideal, but there is no struggle, no temptation, only 'almost perfect peace'.

In *The Manliness of Christ*, Thomas Hughes struggles with another problem that was raised about these years in the life of Jesus, the accusation that in these years he was 'idling, doing nothing, while there was work that waited to be done'.[77] Hughes suggests that Jesus prepared himself for the future by waiting patiently.[78]

Against the background of Farrar's idyllic Nazareth and Hughes' pedestrian moralistic interpretation, Smith's construction becomes much more pointed; he describes the possibility of moral behaviour within a geography of temptation.

Jesus becomes an example of the general point of Smith's *Historical Geography:* in Jesus the audience can see what moral and spiritual forces contribute to the building of character against surrounding adverse influences.

Building character

In the section on Jesus in Nazareth, Smith presents the basic outline of a programme for building *character*, which was an important issue in Victorian Britain. The idea of character was central to political thinking; it determined much of the discussion about social improvement, and it was part of a shared intellectual and moral discourse. The form and particular notions of that discourse were, to a large extent, a result of the impact of evangelical Christianity, described as: 'the vision of life as a perpetual struggle in which one's ability to resist temptation and overcome obstacles needed to be subject to constant scrutiny'.[79]

Smith belonged to this evangelical Christianity. He made his reflections about Jesus and his resistance to temptations relevant for the present day when he says of Nazareth that, as quoted in the previous section, 'Here He grew up and suffered temptation, Who was tempted in all points like as we are.' This is an illustration of Smith's point about how historical geography supports faith in incarnation. On the one hand this represented an identification of Christ with human beings. On the other hand, it encouraged readers to imitate Jesus. That Jesus represented a 'spotless youth' who preserved a perfect purity could not be ascribed to the contribution of his physical nature; on the contrary, it was a result of his moral and spiritual forces and therefore something that was possible for others, too. The underlying presupposition was that Jesus *struggled* against temptation and was victorious.[80] Struggle was an important part of the ethical Christianity of Smith; his conclusion to the section on Jesus encourages the reader to enter into the same struggle against temptations: 'the chief lesson which Nazareth teaches is the *possibility* [my italics] of a pure home and a spotless youth in face of the evil world'.

Struggle against temptation was also the topic of many of Smith's sermons, especially those addressed to young men and women.[81] Smith's saw temptations as being of two kinds. One exploited former weaknesses; Smith speaks of them as 'old indulgences', most likely a reference to the breaking of sexual purity codes. The other type of temptation was of the sort that Jesus experienced, 'opportunities and tests, the visions to us of our greatness that two worlds are in contest for our souls'. Here Smith will speak 'frankly to young men. You have now the temptations of your manhood in your own power. Manhood is coming to you with the discovery of destiny and a vocation, with its clear issues and responsibilities.'[82] That the temptations are 'in your own power' shows Smith's confidence in the possibility of building character; by withstanding small temptations, one built up power to resist later temptations. Likewise, if one gave in to temptations, one weakened one's power to resist and thereby weakened one's character. Therefore the struggle was important, and as a result, one carried the responsibility for one's own character.[83]

Through Smith's description of the temptations of Jesus we read an evangelical perception of the modern world and its dangers. It was characterized by 'rumour and scandal with every provocation to unlawful curiosity[84] and premature ambition', as well as by 'pressure and problems of the world outside'.[85] Here we see central aspects of perceived dangers in a modern society like Scotland at the end of the nineteenth century: sexual and other temptations (e.g. ambition) that characterized a society where especially many young men had to leave home at an early age.

'A pure home'

The presentation of Jesus as a young boy in Nazareth gave Smith the opportunity to present Jesus as an ideal in an area of great significance in the Victorian period: home and the upbringing of youths.[86] In the moral geography of nineteenth-century Britain, the home had a special place. The Industrial Revolution and other social changes in the early nineteenth century brought with them great economic and social upheaval, with a growing urbanism. House and work were no longer linked; the workplace became separated from the family dwelling. In the rising middle classes, the home represented a haven away from work, whereas industrialization and deplorable living conditions threatened the social stability of a home for the working classes.[87] The phrase 'a pure home' summed up the desires and hopes of many in the late nineteenth century across religious and class boundaries.

For the middle classes, *home* became the signal metaphor for the private shelter away from the pressures and noise of work, and from the evils and vices of the city. Home was associated with wife and children. Women did not work outside the home but became 'the angel in the house',[88] representing all the ideals of quietness, purity and peace. At the same time the father was the patriarch of the house, with prestige and authority, supported by the image of a powerful God. This modern notion of home was particularly strong in English culture; it is easy to see how Smith employs a well-known value system when he sets up the pressures, vices and temptations of the world in contrast to the 'pure home'. However, this domestic system, and in particular the authority of the patriarch, came under strain in the last part of the nineteenth century.[89] It suffered public criticism, and, significant for our discussion, a loss of support from religion, brought about by changes in the religious climate. The traditional, authoritarian beliefs, especially in the evangelical traditions, lost ground.

Even if the ideology of family and its social relations underwent changes, the idea of 'the pure home' in Smith's passage on Jesus in Nazareth resonated with

readers over a broad spectrum. Early sociologists, medical doctors and social reformers in the nineteenth century were concerned about homes in the context of
the social and moral geography of the cities. They shared the same ideas about
how the environment influenced human behaviour as the historical geographers
who studied ancient societies. Therefore, environmental conditions such as over-
crowding, bad housing, lack of water and sanitation, etc., were directly related to
poverty, ill-health, drunkenness and delinquency. Thus, 'the mapping of the moral
geography of the city, in particular, provided a basis for social intervention'.[90]

Housing for the poor was an area of special concern. It was felt that the spatial
economy of the household in terms of separate housing for families, with sanitation and washing facilities, should help to improve their situation and thereby
reform individuals. Health and virtue were linked. Social reformers saw the relationship between a poor home and the problems of youths. They considered
juvenile delinquency to be a result of particular types of family and homes – for
example, the absence of a father figure, poverty in the household, and lack of sufficient space in the home.

The concept of home' was not just a middle-class idea, however, that social
reformers tried to bring to the working classes. Neville Kirk shows that what he
calls the 'deification of the home' was a central aspect of the ideology of organized
labour in the mid-nineteenth century.[91] Organized labour represented primarily
'the respectable' workers and emphasized the importance of familial strength and
social stability centred on the home.

The Scottish reformed churches had to a great extent ignored these problems
for the most part in the nineteenth century; the preaching of the gospel to the
poor was combined with an acceptance of the economic system and the enormous
inequalities that it produced.[92] Smith participated in a movement of social criticism in the Free Church; in his 1885 address, 'Christianity and Labour', he also
addresses the problems of working class homes. He deplores the fact that because
of the demands of the workplace, 'the security of a home and the health of the
family became simply impossible'. In a direct criticism of rich Christians as own-
ers of the workplaces, he says that 'you keep education from them, and the possibility of *pure homes*'.[93] Thus, the term 'a pure home' in the description of Jesus'
youth, carried meaning both for the middle class readership of Smith's book, and
for the working-class poor.

Thus the function of the reference to a 'pure home' is obviously to serve as a
symbol of the moral character of the home. Unlike Farrar, Smith does not use
the opportunity to describe Jesus' household; there is no sign of Joseph in Smith's
story, nor, maybe more surprisingly, of Mary. The phrase 'a pure home' only by
implication makes a reference to the influence of the mother, and to the father's
responsibility to protect the purity of the home.[94]

'And a spotless youth'

Smith's main emphasis is upon Jesus and how he overcame the temptations of Nazareth and showed 'perfect purity' and a 'spotless youth'. In a middle-class environment these ideals were probably especially associated with sexual purity. Smith's terminology is very close to that used by Edward Benson, headmaster of Wellington College and later Archbishop of Canterbury. In his farewell sermon to the pupils of Wellington College in 1873, Benson gave this final admonition: 'For you will be men. You will seek Purity, that the souls and bodies you offer those you love and to all-seeing God may be white and unspotted.'[95] The ideal of sexual purity was an important part of the moral rhetoric of Victorian educators together with ideals from the sports field such as fair play, team spirit and the discouragement of effeminacy. But even more important than these ideals was the development of *character* in order to withstand temptations and to exercise self-control. The central concepts were 'manliness' and 'courage'. For this reason, the way in which Jesus withstood temptation was presented as proof of his manliness, and as an example to follow.[96]

The purpose of this was to educate boys to become men, both at home and abroad. George Mosse sums up the purpose of this training: 'The typical English public school, on the other hand, was meant to provide a microcosm of state and society, to build the character of those who were destined to rule.'[97] Thus, the boys were educated to become a national elite, exemplifying the character and values of the nation, and also of the Empire. The Empire as administration, the military, commerce and shipping was never far away; it was an underlying social, economic and mental structure.

The churches advocated the ideal of sexual purity until marriage, an ideal that apparently was a reality for many, especially middle-class young couples. However, among working class youths this was not so. Also for young men of the middle classes, the interval between reaching puberty and contracting marriage was often between ten and fifteen years; since young women of their own class were 'off limits', sexual experiences happened with domestic servants or more often with prostitutes.[98] This obviously was a concern for the churches; the founding of the YMCA in 1848 was one of the means to reach out to young men of the lower-middle or upper working classes, to install manliness with a commitment to purity.

In the late Victorian period, this concern in the churches about sexual vice and moral corruption and 'its terrible effects on national welfare' reached a new stage. One example is the establishment of the Church of England Purity Society (CEPS) in 1883, with the explicit goal of promoting male sexual purity; another example is the interdenominational White Cross Army. The primary goals of the CEPS were 'purity, a chivalrous respect for womanhood and protection of the young from contamination'. Clearly this enterprise was seen as part of shaping a national character; the CEPS aimed to 'stir up the manhood of England'. The aim to install a morality of sexual abstention in men, as part of the concept of manhood, was therefore seen as a public, national enterprise.[99]

Smith used historical geography to describe Nazareth as he would describe life in Glasgow, with an emphasis not so much on the horror of the living conditions of the poor working classes[100] as on the moral temptations of city life, especially for the young men in the process of growing up and preparing for adult life. Thus, the goals of a 'pure home' and 'spotless youth' did not need any elaboration in a first-century setting in Nazareth; they were perfectly understandable within a modern British context. That Jesus 'was tempted in all points like as we are' was a picture of Jesus as a youthful figure with whom it was easy to identify. This was a Jesus about whom one could sing, 'What a friend we have in Jesus'.[101] This picture of Jesus brought him out of narrow church confines and made it possible to reach out to a larger following. Also, there was no heavy emphasis on sin and guilt in Smith's lectures and sermons. The way to follow Jesus was by means of character development. This is the significance of the possibility of purity that Jesus exemplified: it was attainable by all who exercised their will and thereby built their character. Except for the reference to 'pure home', the ideal is a *manly* character. Since Smith does not use the obvious opportunity to bring Mary, the mother of Jesus, into the ideal of the home, the focus is placed upon the description of a young man facing the world.

Places of Temptation: Caesarea Philippi

Ambition versus self-sacrifice

Smith's discussion of Jesus' youth in Nazareth emphasized evangelical ideals of sexuality and purity, which today we would easily characterize as 'private morality' but in Victorian Britain they were markers of national character. But in his presentation of the Greek and Roman world as *temptations* Smith was concerned with more than sexuality. In his description of Nazareth, Smith mentions in passing 'the provocation ... to premature ambitions' and 'a vision of all the kingdoms of the world'.[102]

With the term 'premature ambitions', Smith probably alludes to a major problem for young men both of the middle and working classes and their families.[103] For young men of the middle classes, it was difficult to find suitable work to support a family and a home. The old tradition of following in the father's footsteps, with the father introducing his son into the business or his profession, fell apart with growing competitiveness both in business and in the public sector. This situation put greater stress on the individual and his responsibility for his own success. There was growing anxiety among parents, especially among fathers, about the

future of their sons; the growth of enrolment in public schools in this period is
an indication of the felt need to prepare a young boy properly to enter into modern society. The focus of these schools was upon 'independence and manliness
of character', and although there was an emphasis on purity, as discussed earlier,
there was also a growing importance placed on sports, with ideals like competition, toughness, and independence balanced by team play and consideration of
others. We may see this as an attempt to develop the ideal of a gentleman within
a new type of business society, keeping ambitions in check while at the same time
securing success.

However, this was only one of a number of possible paradigms for manhood
within societies with quickly growing industrialization.[104] The 'self-made man' or
the 'entrepreneur' provided another possibility, with competition and the accumulation of power in the workplace as the foremost values. The growth of industry in Scotland in the nineteenth century was to a great extent the product
of men coming from rural or modest urban backgrounds.[105] Many of them had
a sense of social and communal responsibility, although their main concern (and
felt responsibility) was to make their businesses profitable, which meant that the
worker's pay and living conditions were prioritized. 'The enterprising Scot' was
seen as the very personification of progress, although he may have been an ideal
created by the Victorian age.[106] The many popular self-help books of the period
emphasized how a man, by vigorous self-help, might triumph in the struggle with
the world. The third model was the 'artisan paradigm', which stressed autonomous self-sufficiency, independence and self-respect.[107]

It is possible that since Smith combines 'premature ambitions' and 'visions
of the Kingdom', he once more has in mind the middle-class youth, and wants
to shape the gentlemanly ideal when he returns to the story of the temptation of
Jesus. In the first version of his interpretation of that story, Smith interprets the
kingdoms that the devil shows Jesus as 'the marvellous resources of Greece and
Rome'. Smith brings up again the temptation to become ruler of the world when
he describes how Jesus asked his disciples what people thought of him when he
entered Caesarea Philippi (Mark 8:27–30). The location, Paneas, situated in the
Jordan Valley north of the Lake of Gennesaret was a lush place with a strong water
stream and trees; it was an ancient place for worship and had a sanctuary of the
Greek god Pan. More recently, Herod the Great had built a temple to Augustus
there, as shown on ancient coins found at the place, named Caesarea Philippi by
Herod's son, Philip.[108]

It was this archaeological evidence Smith used to construct a context for the
Caesarea Philippi episode as a place where men worshipped 'side by side the forces
of nature and the incarnation of political power'.[109] He finds it striking 'that the
first clear confession of Christ's Divine Sonship was made near the shrine in which

men already worshipped a fellow-man as God'.[110] But it is the human aspect of the divine incarnation that Smith emphasizes, with the contrast between the emperor with 'his rank, his splendour, his power' and Christ who 'turned that very day from the symbol of all this to seek His kingdom by the way of sacrifice and death.'[111]

Smith concludes by saying that at Caesarea, by the sources of Jordan, 'we see' this contrast between Caesar and Christ. As a travel writer, Smith combines his observations at the location with an inner sight and through the use of the inclusive we he suggests that also armchair travellers can share in this sight and insight. Smith employs his power as a preacher, directly addressing his readers, by reminding them that 'this was a contrast on which Christ often dwelt', and inviting them to make their own judgment regarding the importance of this episode: 'nowhere can we better value the alternative which it presented to *that generation*'.[112]

Smith might just as well have said 'this generation', since with the phrase 'where we see' he invites his present-day readers to contemplate 'the apotheosis of the Gentile spirit in the temple raised to an Augustus by the flattery of a Herod, and Christ with His few disciples turning from it to His Cross and Sacrifice'.[113] Cross and sacrifice or flattery of the power of this world: these were the alternatives that Smith put in front of his readers.

That Jesus chose self-sacrifice was not an expression of weakness; it was a way to seek a higher and truer value in the Kingdom of God. In Paneas, it is contrasted with the power of the Roman emperor; his was temporary and possessed only for a short time, while that of Christ was eternal. In Caesarea Philippi, Smith describes the character of Jesus developed in contrast to an environment of power and extravagance. In another setting, Smith describes self-sacrifice as corresponding to the nature of the landscape. In his picture of Judea, Smith ascribes Jesus' self-sacrifice to his role as shepherd in analogy with the shepherds of Judea.[114] In the pastoral landscape of Judea, to be a shepherd was the main occupation. The founder of their dynasty, David, had been a shepherd, and Smith describes the shepherds as stately, conversing with empires. These forceful and manly characteristics are combined with the willingness of the shepherd to sacrifice himself for his sheep. The shepherd with his flock, who looks after his sheep, 'has every one of them in his heart', and therefore Christ took the shepherd as the type of self-sacrifice. In this setting, self-sacrifice is an expression of manly love, and Smith presents Jesus as a manly ideal of how to seek the Kingdom in direct contrast to the world of power-holders and flatterers.

In contrast to the association with war that the notion of sacrifice carried in Prussia and France, in Victorian Britain sacrifice was considered a feminine virtue associated with domesticity and not with men's lives in the workplace or in public. Since sacrifice was so central to the churches' teaching about Christ, that tended to make him irrelevant among men of the business world and of the working class. One of the accusations against the churches in the Victorian period was that Christ had become feminized; he was not portrayed as 'a real man' and therefore he could not be an ideal for working men. In his *Historical Geography*, Smith appears to respond to that problem, both through his picture of Jesus and with his description of the disciples. The setting for this is the presentation of the manly character of the Galileans shaped by the landscape, and the picture of the fishermen–disciples of Jesus at the Lake of Galilee as ideals of manly character.[115] Here Smith moves from a picture of the ideals associated with Jesus as at least implicitly middle class to a discussion of the working classes and their character, arguably also as seen from Smith's middle-class position.

The churches tried in various ways to respond to the claim that Christ was not masculine enough. One response was 'muscular Christianity', emphasizing the manliness of Christ; it was more a trend among writers than an organized movement, being represented especially by Charles Kingsley.[116] Another more organized response was to employ sports and games as, for instance, in the YMCA and the Boys' Brigade.[117] Part of their efforts was to reinterpret what seemed the meekness of Christ in terms of strength and courage. One example is *The Manliness of Christ* by Thomas Hughes, the author of *Tom Brown's Schooldays*, the famous book about how public school education fostered a Christian sporting masculinity.[118]

There were also other responses, however, which tried to introduce feminine values like service, self-sacrifice and love into the male workplace.[119] At the same time as Smith worked among the poor in Glasgow, the WCMA in the USA championed a shift in the understanding of manly character away from entrepreneurial, competitive qualities to a character ideal of 'self-denial, sacrifice and collectivity'. These qualities were integrated into 'the manly life on the model of the Christ man'. Similarly, even in the personal aspects of the man, in family relations and emotional life, there were, even among the 'muscular Christians', attempts to integrate 'the tender passions'.[120]

Imagining a Manly Nation

George Adam Smith's description of Jesus in Galilee illustrates the appropriateness of Benedict Anderson's thesis that nations may be described as imagined communities.[121] In his *Historical Geography of the Holy Land*, Smith constructed Galilee to serve as an imagined mirror of Britain in his time. Smith's stated purpose, to use a study of the 'soil and climate' to enforce the reality of Christ's humanity, amounted to a deliberate re-writing of Jesus as an alternative to prevailing views in the Scottish reformed tradition of a dogmatic Christ without social consciousness. In order to do that, Smith also had to re-imagine the picture of Galilee. He broke with a previously common picture of Galilee as a secluded corner of the world, surrounded by desert landscapes, and with Nazareth as an obscure little place. Instead he drew a picture of Galilee as centrally located, with easy contacts throughout the Roman Empire, and with Greek cities around the Sea of Galilee. This created a picture of Galilee that was much closer to life at home than the previous romantic image – for instance, the exotic landscapes with Oriental scenes illustrated by David Roberts.[122] Smith's Galilee had communication by roads, travel opportunities, businesses and cities of a type that was well known in Britain.

Smith's description, as others before him, made Galilee into familiar territory, into a 'homeland'. The landscape of Galilee fused with that of the Britain of Smith's own day. His *Historical Geography* depicted a *moral landscape* whose issues and problems overlapped with those of his own time. The questions were national, in that they affected the very structure and cohesion of society. It was the pressing problems of an urbanized and industrialized society that concerned Smith – problems that he encountered in his engagement with workers and the poor in the harbour district of Glasgow. Therefore we could say that, as unlikely as it might seem, Smith describes Galilee as Glasgow; this is possible since he has already constructed Galilee as filled with Greek cities, and his concern is with human and social relations.

The contrast that could have been established between Galilee as an 'ideal territory' versus the outside forces of Greece and Rome was not made in that way. With Smith's description of communications by road and geographic proximity, Greece and Rome were not distant 'others'; rather, they infiltrated the landscape of Galilee. This aspect of Smith's description may have been due to the role of Greece and Rome as models for Britain, both in terms of architecture and education, but also in relation to Britain's role as a modern empire. Smith gave an ambiguous presentation of Greece and Rome; he spoke of them with some admiration as 'great powers', but they were also presented as *temptations* within the moral landscape he depicts. Since they were described in scenes familiar to modern life in Britain, however, they were in a way not foreign but *familiar* temptations. They were well known, part of life in the modern world, and not to be attributed to a totally foreign realm. Smith appears to over-emphasize the size of the towns in Galilee to create this similarity with modern Britain. Likewise, he did not emphasize the religious aspect of the contrast between 'Greek' and 'Galilean', but a *moral* difference. Thus, Galilee was a landscape and a geography where contrasts were played out in a moral key. The social issues, the contrast between poor and rich and the despair of life among the masses, were present, but the primary perspective was the moral one, presented as *temptation*.

It was therefore necessary to establish a moral character that could resist temptation and thus represent an ideal. It is here that the image presented of Jesus/Christ had its main role. Since he shared the same temptations experienced by modern readers, Smith described him as an ideal image of humanity, and with a character that represented national values. In describing Jesus, Smith focused on issues that were of central concern in the Britain of his time: namely, home as the main focus of family life in a period of rapid changes and pressures in work life, and the upbringing of youth with the need to shape in them – particularly in young men – a character of purity. Moreover, in a period of aggressive capitalism and competition, Smith's response was to promote altruism, expressed in Christian terminology as self-sacrifice.

The terminology of temptation and struggle belongs to the language of warfare transferred to the moral and spiritual realm. This has a long Christian tradition going back to the Bible, as in the (contested) Pauline letter to the Ephesians (6:10–17), for instance. The language of spiritual warfare was very popular among Protestant groups in early modernity. The Christian is presented as being at war with evils from without and within, and the character required to withstand temptation is couched in the terminology of masculinity, just as in the discourse of 'real' warfare as discussed in *Masculinities in Politics and War*.[123] In many situations of crises and conflicts, there was a competition among various forms of masculinities as to which should be hegemonic.

Therefore we must ask what form of masculinity it was that Smith presented in a time of conflict over hegemonic masculinities. It was very far from the 'muscular Christianity' of Charles Kingsley earlier in the century, who spoke of 'the strong man Jesus Christ'.[124] Smith chose a different route: in Nazareth, Jesus was an innocent youth; in Paneas, he is presented as giving himself up to self-sacrifice. It is only among the shepherds of Judea that Smith finds a truly masculine figure for Jesus, but even so, it is a type for self-sacrifice.[125] The Jesus of Smith's *Historical Geography* is obviously a young man, but he does not present the same type of ambiguity as the representation of Jesus in pictorial works by the Pre-Raphaelites.[126] Instead, as a young man Jesus represents for Smith an ideal for other young men and boys preparing for adult life. The situation of the public schools might provide the most likely setting; here Smith's Jesus seems to play the role of the perfect student, and not the role of the teacher as in Schleiermacher's lectures.

Smith's other addresses and sermon suggests a broader audience, however, also including working-class lads. Although speaking from a middle-class position, Smith represented an effort to extend respectability also to the working classes. In some of his addresses, Smith spoke of Jesus as 'a working man'. Obviously a provocative statement for many, this was part of Smith's effort to make it possible for working men to identify with Jesus.[127] In that way, Jesus could function to integrate the working classes into the nation, and thereby make it possible to imagine a unified nation, not in terms of the different parts of Britain but in terms of the even more serious class divisions in Victorian Britain. The image of Jesus' purity and self-sacrifice in the face of temptation placed him at the centre of a moral discourse that defined national identity in categories that were intended to transcend class and social barriers.

Conclusion

George Adam Smith's picture of Jesus in Galilee stands at the end of the nineteenth century, the last in a line of presentations starting with Schleiermacher in the first part of the century and continuing with Strauss and Renan in the middle of the century. The purpose of this chapter together with the preceding ones has been to investigate how the rise of nationalism and the first quests for the historical Jesus were combined and interacted with one another, so that the result was an image of Jesus as a figure of identification for 'modern' readers, not only as a model for personal identity but also as one for shaping the nation and Europe. For this reason, Jesus was configured differently in different nations and at different times.

Our study has shown that there were three main ideas on areas of study that were combined and worked together to produce paradigmatic pictures of Jesus. The first idea is that of 'the great man' as the main shaper of history and founder of nations. Jesus embodied 'the great man' from antiquity: he provided a putatively direct contact with the classical roots of modern European nations and the origin of their culture whilst at the same time, he represented progress and development. Although critical of the churches' Christology, the quest for the historical Jesus was not introduced as a secular idea. Rather, it represented history under the providence of God. The idea of 'the great man' and history as developing from antiquity under the providence of God represents what Charles Taylor calls a 'social imaginary', or a commonly accepted view of how the world works.[128]

The second idea was the ideology of nationhood and nationalism, which was the cultural and political view of how the world ought to work in a specific context, differing from country to country and over time. Nationalism was the social and political setting of the Lives of Jesus that we have studied. Jesus' historical relationship to the people and territory of Galilee and Palestine provided parallels to issues of nation and national identity in the nineteenth century.

Finally, historical Jesus scholarship was related closely to source criticism of the Gospels, another area of New Testament studies that developed in the nineteenth century. Source criticism started out as a question about whether John's Gospel or the three Synoptic Gospels were the most reliable source. Subsequently, the question was refined, with discussions of the sources behind the Gospels themselves, and of 'the synoptic problem', which is the literary relationship between the three Synoptic Gospels. These questions have played a central role in traditional histories of historical Jesus scholarship. It has been mostly overlooked, however, that the study of literary criticism and the history of tradition were not disinterested scholarly investigations but, rather, part of ideological trends and reflected political interests in the nineteenth century.

These three ideological and cultural areas were variously combined in presentations of the historical Jesus, and thus produced different images of him and of a nation. For Schleiermacher, lecturing at a time when the unified German state did not yet exist, Jesus was portrayed as directing his mission to the 'whole people' and the 'whole land' and thus, so to speak, imagining a nation. The image of King Frederick II as the ideal 'great man' who embodied the people was a model for Schleiermacher's Jesus and contributed to his ideal of a democratic nation. Schleiermacher's choice of John's Gospel as his main source reflected his idea of the unity of the (German) people. In John, Jesus' mission is directed at the whole country, and Jesus therefore could not be located primarily in Galilee.

Schleiermacher wrote in a period before the Synoptic Gospels or their sources were accepted as the best historical basis for a life of Jesus; this later stage is reflected in the books by Strauss and Renan. In these Gospel sources, Galilee was Jesus' main location and Jerusalem and Judea were places of conflict and Jesus' death. Therefore Galilee became an ideal, either because the population there responded positively to Jesus (Strauss), or because the landscape itself inspired Jesus (Renan). In this way, Galilee represented the beginning of Christianity; it was identified with a new humanity, while Jerusalem represented the old faith. This was an old figure of contrasts that was now played out and justified with the modern sciences of geography, philology and literary criticism, and eventually the biology of race.

For both Strauss and Renan, the contrast between Galilee and Jerusalem became a paradigm for modern contrasts related to national unity and characteristics. For Strauss it took the form of the divide between the Protestant North and Catholic South in Germany. In the period of Bismarck's power politics leading up to a unified Germany, Jesus became a non-political Messiah in the shadow of the Roman Empire. For Renan, Galilee and Jerusalem prefigured the contrast between the French nation, representing humanity, versus the Muslim Orient, or even Germany as a nation, based on race. Renan's Jesus was shaped by Galilee, but at the same time he was a 'great man' who initiated a new humanity without racial divisions. However, Renan's ideal carried with it racial prejudices as part of its heritage.

For Smith, Jesus was without discussion placed in Galilee within a vivid description of landscape and geography. Smith shared with Renan the experience of travelling to Galilee, so that the landscape itself became a source for his picture of Jesus, too. The books of both men were examples of an interest in the Holy Land that was so much a part of modern European religion, scholarly activity, growing tourism and politics in the second part of the nineteenth century. More than Renan, Smith shared a tradition of explicit English identification between 'Holy

Land' and 'homeland', but, like Renan, he also represented an imperial gaze when looking at the Holy Land. Smith, like Strauss and Renan, saw Galilee as a model for modern society but the contrast to Jerusalem did not play an important role. Rather, the conflicts are described as internal to Galilee; the Greek and Roman world of commerce, power and sensuality was present within the land, as similar forces were also present in Smith's Britain. These forces represent temptations. Thus, Smith's Galilee is portrayed in terms of a moral geography. Against this background, Smith's picture of Jesus takes its form. The common 'great man' ideal is expressed in the image of Jesus portrayed as a young man who overcomes the temptations of sex and success; he becomes thereby an example of the character that is necessary to build both a person and a nation and with them an empire.

The nineteenth-century constructions of Jesus in Palestine are a form of the historical imagination of Jesus as a 'great man' in communities configured as nations and empires. Rather than looking upon these imaginations as failures, as Schweitzer did, we should consider them as responding to the needs of specific situations and trying to make history relevant for present-day challenges. This is also the challenge for today's images of the historical Jesus; but the specific challenge now is how *not* to paint Jesus as a national figure.

CHAPTER VII

JESUS BEYOND NATIONALISM

Imagining a Post-National World[1]

A map of the world that does not include Utopia is not worth even glancing at
Oscar Wilde[2]

Jesus: a Utopian Biography?

Is it possible to imagine Jesus and his life among people of his day in a way that will make sense for our time? Can a life-writing about him be written in a dialogue also with our world, particularly as we struggle with questions of a new world order?

These are the types of question that seem to have inspired the nineteenth-century authors discussed in this book. Writing the Life of Jesus was a way to go back to the origins not only of Christianity but also of European society and civilization. And in a civilization and societies facing daunting changes and challenges, writing the history of Jesus in his time and society was also a way to look forward, by imagining how the memory of Jesus challenged the present and pointed towards a different future. Writing about Jesus was writing both his own history and a possible future for one's own people or nation. History and utopia were linked in the life of Jesus.

This element of utopia was important in the early historical Jesus studies, with Schleiermacher's imagination of a nation based upon a people of citizens participating in the political process as the best example. This early form of democratic nationalism, based on the writings of some intellectuals and small student movements, seemed insignificant compared to the autocratic powers who were determined to bring Europe back within the old order, before the upheavals caused by Napoleon. However, after the vision of a nation based upon people as citizens first was launched, it caught on and eventually became political reality. Thus, engaging in writing about the life of Jesus was also a way to engage in the larger question of the future of society and nation.

The most pressing question today goes beyond the nation; it is the need to think of a future for all of humanity. It is difficult to get to grips with this challenge within structures and systems that are designed to administer the current arrangement. To imagine a future that is different from a prolongation of the present is almost beyond comprehension. That is why utopias are so necessary, as Oscar Wilde pointed out succinctly more than a hundred years ago. I think that if there will be any sense in continuing to engage with the question of Jesus, it is because of this element of utopia in writing about his life, which is both a challenge and a promise to move us into the future.[3]

I will take a recent discussion of biography as my starting point for a reflection on what I see as the challenge of life-writing about Jesus today. Representing the 'New Biography', Jo Burr Margadant states that 'culture politics are most easily examined as well as emphatically imagined in the individual'.[4] I understand culture politics here to be the ideals, visions and practices of a society, which may find a focusing point in the biography of an individual. A biography is about imagination, how we construct a life within a society; it is a question of the terms, categories and visions that help us to see, understand and make a past life relevant for our own time and society. Therefore, to write about Jesus is to engage in an examination of culture and politics through the lenses of the life of one person who embodies the issues of that period. To place a person in a context always involves imagining and presenting this context with the help of modern categories and terms; thus, a biography presents analogies and inspiration by which we as readers can understand and construct our own lives.[5]

It is these categories that help us to see, to describe and to analyse; what falls outside these categories we do not see. The task of examining the culture politics of Jesus and his society necessitates a self-reflection by the author upon the theories and methods we use to examine ancient societies. Throughout this book, I have pointed out how Schleiermacher, Strauss, Renan and Smith employed the modern understandings of categories like 'people', 'nation', and increasingly 'empire' and 'race', to interpret Jesus in his setting in Palestine. Since Jesus was viewed as an ideal for European society, as a 'great man' who represented divine inspiration for the progress of history, these categories presented the society of Jesus in terms that were recognizable and relevant for the authors' own societies.

Margadant's view of an individual as embodying the cultural politics of a society has similarities to Schleiermacher's idea of the goal of biography as placing an individual within his or her social context. However, compared to the way Schleiermacher and other nineteenth-century scholars spoke of writing a biography of Jesus, there are significant problems with speaking of a 'biography'. Common criteria for a biography are that it shall span the whole of a person's life and be based on factual evidence. Both these criteria are difficult to fulfil when writing about Jesus. For most of his life, between his birth and the start of his public career, there are no reliable sources. Even for his public life, the Gospels, although maybe modelled after ancient biographies, are quite fragmentary. These limitations put certain restrictions on what it is possible to do; a full-scale biography of Jesus would present biographical fiction more than historical biography.

Instead I suggest that it is possible to do *life-writing* about Jesus. The phrase 'life-writing' is associated with the English literature professor and biographer Hermione Lee, who uses it of writing about a life based on 'relics, legends and fragments, with the parts and bits and gaps which are left over after the life has ended'.[6] To create a life-writing about a person may therefore include reconstructions of certain activities of their life, or of certain thematic aspects of it. It is this type of life-writing that I think it is possible to do about Jesus. On historical criteria, the Gospels provide enough material to give a characteristic profile of who he was perceived to be, and of his main activities in Galilee: the main themes of his message, his associations with people, and his attitudes to local authorities. In the following I will attempt to give an outline of what such a life-writing might include.

Life-writing shares with biography the need to see the individual in his or her social context. Within writings about biography, there has been a discussion of which is the most significant, the individual or the collectivity, and of the relationship between the two.[7] The nineteenth-century idea of the 'great man' emphasized the role of the leader, whereas present-day views focus more on collective social forces. I think David Nasaw strikes a good balance when he says that the historian as biographer 'proceeds from the premise that individuals are situated but not imprisoned in social structures and discursive regimes'; another premise is that human beings have the 'capacity of going beyond created structures in order to create others'.[8]

In terms of writing about the historical Jesus, this means to focus on Jesus as an active agent in his life and in his society. I have applied this perspective in a previous study of the historical Jesus and how he was placed in Galilee.[9] The relationship between place and people has frequently been understood as a one-way direction, with place (nature, social places) influencing the identity of persons – putting people into place, so to speak. Instead, I took my starting point from a statement by Jonathan Z. Smith: 'Human beings are not placed, they bring place into being'.[10] I suggest that to place Jesus in Galilee is also to ask how he, with his actions and words, represented a way to shape and re-imagine Galilee as a society. Instead of reading Jesus 'backwards', against the determination by his context, I suggest reading him 'forwards', in terms of *what he aimed to do*.[11] Thus, in the words of Margadant, I will use a life-writing about Jesus to 'emphatically imagine' in Jesus the possibilities of a culture politics for the future.

Applied to the issue under discussion in this book, this suggestion presupposes that writing about Jesus can be a resource for thinking about the political future and not just for personal inspiration. The modern compartmentalization of society into different spheres has placed Jesus, together with Christianity, in a religious and private sphere, separate from the political and public sphere. This form of compartmentalization means that each sphere becomes more limited and has fewer resources for cross-fertilization. This separation has made politics less visionary and religion less relevant to social life, to the detriment of both. Therefore writing about the life of Jesus must renew an explicit awareness of the political context of such writing. But I question whether the terms for describing society that originated with nationalism in the nineteenth century are appropriate or sufficient today.

What Would Jesus Deconstruct?

It is at this point I ask with Foucault if it is possible to 'think otherwise' than we have traditionally been thinking.[12] Can writings about Jesus present an alternative form of thinking that can provide ways of imagining societies differently from the present world structures based on nation states? This suggestion requires that it is possible to break the picture of Jesus away from its identification with nation, the nation state and national values that have been part of biblical interpretation since the nineteenth century. Here I borrow a phrase from John D. Caputo's book, *What Would Jesus Deconstruct?*[13] This title plays on a book very popular with evangelical Christians in America at the end of the nineteenth century, *What Would Jesus Do?*[14] This book described what would happen if Jesus returned to a small town in America, and imagined how he would represent a challenge of radical social justice. From this book came the idea for the title of Caputo's book, an introduction to post-modernism in a church context. The central piece of Caputo's book is a reading of Jesus' radical message of the Kingdom of God that literally deconstructs the complacency of modern Christians.[15] They have made family values, the protection of property and individual freedom central aspects of their reading of the Gospels, and that is what Caputo's presentation of the 'true' Jesus brilliantly deconstructs.

These supposedly Christian values are part of what many, not only in America but also in Europe, perceive to be 'naturally' part of 'national values'. And I take Caputo's question, directed at commonly held Christian views, also to be directed at present-day historical Jesus studies, which have been shaped by the 'naturalness' of nations and nationhood. Thus, I suggest that it is necessary to deconstruct these associations between Jesus and the concerns of the nation and national identities that seem to underlie many presentations of the historical Jesus today. So I propose to raise the same questions as Schleiermacher and the other Jesus scholars of the nineteenth century: What is a people? What are communal values? How should an organization of society that serves the good of the people be imagined? However, I suggest raising these questions *not* in the national key of the nineteenth century, but as relevant for a global context. Thus, I raise the question of how writing about Jesus may be relevant for a vision of a new world order.

An obvious question may be, why it is necessary to think 'beyond nationalism'? The biographers of Jesus in the nineteenth century described him in light of the political, social and economic crises in their own societies. Together with many others, they saw nationalism as the solution to the political problems of Europe,[16] and this became a dominant pattern of interpretation for nineteenth century writers.

In the twenty-first century, our crises and challenges are global; they affect not only Europe but the world in its totality. However, even when these global challenges are recognized, there is a strong resistance to address the problems caused by the present political system based on nation states. The Toronto *Globe and Mail*, for example, recently published an essay under the heading, 'Another New World Order'.[17] The essay identified four core structural trends driving the changes that are reshaping economics, societies and politics: namely, globalization, demographics, the information revolution and climate change. Together with events like 9/11 and the Iraq war these forces are without a doubt changing the present world order. Nevertheless, despite the focus on 'another new world order', the essay did not question the old order of the world divided into nations and states, or ask whether these structures are able to respond to such global challenges.

Moreover, written by a politician and bureaucrat, the essay spoke of the world's problems in the abstract terms of 'globalization, demographics, the information revolution and climate change.' But behind these abstract terms are human beings: the families who lost their homes and livelihoods because of the global financial crisis; the young African men who, driven by extreme poverty, try to get into the 'fortress of Europe'; the islanders in the Pacific who will see their low-lying islands drown if climate change continues. It is obvious that in the present world order the nation states and their military and political organizations have not been able or willing to solve these problems. It is also obvious that ideas for possible new ways to order the world will not come from such 'responsible' politicians.

To imagine an inclusive 'world people' instead of the common division into nations and nation states seems impossible. In his incisive book, *Contemporary Debates on Nationalism*,[18] Umut Özkirimli argues that 'the complacency with the existing order' is the most serious problem within literature on nationalism as a political system. Özkirimli points out how alternative ways of political thinking, especially that of a single world community, have been argued for by political thinkers from the Stoics via Rousseau and Kant to the internationalist Socialists of the early twentieth century. However, since the nationalist discourse has been so successful at imposing itself, it has suppressed alternative forms of political thinking and continues to present itself as the 'natural' way of doing politics and of understanding the world. [19]

I do not argue for an imagination of a new world order out of a theoretical interest in political systems, but because of the need to secure for all people in the world a decent life, fulfilling their basic material needs and their social and political rights. I do not think that life-writings about Jesus will solve these questions, but I do think that they can help our imaginations of what might be possible.

What is a (World) People?

My first question is: How can we break away from thinking only in terms of 'a nation people' and instead imagine a 'world people'? The strong link between 'people' and 'nation' today perpetuates inequalities among people. The system of nations and nation states is not only inadequate in its response to the present crises; the system of nation states and the ideology of national identities are themselves causing many of the problems and conflicts of today's world. This becomes especially visible in many European countries with recent and growing groups of minorities as refugees, asylum seekers and 'guest workers'. Many countries experience culturally complex situations that represent fluidity over a previous situation of real or imagined social and cultural stability. In many parts of Europe, the result has been a resistance to an increasing cultural complexity that, somewhat falsely, is attributed to the increased presence of minorities.[20] Many, especially those who have belonged to a dominant majority, experience this development as a crisis; they feel that the practices, symbols and values associated with their national identities are challenged, and that established borders and the traditional order of society are threatened.[21]

This reaction has been expressed to a large extent in a new wave of nationalism, which has taken the form of a 'neo-ethnification of national identity'.[22] The concept of *ethnification* focuses on specific ideas about language, culture, religion, descent and territory as central to processes of identification. This linkage between nations and ethnicity strengthens divisions between 'us' and 'them' and often leads to discrimination. It has also led to a proliferation of state break-ups in order to create ethnically 'pure' nation states with the increased danger of discrimination against minorities, or even instances of ethnic cleansing.

This situation may seem far away from anything associated with historical Jesus studies, but one of the sources of this ethno-nationalism in Europe is the idea of Europe as a Christian region. This notion has played an important part in arguments against including Turkey in the EU. Conceptions of Christianity as a 'national religion' have also contributed to the constructions of national identities, as for instance with the recent break-up of the former Yugoslavia into ethnically based independent states.

Jesus and an ethnic people

In this context it matters how the historical Jesus is imagined, and whether his social context is 'naturally', as a matter of fact, imagined in terms that reinforce national categories. One example is the discussion of the identity of Galilee and Jesus. The question is the same as in the nineteenth century – whether the Galileans and Jesus were similar to or different from the Jews of Jerusalem and Judea – only the concepts used for identity have changed. Strauss and Renan used the terminology of 'race' in discussions of the identity of the Galileans and Jesus. However, after the Second World War with the Holocaust and the end of the European colonial era, the term 'race' was discredited and anthropologists created the new term 'ethnicity', a terminology that is linked closely to the identity of nations and ideologies of nationalism.[23] This term has been taken over by biblical scholars as well; as a result, the renewed discussion of the identity of Galilee and of Jesus is now raised as a question of *ethnicity*.[24] However, the customary positions of the nineteenth century are now turned upside down, with the dominant view being that Galilee unquestionably was ethnically Jewish.

As in the nineteenth century, the identity of Galilee is important because it is taken to determine the identity of Jesus. Therefore defenders of a Jewish Galilee have harsh criticisms for scholars who argue for a more diverse or complex Galilean identity,[25] claiming that such scholarship 'by de-Judaizing Galilee distorts Jesus, the Jesus movement, and their Galilean context'.[26] What makes this criticism so remarkable is that the scholars who are criticized do not argue that Galileans – or Jesus – were not Jewish, but only that to be Jewish might include a large degree of diversity and differences. From the strong criticism, one gets the sense that what is defended is an ethnic identity that does not allow for complexities or mixtures.[27] Even if diversities in some areas such as the economy and social structures are recognized, when it comes to religion as *the* significant factor in ethnicity, there does not seem to be any room for diversity.[28] It appears that the historical reconstruction of the ethnic identity of Galilee and Jesus has an almost existentialist relevance; the picture of Jesus becomes a symbol for modern identities.[29]

In *The Symbolic Jesus*, William E. Arnal has analysed the relationship between these discussions of the Jewishness of Jesus and constructions of contemporary identity.[30] He finds structural similarities between the constructions of Jesus and attitudes to the cultural complexities of today's world.[31] The responses to such complexities seem to influence the ways in which the historical Jesus is constructed. One reaction, according to Arnal, is 'to embrace *the fluidity of identity* that marks the present'. That appears to be the attitude that can be surmised from the image of Jesus in a Galilee of mixed identities. The other reaction, Arnal finds, is 'to construct the historical Jesus as an archetype for a fairly rigidly defined identity, consequently identifying identity itself with clear boundaries, limited cultural options, and, in short, coherence and homogeneity'.[32] The descriptions of Jesus and Galilee in such terms are similar to many reactions to the changes that have affected the nation states. Arnal finds that behind the debate of a Jewish Jesus it is possible to see 'an identity-related dispute, in which "Jewish" is being offered as a cipher for the reification of cultural identity, religious, national, or otherwise'.[33]

It is probably necessary once more to emphasize that the recent discussion has not questioned that Jesus was Jewish: that makes this discussion different from the attempts in the nineteenth century and in twentieth-century Germany to distance Jesus from Judaism. As I think Arnal has succeeded in pointing out, the issue is relevant for all instances of strictly defined ethnic and religious identities, and how these identities are associated with boundaries and thereby with creating insiders and outsiders. Therefore, the discussion of the ethnic identity of Jesus is a test case of how to define a people.

People at the borders

Within a short period of time, ethno-nationalism has become 'naturalized' as the way to think of people, and as the obvious way to imagine people as a nation within established borders. Most scholars who work on the historical Jesus come, like me, from secure positions within established nation states, and we are, of course, also embedded in this way of envisioning the world. We belong to that privileged group of people who can travel all over the world, wave our passports at border controls, and pass by less fortunate travellers, with less established identities, who get endlessly checked, controlled and sometimes returned. The recent increase in immigrants, refugees and foreign workers in European and also North American countries has resulted in discussions of increased border control, the need for boundaries and preserving the 'purity' of the nation in terms of culture, religion, language and customs. Can we imagine a history of Jesus written from the experience and perspective of immigrants and refugees, with a hope for a world that is not ruled by boundaries of ethnicity, nationality and religion?

It was such a situation of marginality that inspired Virgilio Elizondo's *Galilean Journey*.[34] Elizondo's reading of the Gospels represents an interaction between the identity and experiences of Mexican Americans and the foundational events of Jesus in Galilee as they are recorded in the Synoptic Gospels. Read from the marginal place of Mexican Americans in the USA, the Spanish terms *mestizaje* and *frontera* add new dimensions to the categories of 'mixing' and 'borders'. *Mestizaje*, or race-mixture, became a regular feature of the European–Amerindian encounter after the fifteenth century. But both the process and the persons of mixed race, those who are *mestizo*, were looked down upon, and were rejected as impure by the parent groups. In the USA, Mexican *mestizos* were treated as inferior, and mixed marriages were prohibited in many states. Thus, this form of mixing was not without danger; it encountered violence and discrimination. When Elizondo started his work in the 1960s, the Mexican American people were not only poor, discriminated against and marginalized, but also without a voice, without an identity.

In his reading of Jesus in Galilee in light of these experiences, Elizondo found a voice for his people. He had noticed the many references to Galilee and Jesus as a Galilean in the Gospels, and asked about the *meaning* of Galilee. Since there were few answers in the Bible, he found the meaning in the historical situation of Galilee and Jesus' historical experiences.[35] Galilee was a crossing point for travel and commercial routes, which also made it open for multiple invasions and migration. In consequence, a 'natural, ongoing biological and cultural *mestizaje* was taking place',[36] but this was a *mestizaje* that resulted in rejection and disparagement from both Jews and the Greco-Roman population.

In this situation the role of Jesus was significant for the Galileans. Elizondo sees Jesus the Galilean as 'a borderland reject', that is, he identified with the rejected and showed his love for them. The key term of Jesus' message was the Kingdom of God, to which he invited all who were rejected. Jesus had a unique relationship to God, and through this relationship he revealed a new anthropology that gave people 'dignity, confidence, security, docility, and self-respect based on freely chosen dependence on the absolute God'.[37]

The story of Jesus in Galilee brought Mexican Americans into being as a people. This act of creation had exemplary importance, in that Jesus' vision of a people

> could serve as a prototype of the *fronteras* of the world – whether they be nations or neighbourhoods – where diverse peoples encounter one another not to fight, humiliate, or exclude one another, but to form new friendships and families in space where the 'impure' and excluded can find new possibilities and inaugurate new beginnings.[38]

Elizondo has been criticized that his picture of Galilee reflects the traditional pattern of a contrast between Galilee and Judea/Jerusalem,[39] and we recognize elements from the descriptions by Renan, Strauss and Smith. However, at the time when Elizondo wrote his book, this was the dominant scholarly picture.[40] Although to a large extent Elizondo takes over the picture of a mixed Galilee, his own experience of a situation of mixture and hybridity as one of marginality and discrimination makes him see the picture in a different way. It becomes a very different history and a very different model for a contemporary social imaginary.

Elizondo's vision of a new humanity is *not* centred in nations, but at the borders, the *fronteras*. Elizondo sees a parallel between Jesus' constant border crossings in Galilee, and the *mestizo* experience of daily border crossings. Therefore, Elizondo's vision of *mestizo* peoples is not that of a separate nation, and not to speak of a nation state, but of people who inhabit the 'in-between' of nations and cultures, playing a painful but creative mediating role in the processes of intercultural encounter that foster a gradual movement 'from closed particularities to a more open universality'.[41] Elizondo's interpretation of Jesus and Galilee represents a questioning of the nation as the main category for group identity from the position of *mestizaje*.

A new people within boundaries

The difference between the construction of Galilee as ethnically Jewish and Elizondo's Galilee of the *mestizos* at the boundaries cannot be explained as matter of who is right and who is wrong. It is a matter of what one is looking for and what categories one uses to define the identity of a people. In terms of a life-writing of the historical Jesus, it is also a matter of how much importance one ascribes to the context, and how much to Jesus as an independent agent. Renan saw Jesus as determined by the landscape and nature of Galilee. Much of the most recent discussion of Galilean identity is described in ethnic categories, based on historical and archaeological evidence; it follows, therefore, that Jesus' identity also seems to be determined externally by such things.

However, granted that Jesus was Jewish, and lived within a society where being Jewish was a matter of normalcy and of obeying the given authorities, the question of ethnic identity, with its overtones of the national identity of Jesus, might not be the most relevant question. It may be more relevant to use not ethnic, but social categories to describe how Jesus acted within his context. Within the last generation methods and perspectives from the social sciences have become an important resource in biblical studies, to imagine the social systems and structures of ancient societies. In historical Jesus studies this has resulted in the recognition of the dominant social and normative systems of Palestinian society, the importance of household and kinship, and the domination and power of the elite over the peasant population.[42] To know these structures and their basis in customs and the religious authorities provides a social setting for imagining the aims of Jesus' activities and his preaching.

Viewed from this perspective, the role of Jesus as an actor in society, in his engagement with the world, was not concerned with the usual definition of boundaries of ethnicity, nationality and religion. In terms of a life-writing of Jesus I would question what this type of external classification contributes to our understanding of him. It makes more sense to say that Jesus saw society from the perspective of social categories of outsiders versus elite and margins versus centre. This does not mean that it is sufficient to describe Jesus as a 'social activist'; his was a message of how God would act, and it is reasonable to imagine that he saw himself as carrying out God's work. When Jesus placed himself together with the outsiders, with those at the margins, he seemed to suggest, at least in view of his followers, that this was where God was. He was clearly aware of and concerned about relations between people, between rich and poor, and elites and outcasts, always taking the position of those who suffered exclusion.[43]

If we ask about Jesus' specific contribution, his heritage, it is not best described in creating a new ethnicity; he did not, in the manner of Paul speak of breaking down boundaries between Jews and Greeks. Rather he broke down divisions based on social or moral positions, giving priority to the outsiders and the marginalized; he invited all to an inclusive fellowship around meals. Sociology might describe this as an alternative community, a beginning of a new sociability that would link people together in a new way, across boundaries and other distinctions, and being stronger than other social structures.

A people across boundaries

I find that using categories like given social structures and alternative communities to describe Jesus' activity in his society also inspires a look at the world today for beginnings of new ways of imagining linkages between people. In modern categories, I would say that the way Jesus related to people can be interpreted through the approach known as 'intersectionality'. This is a term that has its background in feminist approaches to discrimination and inequality, and looks at the fluid relationship between socio-cultural categories and identities and how they work together.[44] Intersectionality helps to identify important categories for identities on a much broader scale than nation, people and ethnicity; it considers, for example, race, religion, gender, social class, age, disability (health/illness), bodies, place and the position of the majority or minority. The United Nations uses intersectionality in its work on discrimination on the basis of gender and race.[45] Intersectionality makes it possible to be both specific and universal; it does not speak of women 'in general', but helps to identify situations that affect many women worldwide in similar ways – for instance, the situation of women in war zones and refugee camps, exposed to oppression, poverty, lack of food, rape, illness, death and loss of children. These are familiar situations in many parts of the world and their plights do not stop at national borders. These women represent just one of a number of groups of people whose sufferings place them in similar situations; they make up a worldwide community.

Intersectionality provides a way to see the interconnectedness of discrimination in many areas, and all over the world. These are issues that go across and beyond individual nations and they require global solutions. It is a way to look at human lives without being limited by national boundaries, and to identify a people by starting from those most in need. Instead of the present policy whereby many nation states exclude the weakest 'others', a global society would start precisely among them. Thus, intersectionality emphasizes the universality of some human rights as a basis for a global society.

However, it is not only suffering, wars and poverty that represent universal linkages among people. There are also other hopeful signs, as Özkirimli points out, in the new networks and interactions among people that cross over national boundaries:

> The world in which we live is formed of forms of consociation, identification, interaction and aspiration which regularly cross national boundaries. Refugees, global labourers etc. ... constitute large blocks of meaningful association that do not depend on the isopomorphism of citizenship with cultural identity, of work with kinship, of territory with soil, or of residence with national identification.[46]

It is this loosening of ties with the structures and ideologies of nation states that many people experience which Özkirimli finds distinctive about the present era of globalization. He speaks of it as *delinkages* from the structures and mentalities of nationalism. In the 'refugees, global labourers etc.' we can see the contours of a people based on 'meaningful association', which may point to a new way of thinking about a people in a global era.

Our new ways of communicating – via mobile phones, the Internet, Facebook, Twitter, etc. – create contacts and virtual communities that span the globe and that may create strong, partial identities. There are also other, maybe more traditional ways of building communal identities. The international community of scholars and students is one example of how the local is connected globally. Universities are increasingly becoming places where a diversity of people work together and students who travel between universities in different parts of the world become part of international networks. The important question is whether these new forms of associations that bind individuals and groups together in people-like ways can be sources for new forms of organization that will be politically effective on a global level.

The criticism of such a position is, of course, that it represents a naive utopianism. But this is an argument that only serves to stop the imagining of alternative possibilities. The problem today, however, is the lack of a vision of what an alternative order might look like. Is it naive to try to renew words like 'imagining', 'vision' and 'utopia' and bring them into the present discussion? Maybe it is naive, but it is necessary; as Özkirimli reminds us:

> We should never forget that imagination has been central to agency for most of human history. It was the imagination, in its collective forms, that created the idea of nationhood; the seeds of a post-national order will also be sown by the imagination.[47]

Family Values in a Global World

In *What Would Jesus deconstruct?* Caputo argues that many Christians have made family values, the protection of property and individual freedom central aspects of their reading of the Gospels. This is a situation that not only applies to the USA, the society that Caputo primarily addresses, but is also true in many other places. What may be different in the USA, however, is the degree to which these values have been identified as Christian and national, so that they make up a civil religion. At the centre of these values are family and patriarchy. This normative system of household and patriarchy is deeply ingrained in traditional Christian culture. Household, family and masculine strength were important metaphors for nineteenth-century ideas about nation and national identity. This continues to be the case; these everyday practices and norms are still linked to the social imaginaries of nation and a structured society.[48] Therefore, when many biblical scholars emphasize that Jesus supported the patriarchal family and the established rules of masculinity, they are actually presenting Jesus within a traditional pattern of patriarchy and national identity.[49]

Elisabeth Schüssler Fiorenza has strongly criticized reading the biblical material about Jesus within such a preconceived pattern of patriarchy. She sees a correspondence between the defence of patriarchy and the image of Jesus as 'the great heroic man and charismatic leader or as the Divine Man and G*d striding over the earth'. The presentation of Jesus as 'a great man' has been based on a model that marginalizes women or non-elite men as historical agents. Instead, Schüssler Fiorenza introduces a critical feminist reconstructive model based on the assumption of women's presence and agency within a movement patterned after 'grass-roots social movements for change', such as, for instance, 'the workers' movement, the civil rights movement, the feminist movement, or the ecological movement'. Common to such movements is that they 'envision a different world' in order to mobilize resistance and revolt against unjust situations and oppressive structures.[50]

In her criticism of 'the great man' as a model for Jesus, associated with the structures and norms of patriarchy and family, the criticism of Schüssler Fiorenza and many other feminist scholars strikes at a central aspect of 'national values', while an alternative model for Jesus and his group, namely that of 'grass-roots social movements,' points towards a formation that goes beyond national boundaries.

It is surprising how the question of Jesus' position on family, primarily as a question of his views on marriage and divorce, has played such a large role in discussions about the historical Jesus. Since these issues are hardly at the centre of the Gospel reports about Jesus, it is plausible that present-day interests in defending the social institution of (heterosexual) marriage and family are partly responsible for these positions.

This is not to say that Jesus was not interested in the household, but his interests seem to have been different from that of the present day's defenders of family values.[51] The household was the basis for Palestinian society, as it is in any peasant society. So this was the given position of Jesus, that it was something he was born into and that he must have taken for granted. Therefore something dramatic must have happened in his, and in his disciples', relationship to their household of origin, since so many sayings ascribed to Jesus refer to conflicts with or to leaving household and family. Several of these sayings suggest exclusion from family and the despair that accompanies such experiences. It is no wonder, therefore, that Jesus' images of a new social form of community for his followers were couched in the language of household and family relationships.

If this was the situation behind many of Jesus' statements on household and family, it is understandable that it was not marriage and divorce that was the prominent topic, but the social role of families, as groups of support, nourishment and sharing. Again, this is a matter of what categories scholars use when writing about Jesus. I will suggest that economic categories are most useful to investigate Jesus' attitudes to these aspects of household and families as 'economic' communities'. However, this requires an explanation of my usage of the ancient term 'economy', which has quite different meanings from the way it is presently used.

The ancient Greek term *oikonomia* was more comprehensive than the modern term economy; it meant 'householding' in a broad sense, both at the small level of the household and at the level of city-state politics.[52] It is in this sense that I have used the term in a previous study, *The Economy of the Kingdom*. I coined the term 'the economy of the kingdom' to explore the way Jesus uses the economic terminology of exchange to present an alternative to the dominant system of a Hellenized economy.[53] This way of speaking of 'economy' was not restricted to exchange of money, it included all forms of exchange in terms of resources, whether they were material, social or political. This exchange was a system based on balanced reciprocity, that is, an exchange where giving and receiving should balance. At its worst, the system was one wherein the weak and poor were exploited by the powerful without getting anything in return; that is called negative reciprocity. In Jesus' rhetoric of woes and blessings, parables and narratives, the rich and powerful are not the ones to create a just world; rather, they combine extortion of the poor with rejection of God (does this sound familiar?).

Households and families were based on 'generalized reciprocity', that is, of a giving of food, clothing, shelter and assistance without expectation of a quick return or balance. This was an 'economy' like householding that supported children, that gave household members security, and which, of course, was based on the authority of the father and distinctive gender roles.

I suggest that this form of household economics also represents family values. They cannot so easily as those ideas of family, heterosexuality and marriage be used or misused to make distinctions *vis-à-vis* 'others'; moreover, they cannot be lifted into a cultural realm that is oblivious to economic differences and difficulties. To start our thinking about family values in terms of support and care for children around the world who live in poor households or without a household might turn that misused term into a vision for the future of the world.

A Moral World Geography

Nationalism is rooted in ideas about the importance of culture and politics, the politics of the French Revolution, and writings by German philosophers on culture and language forming a common identity. The nineteenth and the first part of the twentieth century was a time when politics, expressed in colonialism and imperialism, seemed to rule the world. Today the major power player is the economy, through that empire that is called 'the Market'.

The global economy, in many ways, is a global marketplace beyond the control and regulation of individual states. Thus industry and employment may be moved away from their traditional locations to places with cheap labour; a banking crisis in the USA or Greece may have repercussions all over the world; poor countries lose out as prices for export of their natural resources drop. National governments as well as international organizations are more or less helpless – even the USA can no longer have a dominating influence on the world economy.

On the other hand, the economy and nation states are also often working together against the interest of the people of these states. In many ways and in many countries, the economy (that is, the market and capitalism) and the nation state combine to rob ordinary people of resources and livelihood (for instance, homes, pensions, health care) while official and unofficial corruption is rampant.[54]

This double crisis represented by the globalized market seems to me to be the most serious problem in the world today. Where can we find imaginations for a possible solution? This seems to be a truly utopian quest. Still, I will attempt to try it out on the quest for the historical Jesus, but not on that alone, I will also bring into the discussion the German philosopher Jürgen Habermas. I will compare a reading of Jesus' vision of the Kingdom of God as household solidarity with Habermas' writings on a global house holding.

Kingdom as a solidary place

Jesus had a political word for utopia; he called it the Kingdom of God. Strangely, it is not included in that marvellous book, *Dictionary of Imaginary Places*,[55] which lists a large number of 'worlds created to satisfy an urgent desire for perfection'.

Some of the sources, such as Thomas More's *Utopia* or Jonathan Swift's *Gulliver's Travels*, create ideal places that also serve as criticism of the current order of the world. I think that the Kingdom of God similarly represents such an ideal place that at the same time serves as a criticism of the present world.[56]

This is not an uncontested view. The meaning of the term 'the Kingdom of God' has always been contested. Schleiermacher probably was the first to emphasize its central place in Jesus' message; since Schweitzer it has regularly been understood in terms of time, most often referring to a (distant) future. Consequently, much of the discussion among scholars has been about 'when' the Kingdom would come. In a previous work, *Putting Jesus in His Place*, I have proposed to investigate Jesus' sayings about the Kingdom of God in terms of *place*,[57] that is, raising the question 'What is it that is expected to arrive?' If the Kingdom of God represents something different from the present world, as is generally accepted, how does Jesus present it? I am suggesting that this difference is imagined in terms of how the world is structured, what power it is that rules the world, and what characterizes this form of rule.

In *The Economy of the Kingdom* I have suggested, as I outlined above, that Jesus saw life in households and families in terms of *economy*, in the meaning of householding; and that this term was also used for politics, for the 'householding' of the city state or the domain of a ruler. Therefore, I argued, to analyse Jesus' statements of the Kingdom of God might show what Jesus saw as characteristic of God's rule in contrast to that of life under the present rulers.

The very term that Jesus chose, Kingdom of God, makes it plausible that he saw it in contrast to his present-day rulers. With this term Jesus employed political language. In ancient Mediterranean societies, government was conducted by individual rulers, and *basileia* (kingdom, empire) named the area and authority of a king or emperor. Therefore, the term 'Kingdom of God' could not avoid invoking associations with the present situation and throwing light on the human condition and the relationship between rulers and ruled.

'Kingdom of God' appears to be a term that was coined by Jesus; it turns up in Jesus' parables, narratives and paradoxical sayings that in various ways illustrate the meaning of the term but never give a definition for it. It sounded familiar, being close to well-known language from Israel's history about God as king, but in these ancient sayings God as king was not combined with the word 'kingdom'. And when Jesus speaks of the Kingdom of God, he does not at the same time speak of God as king. So this new combination of 'God' and 'kingdom' is effectively a mystery. What can it mean?

Jesus does not use the term 'Kingdom' in such a way that it supports the ambitions of rulers or even the dreams of people for a kingdom that would fulfil their usual hopes. Instead he speaks of kingdom in a way that turns such expectations upside down.[58] Thus, I find it more plausible to think that Jesus with the phrase 'Kingdom of God' in a new, paradoxical way combined God with the well-known contemporary political term *kingdom* normally used to refer to the Roman Empire and small Hellenistic princedoms. The combined term 'Kingdom of God' was Jesus' critical alternative to current kingdoms and empires and it deconstructed their power symbolically. This interpretation sees Jesus' message of the Kingdom of God as directed to people with experiences of poverty, exclusion and other pressures from the Roman Empire and the princedom of Herod Antipas in Galilee.

The Kingdom of God is not a 'realistic' political programme, but it posed a critical alternative to the basic structures of Jesus' society. As I discussed in the previous section of this chapter, Jesus' alternative was modelled on ideal behaviour in a household but extended beyond its boundaries. The central image of God in the parables of the Kingdom is God not as king, but as a father who gives his children what they need. It has been argued that this image upholds the patriarchal structure of the household, and in a first-century traditional society there is probably no way that this could be avoided. However, it is significant that compared to, for instance, the advice to parents and children in the post-Pauline letters of the New Testament,[59] there is no mention by Jesus of obedience or subservience on the part of the children. It is parental giving and care that is emphasized as God's role. Trust in that care and providence is encouraged in those who are addressed, who are those in need.

Thus, Jesus promises a Kingdom where the ideals of security and support associated with the home were extended to those who had left or fallen out of their household and village network, followers of Jesus who were marginalized. The 'economy', understood in the classical tradition as householding, now could stand for the total range of human relations. The critical alternative to the rule of the unjust system included, for instance, non-resistance, non-violence, forgiveness, mercy and compassion. These were attitudes and interactions that characterized God and that also represented the goal of human relations. This was the vision Jesus expressed in the language of the Kingdom.

Christians have often used the words of Jesus on the economy as binding for or as challenges to their own private behaviour, but I think that is an application that limits their possibility to pose challenges on a structural level. It is true that Jesus did not speak in terms of systems and structures, but that does not mean that his words were limited only to individual persons. We have to see Jesus' sayings about the Kingdom of God and what it required within the political structures of his time.[60] Within a society that functioned along personal relations and power, Jesus addressed individuals as 'types' (the rich, the tax collector, etc.) or in typical situations; therefore, his sayings were directed at the ways society generally worked.

The Kingdom of God deconstructed the rule of the kingdoms of Jesus' day; it presented a picture of human society and forms of social interaction that were totally opposite to the rule of the day, which was characterized by exploitation and oppression. What I have argued here, as a way to look at the Kingdom sayings of Jesus in a historical context, John D. Caputo has said in terms of a contemporary understanding of these sayings. He speaks of the 'logic of the world' and the 'poetics of kingdom' as antagonists. The kingdom contradicts the 'world of calculus and balanced payments', a term that corresponds to the way I have presented the 'economics' as the order of the day in ruling the ancient understanding. Likewise, Caputo also rejects the way the Kingdom of God is often put into the future, as at a distance and therefore not a challenge to the present world. Caputo says that this contrast between the 'logic of the world' and the 'poetics of the kingdom' cannot be solved by placing them in two different 'wheres'; they are 'two different "hows", whose differences must be negotiated in the one and only world we know'.[61]

In the context of the present world crisis I find that the ancient understanding of economy as 'house holding' in connection with Jesus' message of the Kingdom takes on a new and sharpened meaning. I suggest that Jesus' 'economy of the Kingdom' represents a challenge to bring together what today is split apart – economy and politics – under the moral domain of social solidarity.

Habermas: A global 'householding'

It is this problem, of how economy and politics can be brought together under the moral domain of social solidarity, that Jürgen Habermas addresses in his essay, 'The postnational constellation and the future of democracy'.[62] Like Schleiermacher, Habermas has been engaged with the question 'What is a people?', seeing the development of a citizens' democracy as the lasting result of the nation state.[63] His present concern is how this democracy can be preserved and developed in a postnational situation. Globalization with globalized markets has threatened the autonomy of nation states and limited their possibility to shape policies of social solidarity; it is a situation that makes a postnational organization necessary. Habermas first discusses the possibility that the European Union could develop a self-understanding of egalitarian universalism, before he considers the global scene under the framework of a restructured United Nations. The goal for such a global community would be a politics that can 'catch up with global markets', to enact a 'political closure of an economically unmastered world society' and instead 'make a change of course toward a world domestic policy'.[64]

The terminology of 'a world domestic policy' is significant, in that it combines two terms that seem to be at different ends of a spectrum; domestic policy is normally something quite different to world politics. The indicated 'domestic policy' represents the social solidarity that is the mark of Habermas' idea of national democracy. When he combines the two terms into 'a world domestic policy', this suggests that such domestic solidarity should be extended to the world as a whole in a global society. Habermas does not envisage a 'world state' organized from the top down with a world government, but he suggests the creation of an international negotiation system. In such a system, nation states would have to broaden their perspectives beyond national interests and see negotiation with other states not as international relations but as part of global governance in the key of domestic policy. This means transforming the way in which we view the world, not now as different from but precisely as our home, as a domestic arrangement.

The greatest challenge as Habermas sees it is to create a sense of world solidarity and the corresponding political practice that presently exists on a national level as solidarity among citizens. Such a development needs the support of people; it requires them to act as world citizens in support of their national governments. Habermas does not support the idea of creating a new political status of 'world citizens' with voting rights for a world parliament. Instead, he thinks in terms of the extended participation of non-governmental organizations, decision-making procedures at the grass root level, and the extended use of referendums on important issues. This way of supporting communication and decision-making processes, which is a main concern for Habermas, will give democratic legitimacy to the global negotiation process toward a global domestic policy.

Jesus and Habermas

I find this an interesting proposal from one of the world's leading philosophers who dares to imagine a world structure beyond nationalism and who spells out possible ways to implement such a utopian vision. There is a structural similarity between Jesus' paradoxical sayings of household as kingdom and kingdom as household and Habermas' vision of a 'world domestic policy'. In both instances, the domestic solidarity of home is transferred from the local to a larger scene; in Jesus' parables from household to kingdom and in Habermas' case from the nation to the world. In both instances, the goal is to create a new identity and sense of belonging based on a different and larger collectivity than the original one, whether that is a household or a nation.

This is an aspect where the utopian vision of Jesus' Kingdom sayings has obvious political implications, and where a historical reading actually may be a more effective way of pointing to another possible future than a reading of most contemporary political writings. In fact, Jesus' Kingdom sayings bring political thinking back to its primary task: to view human life and society in light of the ultimate aims of politics, to work towards a good life for all, and to engage in democratic discussions of the responsibility of society.

The problem for Habermas is how the sense of civic solidarity among citizens that has been created by the nation state can be developed and sustained on a world level. In typical Habermas fashion, he sees this possibility in the question of involvement by citizens in organizations and movements, and in processes of communication. However, I think a problem remains. For a sense of world community among world citizens to develop, there is a need for an emotive response, a sense of belonging together that can form the basis for solidarity. Here I suggest that the Kingdom vision of Jesus with its images of close relations between God and human beings represents such an emotional imagination that might create not only insight at the level of political philosophy but also personal identification and commitment.

Since the ideologies of nationalism have cleverly used or exploited the rhetoric and symbols of belonging and unity, attempts to create a world community that goes beyond nationalism must also find an imagination and vision that can build solidarity. I am not suggesting that this possibility is something associated exclusively with Jesus and Christianity; I think all religions have the potential to touch people in a deeper way than philosophical and political discourses. But in this book I have been concerned to show that the search for Jesus as a historical person in the nineteenth century inspired the imagination of another way to build and sustain human societies, as a people and a nation. These efforts had both positive and negative effects; in the long run the negative effects linked to the ideologies and mentalities of the nation state, that peculiar nineteenth-century creation, may weigh the heaviest. This is a criticism of the political results of the Life of Jesus writings in the nineteenth century but not of the attempt to write about the historical Jesus in a hermeneutics of political imagination. The task now is to go beyond notions of nation, people and empire as models for writing about Jesus and to write about him in the context of a global community.

As I do the final proof-reading of these pages (22 July 2011) my hometown, Oslo, is shaken by a bomb that destroyed many Norwegian government buildings and by a massacre at a political youth camp, killing a total of 77, mostly youths. The man who carried out these gruesome acts, an 'ethnic' Norwegian, justified them as a protest against a political system that had allowed Norway to become a multicultural society, in particular by immigration of Muslims. These horrible acts based on reactionary nationalism gone mad strengthen my conviction that we must invisage a Jesus for a future 'beyond nationalism', a future that includes people from a variety of ethnic and class backgrounds, beliefs, social contexts and sexual orientations. A hope that includes people is the only response to hate that kills.

Notes

Introduction

1   Friedrich Schleiermacher, *Das Leben Jesu*, ed. by K. A. Rütenik, Sämmtliche Werke I/6 (Berlin: Georg Reimer, 1864); J. C. Verheyden (ed.), *The Life of Jesus* (Philadelphia: Fortress, 1975; Repr. Mifflintown: Sigler, 1997).

2   David Friedrich Strauss, *Das Leben Jesu kritisch bearbeitet* (Tübingen: Osiander, 1835); *The Life of Jesus, Critically Examined*, transl. from the 4th German edn by George Eliot (London: Swan Sonnenschein, 1st edn 1848; new edn 1898).

3   David Friedrich Strauss, *Das Leben Jesu für das deutsche Volk bearbeitet* (Leipzig: Brochaus, 1864); *A New Life of Jesus*, authorized translation, 2 vols (London: Williams and Norgate, 1865); and *The Life of Jesus: For the People*, 2nd edn (London: Williams and Norgate, 1879).

4   Ernest Renan, *Vie de Jésus* (Paris: Michel Lévy, 1863); *The Life of Jesus* (New York: Modern Library, 1927).

5   George Adam Smith, *Historical Geography of the Holy Land* (London: Hodder and Stoughton, 1st edn 1894; 16th edn 1910).

6   Albert Schweitzer, *Von Reimarus zu Wrede: Eine Geschichte der Leben Jesu Forschung* (Tübingen: Mohr/Siebeck, 1906, 2nd edn *Geschichte der Leben Jesu Forschung*, 1913); idem, *The Quest of the Historical Jesus*, 1st complete edn, transl. of 2nd German edn, ed. by John Bowden (Minneapolis: Fortress, 2001).

7   Ward Blanton, *Displacing Christian Origins: Philosophy, Secularity and the New Testament* (Chicago: Chicago University Press, 2007), pp.129–65; see also Simon J. Gathercole, 'The critical and dogmatic agenda of Albert Schweitzer's *The Quest of the Historical Jesus*', *Tyndale Bulletin* li/2 (2000), pp.261–83. The following sections are inspired by Blanton's analysis.

8   Schweitzer, *Quest of the Historical Jesus*, pp.59–64.

9   Ibid., pp.74–90.

10 Ibid., pp.168–73.

11 Ibid., pp.158–67.

12 His criticism partly amounts to a Protestant abhorrence of Catholic piety, cf. his characterization of Renan's picture of 'the gentle Jesus, the beautiful Mary, the fair Galileans' that 'might have been taken over in a body from the shop-window of an ecclesiastical art emporium in the Place St Sulpice' in Paris (*The Quest of the Historical Jesus*, pp.159–60).

13 I owe this insight to a suggestion by Jonathan C. P. Birch of Glasgow University.

14 Schweitzer, *Quest of the Historical Jesus*, p.3.

15 See Joep Leersen, *National Thought in Europe: A Cultural History* (Amsterdam: Amsterdam University Press, 2006).

16   Schweitzer, *Quest of the Historical Jesus*, p.479. This is another instance of the expression of a feeling of national superiority, at odds with Schweitzer's criticism of national inwardness.

17   Schweitzer, *Quest of the Historical Jesus*, pp.478–9.

18   Ibid., p.483.

19   Ibid., p.483.

20   Ibid., p.486.

21   See for example Diane B. Stinton, *Jesus of Africa: Voices of Contemporary African Christology* (Maryknoll, NY: Orbis, 2004); R. S. Sugirtharajah (ed.), *Asian Faces of Jesus* (London: SCM, 1993); and Jon Sobrino, *Jesus in Latin America* (Maryknoll, NY: Orbis, 1987).

22   Recently two books have appeared on Jesus in America: Richard W. Fox, *Jesus in America: Personal Savior, Cultural Hero, National Obsession* (San Francisco: Harper, 2004) and Stephen Protero, *The American Jesus: How the Son of God Became a National Icon* (New York: Farrar, Straus and Giroux, 2003).

23   Elisabeth Schüssler Fiorenza, *Jesus and the Politics of Interpretation* (New York: Continuum, 2000).

24   This is the perspective of a broad overview of presentations of the life of Jesus throughout history in Dieter Georgi, 'The interest in Life of Jesus theology as a paradigm for the social history of biblical criticism', *HTR* 85 (1992), pp.51–83.

25   Shawn Kelley, *Racializing Jesus: Race, Ideology and the Formation of Modern Biblical Scholarship* (London and New York: Routledge, 2002).

26   Susannah Heschel, *The Aryan Jesus: Christianity, Nazis and the Bible* (Princeton: Princeton University Press, 2007).

27   Blanton, *Displacing Christian Origins*.

28   John Breuilly, 'Nationalism and the history of ideas', *Proceedings of the British Academy* (Oxford: Oxford University Press, 2000), p.200.

29   Susan Tridgell, *Understanding Our Selves: The Dangerous Art of Biography*, European Connections 12 (Frankfurt: Peter Lang, 2004), pp.103–7.

30   Umut Özkirimli, *Contemporary Debates on Nationalism: A Critical Engagement* (Basingstoke and New York: Palgrave MacMillan, 2005), pp.195–205.

31   Ernest Renan, *Qu'est-ce qu'une nation? What is a Nation?*, Introduction by Charles Taylor, transl. W. R. Taylor (Toronto: Tapir, 1996).

32   John Breuilly, 'Nationalismus als kulturelle Konstruktion', in Jörg Echternkamp and Sven Oliver Müller (eds), *Die Politik der Nation: Deutscher Nationalismus in Krieg und Krisen 1760–1960* (Munich: R. Oldenborg, 2002), pp.247–68; Benedict Anderson, *Imagined Communities: Reflections on the Origin and Spread of Nationalism* (London and New York: Verso, 1983).

33   E. Kedourie, *Nationalism* (London: Hutchinson, 1960), p.1; quoted in Breuilly, 'Nationalism and the history of ideas', p.187.

34   Notice the opinion by Ernest Renan, regarded as one of the initiators of the discussion of nations and nationhood, that 'the sentiment of nationalities is not even a hundred

years old.' ('Nouvelle lettre à M. Strauss', in Ernest Renan, *Oeuvres complètes* I, Henriette Psichari (ed.) (Paris: Calmann-Lévy, 1947), p.453). He attributes the creation of this consciousness among the European peoples to the French Revolution.

35 Breuilly, 'Nationalism and the history of ideas', p.209.

36 Cf. Bruce Lincoln, who states that, 'when previously persuasive discourses no longer persuade ... society enters a situation of fluidity and crisis ... competing groups ... struggle ... to reshape the borders and hierarchic order of society itself.' (*Discourse and the Construction of Society* (New York and Oxford: Oxford University Press, 1989), p.174).

37 Breuilly, 'Nationalismus als kulturelle Konstruktion', pp.252–3.

38 Leersen, *National Thought in Europe*, p.86.

39 Ibid., pp.86–8.

40 Renan, *Qu'est-ce qu'une nation? What is a Nation?*

41 Leersen, *National Thought in Europe*, pp.97–101.

42 Jürgen Habermas, *The Postnational Constellation: Political Essays*, trans. edn with Introduction by Max Pensky (Cambridge: Polity, 2001), pp.1–25.

43 They represented German law, German history and German language.

44 Max Pensky in 'Editor's Introduction' to Habermas: *The Postnational Constellation* xv.

45 Habermas, *The Postnational Constellation*, p.7.

46 Breuilly, 'Nationalism and the history of ideas', pp.213–14.

47 Cf. Simon Schama, *Landscape and Memory* (London: HarperCollins, 1995).

48 Halvor Moxnes, *Putting Jesus in His Place: A Radical Vision of Household and Kingdom* (Louisville: Westminster John Knox, 2003).

49 Halvor Moxnes, 'Constructing the Galilee of Jesus in an age of ethnic identity', in M. Zetterholm and S. Byrskog (eds), *The Making of Christianity: Conflict, Contacts, and Constructions: Essays in Honor of Bengt Holmberg* (Winona Lake: Eisenbrauns, forthcoming).

50 Halvor Moxnes, 'The construction of Galilee as a place for the historical Jesus,' *BTB* 31 (2001), pp.26–37, 64–77.

51 George L. Mosse, *Nationalism and Sexuality: Middle-Class Morality and Sexual Norms in Modern Europe* (Madison: University of Wisconsin Press, 1985).

52 See for example Andrew Parker, Mary Russo, Doris Sommer and Patricia Yeager (eds), *Nationalism and Sexualities* (London: Routledge, 1992).

53 Stefan Dudink, Karen Hagemann and John Tosh (eds), *Masculinities in Politics and War: Gendering Modern History* (Manchester: Manchester University Press, 2004).

Chapter I: Writing a Biography of Jesus in an Age of Nationalism

1 Friedrich Schleiermacher, *The Life of Jesus*, ed. by J. C. Verheyden (Mifflintown: Sigler, 1997), p.3. Schleiermacher gave these lectures first in 1819 and several times until 1832. Student notes from 1832 served as the basis for the publication in 1864.

2   Schleiermacher, *Life of Jesus*, p.3. The German term is *Lebensbeschreibung*, one of the common terms for biography. Since Schleiermacher uses a biography as a model for his presentation, and stresses that he is speaking of the human person, I use the term 'Jesus', which today is common when speaking of the historical Jesus, although Schleiermacher uses 'Christ' throughout.

3   Note that the German terms, '*bedeutende Vorfragen*' and '*die Sache*' have a significance that is not completely rendered by the English translations.

4   Ernest Renan speaks of 'the biographical form which my work has thus taken' (*The Life of Jesus* (New York: Modern Library, 1927), pp.31–2). In England John Robert Seeley described his work as a biography of Jesus and also spoke of the Synoptic Gospels as biographies, see *Ecce Homo: A Survey of the Life and Work of Jesus Christ* (London: Macmillan, 1865), p.xxi.

5   David Friedrich Strauss, *A New Life of Jesus*, I (London: Williams and Norgate, 1865) pp.1–4.

6   Other biographies were on A. J. Kerner, Eduard Mörike, J. L. Uhland, C. F. Schubart, and Voltaire; see R. S. Cromwell, *David Friedrich Strauss and His Place in Modern Thought* (Fair Lawn, NJ: Burdock, 1974), pp.121–30.

7   Strauss, *New Life of Jesus*, I, p.1.

8   Ibid.

9   Elisabeth M. Lillie, 'Heroes of the mind: The intellectual elite in the work of Ernest Renan', in Graham Gargett (ed.), *Heroism and Passion in Literature: Studies in Honour of Moya Longstaffe* (Amsterdam: Rodopi, 2004), pp.133–4.

10 Geir Hellemo, *Adventus Domini: Eschatological Thought in 4th-Century Apses and Catecheses*, supplements to *Vigiliae Christianae* vol. 5, trans. Elinor Ruth Waaler (Leiden: Brill, 1989).

11 Cf. Jonathan C. P. Birch, 'The Road to Reimarus: History, Morality and Political Theology', in K. Whitelam (ed.) *Holy Land as Homeland? Models for constructing the historic landscapes of Jesus* (Sheffield: Sheffield Phoenix Press, forthcoming).

12 John Horne, 'Masculinity in politics and war in the age of the nation-state and world wars, 1850–1950', in Stefan Dudink, Karen Hagemann and John Tosh (eds), *Masculinities in Politics and War: Gendering Modern History* (Manchester: Manchester University Press, 2004), p.23. It seems as though Horne sets up a contrast between the symbolic power in monarchy and religious authority and that in citizenship and nation, in which religion no longer played a role. For the nineteenth-century authors of historical Jesus studies it seems more relevant to speak of a transfer of religious symbols, from Christ to the human Jesus, and of the political effects that this had in relation to citizenship and nations that were not yet secularized.

13 Hayden White, *Metahistory: The Historical Imagination in Nineteenth-Century Europe* (Baltimore: Hopkins University Press, 1973), pp.5–7.

14 Georg G. Iggers, *German Conception of History: The National Tradition of Historical Thought from Herder to the Present* (Middletown, CT: Wesleyan University Press, 1968), pp.65–6.

15 White: *Metahistory*, pp.142–3.

16 Schleiermacher's exposition here seems to be drawn from one of his earliest studies, 'Teaching history' from 1793; KGA I.1., pp.489–97; see Kurt Nowak, 'Theorie der Geschichte. Schleiermachers Abhandlung "Über den Geschichtsunterricht" von 1793', in G. Meckenstock and J. Ringleben (eds), *Schleiermacher und die wissenschaftliche Kultur des Christentums* (Berlin and New York: de Gruyter, 1991), pp.419–39.

17 Schleiermacher, *Life of Jesus*, p.4.

18 Ibid., p.5.

19 Markus Schröder, *Die kritische Identität des neuzeitlichen Christentums,* BHT 96 (Tübingen: Mohr, 1996), pp.1–11; see also Wilhelm Pauck, 'Schleiermacher's conception of history and Church history,' in his *From Luther to Tillich* (San Francisco: Harper, 1984), pp.67–79.

20 Iggers, *German Conception of History*, pp.3–25; White: *Metahistory*, esp. pp.135–9.

21 Schleiermacher, *Life of Jesus*, p.8.

22 Kurt Nowak, *Schleiermacher und die Frühromantik* (Göttingen: Vandenhoeck and Ruprecht, 1986), pp.245–6.

23 For the larger context of this discussion in the works of Schleiermacher, see Jaqueline Mariña, *Transformation of the Self in the Thought of Friedrich Schleiermacher* (Oxford: Oxford University Press, 2008).

24 Schleiermacher, *Life of Jesus*, p.13.

25 Ibid.

26 Jaqueline Mariña, 'Christology and anthropology in Friedrich Schleiermacher', in J. Mariña (ed.), *The Cambridge Companion to Friedrich Schleiermacher* (Cambridge: Cambridge University Press, 2005), pp.151–70.

27 Strauss, *New Life of Jesus*, pp.1–4. Strauss' extended criticism was also published as a separate book, *The Christ of Faith and the Jesus of History: A Critique of Schleiermacher's Life of Jesus* (Philadelphia: Fortress, 1977); trans. of *Christus des Glaubens und der Jesus der Geschichte. Eine Kritik des Schleiermacher'schen Leben Jesu* (Berlin: F. Duncker, 1865).

28 For an extensive discussion of Strauss' relationship to Schleiermacher, see Friedrich Wilhelm Graf, *Kritik und Pseudo-Spekulation: David Friedrich Strauß als Dogmatiker im Kontext der positionellen Theologie seiner Zeit*, Münchner Monographien zur historischen und systematischen Theologie 7 (München: Keiser, 1982), pp.113–24, 149–70, 250–315.

29 This corresponds to the Hegelian-inspired three stages of hermeneutics that Strauss follows in his first *Life of Jesus*; Ward Blanton, *Displacing Christian Origins: Philosophy, Secularity and the New Testament* (Chicago: University of Chicago Press, 2007), pp.54–9.

30 Strauss finds a small detail in Schleiermacher's lectures that reveals how Schleiermacher combines faith and history. Although Schleiermacher called his lectures *The Life of Jesus*, he almost invariably uses the name 'Christ', which is the honorary title used in the church. That Schleiermacher does not use the human and historical name 'Jesus' in a study of the historical Jesus therefore runs counter to the very idea of a biography; see Strauss, *Der Christus des Glaubens*, pp.25–6.

31 Albert Schweitzer, *The Quest of the Historical Jesus*, 1st complete edn, transl. of 2nd German edn (Minneapolis: Fortress, 2001), pp.59–61.

32   J. Appleby, L. Hunt and M. Jacob, *Telling the Truth about History* (New York: Norton, 1994), pp.52–5.

33   Strauss, *Der Christus des Glaubens*, p.4.

34   Halvor Moxnes, 'The historical Jesus: From master narrative to cultural context', *BTB* 28 (1999), pp.135–49.

35   Susan Tridgell, *Understanding Our Selves: The Dangerous Art of Biography* (Frankfurt: Peter Lang, 2004), p.187.

36   See for instance how the image of Abraham Lincoln has shifted with social and political changes in the USA throughout the nineteenth and twentieth centuries; Barry Schwartz, *Abraham Lincoln and the Forge of National Memory* (Chicago: University of Chicago Press, 2000).

37   See an overview of bibliographies of European biographies in the eighteenth and nineteenth centuries in *Brockhaus' Konversationslexikon*, vol. 3 (1894), pp.16–17.

38   See Michael Maurer, *Die Biographie des Bürgers: Lebensformen und Denkweisen in der formativen Phase des deutschen Bürgertums (1680–1815)* (Göttingen: Vandenhoeck and Ruprecht, 1996); Helmut Scheuer, *Biographie. Studien zur Funktion und zum Wandel einer literarischen Gattung vom 18. Jahrhundert bis zur Gegenwart* (Stuttgart: Metzlersche Verlagsbuchhandlung, 1979).

39   Nowak, *Schleiermacher und die Frühromantik*, pp.231–2.

40   Blanton, *Displacing Christian Origins*, pp.2–5.

41   See Maurer, *Die Biographie des Bürgers*.

42   John Breuilly, 'Nationalism and the history of ideas', *Proceedings of the British Academy* (Oxford: Oxford University Press, 2000), p.200.

43   Maurer, *Die Biographie des Bürgers*, p.617.

44   Ibid., pp.97–104. These examples of specific types of biographies are taken from a German context, but they can be used heuristically to investigate typical forms in other contexts such as France and Great Britain.

45   In the biographical sketches by J. G. Herder in the late eighteenth century there are frequent references to the nation, e.g. on Luther as 'teacher to the nation' and similar terms, such as 'love of the Fatherland'. Especially in the second part of the nineteenth century biographies served an important function to support a Prussian nationalism. See Helmut Scheuer, *Biographie*, pp.32–5, 62–77.

46   Schleiermacher, *Life of Jesus*, p.9

47   Ibid., p.8 [my emphasis].

48   Celia Applegate, *A Nation of Provincials: The German Idea of Heimat* (Berkeley: University of California Press, 1990), pp.2–20.

49   Christian Jansen, 'Deutsches Volk und Deutsches Reich. Zur Pathologie der Nationalstaatsidee im 19. Jahrhundert', in W. Bialas (ed.), *Die nationale Identität der Deutschen* (Frankfurt: Peter Lang, 2002), pp.171–5. The time around 1800 was a transitional period in the use of '*Volk*'. Among younger contemporaries of Schleiermacher, F. Schlegel and J. G. Fichte were influenced by Herder in their use of '*Volk*', but J. W. Goethe continued to use it in the sense of lower classes or 'common people'; E. Bahr, 'Goethes

Volkbegriff und der deutsche Nationalismus um 1808,' in Bialas: *Die nationale Identität*, pp.195–212.

50   Roger Paulin, 'Adding stones to the edifice: Patterns of German biography', in P. France and W. St Clair (eds), *Mapping Lives: The Uses of Biography* (Oxford: Oxford University Press, 2002), pp.104–5.

51   Benedict Anderson, *Imagined Communities: Reflections on the Origin and Spread of Nationalism* (London: Verso, 1983).

52   See also the work of Moretti, who investigates the role of geography and space in the novel to create the nation state in the nineteenth century, in F. Moretti, *The Atlas of the European Novel 1800–1900* (London: Verso, 1998). Cf. p.45: 'the novel is truly the symbolic form of the nation-state'.

53   It is the date of publication, e.g. 8 March, that represents the governing principle that unites reports of all sorts of unrelated events (Anderson, *Imagined Communities*, p.33).

54   Ibid., p.24–5

55   Ibid, p.36.

56   Elinor S. Shaffer, 'Shaping Victorian biography', in France and St Clair (eds): *Mapping Lives*, pp.115–21.

57   The translation of Goethe's *Wilhelm Meister* had a major influence on nineteenth-century writings in England. The biography by George Henry Lewes, *Life of Goethe* (London: Routledge, 1855), based on the influence of Goethe's own biographies, had a formative function upon English biographies in the Victorian period. See ibid., pp.118–21.

58   See Goethe's 'A word for young writers' ('*Ein Wort für junge Dichter*'), discussed in Shaffer, 'Shaping Victorian biography,' p.118.

59   Schleiermacher, *Life of Jesus*, p.5.

60   Anderson, *Imagined Communities*, p.30.

61   Cf. Jaroslav Pelikan, *Jesus Through the Centuries: His Place in the History of Culture* (New Haven, Yale University Press, 1985).

62   Schwartz, *Abraham Lincoln*.

63   Ibid., p.304.

64   From Alexis de Tocqueville's *Democracy in America*, 1835, cited in Schwartz, *Abraham Lincoln*, p.305.

65   Thomas Carlyle, *On Heroes, Hero-Worship, and the Heroic in History*, ed. and with intro. by Carl Niemeyer (Lincoln, NE: University of Nebraska Press, 1966); orig. 1841. S. S. Abverintsev observes that Carlyle's essays do not belong to the genre of modern biographies, but represent an epilogue to the long tradition of Classical biographies, including Plutarch's Lives, that were looking for general types and categories that represented the individual as an exemplum ('From Biography to Hagiography', France and St Clair (eds): Mapping Lives, pp.35–6).

66   Carlyle, *On Heroes*, p.1.

67   Ibid., p.13.

68   Niemeyer, 'Introduction' to Carlyle, *On Heroes*, p.xix.

69   Renan, *Life of Jesus*, p.32

70   Ernest Renan, *Qu'est-ce qu'une nation? [What is a Nation?]* Intro. by Charles Taylor, transl. W. R. Taylor (Toronto: Tapir, 1996), pp.46–7.

71   Renan was not the only one to receive criticism on this point. Foremost among the critics of Carlyle was Herbert Spencer (1820–1903).

72   'Address to the Lyceens of Sens 1883', in Robert N. Bellah (ed.) *Emile Durkheim on Morality and Society* (Chicago: CUP, 1973), pp.26–33.

73   See Chapter III, pp.70–71.

74   Jo Burr Margadant, 'Introduction' in Jo Burr Margadant (ed.), *The New Biography: Performing Femininity in Nineteenth-Century France* (Berkely and Los Angeles; London: University of California Press, 2000), pp.1–3.

75   John Tosh, 'Hegemonic masculinity and the history of gender', in Dudink et al. (eds): *Masculinities in Politics and War*, p.48.

76   Ibid., p.49.

77   I realize that although seeing this aspect of the biographies I have not been able to follow it up sufficiently and integrate it to the degree that I had hoped. This is an aspect that should be followed up; *Masculinities in Politics and War* gives an excellent example of how such a study could be done.

78   Ibid.

79   Stefan Dudink and Karen Hagemann, 'Masculinity in politics and war in the age of democratic revolution, 1750–1850', in Dudink et al. (eds): *Masculinities in Politics and War*, pp.3–21.

80   K. Hagemann, 'German heroes: The cult of the death for the fatherland in nineteenth-century Germany', in Dudink et al. (eds): *Masculinities in Politics and War*, pp.116–34.

81   Tosh, 'Hegemonic masculinity', pp.41–58.

82   Dudink and Hagemann, 'Masculinity in politics and war', p.15.

83   Ibid.

84   Horne, 'Masculinity in politics and war', pp.22–40.

85   Cf. the famous painting, *Liberty Leading the People*, by Eugène Delacroix, 1830.

86   Hagemann, 'German heroes', pp.123–4.

87   G. Sluga, 'Masculinities, nations and the New World Order,' in Dudink et al. (eds): *Masculinities in Politics and War*, p.241.

88   George L. Mosse, *The Image of Man: The Creation of Modern Masculinities* (Oxford: Oxford University Press, 1996).

89   Ibid., pp.50–5.

90   George L. Mosse, *Nationalism and Sexuality: Respectability and Abnormal Sexuality in Modern Europe* (New York: H. Fertig, 1985), pp.81–9.

91   Tosh, 'Hegemonic masculinity', p.49.

92   Susannah Heschel, *The Aryan Jesus: Christianity, Nazis and the Bible* (Princeton: Princeton University Press, 2007), pp.34–5.

Chapter II: Holy Land as Homeland

1   Benedict Anderson, *Imagined Communities: Reflections on the Origin and Spread of Nationalism* (London: Verso, 1983), p.30.

2   James Duncan and David Ley (eds), *Place, Culture, Representation* (London: Routledge, 1993); quotations from pp.1–2.

3   The *Oxford Universal Dictionary* explains 'survey' as 'the act of looking at something as a whole, or from a commanding position'; thus the surveyor has the power of observation.

4   Duncan and Ley, *Place, Culture, Representation*, pp.1–2.

5   Edward W. Said, *Orientalism* (New York: Random House, 1978), p.43.

6   See Lisa Lowe, *Critical Terrains: French and British Orientalism* (Ithaca and London: Cornell University Press, 1991), pp.5–10.

7   Eitan Bar-Yosef, *The Holy Land in English Culture 1799–1917: Palestine and the Question of Orientalism* (Oxford: Oxford University Press, 2005), see esp. pp.5–10; quotation from p.4.

8   The quotations are from a speech at the opening meeting of PEF in 1865; Bar-Yosef, *The Holy Land in English Culture*, p.6.

9   Beshara B. Doumani, 'Rediscovering Ottoman Palestine: writing Palestinians into history,' *Journal of Palestine Studies* xxi/2 (1992), p.7; see also the discussion of the PEF below.

10 Edward Said has made the observation that 'the interrelationships between scholarship (and literature, for that matter) and the institutions of nationalism have not been as seriously studied as they should' (Edward W. Said, *Culture and Imperialism* (New York: Vintage 1993), p.51). Old Testament scholars have taken up the study of the interrelationship between modern nationalism and presentations of ancient Israel as a state, but so far there have been no comparable studies of presentations of Jesus in the context of Palestine.

11 Paul Readman, *Land and Nation in England: Patriotism, National Identity, and the Politics of the Land* (Woodbridge, UK and Rochester, NY: Boydell Press, 2008).

12 Celia Applegate, *A Nation of Provincials: The German Idea of Heimat* (Berkeley: University of California Press, 1990).

13 Ibid., see pp.7–11, quotation from p.11.

14 Ibid., p.9.

15 Lisa Lowe, *Critical Terrains*, pp.30–1.

16 Doumani, 'Rediscovering Ottoman Palestine', p.7.

17 Ibid., p.7.

18 Said, *Orientalism*, p.43.

19 For further details on what follows see Robert L. Wilken, *The Land Called Holy: Palestine in Christian History and Thought* (New Haven: Yale University Press, 1992), pp.24–7, 56–8, 124–5, 168–70.

20 See Colin Morris, *The Sepulchre of Christ and the Medieval West* (Oxford: Oxford University Press, 2005), pp.47–58.

21 See for example the Harvard dissertation by Adam Beaver, 'A Holy Land for the Catholic Monarchy: Orientalism in the Making of the Spanish Renaissance', Ph.D. diss., Harvard University, 2008, to be published as a monograph.

22 See Nathan Schor, *Napoleon in the Holy Land* (London: Greenhill, 1999).

23 Alexander Schölch, *Palestine in Transformation: Studies in Social, Economic and Political Development*, trans. W. C. Young and M. C. Garrity (Washington: Institute for Palestine Studies, 1993), pp.47–75; see also Vivian D. Lipman, 'Britain and the Holy Land: 1830–1914,' in M. Davis and Y. Ben-Arieh (eds), *With Eyes towards Zion III: Western Societies and the Holy Land* (New York: Praeger, 1991), pp.195–207.

24 Said, *Orientalism*, pp.80–8.

25 Gilles Néret (ed.), *Description de l'Egypte. Publiée par les ordres de Napoléon Bonaparte*, English trans. C. Miller, German trans. B. Blumenberg (Köln: Benedikt Taschen, 1997).

26 Eitan Bar-Yosef surveyed the number of publications between 1775 and 1915, as well as their circulation, and found that they were largely limited to the middle class (*The Holy Land in English Culture*, pp.94–104). On works focused more narrowly on the geography of the Holy Land see Edwin J. Aiken, *Scriptural Geography: Portraying the Holy Land* (London: I.B.Tauris, 2010), pp.18–56.

27 See Morris, *The Sepulchre of Christ*, pp.306–27, 363–83.

28 There have been many studies of American travel writing: cf. John Davis, *The Landscape of Belief: Encountering the Holy Land in Nineteenth-Century American Art and Culture* (Princeton: Princeton University Press, 1996); Burke O. Long, *Imagining the Holy Land* (Bloomington: Indiana University Press, 2003); Hilton Obenzinger, *American Palestine: Melville, Twain and the Holy Land Mania* (Princeton: Princeton University Press, 1999); Michael B. Oren, *Power, Faith and Fantasy: America in the Middle East 1776 to the Present* (New York: Norton, 2007); and Brian Yothers, *The Romance of the Holy Land in American Travel Writing 1790–1876* (Aldershot: Ashgate, 2007).

29 I have used mostly books by British travellers; for German and French travellers and explorers see Yehoshua Ben-Arieh, *The Rediscovery of the Holy Land in the Nineteenth Century* (Jerusalem: Magnum, 1979).

30 A. P. Stanley, *Sinai and Palestine in Connection with their History*, new edn (New York: Armstrong, 1885).

31 John James Moscrop, *Measuring Jerusalem: The Palestine Exploration Fund and the British Interests in the Holy Land* (Leicester and New York: Leicester University Press, 2000), pp.46–8.

32 See Bar-Yosef for a similar analysis of the relation between Englishness and the Holy Land in a sermon by Stanley from 1862 (*The Holy Land in English Culture*, pp.76–8).

33 Stanley, *Sinai and Palestine*, p.9 [my emphasis].

34 See ibid., pp.9–29.

35 Keith W. Whitelam, *The Invention of Israel: The Silencing of Palestinian History* (London: Routledge, 1996), pp.13–23. Even in very critical reviews of Whitelam's overall thesis,

this point has been recognized; cf. Iain Provan: 'It is, for example, important to consider whether and to what extent in past reconstructions of ancient Israel modern scholars have indeed been working anachronistically with a model in their minds of the modern European nation state and modern expressions of imperial power' in 'The end of (Israel's) history? K. W. Whitelam's *The Invention of Ancient Israel*. A review article', *Journal of Semitic Studies* xlii/2 (1997), p.287, n.8.

36 This is a main point in Bar-Yosef's *The Holy Land in English Culture*, see especially pp.18–60.

37 Stanley, *Sinai and Palestine*, p.16.

38 Quoted in Ben Halpern, *The Idea of the Jewish State*, 2nd edn (Cambridge, MA: Harvard University Press, 1969), p.170; see also Oren: *Power, Faith and Fantasy*, pp.362–4.

39 Stanley, *Sinai and Palestine*, pp.25–26.

40 Simon Schama, *Landscape and Memory* (London: HarperCollins, 1995).

41 Aiken, *Scriptural Geography*, pp.27–34.

42 Stanley, *Sinai and Palestine*, p.26.

43 William Thompson, speech made on 22 June 1865, as quoted in Moscrop, *Measuring Jerusalem*, p.71.

44 Davis, *Landscape of Belief*, pp.16–17.

45 Billie Melman, *Women's Orients: English Women and the Middle East, 1718–1918* (London: MacMillan, 1992).

46 Ibid., pp.165–231.

47 Ibid., pp.172–4.

48 Mary Eliza Rogers, *Domestic Life in Palestine* (London: Belle and Daldy, 1862). For the information discussed here see Melman, *Women's Orients*, pp.191–209.

49 See Melman, *Women's Orients*, pp.210–31.

50 Ibid., p.221.

51 Anderson, *Imagined Communities*, pp.163–85.

52 See Moscrop, *Measuring Jerusalem*; for the political context of archaeology in Palestine, see Nadia Abu El-Haj, *Facts on the Ground: Archaeological Practice and Territorial Self-Fashioning in Israeli Society* (Chicago and London: Chicago University Press, 2001), pp.22–45.

53 A. P. Stanley in 'Introduction' to W. Morrison (ed.), *The Recovery of Jerusalem: A Narrative of Exploration and Discovery in the City and the Holy Land* (London: Bentley, 1871), pp.xxii.

54 Umut Özkirimli, *Contemporary Debates on Nationalism: A Critical Engagement* (Basingstoke and New York: PalgraveMacMillan, 2005), p.180.

55 Moscrop, *Measuring Jerusalem*, p.123.

56 Ibid., p.1.

57 Ibid., p.219.

58   Dov Gavish, *A Survey of Palestine under the British Mandate 1920–1948* (London: Routledge, 2005), p.259.

59   For what follows see Schölch, *Palestine in Transformation*, pp.9–17 and El-Haj: *Facts on the Ground*, pp.23–32. Gideon Biger also describes the various administrative divisions, but writes from the perspective of Eretz-Israel as 'a geohistorical concept rooted in historical consciousness' ('The names and boundaries of Eretz-Israel (Palestine) as reflections of stages in its history', in Ruth Kark (ed.), *The Land that Became Israel: Studies in Historical Geography*, trans. M. Gordon (New Haven: Yale University Press, 1990), pp.11–22).

60   C. Conder, 'The Survey of Palestine', in *Palestine Exploration Fund Quarterly Statement* (1874), p.242; quoted from El-Haj: *Facts on the Gound*, p.28.

61   N. A. Silberman, 'Nationalism and archaeology', in Eric M. Meyers (ed.), *Oxford Encyclopaedia of Archaeology in the Near East* vol. iv (New York: Oxford University Press, 1997), p.105.

62   Dov Gavish, 'French cartography of the Holy Land in the nineteenth century', in *Palestine Exploration Quarterly* 126 (1994), pp.24–31.

63   See Chapter VI, pp.151–155.

64   George Adam Smith, *Historical Geography of the Holy Land*, 25th edn (London: Hodder and Stoughton, 1931), pp.408–11.

65   Doumani, 'Rediscovering Ottoman Palestine', p.24, n.5.

66   See Schölch, *Palestine in Transformation*, pp.61–5 and Bar-Yosef, *The Holy Land in English Culture*, pp.182–246.

67   Bar-Yosef holds a critical view of the influence of the millenarian restorationists upon the political decisions behind the Balfour declaration (see *The Holy Land in English Culture*, pp.182–4, 243–6).

68   Schölch stipulates that before 1880 there were only 24,000 Jews living in Palestine (*Palestine in Transformation*, p.75, see also pp.19–43).

69   Bar-Yosef, *The Holy Land in English Culture*, pp.81–5.

70   Doumani, 'Rediscovering Ottomanian Palestine', p.7.

71   Yehoshua Ben-Arieh, 'Holy Land views in nineteenth century Western travel literature', in Davis and Ben-Arieh (eds): *With Eyes towards Zion III*, p.22.

72   See Doumani, 'Rediscovering Ottoman Palestine'.

73   See a summary of the main ideas of Zionism held by Theodor Herzl and others in Boas Evron, *Jewish State or Israeli Nation?* (Bloomington, IN: Indiana University Press, 1991), pp.41–2.

74   The wording of the Balfour declaration, 'a national home for the Jewish people', was consciously ambiguous; a clarification by Balfour said that 'It did not necessarily involve the early establishment of an independent Jewish State, which was a matter of gradual development in accordance with the ordinary laws of political evolution' (Halpern: *The Idea of the Jewish State*, pp.168–9; see also Oren: *Power, Faith and Fantasy*, pp.362–4).

75   Nils Butenschøn, *Midtøsten. Imperiefall, statsutvikling, kriger* (Oslo: Universitetsforlaget, 2008), pp.121–7.

76 Rashid Khalidi, *Palestinian Identity: The Construction of Modern National Consciousness* (New York: Columbia, 1997), pp.150–5, 218, nn.36, 37.

77 Cf. Issam Nassar, 'The trauma of al-Nakba: Collective memory and the rise of Palestinian national identity', in A. Sarat. N. Davidovitch and M. Alberstein (eds), *Trauma and Memory: Reading, Healing and Making Law* (Stanford, CA: Stanford University Press, 2007), p.69.

78 Schölch, *Palestine in Transformation*, pp.16–17.

79 Bar-Yosef, *The Holy Land in English Culture*, pp.76–81.

80 Yothers, *Romance of the Holy Land*, pp.22–5.

81 Ibid., pp.25–6.

82 Morris, *The Sepulchre of Christ*, pp.321–2.

83 See n. 40.

84 William M. Thomson, *The Land and the Book; or, Biblical Illustrations Drawn from the Manners and Customs, the Scenes and the Scenery of the Holy Land*, 2 vols (London: T. Nelson and Sons, 1859).

85 Thomson, *Land and the Book* vol.1, p.xv, quoted in Davis, *Landscape of Belief*, p.47.

86 Thomson, *Land and the Book* vol. 2, p.xv, quoted in Yothers, *Romance of the Holy Land*, p.29.

87 Renan, *Life of Jesus*, p.61.

88 Moscrop, *Measuring Jerusalem*, p.120.

89 Moscrop, *Measuring Jerusalem*, pp.54–5.

90 I must admit that I, too, found the view fascinating. This hill may be the 'brow of the hill upon which their city was built', mentioned in Luke 4:29 as the place from which the people of Nazareth would throw Jesus down.

91 Renan, *Life of Jesus*, p.87.

92 Smith, *Historical Geography*, p.433.

93 H. V. Morton, *In the Steps of the Master* (London: Rich and Cowan, 1935), p.178. In the two first years alone 235,000 copies of the book were printed, and it has been reprinted enumerable times since its first appearance in 1934.

94 Frances Power Cobbe, *Cities of the Past* (London: Trübner, 1864), p.174; quoted in Melman, *Women's Orients*, p.170.

95 Bar-Yosef, *The Holy Land in English Culture*, p.9.

Chapter III: Imagining a Nation

1 Friedrich Schleiermacher, *The Life of Jesus*, ed. by J. C. Verheyden (Mifflintown: Sigler, 1997), p.11.

2 Cf. Friedrich Schleiermacher, 'Über den Geschichtsunterricht', KGA i/1 (Berlin: de Gruyter, 1998), p.493; Kurt Nowak, 'Theorie der Geschichte. Schleiermachers Abhandlung "Über den Geschichtsunterricht" von 1793', in Günter Meckenstock and J. Ring-

leben (eds), *Schleiermacher und die wissenschaftliche Kultur des Christentums* (Berlin and New York: de Gruyter, 1991), pp.419–39.

3   Friedrich Schleiermacher, *On Religion: Addresses in Response to its Cultured Critics*, trans. and intro. by T. N. Tice (Richmond: John Knox, 1969).

4   Friedrich Schleiermacher, *Der Christliche Glaube* i–ii, 2nd edn, ed. by M. Redeker (Berlin: de Gruyter, 1960); Friedrich Schleiermacher, *The Christian Faith*, trans. and ed. by H. R. Mackintosh and J. S. Stewart (Edinburgh: T. and T. Clark, 1928).

5   See a full documentation in Dankfried Reetz, *Schleiermacher im Horizont preussischer Politik* (Waltrop: Spenner, 2002); see especially the section on Schleiermacher in a larger report required by the king, Frederick Wilhelm III, on university teachers who represented a dangerous influence on the youth, pp. 238–40.

6   For a presentation of Schleiermacher's *Life of Jesus* from the perspective of Christology, see C. L. Kelsey, *Schleiermacher's Preaching: Dogmatics and Biblical Criticism. The Interpretation of Jesus Christ in the Gospel of John* (Eugene, OR: Pickwick, 2007). For a larger and more detailed study that also discusses the negative evaluations by D. F. Strauss and A. Schweitzer, see D. Lange, *Historischer Jesus oder mythischer Christus: Untersuchungen zu dem Gegensatz zwischen Friedrich Schleiermacher und David Friedrich Strauss* (Gütersloh: Gerd Mohn, 1975).

7   Susan Tridgell, *Understanding Ourselves: The Dangerous Art of Biography* (Frankfurt: Peter Lang, 2004), p.187.

8   However, see the early work by Jerry F. Dawson, *Friedrich Schleiermacher: The Evolution of a Nationalist* (Austin: University of Texas Press, 1966).

9   W. Dilthey, *Leben Schleiermachers* vol. i (Berlin: Reimers, 1870); see now Kurt Nowak, *Schleiermacher* (Göttingen: Vandenhoeck and Ruprecht, 2001).

10   Friedrich Schleiermacher, *Vorlesungen über die Lehre vom Staat* ed. by W. Jaeschke, KGA ii/8 (Berlin: de Gruyter, 1998).

11   Matthias Wolfes, *Öffentlichkeit und Bürgergesellschaft: Friedrich Schleiermacher's politische Wirksamkeit* 2 vols, Arbeiten zur Kirchengeschichte xviii/1–2 (Berlin: de Gruyter, 2004). Wolfes' work has provided the main inspiration for my reading of Schleiermacher's *Life of Jesus* in this chapter. For a brief version of his argument, see M. Wolfes, 'Sichtweisen. Schleiermachers politische Theorie zwischen dem autoritären Nationalstaatsethos der Befreiungskriegszeit und dem deliberativen Konzept einer bürgerlichen Öffentlichkeit', in Andreas Arndt, Ulrich Barth and Wilhelm Gräb (eds), *Christentum – Staat – Kultur: Akten des Kongresses der Internationalen Schleiermacher-Gesellschaft in Berlin, März 2006*, Schleiermacher-Archiv 22 (Berlin: Gruyter, 2008), pp.375–93.

12   Nowak, *Schleiermacher*, pp.57–8.

13   See Ute Planert, 'Wann beginnt der "moderne" deutsche Nationalismus?' in Jörg Echternkamp and Sven Oliver Müller (eds), *Die Politik der Nation. Deutscher Nationalismus in Krieg und Krisen 1760–1960* (Munich: R. Oldenborg, 2002), pp.25–59.

14   For Schleiermacher's activities and writings of 1808–13, see Wolfes, *Öffentlichkeit und Bürgergesellschaft* I, pp.209–541.

15   Christian Nottmeier, 'Zwischen Preußen und Deutschland. Nation und Nationalstaat bei Friedrich Schleiermacher', in Arndt et al., *Christentum – Staat – Kultur*, pp.337–53.

16 Dawson, *Friedrich Schleiermacher*, pp.144–59.

17 See for instance the influence of the painter and architect Karl Friedrich Schinkel (1781–1841), who was a major agent behind many of the central public buildings and monuments in Berlin at the time; see J. Cramer, U. Laible and H. D. Nägelke, *Karl Friedrich Schinkel. Führer zu seinen Bauten. Band I: Berlin und Potsdam* 3rd edn (Munich and Berlin: Deutsche Kunstverlag, 2008), pp.9–13.

18 H. A. Winkler, *Germany: The Long Road West*, vol. 1, 1789–1933, trans. A. J. Sager (New York: Oxford University Press, 2006), pp.52–61.

19 Wolfes, *Öffentlichkeit und Bürgergesellschaft* II, p.415.

20 Especially in relation to Schleiermacher's views on Judaism; see ibid., pp.326–90.

21 Frederick Herzog, 'Schleiermacher and the Problem of Power,' in his *Justice Church: The New Function of the Church in North American Christianity* (Maryknoll, NY: Orbis, 1980), pp.55–69.

22 Joerg Rieger, *Christ and Empire* (Minneapolis: Fortress, 2007), pp.197–237.

23 Schleiermacher, *Life of Jesus*, p.158.

24 Ibid., p.159 [my emphasis].

25 From Schleiermacher's own notes as his introduction to lecture 53, *Life of Jesus*, p.355 [emphasis in original]. The words in parentheses are not in the German text, but most likely inserted by the translator to provide a full meaning.

26 Schleiermacher, *Life of Jesus*, pp.160–61.

27 Ibid., p.11.

28 See similarly Lange, *Historischer Jesus*, pp.63–9.

29 The German terms are *der einzelne* and *gemeinsames Leben* or *Gesamtleben*. See Schleiermacher, *Leben Jesu*, pp.7–8.

30 Schleiermacher, *Life of Jesus*, p.12. The editor of the English translation, Jack C. Verheyden, explains that he has chosen 'directing' for the German *dominierend* since 'dominating' has 'now gained connotations of psychological coercion which would mislead in understanding Schleiermacher's meaning in this lecture' (pp.8–9, n.1).

31 Ibid., pp.13–14.

32 For Schleiermacher it was above all Jesus' consciousness of God that made him unique and an example of authentic existence, but that is a point that Schleiermacher brings in only after he has completed his discussion of the relation between the individual and the common life in general terms. Schleiermacher's attempt to combine a general anthropology with a more specific Christological argument of Christ as redeemer is spelled out in his *Christmas Eve*. In this book the influence that Christ exerts upon the common life is understood in terms of an organic community: the Spirit forms the presence of Christ 'within the genuine self-consciousness of individual persons'; see *Christmas Eve*, trans. T. N. Tice (Richmond: John Knox, 1967), p.84.

33 Friedrich Schleiermacher, 'Rede am Geburtstage Friedrich des Großen am 24sten Januar 1817 in der Akademie der Wissenschaften', in Friedrich Schleiermacher, *Akademievorträge*, ed. by Martin Rössler, KGA i/11 (Berlin: de Gruyter, 2002), pp.241–50.

34   Friedrich Schleiermacher, 'Über den Begriff des großen Mannes, Am 24.Januar 1826', in Friedrich Schleiermacher, *Werke. Auswahl in vier Bänden*, Band I (Leipzig: Eckhardt, 1910), pp.520–31.

35   Wolfes, 'Sichtweisen', pp.384–8.

36   Schleiermacher, 'Rede 1817', p.243; see Wolfes, *Öffentlichkeit und Bürgergesellschaft* II, pp.402–3.

37   Schleiermacher, 'Rede 1817', p.245.

38   Schleiermacher, 'Über den Begriff des grossen Mannes', p.527. In his Academy lecture from 1817 Schleiermacher spoke of the participation that made it possible for the peasant population to move out of their situation of dependency and to build that political consciousness among citizens that was necessary for the state; see Wolfes, 'Sichtweisen', p.387.

39   See Chapter I, p.34.

40   Schleiermacher, 'Über den Begriff des grossen Mannes', p.531.

41   Schleiermacher, *Life of Jesus*, p.13 [emphasis in original]. Cf. Jacqueline Mariña on the relation between Christ and all persons in the Christology of Schleiermacher: 'The self-consciousness of one individual can transform the self-consciousness of all.' in *Transformation of the Self in the Thought of Friedrich Schleiermacher* (Oxford: Oxford University Press, 2008), p.187.

42   Schleiermacher, *Life of Jesus*, pp.169–71.

43   Ibid., pp.171–2.

44   David Harvey, 'Space as a key word', in Noel Castree and Derek Gregory (eds), *The David Harvey Reader* (Oxford: Blackwell, 2006), pp.272–4.

45   Schleiermacher, *Life of Jesus*, p.161.

46   Ibid., pp.159–60.

47   J. Z. Smith, *To Take Place: Toward Theory in Ritual* (Chicago: Chicago University Press, 1987), p.30.

48   I have used 'land' for 'zu der Gesammtheit des jüdischen Landes' instead of 'country' in the 1975 translation; Schleiermacher, *Life of Jesus*, p.172.

49   I have used 'the Jewish land' instead of 'Palestine' in the English translation in Schleiermacher, *Life of Jesus*, p.172, which does not render the meaning of the German 'dies', referring back to 'das jüdische Land'.

50   Schleiermacher, *Life of Jesus*, pp.172–4 [my emphasis].

51   After Herods' death, Rome divided the areas between his sons. Archelaus, who got Judea (and Samaria and Idumea) was deposed by the Romans, and therefore Judea was put under direct Roman rule as a province. Herod Antipas ruled two disconnected areas, Galilee and Perea, while Philip ruled Gaulantitis and Trachonitis Batanea.

52   The English translation of the book does not catch the fine distinctions between 'rule' from above, and the division that is made 'in ordinary life' that Schleiermacher makes when he contrasts 'die herrschende Eintheilung' with 'im gewöhnlichen Leben geltende Bezeichnung'.

53 K. R. Olwig, 'Recovering the substantive nature of landscape', *Annals of the Association of American Geographers* 84 (1996), pp.630–53.

54 Note how Schleiermacher's mention of the 'totality of the Jewish land' appears at structurally significant locations in this paragraph, in the first statement, as a summary of the first section, and then in the conclusion of the discussion; see Schleiermacher, *Life of Jesus*, pp.172–4.

55 Ibid., pp.104–5.

56 In only two instances Schleiermacher uses *Palästina* in parallel statements to '*das jüdische Land*', see *Das Leben Jesu*, p.180 line 19 from the top and p.183 l.24. On p.183 l.26 it has a more local, geographical meaning.

57 From Schleiermacher-Nachlass 766/27, Bl.1–2; quoted in Wolfes, *Öffentlichkeit under Bürgergeschellschaft* I, p.369. For the friendship between Schlegel and Schleiermacher and their political estrangement see pp.366–73.

58 Schleiermacher envisages a unified Germany as 'a united empire' that seems to include Austria, under the Austrian emperor, but Wolfes suggests under Prussia (*Öffentlichkeit under Bürgergeschellschaft* II, p.401).

59 Schleiermacher, 'Über den Begriff des grossen Mannes', p.530.

60 At this time, 1826, Schleiermacher imagines a union that was termed a Small-German Empire, based on Prussia (in contrast to a Great-German Empire centred around Austria), but his ideas of the role of the king in relation to his people are similar to that of the letter from 1813; see Nottmeier: 'Zwischen Preußen und Deutschland', p.353.

61 Ulrich Hermann, 'Einleitung,' in Ulrich Hermann (ed.) *Volk – Nation – Vaterland* Studien zum achtzehnten Jahrhundert 18 (Hamburg: Meiner, 1996), pp.11–18.

62 Schleiermacher, *Life of Jesus*, pp.13–14; *Leben Jesu*, pp.12–14.

63 Joep Leersen, *National Thought in Europe: A Cultural History* (Amsterdam: Amsterdam University Press, 2006), pp.109–11.

64 Schleiermacher, *Life of Jesus*, p.14; *Leben Jesu*, p.13.

65 Bernhard Giesen, *Intellectuals and the Nation: Collective Identity in a German Axial Age*, trans. by N. Levis and A. Weisz (Cambridge: Cambridge University Press, 1998).

66 Ibid., pp.90–1.

67 Ibid., pp.103–20.

68 Ibid., pp.105–6 [my emphasis].

69 For a full discussion of Schleiermacher's theology and his view of how the divinity was incorporated into the human Jesus, *The Life of Jesus* must be read together with the relevant sections of his *Christian Faith*, but this falls outside the perspectives of this study; see also Lange, *Historischer Jesus*.

70 Schleiermacher, *Life of Jesus*, pp.45–155.

71 Ibid., pp.102–21.

72 Ibid., pp.104–5.

73   Artisans in the towns belonging to guilds were in a different and much more advanta-
      geous situation; Eda Sagarra, *A Social History of Germany 1648–1914* (London: Methuen,
      1977), pp.323–35.

74   Marion W. Gray, *Prussia in Transition: Society and Politics under the Stein Reform Ministry
      of 1808* (Philadelphia: The American Philosophical Society, 1986), pp.19–20.

75   Giesen, *Intellectuals*, pp.105–6.

76   Cf. Schleiermacher's remarks about the scribes in the previous quotations, from Schlei-
      ermacher, *Life of Jesus*, p.105 and p.117.

77   Mary Ann Perkins, *Nation and Word, 1770–1850: Religious and Metaphysical Language in
      European National Consciousness* (Aldershot: Asgate, 1999), p.150; J. Habermas, 'What
      is a people? The Frankfurt "Germanists' Assembly" of 1846 and the Self-Understanding
      of the Humanities in *Vormärz*', in J. Habermas, *The Postnational Constellation: Political
      Essays*, trans, ed. and with intro. by Max Pensky (Cambridge: Polity, 2001), pp.1–5.

78   Schleiermacher, *Life of Jesus*, p.112.

79   Verheysen, in ibid., p.106, n.19.

80   Ibid., pp.105–6.

81   Ibid., pp.107, 121.

82   Ibid., p.117; Lange, *Historischer Jesus*, p.104.

83   Schleiermacher, *Life of Jesus*, pp.228–31.

84   A caution is necessary: Schleiermacher's position may depend on the context – in other
      instances he does seem to recognize more of a special role for the apostles.

85   Schleiermacher, *Life of Jesus*, p.299.

86   Ibid., pp.358–65.

87   Ibid., p.365.

88   Ibid., p.175.

89   Ibid., p.180; cf. a similar statement on p.181.

90   For a similar suggestions, see Reetz: *Schleiermacher*, p.106.

91   See Giesen, *Intellectuals*, pp.105–6.

92   Friedrich Schleiermacher, 'Promemoria des Bischof's Eylert über einen Reform des
      Schul- und Kirchenwesens, 16 Oktober 1819', in J. Rachold (ed.) *Friedrich Schleierma-
      cher – eine Briefauswahl* (Frankfurt: PeterLang, 1995), pp.307–17.

93   Schleiermacher, *Life of Jesus*, pp.177–80. Schleiermacher does not discuss the Gospel
      sayings addressed to the disciples about leaving everything to follow Jesus; his picture of
      the disciples is that they attended to the business of their households and sometimes they
      went with Jesus on shorter trips.

94   'Hofmeister'; see Michael Maurer, *Die Biographie des Bürgers: Lebensformen und Denk-
      weisen in der formativen Phase des deutschen Bürgertums (1680–1815)* (Göttingen:
      Vandenhoeck and Ruprecht, 1996), pp.457–9.

95   Verheyden in Schleiermacher, *Life of Jesus*, p.235, n.29.

96 The so-called Wolfenbüttel Fragments were first published by G. E. Lessing in 1774–8. For a useful English translation with an introduction in The Life of Jesus series, see Hermann Samuel Reimarus, *Fragments*, ed. by Charles H. Talbert (Philadelphia: Fortress, 1970).

97 Schleiermacher probably referred to Reimarus and Karl Bretschneider (see Verheyden in ibid., pp.256–7, nn.32, 33), but he rejected their views, pp.255–6, 279–80.

98 Ibid., p.290.

99 Giesen speaks of different codes, that is, patterns that make it possible to give outlines of the world or situations (*Intellectuals*, p.13). He speaks of the Romantic code as 'the transcendental code' (pp.80–102) and includes Schleiermacher in this section (p.88).

100 Giesen, *Intellectuals*, p.90.

101 Ibid., p.91.

102 Extensively documented in Wolfes, *Öffentlichkeit*.

103 Paul E. Capetz, 'Friedrich Schleiermacher on the Old Testament', *HTR* 102 (2009), pp.297–326.

104 See Wolfes, *Öffentlichkeit* I, pp.360–91.

105 Schleiermacher, *Life of Jesus*, p.276 [my translation].

106 Ibid., p.277.

107 Ibid., pp.277–8.

108 The German terms are 'gänzlich umzugestalten und zu modifiziren', Schleiermacher, *Leben Jesu*, p.297.

109 Horne, John, 'Masculinity in politics and war in the age of the nation-state and world wars, 1850–1950', in S. Dudink, K. Hagemann and J. Tosh (eds), *Masculinities in Politics and War: Gendering Modern History* (Manchester: Manchester University Press, 2004), p.23.

110 'Ein Gegensatz von Obrigkeit und Untertanen', quotations from Schleiermacher's lectures on Ethics, pp.93–4, cited in Wolfes, *Öffentlichkeit* I, p.29.

111 Wolfes, *Öffentlichkeit* I, pp.28–31.

112 Schleiermacher's presentation of the household as an ideal can also be read as an implicit criticism of the existing household structure in Germany of the time, which could be a very autocratic place; see Brendan Simms, *The Struggle for Mastery in Germany, 1779–1850* (London: MacMillan, 1998), pp.17–19.

113 K. Palonen, *The Struggle With Time: A Conceptual History of 'Politics' as an Activity*, vol.1 (Hamburg: Lit, 2006), p.43.

114 Schleiermacher, *Life of Jesus*, pp.290–1. This position is repeated many times in his lectures, see also pp.255–6, 298–300.

115 Ibid.

116 These quotations are from ibid., pp.299–300.

117 Schleiermacher, 'Über den Begriff des grossen Mannes', p.527.

118 Wolfes, *Öffentlichkeit* II, pp.326–90.

119 Cf. the book burning by a group of young liberal nationalists at Wartburg in 1817, which included books by the Jewish author Saul Asscher who had criticized extreme nationalism; Simms: *Struggle for Mastery*, p.138.

120 Schleiermacher, *Life of Jesus*, p.355.

121 Ibid., pp.358–9.

122 Ibid., pp.359–61.

123 Ibid., p.359, also p.255.

124 Ibid., p.360.

125 Schleiermacher, *Life of Jesus*, p.361.

126 Wolfes, *Öffentlichkeit*, II, pp.330–43.

127 Theodore Vial, 'Schleiermacher and the state', in J. Mariña (ed.) *Cambridge Companion to Friedrich Schleiermacher* (Cambridge: Cambridge University Press, 2005), pp.280–2.

128 Vial says that 'Schleiermacher's theory of the state is intimately connected to his Christology' ('Schleiermacher and the state', p.273). Based on Schleiermacher's theological writings and his sermons Vial draws many conclusions similar to the present study with regard to Schleiermacher's view of nation and state.

129 John Tosh, 'Hegemonic masculinity and the history of gender', in S. Dudink, K. Hagemann and J. Tosh (eds), *Masculinities in Politics and War: Gendering Modern History* (Manchester: Manchester University Press, 2004), p.48.

Chapter IV: A Protestant Nation

1   David Friedrich Strauss, *Das Leben Jesu kritisch bearbeitet* (Tübingen: Osiander, 1835); *The Life of Jesus, Critically Examined*, 3 vols, trans. from the 4th German edn by George Eliot (London: Swan Sonnenschein, 1846).

2   The quotes from Heinrich Heine and Ferdinand Christian Baur are taken from M. C. Massey's 'Introduction' to David Friedrich Strauss, *In Defense of My Life of Jesus Against the Hegelians*, trans. and ed. by Marilyn Chapin Massey (Hamden, CT: Archon, 1983), p.ix.

3   John Horne, 'Masculinity in politics and war in the age of the nation-state and word wars, 1850–1950', in S. Dudink, K. Hagemann and J. Tosh (eds), *Masculinities in Politics and War: Gendering Modern History* (Manchester: Manchester University Press, 2004), p.23.

4   Cf. David Friedrich Strauss, *Die christliche Glaubenslehre in ihrer geschichtlichen Entwicklung und im Kampfe mit der modernen Wissenschaft* (Tübingen: C. F. Osiander, 1840–1).

5   Cf. Strauss' statement in *The Old Faith and New*: 'I am a Bourgeois and I am proud to be one', quoted in F. W. Graf, 'The Old Faith and the New: The late theology of D. F. Strauss', in H. Graf Reventlow and W. Farmer (eds), *Biblical Studies and the Shifting of Paradigms, 1850–1914* (Sheffield: Sheffield Academic Press, 1995), p.223.

6   Some of his liberal friends encouraged him to enter into politics, and Strauss became a member of the popularly elected Württemberg Diet (state assembly) in 1848. But he turned out to be a disappointment for the anti-establishment movement that had

supported him. He sided more and more with the moderates and outright political conservatives and after a short period resigned from his political office. See Horton Harris, *David Friedrich Strauss and His Theology* (Cambridge: Cambridge University Press, 1973), pp.170–4.

7 Ward Blanton, *Displacing Christian Origins: Philosophy, Secularity and the New Testament* (Chicago: University of Chicago Press, 2007), pp.67–103.

8 Marilyn C. Massey, *Christ Unmasked: The Meaning of The Life of Jesus in German Politics* (Chapel Hill, NC: University of North Carolina Press, 1983).

9 The period between the Restoration of 1815 and the Revolution of March 1848; see Bernhard Giesen, *Intellectuals and the Nation: Collective Identity in a German Axial Age*, trans. by N. Levis and A. Weisz (Cambridge: Cambridge University Press, 1998), p.10.

10 Massey, *Christ Unmasked*, p.12; Friedrich Wilhelm Graf, 'D. F. Strauss' radikaldemokratische Christologie', *TRu* 54 (1989), pp.190–5.

11 Massey, *Christ Unmasked*, pp.5–6.

12 Graf, 'The old faith and the new', pp.223–4. Graf indicates such a socio-political interpretation in the last part of his massive study of Strauss as theologian, *Kritik und Pseudo-Spekulation: David Friedrich Strauss als Dogmatiker im Kontext der positionellen Theologie seiner Zeit*, Münchener Monographien zur historischen und systematischen Theologie 7 (Munich: Kaiser, 1982), pp.574–606.

13 Graf, *Kritik und Pseudo-Spekulation*, pp.36–47, 81–87; 104–5.

14 Apart from Blanton's study, not much seem to have happened to follow up the initiatives by Graf and Massey; see the bibliographic essay by Thomas K. Kuhn, 'Strauss, David Friedrich,' *TRE* 32 (2001), p.245.

15 See Thomas Nipperdey, *Germany from Napoleon to Bismarck* (Dublin: Gill and MacMillan, 1996), pp.237–50.

16 Marilyn C. Massey in the 'Introduction' to Strauss, *In Defense of my Life of Jesus*, pp.xi–xii.

17 Information and quotations from Marilyn C. Massey, 'The literature of young Germany and D. F. Strauss's *Life of Jesus*', *JR* 59 (1979), pp.298–9.

18 Nipperdey, *Germany from Napoleon to Bismarck*, p.380.

19 See D. Lange for Strauss' original plan to divide the work into a traditional part (Life of Jesus in the Gospels and in Christian faith), a critical part (a study of the sources and their lack of historical basis), and a dogmatic part (on the truth based on the results) – *Historischer Jesus oder mythischer Christus: Untersuchungen zu dem Gegensatz zwischen Friedrich Schleiermacher und David Friedrich Strauss* (Gütersloh: Gerd Mohn, 1975), pp.177–81. This reflects a Hegelian model of thesis, anti-thesis and synthesis. But in the actual book the first part was dropped and the third part is very brief (pp.757–84); as a result the critical analysis based on 'the mythical point of view' dominates the book.

20 Strauss, *Life of Jesus*, pp.779–81.

21 Ibid., pp.781–4.

22 This was Karl Barth's evaluation in his *From Rousseau to Ritschl* (London: SCM, 1959), pp.362–89.

23   Strauss, *Life of Jesus*, p.780 [my emphasis].

24   Ibid.

25   Graf, *Kritik und Pseudo-Spekulation*, pp.574–97.

26   G. W. F. Hegel, *Philosophy of Right*, § 279, in Karl Marx, *Critique of Hegel's 'Philosophy of Right'*, trans. from the German, ed. and with intro. by Joseph O'Malley (Cambridge: Cambridge University Press, 1970), p.23.

27   Ibid., pp.28–9.

28   Cf. Nipperdey's statement that 'Christian concepts such as revelation, rebirth, resurrection and salvation took on a secular, politico-ethical and nationalist meaning' in *Germany from Napoleon to Bismarck*, p.387.

29   One of his readers was Friedrich Engels. Cf. his letter to Wilhelm Graeber, 8 October 1839: 'now you're going to hear something: I am now an enthusiastic Straussian' (available online at www.marxists.org/archive/marx/works/1839/letters/39_10_08.htm). But Graf is correct when he says that Massey has shown the influence of Strauss' argument upon some intellectuals, but not for the 'masses' of the democratic nationalist movement ('D. F. Strauss' radikaldemokratische Christologie', p.194).

30   Strauss, *Life of Jesus*, p.781 [my emphasis].

31   The most important of which was his *In Defense of My Life of Jesus Against the Hegelians*, as part of his *Streitschriften zur Verteidigung meiner Schrift über das Leben Jesu und zur Charakteristik der gegenwärtigen Theologie*, 3 parts (Tübingen: Osiander, 1837).

32   *Das Leben Jesu, kritisch bearbeitet*, 3.ed. mit Rücksicht auf die Gegenschriften verbesserten Auflage, 2 vols (Tübingen: Osiander, 1838–9). Strauss accepted many criticisms directed at the first edition, but ascribed the changes that he made primarily to a more positive view of the authenticity and credibility of John's Gospel, see pp.iv–v.

33   Strauss, *Leben Jesu*, 3.ed., pp.771, 779.

34   Blanton, *Christian Origins*, p.65.

35   Massey, *Christ Unmasked*, pp.113–14.

36   Ibid., p.124; for the larger context see Jochen Schmidt, *Die Geschichte des Genie-Gedankens in der deutschen Literatur, Philosophie und Politik 1750–1945*, vol. 1, 3rd edn (Heidelberg: Winter, 2004 (1st edn 1985)).

37   Massey, *Christ Unmasked*, p.126.

38   Ibid., p.141.

39   Strauss, *The Life of Jesus*.

40   Nipperdey, *Germany from Napoleon to Bismarck*, pp.527–98.

41   Ibid., pp.633–4.

42   Giesen, *Intellectuals*, pp.123–7; Nipperdey, *Germany from Napoleon to Bismarck*, pp.457–60.

43   Giesen, *Intellectuals*, pp.133–4.

44   Ibid., p.134.

45   Nipperdey, *Germany from Napoleon to Bismarck*,, 458-59.

46 Schweitzer, *The Quest of the Historical Jesus*, 1st complete edn, trans. of 2nd German edn, ed. by John Bowden (Minneapolis: Fortress, 2001), pp.168, 169.

47 Graf, *Kritik und Pseudo-Spekulation*, pp.17–18.

48 Harris, *Strauss and His Theology*, pp.200–12.

49 David Friedrich Strauss, *A New Life of Jesus*, 2 vols (London: Williams and Norgate, 1865).

50 David Friedrich Strauss, *The Life of Jesus: For the People*. 2 vols, 2nd edn (London: Williams and Norgate, 1879).

51 Giesen points out how academics used a direct form of addressing their audiences, to attract attention and to compete with other academics. Strauss uses many of these elements in his preface (*Intellectuals*, pp.127–32).

52 Graf, *Kritik und Pseudo-Spekulation*, p.22.

53 Strauss, *New Life of Jesus* I, p.xiii.

54 Blanton, *Christian Origins*, pp.179–80, n.16.

55 Strauss, *New Life of Jesus* I, pp.xiv–xv.

56 Ibid. This is in explicit contrast to his main argument in *The Life of Jesus, Critically Examined*.

57 Conservative, or new orthodox Protestants would have none of the radical interpretation of Jesus and religion that Strauss represented, nor of political nationalism; Nipperdey, *Germany from Napoleon to Bismarck*, pp.387–8.

58 See Leopold von Ranke, *Deutsche Geschichte im Zeitalter der Reformation*, 3rd edn (Berlin: Duncker, 1852); Thomas A. Brady, Jr., 'The Protestant Reformation in German History', Occasional Paper No. 22 (Washington, DC: German Historical Institute, 1998); and Karl Kupisch, 'The "Luther Renaissance"', *Journal of Contemporary History* 2 (1967), pp.29–49.

59 Kupisch, "Luther Renaissance", pp.39–41.

60 Nipperdey, *Germany from Napoleon to Bismarck*, pp.387–8.

61 Brady, 'The Protestant Reformation', pp.12–15, quotation from p.13.

62 However, the concept 'From Luther to Bismarck' as the master narrative of how modern Germany came into being came to an end with Germany's defeat in the Great War (1914–18); Brady, 'The Protestant Reformation', pp.17–18.

63 Strauss, *Life of Jesus: For the People* I, p.xvii.

64 Jean-Marie Paul, *D. F. Strauss (1808–1874) et son époque*, Publications de l'université Dijon LXI (Paris: Société les belles lettres, 1982), pp.392–3.

65 Strauss, *New Life of Jesus* I, p.xvii.

66 Strauss, *New Life of Jesus* I, pp.xvi–xvii [my emphasis].

67 Ibid., p.xvi.

68 Ibid., p.xviii.

69 Strauss considered Matthew to be the oldest Gospel (*New Life of Jesus* I, pp.150–7), one of the reasons being that it 'bears, more than any other, the stamp of Jewish national-

ity (*das jüdisch-nationale Gepräge*)' (p. 152). According to Strauss, this Jewish character disappeared over time as Christianity spread. Schleiermacher also based his preference for John's Gospel on its focus on Jesus' relation to the nation.

70   Strauss, *New Life of Jesus*, p.334. This description is similar to that in *The Life of Jesus*, 4th edn, with a significant addition in the designation of Antipas and Philip as 'Roman vassal princes'.

71   The name Palestine was introduced as a name for the Roman province in the second century to eradicate traces of the Jewish inhabitants. However, Palestine was not used by the inhabitants or by the Ottoman administration until late in the nineteenth century; Alexander Schölch, *Palestine in Transformation: Studies in Social, Economic and Political Development*, trans by W. C. Young and M. C. Garrity (Washington: Institute for Palestine Studies, 1993), pp.9–12.

72   See Strauss, *New Life of Jesus* I, pp.261–8.

73   Ibid., p.345.

74   Ibid., p.263.

75   The translation 'full privileges of the Jews' seems not quite adequate for the German '*vollwichtige Juden*.'

76   David Friedrich Strauss, *The Old Faith and the New*, 3rd English edn, trans. by Mathilde Blind (London: Asher and Co., 1874); trans. of *Der alte und der neue Glaube Ein Bekenntnis* (Leipzig, 1872).

77   Strauss, *The Old Faith and the New*, p.302.

78   Richard Weikart, 'The origins of social Darwinism in Germany, 1859–1895', *Journal of the History of Ideas* 54 (1993), pp.483–4.

79   Clive Christie, *Race and Nation: A Reader* (London: I.B.Tauris, 1998), p.37.

80   Strauss, *New Life of Jesus* I, pp.345–6.

81   Bo Reicke, 'From Strauss to Holtzmann and Meijboom: Synoptic theories advanced during the consolidation of Germany, 1830–70', *NovT* 29 (1987), pp.1–21.

82   See John S. Kloppenborg Verbin, *Excavating Q: The History and the Setting of the Sayings Gospel* (Edinburgh: T. and T. Clark, 2000), pp.271–328.

83   The Jewish scholar Abraham Geiger, who was inspired by Strauss' method of historical criticism of myths about Jesus, criticized him for not applying the same type of deconstruction of New Testament myths of Judaism. See Susannah Heschel, *Abraham Geiger and the Jewish Jesus* (Chicago: Chicago University Press, 1998), pp.117–18.

84   H. J. Schmitz, *Frühkatholizismus bei Adolf von Harnack, Rudolph Sohm und Ernst Käsemann* (Düsseldorf: Patmos, 1977).

85   Strauss, *New Life of Jesus* I. The first section, pp.241–9, deals with Greek philosophy and how it points towards Jesus, with a comparison with Socrates.

86   Ibid., p.250.

87   Ibid., p.313.

88   Ibid., p.281.

89   Ibid., p.283.

90   See the discussion in Blanton, *Christian Origins*, pp.67–103 and Graf, 'The Old Faith and the New'.

91   Herbert Golder, 'Introduction. David Strauss, Writer and Confessor', in Friedrich Nietzsche, *Unmodern Observations*, ed. by William Arrowsmith (New Haven: Yale University Press, 1990), pp.5–11.

92   Strauss, *Old Faith and New*, p.75 [my emphasis].

93   Ibid., pp.312–13.

94   Arthur Gobineau, *Essai sur l'inégalité des races humaines* (Paris: Firmin Didot Frères, 1853–5). On the influence of Gobineau in Germany, see Schmidt: *Die Geschichte des Genie-Gedankens*, pp.141–4; 215–20.

95   See Weikart, 'Social Darwinism in Germany.'

96   Ibid., pp.483–4.

97   Blanton, who draws on letters from Strauss during the French–German war, finds that Strauss is more troubled by this oscillation 'between literary and military productions', and sees the military establishment as a troublesome 'other self' (*Christian Origins*, pp.67–70).

98   Giesen, *Intellectuals*.

99   Strauss, *Old Faith and the New*, pp.295–6.

100 See the interpretation of the picture of Jesus here in Graf, 'The Old Faith and the New', pp.235–7.

101 Strauss, *Old Faith and the New*, pp.53–95 within the section pp.13–107.

102 Strauss rejects the arguments that moral values like charity, compassion, love, etc., were introduced by Christ by pointing to their sources in other religions and philosophies. Even if Christianity initiated the idea of humanity, it was only brought into a pure form by 'the philosophical–secular civilization of the sceptical eighteenth century'; *Old Faith and the New*, pp.95–8.

103 The German term is *Schwärmer*.

104 Strauss, *Old Faith and the New*, pp.93–4.

105 Ibid., p.86.

106 Giesen, *Intellectuals*, p.140.

107 Susannah Heschel, *The Aryan Jesus: Christianity, Nazis and the Bible* (Princeton: Princeton University Press, 2007), p.32.

108 Paul de Lagarde, *Deutsche Schriften*, 2nd print (Göttingen: Dieterische Verlagsbuchhandlung, 1891 (1878)).

109 Houston S. Chamberlain, *Foundations of the Nineteenth Century*, 2 vols (London: J. Lane, The Bodley Head, 1913), trans. of *Die Grundlagen des Neunzehnten Jahrhunderts* (München: Bruckmann, 1899).

110 Heschel, *Aryan Jesus*, pp.152–63.

111 Rachel Cusk, 'Shakespeare's daughters', *The Guardian*, 12 December 2009, Review section, p.2.

112   Strauss, *Life of Jesus*, p.781.

113   Strauss, *Leben Jesu*, 3rd edn, vol.2, pp.770–2.

114   See Tosh, 'Hegemonic masculinity'.

115   Joep Leersen, *National Thought in Europe: A Cultural History* (Amsterdam: Amsterdam University Press, 2006), p.64.

Chapter V: 'Familiar and Foreign'

1   H. W. Warman, *Ernest Renan: A Critical Biography* (London: Athlone Press, 1964), pp.77–8.

2   Ernest Renan, *Vie de Jésus* (Paris: Michel Lévy, 1863), quotations from *Vie de Jésus* are taken from Henriette Psichari (ed.), *Oeuvres complètes de Ernest Renan* IV (Paris: Calmann-Lévy, 1947), pp.11–371; quotations in English are from the translation of the 1863 edition, *The Life of Jesus*, Intro. by J. H. Holmes (New York: Modern Library, 1927). Renan also issued a popular version, titled *Jesus*, in 1864; to add confusion, from the 32nd edition this was titled *Vie de Jésus, Édition Populaire* – see Georges Pholien, *Les deux 'Vie de Jésus' de Renan*, bibliothèque de la Faculté de Philosophie et Lettres de l'Université de Liège (Paris: 1983), fasc.239.

3   Charles Darwin, *On the Origin of the Species* (London: Murray, 1859).

4   J. G. Herder, *Abhandlung über den Ursprung der Sprache* (Berlin: Voss, 1772).

5   Ernest Renan, *De l'origine du langage* (1848, 1858); see Maurice Olender, *The Languages of Paradise*, rev. edn (New York: Other, 2002), pp.51–81.

6   Keith Gore, *L'idée de progrès dans la pensée de Renan* (Paris: Nizet, 1970), pp.171–9.

7   See the discussion of similarities and differences between Strauss and Renan in Laudyce Rétat, *Religion et imagination religieuse: Leur formes et leurs rapports dans l'oeuvre d'Ernest Renan* (Paris: Klincksieck, 1977), pp.181–4, 201–4.

8   See the chapter on 'Fiction Christ' in David C. J. Lee, *Ernest Renan: In the Shadow of Faith* (London: Duckworth, 1996), pp.187–206.

9   David Friedrich Strauss, *A New Life of Jesus*, I (London: Williams and Norgate, 1865), p.xviii.

10   Albert Schweitzer, *The Quest of the Historical Jesus*, 1st complete edn, trans. of 2nd German edn, edited by John Bowden (Minneapolis: Fortress, 2001), pp.167, 479.

11   Rogers Brubaker, *Citizenship and Nationhood* (Cambridge, MA: Harvard University Press, 1992), pp.101–2.

12   Schweitzer, *Quest of the Historical Jesus*, p.167.

13   Edward W. Said, *Orientalism* (New York: Random House, 1978), pp.131–50.

14   Said discusses Renan's *Life of Jesus* briefly, but only with regard to the relation between narrative form and history, in Edward Said, *Beginnings: Intention and Method* (New York: Columbia University Press, 1975), pp.215–22.

15   Susannah Heschel, *Abraham Geiger and the Jewish Jesus* (Chicago: Chicago University Press, 1998), pp.154–8.

16 See T. R. Wright, 'The letter and the spirit: Deconstructing Renan's *Life of Jesus* and the assumptions of modernity', *Religion and Literature* 26 (1994), pp.55–74; Eben Scheffler, 'Ernest Renan's Jesus: an appraisal', *Neotestamentica* 33 (1999), pp.179–97.

17 Renan, *Life of Jesus*, p.297.

18 Said, *Orientalism*, pp.42–3, 76–88.

19 9 November 1860; Ernest Renan, *Letters from the Holy Land*, trans. by Lorenzo O'Rourke (New York: Doubleday, 1904), p.148.

20 12 September 1861; E. Renan and M. Berthelot, *Correspondance: 1847–1892* (Paris: Calmann-Lévy, 1898), pp.283–5.

21 25 January 1861; Renan, *Letters*, p.155.

22 9 November 1860; Ibid., p.147.

23 See Renan, *Letters* and Renan and Berthelot: *Correspondance*.

24 Quotations are from Renan, *Life of Jesus*, p.61 [my italics].

25 Ibid.

26 Ibid.

27 Ibid., p.62.

28 Renan, *Life of Jesus*, pp.62–4.

29 Lee, *Ernest Renan*, pp.188, 292, n. 3–4.

30 Renan, *Life of Jesus*, pp.62–4.

31 Said, *Orientalism*, p.143.

32 Cf. Said who speaks of it as 'a dead … Oriental biography' (*Orientalism*, p.146).

33 Daniel L. Pals, *The Victorian 'Lives' of Jesus* (San Antonio: Trinity University Press, 1982), p.37.

34 Said, *Orientalism*, pp.149–50.

35 Henri Baudet, *Paradise on Earth: Some Thoughts on European Images of Non-European Man* (New Haven and London: Yale University Press, 1965), p.vi.

36 Thomas Hauschild, 'Christians, Jews and the Other in German Anthropology', *American Anthropologist* 99 (1997), p.746.

37 Olender, *The Languages of Paradise*, p.16.

38 8 March 1861, Renan, *Letters*, pp.163–5.

39 19 April 1861, ibid., p.170.

40 Ibid.

41 Schweitzer, *Quest of the Historical Jesus*, pp.159–60.

42 Yehoshua Ben-Arieh, 'Nineteenth-century historical geographies of the Holy Land', *Journal of Historical Geography* 15 (1989), pp.69–79.

43 From Herder's *Reason in History* (1830) as quoted by Olender, *The Languages of Paradise*, pp.10–11.

44 Renan, *Life of Jesus*, p.86.

45 Ibid.

46   Ibid., p.173.

47   Ibid., p.187.

48   9 November 1860, Renan, *Letters*, p.155.

49   Said, *Orientalism*, pp.228–9.

50   Renan, *Life of Jesus*, p.173.

51   Ibid., p.173.

52   Ibid., p.116.

53   Ibid., p.118.

54   Ibid., p.87.

55   Ibid., p.214.

56   Ibid.

57   Ibid., pp.114–15.

58   Ibid., p.170.

59   Rétat, *Religion et imagination religieuse*, p.186. On the history of the relation between climate and national character see Joep Leersen, *National Thought in Europe: A Cultural History* (Amsterdam: Amsterdam University Press, 2006), pp.65–70.

60   Renan, *Life of Jesus*, p.87.

61   Ibid., p.89.

62   Ibid., pp.64–5.

63   Ibid., see chs 7, 11 and 17.

64   Ibid., p.269.

65   Ibid., p.116.

66   Ibid., pp.198–204.

67   References to Renan, *Oeuvres*, vol. 8, pp.150, 581 are from Olender, *Languages of Paradise*, pp.64–5.

68   Susannah Heschel, *The Aryan Jesus: Christianity, Nazis and the Bible* (Princeton: Princeton University Press, 2007), pp.34–5.

69   Renan, *Life of Jesus*, pp.194–5.

70   Mark 12:13–17.

71   Ernest Renan, *Qu'est-ce qu'une nation? What is a Nation?* Intro. by Charles Taylor, trans. by W. R. Taylor (Toronto: Tapir, 1996).

72   Renan, *What is a Nation?*, pp.42–5; quotations are from pp.48–50.

73   Glenn H. Roe, 'Contre Taine et Renan: Charles Péguy and the metaphysics of modern history', *French Forum* xxxiv/2 (2009), pp.17–37.

74   Renan, *Life of Jesus*, p.116.

75   Ibid., p.154.

76   Ibid., pp.154–55.

77   Ibid., p.157.

78   Ibid., p.116.

79   Renan, *Life of Jesus*, pp.157–58 [my emphasis].

80   Albert Schweitzer, *The Mystery of the Kingdom of God* (New York: Dood, Mead and Co., 1914), p.122.

81   Albert Schweitzer, *The Kingdom of God and Primitive Christianity*, ed. by U. Neuenschwander (London: Adam and Charles Black, 1968), p.100.

82   John D. Caputo, *The Weakness of God: A Theology of the Event* (Bloomington, IN: Indiana University Press, 2006), p.107.

83   Renan, *Life of Jesus*, pp.89–90.

84   See above pp.43–44.

85   Renan, *Life of Jesus*, p.83.

86   See Chapter IV, pp.115–118.

87   So also Strauss; see Chapter IV, p.111.

88   See Heschel, *Aryan Jesus*.

89   Renan, *What is a Nation?*, pp.26–35.

90   Ibid., pp.34–5 [my emphasis].

91   Renan, *Life of Jesus*, pp.81–8.

92   Ibid., pp.213–26.

93   Ibid., p.218.

94   Renan, *Life of Jesus*, pp.225–6.

95   W. D. Whitney, 'On the so-called science of religion', *Princeton Review* 57 (1881), pp.429–52; from J. Z. Smith, 'Religion, religions, religious', in M. C. Taylor (ed.), *Critical Terms for Religious Studies* (Chicago: Chicago University Press, 1998), pp.276–9.

96   See Brubaker, *Citizenship and Nationhood*, pp.101–2.

97   Warman, *Ernest Renan*, pp.117–28.

98   D. F. Strauss, *Krieg und Friede: Zwei Briefe an Ernst [sic] Renan, Nebst dessen Antwort auf den Ersten* (Leipzig: Hirzel, 1870), p.53.

99   Ernest Renan, 'Nouvelle lettre à M. Strauss,' in Henriette Psichari (ed.), *Oeuvres complètes* I (Paris: Calmann-Lévy, 1947), p.456 [my trans].

100 I. Geiss, *The Question of German Unification 1806–1996* (London and New York: Routledge, 1997), pp.35–68.

101 Renan, 'Nouvelle lettre à M. Strauss', p.456. See Hannah Arendt, *The Origins of Totalitarianism*, new edn (New York: Harcourt, Brace and World, 1966), pp.158–61.

102 Brubaker, *Citizenship and Nationhood*, pp.50–72, 114–15.

103 Shawn Kelley, *Racializing Jesus: Race, Ideology and the Formation of Modern Biblical Scholarship* (London and New York: Routledge, 2002), pp.35–9.

104 Jürgen Habermas, *The Postnational Constellation: Political Essays*, trans, ed. and with intro. by Max Pensky (Cambridge: Polity, 2001), pp.5–14.

105 Renan, *What is a Nation?*, pp.10–11.

106 Brubaker, *Citizenship and Nationhood*, p.2.

107 Ibid., pp.98–102.

108 The (false) conviction of Alfred Dreyfus, a French officer of Alsatian Jewish descent, for treason by giving military secrets to the Germans created a political scandal in France in the 1890s and early 1900s, and revealed a strong antisemitism in France. See A. S. Lindemann, *The Jew Accused: Three Anti-Semitic Affairs: Dreyfus, Beilis, Frank, 1894–1915* (Cambridge: Cambridge University Press, 1991), pp.88–93.

109 See the statement by Viviane Reading, EU Commissioner for Justice, Fundamental Rights and Citizenship, press briefing on 14 September 2010, online at http://europa. eu/rapid/pressReleasesAction.do?reference=SPEECH/10/428&format=HTML&aged= 0&language=EN&guiLanguage=en.

110 Kenan Malik, *The Meaning of Race: Race, History and Culture in Western Society* (London: MacMillan, 1996), pp.130–3.

111 Olender, *Languages of Paradise*, pp.57–63; S. Almog, 'The racial motif in Renan's attitude to Jews and Judaism', in S. Almog (ed.), *Anti-Semitism Through the Ages* (Oxford: Pergamon Press, 1988), pp.255–78; esp. pp.268, 273–5.

112 Malik, *The Meaning of Race*, pp.71–100.

113 See Olender, *Languages of Paradise*.

114 Renan, *Life of Jesus*, p.70, n.1.

115 Said, *Orientalism*, pp.141–2, 150; Heschel, *Abraham Geiger*, pp.154–8.

116 Heschel, *Aryan Jesus*, pp.33–8; quotation from p.36.

117 Renan, *Life of Jesus*, p.225.

118 Renan, *What is a Nation?*, pp.27–8.

119 See Chapter II, pp.43–44.

120 Brubaker, *Citizenship and Nationhood*, pp.119–22.

121 Olender, *Languages of Paradise*, pp.63–8; Said, *Orientalism*, pp.145–8.

122 See Chapter IV.

123 See Kelley, *Racializing Jesus*.

124 Ibid., p.213.

125 Ibid., p.214.

126 However, Kelley, who presents Renan's system of Indo-European versus Semitic languages and races, does not discuss his *Life of Jesus* (*Racializing Jesus*, pp.84–7).

127 Mike Hill, *After Whiteness: Unmaking an American Majority* (New York: New York University Press, 2004), p.7.

128 For an insightful discussion of this dilemma, see Marianne Gullestad, *Plausible Prejudice: Everyday Experiences and Social Images of Nation, Culture and Race* (Oslo: Universitetsforlaget, 2006).

Chapter VI: The Manly Nation

1 Björn Hettne, Sverker Sörlin, Uffe Østergård, *Den globala nationalismen: nationalstatens historia och framtid*, 2nd edn (Stockholm: SNS Förlag, 2006), pp.24–6.

2 Linda Colley, *Britons: Forging the Nation 1707–1837* (London: Pimlico, 2003), p.54.

3 John Horne points out how in the nineteenth century national identities were frequently described by help of male roles and characteristics; see John Horne 'Masculinity in politics and war in the age of the nation-state and word wars, 1850–1950', in S. Dudink, K. Hagemann and J. Tosh (eds), *Masculinities in Politics and War: Gendering Modern History* (Manchester: Manchester University Press, 2004), pp.23–30.

4 John Tosh, 'Hegemonic masculinity and the history of gender', in S. Dudink, K. Hagemann and J. Tosh (eds), *Masculinities in Politics and War: Gendering Modern History* (Manchester: Manchester University Press, 2004), p.47.

5 George L. Mosse, *Nationalism and Sexuality: Respectability and Abnormal Sexuality in Modern Europe* (New York: H. Fertig, 1985), p.182. See also Peter Caminos, 'Late-Victorian sexual respectability and the social system', *International Review of Social History* 8 (1963), pp.18–48.

6 George Adam Smith, *The Historical Geography of the Holy Land* (London: Hodder and Stoughton, 1st edn 1894; 16th edn 1910).

7 Somewhat surprisingly, except for his wife's memoir – Lilian Adam Smith, *George Adam Smith: A Personal Memoir and Family Chronicle* (London: Hodder and Stoughton, 1943) – there has been no major study of his life and career before Iain D. Campbell, *Fixing the Indemnity: The Life and Work of Sir George Adam Smith (1956–1942)* (Milton Keynes: Paternoster, 2004). Edwin J. Aiken discusses Smith's *The Historical Geography of the Holy Land* in the context of how geographies of the Holy Land in the nineteenth century responded to the intellectual and social situation of the time, especially the dissonance between faith and science, in *Scriptural Geography: Portraying the Holy Land* (London: I.B.Tauris, 2010), pp.133–85.

8 See Hermione Lee, *Body-Parts: Essays on Life-Writing* (London: Chatto and Windus, 2005), pp.1–5.

9 Benedict Anderson, *Imagined Communities: Reflections on the Origin and Spread of Nationalism* (London: Verso, 1983), p.30.

10 For a review of these books, see Daniel L. Pals, *The Victorian 'Lives' of Jesus* (San Antonio, TX: Trinity University Press, 1982).

11 John Robert Seeley, *Ecce Homo: A Survey of the Life and Work of Jesus Christ* (London: MacMillan, 1865).

12 Pals, *Victorian 'Lives' of Jesus*, pp.39–50.

13 Frederic W. Farrar, *The Life of Christ* (London: Cassell, Petter and Galpin, 1874). In the Preface, Farrar explicitly states that 'this Life of Christ is avowedly and unconditionally the work of a believer' (p.9).

14 Later books by Smith include *Jerusalem: The Topography, Economics and History from the Earliest Times to A.D. 70* (London: Hodder and Stoughton, 1907–8) and *Atlas to The Historical Geography* (London: Hodder and Stoughton, 1915).

15   See Chapter II, pp.46–50.

16   See Robin Butlin, 'George Adam Smith and the historical geography of the Holy Land: Contents, contexts and connections', *Journal of Historical Geography* 14 (1988), pp.392–6.

17   Ibid., pp.387–9.

18   This and the quotation that follows are from Smith, *Historical Geography*, p.112.

19   See Campbell: *Fixing the Indemnity*, pp.214–17.

20   Stephen Reicher and Nick Hopkins, *Self and Nation: Categorization, Contestation and Mobilization* (London: Sage Publications, 2001).

21   Ibid., pp.100–30.

22   Ibid., p.117.

23   Smith, *Historical Geography*, pp.29–34.

24   Ibid., p.21.

25   Ibid., p.19 [my emphasis].

26   Beshara B. Doumani, 'Rediscovering Ottoman Palestine', p.24, n.5.

27   Smith, *Historical Geography*, p.112. Notice the similarities between this description of Israel and Smith's description of Scotland in his farewell remarks at a dinner in his honour when he left Glasgow for Aberdeen in 1910: 'We, almost the smallest people on earth ... Much of the eloquence and humanity of Scottish literature has sprung from the national experience of migration and of exile. We Scots have been, as much as Israel, "a people of dispersion". In addition we have had our share in building an Empire resting on all the continents'; Lilian Adam Smith, *George Adam Smith*, pp.110–11.

28   See Smith, *Historical Geography*, pp.34–9.

29   See Chapter V.

30   In the 25th edn of *Historical Geography* (1931), Smith writes about the war in 1914–18, especially about Allenbys' campaign (pp.408–11).

31   R. D. Kernohan, *The Road to Zion: Travellers to Palestine and the Land of Israel* (Edinburgh: Handsel Press, 1995), pp.111–12.

32   George Adam Smith, *Modern Criticism and the Preaching of the Old Testament* (London: Hodder and Stoughton, 1901), pp.272–4.

33   Smith, *Modern Criticism*, p.273.

34   See George Adam Smith, *Jeremiah: Being the Baird Lecture for 1922* (London: Hodder and Stoughton, 1923), p.7

35   Patrick Joyce, *Democratic Subjects: The Self and the Social in Nineteenth Century England* (Cambridge: Cambridge University Press, 1994), p.19.

36   Stefan Collini, *Public Moralists: Political Thought and Intellectual Life in Britain 1850–1930* (Oxford: Clarendon, 1991), pp.60–90; quotations from pp.62–3.

37   Ibid.

38   Campbell (*Fixing the Indemnity*, pp.61–2) emphasizes that 'Smith was concerned to draw a distinction between altruism and evangelicalism', in that he held that one should

first establish a relation to God before that to one's fellow men. But Campbell also underlines how social concern grows out of faith, and the Gospel brings a 'new sacredness upon common life'. It is this direction of faith towards 'common life' that makes it relevant to see in Smith's writing a contribution to the discussion of altruism from an evangelical perspective.

39   Smith, *Historical Geography*, p.114.

40   Ibid., pp.34–5.

41   Ibid., p.36.

42   This was a popular religious topic in that period. See a number of contemporary British books on the subject: Norman Macleod, *The Temptation of Our Lord* (London: Strahan and Co., 1873); George S. Barrett, *The Temptation of Christ* (Edinburgh: Macniven and Wallace, 1883); and Stewart A. Morris, *The Temptation of Jesus: A Study of Our Lord's Trial in the Wilderness* (London: Andrew Melrose, 1903).

43   Smith, *Historical Geography*, p.114. Galilee is presented in two chapters in Smith's *Historical Geography*. Chapter XX provides an overview of all of Galilee (pp.413–35), then Chapter XXI takes a closer look of the Lake of Galilee as the central part of the region (pp.439–63).

44   See discussions of Schleiermacher in Chapter III and Strauss in Chapter IV. Cf. Smith's treatment of the political situation in *Jerusalem* I, pp.411–34.

45   Smith discusses this briefly in *Historical Geography*, p.414.

46   Ibid., pp.425–31.

47   Notice how Smith made use of the previously unused records of Napoleon's invasion in Syria in 1799 (*Historical Geography*, p.xiii), and his descriptions of Allenby's warfare, *Historical Geography* (25th rev. edn, 1931), pp.285–6, 408–11.

48   Smith, *Historical Geography*, pp.431–2 [my emphasis].

49   Ibid., pp.591–608. The title of this chapter indicates Smith's perspective: 'Greece Over Jordan: The Decapolis'.

50   Ibid., p.608, my italics.

51   None of the contemporary meanings of 'gay' were present in the word at the time of Smith.

52   Smith, *Historical Geography*, pp.431–2 [my emphasis].

53   See R. Jenkyns, *The Victorians and Ancient Greece* (Oxford: Blackwell,1980).

54   Tristram Hunt, *Building Jerusalem: The Rise and Fall of the Victorian City* (London: Weidenfeld and Nicolson, 2004).

55   Jenkyns, *The Victorians and Ancient Greece*, pp.67–73.

56   For the following see Linda Dowling, *Hellenism and Homosexuality in Victorian Oxford* (Ithaca: Cornell University Press, 1994), esp. pp.5–25, 56–62.

57   David J. DeLaura, *Hebrew and Hellene in Victorian England: Newman, Arnold and Pater* (Austin,TX: University of Texas Press, 1969). Cf. how the relation between emotions and landscape is reflected in paintings in A.Wilton and R. Upstone (eds), *The Age of*

Rossetti, Byrne-Jones and Watts: Symbolism in Britain 1860–1900 (London: Tate Gallery, 1997), pp.174–85.

58   G. Murray, *A History of Ancient Greek Literature* (New York: Appleton and Company, 1897), Preface, quoted in Jenkyns, *The Victorians and Ancient Greece*, p.294.

59   A phrase attributed to Pater in Jenkyns, *The Victorians and Ancient Greece*, p.295.

60   John Addington Symonds in ibid., p.297.

61   Robert W. Buchanan, 'The Fleshy School of Poetry: Mr. D. G. Rossetti', *The Contemporary Review* 18 (1871), now available online at http://www.victorianweb.org/authors/buchanan/fleshy.html.

62   Smith, *Historical Geography*, p.432.

63   George Adam Smith, *Christianity and Social Life: A Course of Lectures* (Edinburgh: Macniven and Wallace, 1885), pp.69–70.

64   Smith, *Historical Geography*, p.30.

65   Ibid., p.433.

66   Cf. the way Renan spoke of Galilee as 'the fifth Gospel', see Chapter V.

67   See Chapter V, pp.132–134.

68   Smith, *Historical Geography*, p.433.

69   Ibid., p.434.

70   See Halvor Moxnes, 'The construction of Galilee as a place for the historical Jesus', *BTB* 31 (2001), pp.64–77.

71   Smith, *Historical Geography*, pp.434–5, my italics.

72   See Farrar, *Life of Christ*; see also Pals, *Victorian 'Lives'*, pp.81–5.

73   See, for example, Farrar, *Life of Christ*, p.65: 'in some recess in the wall is placed the wooden chest, painted with bright colours, which contains the books or other possessions of the family'.

74   Farrar, *Life of Christ*, p.83.

75   Ibid., p.87.

76   Quotations from ibid., p.82

77   Thomas Hughes, *The Manliness of Christ* (London: Macmillan and Co.,1879), pp.56–7.

78   Peter Gay, 'The manliness of Christ,' in R. W. Davis and R. J. Helmstadter (eds), *Religion and Irreligion in Victorian Society: Essays in Honour of R. K. Webb* (London: Routledge, 1992), pp.102–16.

79   Collini, *Public Moralists*, p.105.

80   Richard Allan Riesen, *Criticism and Faith in Late Victorian Scotland: A. B. Davidson, William Robertson Smith and George Adam Smith* (New York and London: Lanham, 1985), p.43.

81   See George Adam Smith, *The Forgiveness of Sins and Other Sermons* (London: Hodder and Stoughton, 1904).

82   Smith, *Forgiveness of Sins*, pp.66–7.

83 Walter E. Houghton, *Victorian Frame of Mind 1830–1870* (New Haven: Yale University Press, 1957), pp.233–4.

84 The phrase 'unlawful curiosity' is possibly a reference to witchcraft and demonology, to try to get insight by illegal means. This terminology is used in Walter Scott, *Letters on Demonology and Witchcraft*, 2nd edn (London: Routledge, 1885). Smith refers to necromancy as an example of 'base other-worldiness', in *Modern Criticism*, p.269.

85 See n.71.

86 This emphasis upon Jesus as an example and ideal represents a shift in religious attitudes to Jesus, away from an earlier, more dogmatic focus on the atonement through Jesus' suffering and death; John Tosh, *A Man's Place: Masculinities and the Middle-Class Home in Victorian England* (New Haven and London: Yale University Press, 1999), p.147.

87 See Tosh, *A Man's Place* and Neville Kirk, *Change, Continuity and Class: Labour in British Society, 1850–1920* (Manchester and New York: Manchester University Press, 1998), pp.117–20; 254–61.

88 Cf. the well-known poems by Coventry Kersey Dighton Patmore, *The Angel in the House* (London: John W. Parker and Son, 1854–6).

89 Tosh, *A Man's Place*, pp.145–69.

90 See Felix Driver, 'Moral geographies: Social science and the urban environment in mid-nineteenth century England', *Transactions of the Institute of British Geographers* NS 13 (1988), pp.275–87; quotation from p.279.

91 Kirk, *Change, Continuity and Class*, pp.117–20, 254–61.

92 See A. C. Cheyne, *The Transforming of the Kirk: Victorian Scotland's Religious Revolution* (Edinburgh: St Andrew Press, 1983), pp.110–15.

93 Smith, *Christianity and Social Life*, pp.65, 67 [my emphasis].

94 Tosh, *A Man's Place*, p.85.

95 Quotation from F. Knight, '"Male and Female He created Them": Men, Women and the Question of Gender', in J. Wolffe (ed.) *Religion in Victorian Britain, V: Culture and Empire* (Manchester and New York: Manchester University Press, 1997), p.39.

96 See especially Hughes, *The Manliness of Christ*. Notice the structure of the book that shows the importance of this association between resistance to temptations and manliness. Between ch. 1, 'The Holy Land AD30', and ch. 3, 'Christ's Boyhood,' is ch. 2, on 'The Tests of Manliness', pp.23–40.

97 Mosse, *Nationalism and Sexuality*, p.81.

98 Tosh, *A Man's Place*, pp.107–8.

99 Sue Morgan, '"Writing the male body": Sexual purity and masculinity in *The Vanguard*, 1884–94', in Andrew Bradstock, Sean Gill, Anne Hogan and Sue Morgan (eds), *Masculinity and Spirituality in Victorian Culture* (Basingstoke and London: MacMillan, 2000), p.190.

100 See the description of living conditions for the poor in Glasgow in the period between 1841 and 1914, in Andrew Gibb, *Glasgow: The Making of a City* (London: Croom Helm, 1983), pp.115–45.

101 Written by Joseph M. Scriven in 1855.

102 Smith, *Historical Geography*, p.435.

103 See Tosh, *A Man's Place*, pp.115–19.

104 Thomas Winter, *Making Men, Making Class: The YMCA and Workingmen, 1877–1920* (Chicago and London: Chicago University Press, 2002), pp.55–7.

105 See Sydney and Olive Checkland, *Industry and Ethos: Scotland 1832–1914*, The New History of Scotland, VII (London: Edward Arnold, 1984), pp.14–20.

106 See Ian Donnachie, 'The Enterprising Scot', in I. Donnachie and C. Whatley (eds), *The Manufacture of Scottish History* (Edinburgh: Polygon, 1992), pp.90–105.

107 See Winter, *Making Men*, p.56.

108 Smith, *Historical Geography*, pp.473–8.

109 Ibid., p.476.

110 Ibid., p.478.

111 Ibid., p.479.

112 Ibid.

113 Ibid.

114 Ibid., p.312.

115 For a discussion of Smith's presentation of the fishermen at the Lake of Gennesareth see H. Moxnes, 'George Adam Smith and the moral geography of Galilee', in Zuleika Rodgers, Margaret Daly-Denton and Anne Fitzpatrick McKinley (eds), *A Wandering Galilean: Essays in Honour of Seán Freyne* (Leiden: Brill, 2009), pp.237–78.

116 See Donald E. Hall (ed.), *Muscular Christianity: Embodying the Victorian Age* (Cambridge: Cambridge University Press, 1994).

117 P. J. Walker, '"I live not yet I for Christ liveth in me": Men and masculinities in the Salvation Army, 1865–90', in M. Roper and J. Tosh (eds), *Manful Assertions: Masculinities in Britain since 1800* (London and New York: Routledge, 1991), pp.92–112.

118 Hughes, *The Manliness of Christ*; see the discussion in Gay: 'The manliness of Christ'.

119 S. Curtis, 'The Son of Man and God the Father: The social gospel and Victorian masculinity', in Mark C. Carnes and C. Griffin (eds), *Meanings of Manhood: Constructions of Masculinity in Victorian America* (Chicago and London: University of Chicago Press, 1990), p.72; Winter, *Making Men*, pp.58–9.

120 For Charles Kingsley, the 'father' of 'muscular Christianity', see Gay: 'Manliness of Christ', pp.113–15.

121 See Anderson, *Imagined Communities*.

122 See David Roberts, *Jerusalem and the Holy Land Rediscovered: The Prints of David Roberts (1796–1864)*, contrib. by W. D. Davies, Eric M. Meyers and S. Walker Schroth, Foreword by M. P. Mezzatesta (Durham, NC: Duke University Museum of Art, 1996).

123 S. Dudink, K. Hagemann and J. Tosh (eds), *Masculinities in Politics and War: Gendering Modern History* (Manchester: Manchester University Press, 2004).

124 Charles Kingsley, *His Letters and Memoires of his Life*, 12th edn, vol. II (London: Kegan Paul, 1878), p.260. See also Normann Vance, *The Sinews of the Spirit: The Ideal of Christian Manliness in Victorian Literature and Religious Thought* (Cambridge: Cambridge University Press, 1985).

125 Smith, *Historical Geography*, p.311.

126 Cf. the immensely popular *The Light of the World* by Holman Hunt, 1900–04.

127 It is surprising that, in the texts of Smith that I have been able to find, there are few traces of his long collaboration with working-class women and their organizations.

128 See Charles Taylor, *Modern Social Imaginaries* (Durham and London: Duke University Press, 2004), esp. pp.23–30.

Chapter VII: Jesus Beyond Nationalism

1   This chapter is inspired by the contributions in Halvor Moxnes, Ward Blanton and James G. Crossley (eds), *Jesus Beyond Nationalism: Constructing the Historical Jesus in a Period of Cultural Complexity* (London: Equinox, 2009).

2   From Oscar Wilde, 'The Soul of Man under Socialism', quoted in Umut Özkirimli, *Contemporary Debates on Nationalism: A Critical Engagement* (Basingstoke and New York: Palgrave MacMillan, 2005), p.205.

3   See Leif E. Vaage, 'Beyond nationalism: "Jesus the Holy Anarchist"? The Cynic Jesus as eternal recurrence of the repressed', in Moxnes et al. (eds), *Jesus Beyond Nationalism*, pp.92–5.

4   Jo Burr Margadant, 'Introduction: Constructing selves in historical perspective', in J. B. Margadant (ed.), *The New Biography: Performing Femininity in Nineteenth-Century France* (Berkeley: University of California Press, 2000), p.7.

5   Lois W. Banner, 'Biography as history', *American Historical Review* 114 (2009), p.582.

6   Hermione Lee, *Body-Parts: Essays on Life-Writing* (London: Chatto and Windus, 2005), pp.1–5.

7   J. Schläger, 'Biography: Cult as culture', in J. Batchelor (ed.), *The Art of Literary Biography* (Oxford: Carendon, 1995), pp.57–71.

8   David Nasaw, 'Historians and biography: Introduction', *American Historical Review* 114 (2009), p.577.

9   See Halvor Moxnes, *Putting Jesus in His Place: A Radical Vision of Household and Kingdom* (Louisville: Westminster John Knox, 2003).

10   Jonathan Z. Smith, *To Take Place* (Chicago: University of Chicago Press, 1992), p.30.

11   This question reflects that at the same time as a person is situated in a context, he or she is also an agent within a social field; cf. the discussion of Bourdieu on biography in Stephen J. Walton, *Skaff deg eit liv! Om biografi*, 2nd edn (Oslo: Samlaget, 2009), pp.194–6.

12   Michel Foucault, *The Use of Pleasure, The History of Sexuality* II (New York: Pantheon, 1985), pp.9–10.

13   John D. Caputo, *What Would Jesus Deconstruct? The Good News of Post-Modernism for the Church* (Grand Rapids, MI: Baker Academic, 2007).

14   Charles Sheldon, *In His Steps: What Would Jesus Do?* (New York: Grosset and Dunlop, 1896).

15   Caputo, *What Would Jesus Deconstruct?*, pp.81–116.

16   Renan, for instance, saw the idea of nationality that spread from the French Revolution as a major driving force in the liberation movements in southern and eastern Europe in the nineteenth century; see Ernest Renan, 'Nouvelle lettre à M. Strauss', in Henriette Psichari (ed.), *Oeuvres complètes* I, p.453.

17   Kevin Lynch, 'Another New World Order', The Globe essay on 'Drivers of Change'; *Globe and Mail*, 4 September 2010, A.15.

18   Özkirimli, *Contemporary Debates on Nationalism*.

19   Ibid., pp.195–205.

20   Even if it is new practices and symbols of gender roles, family structures and sexuality among the majority population that have introduced the most dramatic changes in European societies, it is the arrival of people from 'the outside' that has sparked the discussion of 'national identity'. See Marianne Gullestad, *Plausible Prejudice: Everyday Experiences and Social Images of Nation, Culture and Race* (Oslo: Universitetsforlaget, 2006), p.122.

21   B. Lincoln, *Discourse and the Construction of Society: Comparative Studies of Myth, Ritual, and Classification* (New York and Oxford: Oxford University Press, 1989), p.174.

22   Gullestad, *Plausible Prejudice*, pp.209–10.

23   See Thomas Hylland Eriksen, *Ethnicity and Nationalism*, 2nd edn (Pluto: London, 2002).

24   See Halvor Moxnes, 'Identity in Jesus' Galilee – From ethnicity to locative intersectionality', *Biblical Interpretation* (2010), pp.390–416.

25   The position of a diverse Galilean identity has been argued in a number of studies by Richard A. Horsley; see *Galilee, History, Politics, People* (Valley Forge: PA: Trinity, 1995). More recently, see M. Moreland, 'The inhabitants of Galilee in the Hellenistic and Early Roman Periods', in J. Zangenberg, H. W. Attridge and D. B. Martin (eds), *Religion, Ethnicity, and Identity in Ancient Galilee* (Tübingen: Mohr Siebeck, 2007), pp.33–59. Related to the theory of a diverse Galilean identity is the suggestion that Jesus could be compared to Cynic preachers, for a summary of that position and of its critics, see Vaage: 'Jesus the Holy Anarchist', pp.86–92.

26   M. Chancey, *The Myth of a Gentile Galilee* (Cambridge: Cambridge University Press, 2002), p.182.

27   John S. Kloppenborg Verbin, *Excavating Q: The History and Setting of the Sayings Gospel* (Edinburgh: T. and T. Clark, 2000), pp.435–6.

28   Jonathan L. Reed, *Archaeology and the Galilean Jesus* (Harrisburg, PA: Trinity, 2000), pp.62–99, 216–18.

29   Sian Jones, in *The Archaeology of Ethnicity: Constructing Identities in the Past and Present* (London: Routledge, 1997), studies and questions how the modern concept of ethnicity is used in contemporary archaeology to construct modern identities, based on a perceived continuity between the past and the present. Jones points out how such construc-

tions are often used to legitimate cultural identities among present people by tracing their imagined origins.

30   See William E. Arnal, *The Symbolic Jesus: Historical Scholarship, Judaism and the Construction of Contemporary Identity* (London: Equinox, 2005).

31   See the description of 'cultural complexity' in Thomas Hylland Eriksen, 'What is cultural complexity?' in Moxnes et al. (eds): *Jesus Beyond Nationalism*, pp.9–10: 'The term connotes the coexistence of two or several cultural traditions, their permutations and their anti-traditions (negations through simple dialectical negotiation). Mixing, reinterpretation and resistance to mixing and reinterpretation are part and parcel of any culturally complex situation and contribute to making it volatile. A challenge for contemporary societies consists in balancing opposing identity claims and creating non-confrontational spaces for encounters and dialogue.'

32   William E. Arnal, 'Jesus as battleground in a period of cultural complexity', in Moxnes et al. (eds): *Jesus Beyond Nationalism*, p.101 [my emphasis].

33   Ibid., p.110.

34   Virgilio Elizondo, *Galilean Journey: The Mexican Promise* (Maryknoll, NY: Orbis, 1983).

35   It is this historical perspective that makes Elizondo's book part of the historical Jesus' debate, even if the book does not represent an independent contribution to historical Jesus research. See the discussion in Michael E. Lee, '*Galilean Journey* revisited: Mestizaje, anti-Judaism, and the dynamics of exclusion', *Theological Studies* 70 (2009), pp.377–400.

36   Elizondo, *Galilean Journey*, p.51.

37   Ibid., p.58.

38   Virgilio Elizondo, 'Jesus the Galilean Jew in Mestizo Theology', *Theological Studies* 70 (2009), p.274.

39   Jean-Pierre Ruiz, 'Good fences and good neighbors? Biblical scholars and theologians', *Journal of Hispanic/Latino Theology* 14 (May 2007), online at http://www.latinotheology.org/2007/fences_neighbors; Jeffrey S. Siker, 'Historizing a racialized Jesus: Case studies in the "Black Christ", the "Mestizo Christ", and white critique', *Biblical Interpretation* 15 (2007), pp.26–53; but see also Lee, '*Galilean Journey* revisited', pp.387–91.

40   The book was based on his doctoral dissertation *Métissage, violence culturelle, annonce de l'évangile* from Institut Catholique in Paris in 1978.

41   Elizondo, 'Jesus the Galilean', p.279.

42   For an introduction to such perspectives, see K. C. Hanson and Douglas E. Oakman, *Palestine in the Time of Jesus: Social Structures and Social Conflicts*, 2nd edn (Minneapolis: Fortress, 2008).

43   See Moxnes, *Putting Jesus in His Place*, pp.91–107.

44   See Jennifer C. Nash, 'Re-thinking intersectionality', *Feminist Review* 89 (2008), pp.1–15; Kathy Davis, 'Intersectionality as buzzword: A sociology of science perspective on what makes a feminist theory successful', *Feminist Theory* 9 (2008), pp.67–83.

45   See the report by Ms Radhika Coomaraswamy, Special Rapporteur of the Commission on Human Rights on Violence Against Women, to the World Conference Against Racism, Racial Discrimination, Xenophobia And Related Intolerance, Geneva, 30 July–

10 August 2001, available online at http://www.unhchr.ch/huridocda/huridoca.nsf/ (Symbol)/A.CONF.189.PC.3.5.En.

The present Rapporteur, Rashida Manjoo, will present a new thematic report to the Human Rights Council in June 2011. Manjoo's report will focus on intersectional forms of discrimination in the context of violence against women, see http://intlawgrrls.blogspot. com/2010/09/intersectionality-and-un-special.html.

46 Özkirimli, *Contemporary Debates on Nationalism*, p.201.

47 Ibid., p.205.

48 See Gullestad, *Plausible Prejudice*, pp.93–125.

49 This combination of national identity and family values may be most vigorously expressed in the USA. See Carolyn Osiek, 'The family in early Christianity: Family values revisited', *Catholic Biblical Quarterly* 58 (1996), pp.1–24.

50 Elisabeth Schüssler Fiorenza, *Jesus and the Politics of Interpretation* (New York and London: Continuum, 2000), quotations from pp.24, 27.

51 See Moxnes, *Putting Jesus in His Place*, pp.22–71.

52 See Herman E. Daly and John B. Cobb, *For the Common Good: Redirecting the Economy toward Community, the Environment, and a Sustainable Future* (Boston: Beacon Press, 1994), pp.138–58.

53 See Halvor Moxnes, *The Economy of the Kingdom: Social Conflict and Economic Relations in Luke's Gospel* (Philadelphia: Fortress, 1988).

54 This is not only true of so-called 'banana-republics'; in the USA 1% of the population earns 23,5% of the nation's income; and there is a very strong political opposition to use public money for systems of health care, pensions and schooling for the poor; see Jacob S. Hacker and Paul Pierson, *Winner-Take-All Politics: How Washington made the Rich richer and Turned its Back on the Middle Class* (New York: Simon & Schuster, 2010).

55 Alberto Manguel and Gianni Guadalupi, *The Dictionary of Imaginary Places*, rev. edn (Toronto: Knopf, 1999).

56 See Moxnes, *Putting Jesus in his Place*, pp.108–24.

57 Ibid.

58 See John D. Crossan, *In Parables: The Challenge of the Historical Jesus* (New York: Harper and Row, 1973).

59 Ephesians 6:1–3; Colossians 3:20.

60 Caputo, *What would Jesus Deconstruct?*, pp.87–8.

61 John D. Caputo, *The Weakness of God: A Theology of the Event* (Bloomington, IN: Indiana University Press, 2006), p.106.

62 Jürgen Habermas, *The Postnational Constellation: Political Essays*, trans, ed. and with intro. by Max Pensky (Cambridge: Polity, 2001), pp.58–112.

63 See Habermas' essay 'What is a people? The Frankfurt "Germanist Assembly" of 1846 and the self-understanding of the humanities in the Vormärz', in *The Postnational Constellation*, pp.1–25.

64 See Habermas, *The Postnational Constellation*, pp.104–112.

Bibliography

ABBREVIATIONS

BTB	*Biblical Theology Bulletin*
HTR	*Harvard Theological Review*
JR	*Journal of Religion*
JSOTS	Journal for the Study of the Old Testament Supplement
KGA	Schleiermacher, Kritische Gesamtausgabe
NovT	*Novum Testamentum*
Rev TheolPhil	*Revue de Théologie et de Philosophie*
TRE	*Theologische Realenzyklopädie*
TRu	*Theologische Rundschau*

Abverintsev, Sergei, S., 'From biography to hagiography', in France and St Clair (eds), *Mapping Lives*, pp.19–36.

Aiken, Edwin J., *Scriptural Geography: Portraying the Holy Land* (London: I.B.Tauris, 2010).

Almog, S., 'The racial motif in Renan's attitude to Jews and Judaism', in S. Almog (ed.), *Anti-Semitism Through the Ages* (Oxford: Pergamon Press, 1989), pp.255–78.

Anderson, Benedict, *Imagined Communities: Reflections on the Origin and Spread of Nationalism* (London: Verso, 1983).

Appleby, Joyce, Lynn Hunt and Margaret Jacob, *Telling the Truth about History* (New York: Norton, 1994).

Applegate, Celia, *A Nation of Provincials: The German Idea of Heimat* (Berkeley: University of California Press, 1990).

Arendt, Hannah, *The Origins of Totalitarianism* (New York: Harcourt, Brace and World, 1966).

Arnal, William E., 'Jesus as battleground in a period of cultural complexity', Moxnes et al. (eds): *Jesus Beyond Nationalism*, pp.99–117.

—— *The Symbolic Jesus: Historical Scholarship, Judaism and the Construction of Contemporary Identity* (London: Equinox, 2005).

Arndt, Andreas, Ulrich Barth and Wilhelm Gräb (eds), *Christentum – Staat – Kultur: Akten des Kongresses der Internationalen Schleiermacher-Gesellschaft in Berlin, März 2006*, Schleiermacher-Archiv 22 (Berlin: Gruyter, 2008).

Bahr, E., 'Goethes Volkbegriff und der deutsche Nationalismus um 1808', in W. Bialas (ed.), *Die nationale Identität der Deutschen* (Frankfurt: Peter Lang, 2002), pp.195–212.

Banner, Lois W., 'Biography as history', *American Historical Review* 114 (2009), pp.579–86.

Barrett, George S., *The Temptation of Christ* (Edinburgh: Macniven and Wallace, 1883).

Barth, Karl, *From Rousseau to Ritschl* (London: SCM, 1959).

Bar-Yosef, Eitan, *The Holy Land in English Culture 1799–1917: Palestine and the Question of Orientalism* (Oxford: Oxford University Press, 2005).

Baudet, Henri, *Paradise on Earth: Some Thoughts on European Images of Non-European Man* (New Haven and London: Yale University Press, 1965).

Beaver, Adam, 'A Holy Land for the Catholic monarchy: Orientalism in the making of the Spanish Renaissance', Ph.D. diss., Harvard University, 2008.

Bellah, Robert N. (ed.) *Emile Durkheim on Morality and Society* (Chicago: CUP, 1973).

Ben-Arieh, Yehoshua, 'Holy Land views in nineteenth century Western travel literature', in Davis and Ben-Arieh (eds), *With Eyes towards Zion III*, pp.10–29.

——— 'Nineteenth-century historical geographies of the Holy Land', *Journal of Historical Geography* 15 (1989), pp.69–79.

——— *The Rediscovery of the Holy land in the Nineteenth Century* (Jerusalem: Magnum, 1979).

Biger, Gideon, 'The names and boundaries of Eretz-Israel (Palestine) as reflections of stages in its history', in Ruth Kark (ed.), *The Land that Became Israel: Studies in Historical Geography*, trans. M. Gordon (New Haven: Yale University Press, 1990), pp.1–22.

Birch, Jonathan C. P., 'The Road to Reimarus: History, Morality and Political Theology', in K. Whitelam (ed.), *Holy Land as Homeland? Models for constructing the historic landscapes of Jesus* (Sheffield: Sheffield Phoenix Press, forthcoming).

Blanton, Ward, *Displacing Christian Origins: Philosophy, Secularity and the New Testament* (Chicago: University of Chicago Press, 2007).

Brady, Thomas A. Jr., 'The Protestant Reformation in German History', *Occasional Paper No. 22* (Washington, DC: German Historical Institute, 1998).

Breuilly, John, 'Nationalismus als kulturelle Konstruktion,' in Echternkamp and Müller (eds), *Die Politik der Nation*, pp.247–68.

———— 'Nationalism and the history of ideas', *Proceedings of the British Academy* (Oxford: Oxford University Press, 2000), pp.187–223.

Brockhaus' Konversationslexikon, vol. 3, 14th edn (Leipzig: Brockhaus, 1894).

Brubaker, Rogers, *Citizenship and Nationhood* (Cambridge, MA: Harvard University Press, 1992).

Buchanan, Robert W., 'The Fleshy School of Poetry: Mr D. G. Rossetti', *The Contemporary Review* 18 (1871).

Butenschøn, Nils, *Midtøsten: Imperiefall, statsutvikling, kriger* (Oslo: Universitetsforlaget, 2008).

Butlin, Robin, 'George Adam Smith and the historical geography of the Holy Land: Contents, contexts and connections', *Journal of Historical Geography* 14 (1988), pp.381–404.

Caminos, Peter, 'Late-Victorian sexual respectability and the social system', *International Review of Social History* 8 (1963), pp.18–48.

Campbell, Iain D., *Fixing the Indemnity: The Life and Work of Sir George Adam Smith (1956–1942)* (Milton Keynes: Paternoster, 2004).

Capetz, Paul E., 'Friedrich Schleiermacher on the Old Testament', *HTR* 102 (2009), pp.297–326.

Caputo, John D., *What Would Jesus Deconstruct? The Good News of Post-Modernism for the Church* (Grand Rapids, MI: Baker Academic, 2007).

———— *The Weakness of God: A Theology of the Event* (Bloomington, IN: Indiana University Press, 2006).

Carlyle, Thomas, *On Heroes, Hero-Worship, and the Heroic in History*, ed. and with intro. by Carl Niemeyer (Lincoln, NE: University of Nebraska Press, 1966).

Chamberlain, Houston S., *Foundations of the Nineteenth Century*, 2 vols (London: J. Lane, The Bodley Head, 1913); trans. of *Die Grundlagen des Neunzehnten Jahrhunderts* (Munich: Bruckmann, 1899).

Chancey, M., *The Myth of a Gentile Galilee* (Cambridge: Cambridge University Press. 2002).

Checkland, Sydney and Olive, *Industry and Ethos: Scotland 1832–1914*, The New History of Scotland, VII (London: Edward Arnold, 1984).

Cheyne, A. C., *The Transforming of the Kirk: Victorian Scotland's Religious Revolution* (Edinburgh: St Andrew Press, 1983).

Christie, Clive, *Race and Nation: A Reader* (London: I.B.Tauris, 1998).

Colley, Linda, *Britons: Forging the Nation 1707–1837* (London: Pimlico, 2003).

Collini, Stefan, *Public Moralists: Political Thought and Intellectual Life in Britain 1850–1930* (Oxford: Clarendon, 1991).

Coomaraswamy, Radhika, 'Special Rapporteur of the Commission on Human Rights on violence against women, to World Conference Against Racism, Racial Discrimination, Xenophobia And Related Intolerance, Geneva, 30 July to 10 August 2001', available online at http://www.unhchr.ch/huridocda/huridoca.nsf/(Symbol)/A.CONF.189.PC.3.5.En.

Cramer, J., U. Laible and H. D. Nägelke, *Karl Friedrich Schinkel: Führer zu seinen Bauten. Band I: Berlin und Potsdam*, 3rd edn (Munich and Berlin: Deutsche Kunstverlag, 2008).

Cromwell, R. S., *David Friedrich Strauss and His Place in Modern Thought* (Fair Lawn, NJ: Burdock, 1974).

Crossan, John D., *In Parables: The Challenge of the Historical Jesus* (New York: Harper and Row, 1973).

Crossley, James G. 'Jesus the Jew since 1967' in Moxnes et al. (eds), *Jesus beyond Nationalism*, pp.119–37.

Curtis, S., 'The Son of Man and God the Father: The social Gospel and Victorian masculinity', in Mark C. Carnes and C. Griffin (eds), *Meanings of Manhood: Constructions of Masculinity in Victorian America* (Chicago and London: University of Chicago Press, 1990), pp.67–78.

Cusk, Rachael, 'Shakespeare's daughters', *The Guardian* (12 December 2009), Review section, pp, 2–3.

Daly, Herman E. and John B. Cobb, *For the Common Good: Redirecting the Economy toward Community, the Environment, and a Sustainable Future* (Boston: Beacon Press, 1994).

Darwin, Charles, *On the Origin of the Species* (London: Murray, 1859).

Davis, John, *The Landscape of Belief: Encountering the Holy Land in Nineteenth-Century American Art and Culture* (Princeton: Princeton University Press, 1996).

Davis, Kathy, 'Intersectionality as buzzword: A sociology of science perspective on what makes a feminist theory successful', *Feminist Theory* 9 (2008), pp.67–83.

Davis, Moshe and Yehoshua Ben-Arieh (eds), *With Eyes towards Zion III: Western Societies and the Holy Land* (New York: Praeger, 1991).

Dawson, Jerry F., *Friedrich Schleiermacher: The Evolution of a Nationalist* (Austin: University of Texas Press, 1966).

DeLaura, David J., *Hebrew and Hellene in Victorian England: Newman, Arnold and Pater* (Austin, TX: University of Texas Press, 1969).

Dilthey, W., *Leben Schleiermachers*, vol. I (Berlin: Reimers, 1870).

Donnachie, Ian, 'The Enterprising Scot', in I. Donnachie and C. Whatley (eds), *The Manufacture of Scottish History* (Edinburgh: Polygon, 1992), pp.90–105.

Doumani, Beshara B., 'Rediscovering Ottoman Palestine: Writing Palestinians into history', *Journal of Palestine Studies* xxi/2 (1992), pp.5–28.

Dowling, Linda, *Hellenism and Homosexuality in Victorian Oxford* (Ithaca: Cornell University Press, 1994).

Driver, Felix, 'Moral geographies: Social science and the urban environment in mid-nineteenth century England', *Transactions of the Institute of British Geographers* NS 13 (1988), pp.275–87.

Dudink, Stefan and Karen Hagemann, 'Masculinity in politics and war in the age of democratic revolution, 1750–1850', in Dudink et al. (eds), *Masculinities in Politics and War*, pp.3–21.

Dudink, Stefan, Karen Hagemann and John Tosh (eds), *Masculinities in Politics and War: Gendering Modern History* (Manchester: Manchester University Press, 2004).

Duncan, James and David Ley (eds), *Place, Culture, Representation* (London: Routledge, 1993).

Echternkamp, Jörg and Sven Oliver Müller (eds), *Die Politik der Nation: Deutscher Nationalismus in Krieg und Krisen 1760–1960* (Munich: R. Oldenborg, 2002).

El-Haj, Nadia Abu, *Facts on the Ground: Archaeological Practice and Territorial Self-Fashioning in Israeli Society* (Chicago and London: Chicago University Press, 2001).

Elizondo, Virgilio, 'Jesus the Galilean Jew in Mestizo Theology', *Theological Studies* 70 (2009), pp.262–80.

——— *Galilean Journey: The Mexican Promise* (Maryknoll, NY: Orbis, 1983).

Eriksen, Thomas Hylland, 'What is cultural complexity?' in Moxnes et al. (eds), *Jesus Beyond Nationalism*, pp.9–24.

——— *Ethnicity and Nationalism*, 2nd edn (Pluto: London, 2002).

Evron, Boas, *Jewish State or Israeli Nation?* (Bloomington, IN: Indiana University Press, 1991).

Farrar, Frederic W., *The Life of Christ* (London: Cassell, Petter and Galpin, 1874).

Fiorenza, Elisabeth Schüssler, *Jesus and the Politics of Interpretation* (New York and London: Continuum, 2000).

Foucault, Michel, *The Use of Pleasure*, The History of Sexuality Vol.2 (New York: Pantheon, 1985).

Fox, Richard W., *Jesus in America: Personal Savior, Cultural Hero, National Obsession* (San Francisco: Harper, 2004).

France, Peter and William St Clair (eds), *Mapping Lives: The Uses of Biography* (Oxford: Oxford University Press, 2002).

Gathercole, Simon J., 'The critical and dogmatic agenda of Albert Schweitzer's *The Quest of the Historical Jesus*', *Tyndale Bulletin* li/2 (2000), pp.261–83.

Gavish, Dov, *A Survey of Palestine under the British Mandate, 1920–1948* (London and New York: Routledge, 2005).

—— 'French cartography of the Holy Land in the nineteenth century', in *Palestine Exploration Quarterly* 126 (1994), pp.24–31.

Gay, Peter, 'The manliness of Christ', in R. W. Davis and R. J. Helmstadter (eds), *Religion and Irreligion in Victorian Society: Essays in Honour of R. K. Webb* (London: Routledge, 1992), pp.102–16.

Geiss, I., *The Question of German Unification 1806–1996* (London and New York: Routledge, 1997).

Georgi, Dieter, 'The interest in Life of Jesus theology as a paradigm for the social history of biblical criticism', *HTR* 85 (1992), pp.51–83.

Gibb, Andrew, *Glasgow: The Making of a City* (London: Croom Helm, 1983).

Giesen, Bernhard, *Intellectuals and the Nation: Collective Identity in a German Axial Age*, trans. by N. Levis and A. Weisz (Cambridge: Cambridge University Press, 1998).

Gobineau, Arthur, *Essai sur l'inégalité des races humaines* (Paris: Firmin Didot Frères, 1853–5).

Golder, Herbert, 'Introduction to "David Strauss: Writer and Confessor"', in Friedrich Nietzsche, *Unmodern Observations*, ed. by William Arrowsmith (New Haven: Yale University Press, 1990), pp.3–14.

Gore, Keith, *L'idée de Progrès dans la Pensée de Renan* (Paris: Nizet, 1970).

Graf, Friedrich Wilhelm, 'La théologie critique au service de l'émancipation bourgeoise: David Friedrich Strauss (1808–1874)', *RevTheolPhil* 130 (1998), pp.151–72.

—— 'The Old Faith and the New: the late theology of D. F. Strauss', in H. G. Reventlow and W. Farmer (eds), *Biblical Studies and the Shifting of Paradigms, 1850–1914*, JSOTS 192 (Sheffield, 1995), pp.223–45.

—— 'D. F. Strauss' radikaldemokratische Christologie', *TRu* 54 (1989), pp.190–5.

—— *Kritik und Pseudo-Spekulation: David Friedrich Strauß als Dogmatiker im Kontext der positionellen Theologie seiner Zeit*, Münchner Monographien zur historischen und systematischen Theologie 7 (München: Keiser, 1982).

Gray, Marion W., *Prussia in Transition: Society and Politics under the Stein Reform Ministry of 1808* (Philadelphia: The American Philosophical Society, 1986).

Gullestad, Marianne, *Plausible Prejudice: Everyday Experiences and Social Images of Nation, Culture and Race* (Oslo: Universitetsforlaget, 2006).

Habermas, Jürgen, *The Postnational Constellation: Political Essays*, trans, ed. and with intro. by Max Pensky (Cambridge: Polity, 2001).

—— 'What is a people? The Frankfurt "Germanist Assembly" of 1846 and the self-understanding of the humanities in the Vormärz', in Habermas, *The Postnational Constellation*, pp.1–25.

Hacker, Jacob S. and Paul Pierson, *Winner-Take-All Politics: How Washington Made the Rich Richer – And Turned Its Back on the Middle Class* (New York: Simon and Schuster, 2010).

Hagemann, Karen, 'German heroes: The cult of the death for the fatherland in nineteenth-century Germany', in Dudink et al. (eds), *Masculinities in Politics and War*, pp.116–34.

—— 'A valorous Volk family: The nation, the military, and the gender order in Prussia in the time of the anti-Napoleonic wars, 1806–15', in I. Blom, K. Hagemann and C. Hall (eds), *Gendered Nations: Nationalisms and Gender Order in the Long Nineteenth Century* (Oxford and New York: Berg, 2000), pp.179–205.

Hall, Donald E. (ed.), *Muscular Christianity: Embodying the Victorian Age* (Cambridge: Cambridge University Press, 1994).

Halpern, Ben, *The Idea of the Jewish State*, 2nd edn (Cambridge, MA: Harvard University Press, 1969).

Hanson, K. C., and Douglas E. Oakman, *Palestine in the Time of Jesus: Social Structures and Social Conflicts*, 2nd edn (Minneapolis: Fortress, 2008).

Harris, Horton, *David Friedrich Strauss and His Theology* (Cambridge: Cambridge University Press, 1973).

Harvey, David, *The David Harvey Reader*, ed. by Noel Castree and Derek Gregory (Oxford: Blackwell, 2006).

Hauschild, Thomas, 'Christians, Jews and the Other in German anthropology', *American Anthropologist* 99 (1997), pp.746–53.

Hellemo, Geir, *Adventus Domini: Eschatological Thought in 4th-Century Apses and Catecheses*, supplements to *Vigiliae Christianae* vol. 5, trans. by Elinor Ruth Waaler (Leiden: Brill, 1989).

Herder, J. G., *Abhandlung über den Ursprung der Sprache* (Berlin: Voss. 1772).

Hermann, Ulrich, 'Einleitung', in Ulrich Hermann (ed.), *Volk – Nation – Vaterland*, Studien zum achtzehnten Jahrhundert 18 (Hamburg: Meiner, 1996), pp.11–18.

Herzog, Frederick, 'Schleiermacher and the problem of power,' in his *Justice Church: The New Function of the Church in North American Christianity* (Maryknoll, NY: Orbis, 1980), pp.55–69.

Heschel, Susannah, *The Aryan Jesus: Christianity, Nazis and the Bible* (Princeton: Princeton University Press, 2007).

—— *Abraham Geiger and the Jewish Jesus* (Chicago: Chicago University Press, 1998).

Hettne, Björn, Sverker Sörlin, Uffe Østergård. *Den globala nationalismen: nationalstatens historia och framtid*, 2nd edn (Stockholm: SNS Förlag, 2006).

Hill, Mike, *After Whiteness: Unmaking an American Majority* (New York: New York University Press, 2004).

Horne, John, 'Masculinity in politics and war in the age of the nation-state and world wars, 1850–1950', in Dudink et al. (eds): *Masculinities in Politics and War*, pp.22–40.

Horsley, Richard A., *Galilee, History, Politics, People* (Valley Forge: PA: Trinity, 1995).

Houghton, Walter E., *Victorian Frame of Mind 1830–1870* (New Haven: Yale University Press, 1957).

Hughes, Thomas, *The Manliness of Christ* (London: Macmillan and Co., 1879).

Hunt, Tristram, *Building Jerusalem: The Rise and Fall of the Victorian City* (London: Weidenfeld and Nicolson, 2004).

Iggers, Georg, G., *German Conception of History: The National Tradition of Historical Thought from Herder to the Present* (Middletown, CT: Wesleyan University Press, 1968).

Jansen, Christian, 'Deutsches Volk und Deutsches Reich: Zur Pathologie der Nationalstaatsidee im 19. Jahrhundert', in W. Bialas (ed.), *Die nationale Identität der Deutschen* (Frankfurt: Peter Lang, 2002), pp.167–94.

Jenkyns, R., *The Victorians and Ancient Greece* (Oxford: Blackwell, 1980).

Jones, Sian, *The Archaeology of Ethnicity: Constructing Identities in the Past and Present* (London: Routledge, 1997).

Joyce, Patrick, *Democratic Subjects: The Self and the Social in Nineteenth Century England* (Cambridge: Cambridge University Press, 1994).

Kelley, Shawn, *Racializing Jesus: Race, Ideology and the Formation of Modern Biblical Scholarship* (London and New York: Routledge, 2002).

Kelsey, C. L., *Schleiermacher's Preaching: Dogmatics and Biblical Criticism. The Interpretation of Jesus Christ in the Gospel of John* (Eugene, OR: Pickwick, 2007).

Kernohan, R. D., *The Road to Zion: Travellers to Palestine and the Land of Israel* (Edinburgh: Handsel, 1995).

Kingsley, Charles, *His Letters and Memories of his Life*, 12th edn, 2 vols (London: Kegan Paul, 1878).

Kirk, Neville, *Change, Continuity and Class: Labour in British Society, 1850–1920* (Manchester and New York: MacMillan, 1998).

Khalidi, Rashid, *Palestinian Identity: The Construction of Modern National Consciousness* (New York: Columbia, 1997).

Kloppenborg Verbin, John S., *Excavating Q: The History and the Setting of the Sayings Gospel* (Edinburgh: T. and T. Clark, 2000).

Knight, Frances, '"Male and Female He created Them": Men, women and the question of gender', in J. Wolffe (ed.), *Religion in Victorian Britain, V: Culture and Empire* (Manchester and New York: Manchester University Press, 1997), pp.24–57.

Kuhn, Thomas K., 'David Friedrich Strauss', *TRE* 32 (2001), pp.241–6.

Kupisch, Karl, 'The "Luther Renaissance"', *Journal of Contemporary History* 2 (1967), pp.29–49.

Lagarde, Paul de, *Deutsche Schriften* 2. Print (Göttingen: Dieterische Verlagsbuchhandlung, 1891).

Lange, D., *Historischer Jesus oder mytischer Christus: Untersuchungen zu dem Gegensatz zwischen Friedrich Schleiermacher und David Friedrich Strauss* (Gütersloh: Gerd Mohn, 1975).

Lee, David C. J., *Ernest Renan: In the Shadow of Faith* (London: Duckworth, 1996).

Lee, Hermione, *Body-Parts: Essays on Life-Writing* (London: Chatto and Windus, 2005).

Lee, Michael E., '*Galilean Journey* revisited: Mestizaje, anti-Judaism, and the dynamics of exclusion', *Theological Studies* 70 (2009), pp.377–400.

Leersen, Joep, *National Thought in Europe: A Cultural History* (Amsterdam: Amsterdam University Press, 2006).

Lewes, George Henry, *Life of Goethe* (London: Routledge, 1855).

Lillie, Elisabeth M., 'Heroes of the mind: The intellectual elite in the work of Ernest Renan', in Graham Gargett (ed.), *Heroism and Passion in Literature: Studies in Honour of Moya Longstaffe* (Amsterdam: Rodopi, 2004), pp.133–44.

Lincoln, Bruce, *Discourse and the Construction of Society* (New York and Oxford: Oxford University Press, 1989).

Lindemann, A. S., *The Jew Accused: Three Anti-Semitic Affairs: Dreyfus, Beilis, Frank, 1894–1915* (Cambridge: Cambridge University Press, 1991).

Lipman, Vivian D. 'Britain and the Holy Land: 1830–1914', in M. Davis and Y. Ben-Arieh (eds), *With Eyes towards Zion III*, pp.195–207.

Long, Burke O., *Imagining the Holy Land* (Bloomington: Indiana University Press, 2003).

Lowe, Lisa, *Critical Terrains: French and British Orientalism* (Ithaca and London: Cornell University Press, 1991).

Lynch, Kevin, 'Another New World Order', The Globe essay on 'Drivers of Change', *Globe and Mail*, 4 September 2010, A.15.

Macleod, Norman, *The Temptation of Our Lord* (London: Strahan and Co., 1873).

Malik, Kenan, *The Meaning of Race: Race, History and Culture in Western Society* (London: MacMillan, 1996).

Manguel, Alberto and Gianni Guadalupi, *The Dictionary of Imaginary Places*, rev. edn (Toronto: Knopf, 1999).

Margadant, Jo Burr, 'Introduction' in Jo Burr Margadant (ed.), *The New Biography: Performing Femininity in Nineteenth-Century France* (Berkely and Los Angeles; London: University of California Press, 2000), pp.1–28.

Mariña, Jaqueline, *Transformation of the Self in the Thought of Friedrich Schleiermacher* (Oxford: Oxford University Press, 2008).

——— 'Christology and anthropology in Friedrich Schleiermacher', in J. Mariña (ed.), *The Cambridge Companion to Friedrich Schleiermacher*, pp.151–70.

——— (ed.) *The Cambridge Companion to Friedrich Schleiermacher*, ed. by J. Mariña (Cambridge: Cambridge University Press, 2005).

Marx, Karl, *Critique of Hegel's 'Philosophy of right'*, trans., ed. and with intro. by Joseph O'Malley (Cambridge: Cambridge University Press, 1970).

Massey, Marilyn C., *Christ Unmasked: The Meaning of The Life of Jesus in German Politics* (Chapel Hill, NC: University of North Carolina Press, 1983).

—— 'Introduction' to David Friedrich Strauss, *In Defense of my Life of Jesus against the Hegelians*, trans. and ed. by M. C. Massey (Hamden, CN: Archon, 1983), pp.ix–xxxix.

—— 'The literature of young Germany and D. F. Strauss's *Life of Jesus*', *JR* 59 (1979), pp.298–323.

Maurer, Michael, *Die Biographie des Bürgers: Lebensformen und Denkweisen in der formativen Phase des deutschen Bürgertums (1680–1815)* (Göttingen: Vandenhoeck and Ruprecht, 1996).

Melman, Billie, *Women's Orients: English Women and the Middle East, 1718–1918* (London: MacMillan, 1992).

Moreland, M., 'The inhabitants of Galilee in the Hellenistic and early Roman periods', in J. Zangenberg, H. W. Attridge and D. B. Martin (eds), *Religion, Ethnicity, and Identity in Ancient Galilee* (Tübingen: Mohr Siebeck, 2007), pp.33–59.

Moretti, Franco, *The Atlas of the European Novel 1800–1900* (London: Verso, 1998).

Morgan, Sue, '"Writing the male body": Sexual purity and masculinity in *The Vanguard*, 1884–94', in Andrew Bradstock, Sean Gill, Anne Hogan and Sue Morgan (eds), *Masculinity and Spirituality in Victorian Culture* (Basingstoke and London: MacMillan, 2000), pp.179–93.

Morris, Colin, *The Sepulchre of Christ and the Medieval West* (Oxford: Oxford University Press, 2005).

Morris, Stewart A., *The Temptation of Jesus: A study of Our Lord's Trial in the Wilderness* (London: Andrew Melrose, 1903).

Morton, H. V., *In the Steps of the Master* (London: Rich and Cowan, 1935).

Moscrop, John James, *Measuring Jerusalem: The Palestine Exploration Fund and the British Interests in the Holy Land* (Leicester and New York: Leicester University Press, 2000).

Mosse, George L., *The Image of Man: The Creation of Modern Masculinities* (Oxford: Oxford University Press, 1996).

—— *Nationalism and Sexuality: Middle-Class Morality and Sexual Norms in Modern Europe* (Madison: University of Wisconsin Press, 1985).

—— *Nationalism and Sexuality: Respectability and Abnormal Sexuality in Modern Europe* (New York: H. Fertig, 1985).

Moxnes, Halvor, 'Constructing the Galilee of Jesus in an age of ethnic identity', in M. Zetterholm and S. Byrskog (eds), *The Making of Christianity: Conflict, Contacts, and Constructions: Essays in Honor of Bengt Holmberg* (Winona Lake: Eisenbrauns, forthcoming).

———— 'Identity in Jesus' Galilee – From ethnicity to locative intersectionality', *Biblical Interpretation* 18 (2010), pp.390–416.

———— 'George Adam Smith and the moral geography of Galilee', in Zuleika Rodgers, Margaret Daly-Denton and Anne Fitzpatrick McKinley (eds), *A Wandering Galilean: Essays in Honour of Seán Freyne* (Leiden: Brill, 2009), pp.237–78.

———— *Putting Jesus in His Place: A Radical Vision of Household and Kingdom* (Louisville: Westminster John Knox, 2003).

———— 'Renan's *Vie de Jésus* as representation of the Orient', in Hayim Lapin and Dale B. Martin (eds), *Jews, Antiquity, and the Nineteenth-Century Imagination*, Studies and Texts in Jewish History and Culture XII (University Press of Maryland, 2003), pp.85–108.

———— 'The construction of Galilee as a place for the historical Jesus', *BTB* 31 (2001), pp.26–37, 64–77.

———— 'The historical Jesus: From master narrative to cultural context', *BTB* 28 (1999), pp.135–49

———— *The Economy of the Kingdom: Social Conflict and Economic Relations in Luke's Gospel* (Philadelphia: Fortress, 1988).

Moxnes, Halvor, Ward Blanton and James G. Crossley (eds), *Jesus Beyond Nationalism: Constructing the Historical Jesus in a Period of Cultural Complexity* (London: Equinox, 2009).

Murray, G., *A History of Ancient Greek Literature* (New York: Appleton and Company, 1897).

Nasaw, David, 'Historians and biography: Introduction', *American Historical Review* 114 (2009), pp.573–78.

Nash, Jennifer C., 'Re-thinking intersectionality', *Feminist Review* 89 (2008), pp.1–15.

Nassar, Issam, 'The trauma of al-Nakba: Collective memory and the rise of Palestinian national identity', in A. Sarat, N. Davidovitch, M. Alberstein (eds), *Trauma and Memory: Reading, Healing and Making Law* (Stanford, CA: Stanford University Press, 2007), pp.65–77.

Niemeyer, Carl, 'Introduction' to Thomas Carlyle, *On Heroes, Hero-Worship, and the Heroic in History* (Lincoln, NE: University of Nebraska Press, 1966), pp.vii–ixx.

Néret, Gilles (ed.), *Description de l'Egypte. Publiée par les ordres de Napoléon Bonaparte*, English trans. C. Miller, German trans. B. Blumenberg (Köln: Benedikt Taschen, 1997).

Nipperdey, Thomas, *Germany from Napoleon to Bismarck, 1800–1866*, trans. by D. Nolan (Dublin: Gill and Macmillan, 1996).

Nottmeier, Christian, 'Zwischen Preussen und Deutschland: Nation und Nationalstaat bei Friedrich Schleiermacher', in Arndt et al.: *Christentum – Staat – Kultur*, pp.337–53.

Nowak, Kurt, *Schleiermacher* (Göttingen: Vandenhoeck and Ruprecht, 2001).

—— 'Theorie der Geschichte. Schleiermachers Abhandlung "Über den Geschichtsunterricht" von 1793', in Günter Meckenstock and J. Ringleben (eds), *Schleiermacher und die wissenschaftliche Kultur des Christentums* (Berlin and New York: de Gruyter, 1991), pp.419–39.

—— *Schleiermacher und die Frühromantik* (Göttingen: Vandenhoeck and Ruprecht, 1986).

Obenzinger, Hilton, *American Palestine: Melville, Twain and the Holy Land Mania* (Princeton: Princeton University Press, 1999).

Oren, Michael B., *Power, Faith and Fantasy: America in the Middle East 1776 to the Present* (New York: Norton, 2007).

Olender, Maurice, *The Languages of Paradise*, rev. edn (New York: Other, 2002).

Olwig, K. R., 'Recovering the substantive nature of landscape', *Annals of the Association of American Geographers* 84 (1996), pp.630–53.

Osiek, Carolyn, 'The family in early Christianity: Family values revisited', *Catholic Biblical Quarterly* 58 (1996), pp.1–24.

Özkirimli, Umut, *Contemporary Debates on Nationalism: A Critical Engagement* (Basingstoke and New York: Palgrave MacMillan, 2005).

Palonen, K., *The Struggle With Time: A Conceptual History of 'Politics' as an Activity*, I (Hamburg: Lit, 2006).

Pals, Daniel L., *The Victorian 'Lives' of Jesus* (San Antonio: Trinity University Press, 1982).

Parker, Andrew, Mary Russo, Doris Sommer and Patricia Yeager (eds), *Nationalism and Sexualities* (London: Routledge, 1992).

Patmore, Coventry Kersey Dighton, *The Angel in the House* (London: John W. Parker and Son, 1854–6).

Pauck, Wilhelm, 'Schleiermacher's conception of history and Church history', in his *From Luther to Tillich* (San Fransico: Harper, 1984), pp.67–79.

Paul, Jean-Marie, *D. F. Strauss (1808–1874) et son époque* (Paris: Société les belles lettres, 1982).

Paulin, Roger, 'Adding stones to the edifice: Patterns of German biography', in France and St Clair (eds): *Mapping Lives*, pp.103–14.

Pelikan, Jaroslav, *Jesus Through the Centuries: His Place in the History of Culture* (New Haven: Yale University Press, 1985).

Pensky, Max, 'Editor's Introduction' to Habermas: *The Postnational Constellation*, pp.vii–xvii.

Perkins, Mary Ann, *Nation and Word, 1770–1850: Religious and Metaphysical Language in European National Consciousness* (Aldershot: Ashgate, 1999).

Pholien, Georges, *Les deux 'Vie de Jésus' de Renan*, (Paris: 1983), fasc.239.

Planert, Ute, 'Wann beginnt der "moderne" deutsche Nationalismus?', in Echternkamp and Müller (eds): *Die Politik der Nation*, pp.25–59.

Protero, Stephen, *The American Jesus: How the Son of God Became a National Icon* (New York: Farrar, Straus and Giroux, 2003).

Provan, Iain, 'The end of (Israel's) history? K. W. Whitelam's *The Invention of Ancient Israel*. A review article', *Journal of Semitic Studies* xlii/2 (1997), pp.283–300.

Ranke, Leopold von, *Deutsche Geschichte im Zeitalter der Reformation*, 3rd edn (Berlin: Duncker, 1852).

Readman, Paul, *Land and Nation in England: Patriotism, National Identity, and the Politics of the Land* (Woodbridge, UK and Rochester, NY: Boydell Press, 2008).

Reed, Jonathan L., *Archaeology and the Galilean Jesus* (Harrisburg, PA: Trinity, 2000).

Reetz, Dankfried, *Schleiermacher im Horizont preussischer Politik* (Waltrop: Spenner, 2002).

Reicher, Stephen and Nick Hopkins, *Self and Nation: Categorization, Contestation and Mobilization* (London: Sage Publications, 2001).

Reicke, Bo, 'From Strauss to Holtzmann and Meijboom: Synoptic theories advanced during the consolidation of Germany, 1830–70', *NovT* 29 (1987), pp.1–21.

Reimarus, Hermann Samuel, *Fragments*, ed. by Charles H. Talbert (Philadelphia: Fortress, 1970).

Renan, Ernest, *Qu'est-ce qu'une nation? [What is a Nation?]*, Intro. by Charles Taylor, trans. W. R. Taylor (Toronto: Tapir, 1996).

——— *Histoire et Parole: Oeuvres Diverses*, ed. by L. Rétat (Paris: R. Laffont, 1984).

——— *Vie de Jésus* in Henriette Psichari (ed.), *Oeuvres complètes de Ernest Renan* IV (Paris: Calmann-Lévy, 1947), pp.11–371.

—— 'Nouvelle lettre à M. Strauss', in Henriette Psichari (ed.), *Oeuvres complètes*, I (Paris: Calmann-Lévy, 1947), pp.449–62.

—— *Letters from the Holy Land*, trans. by Lorenzo O'Rourke (New York: Doubleday, 1904).

—— *Vie de Jésus* (Paris: Michel Lévy, 1863); *The Life of Jesus*, Intro. by J. H. Holmes (New York: Modern Library, 1927).

—— *De l'Origine du Langage*, 2nd edn (Paris: Michel Lévy, 1858).

Renan, E. and M. Berthelot, *Correspondance: 1847–1892* (Paris: Calmann-Lévy, 1898).

Rétat, Laudyce, *Religion et Imagination Religieuse: Leur formes et leurs rapports dans l'oeuvre d'Ernest Renan* (Paris: Klincksieck, 1977).

Rieger, Joerg, *Christ and Empire* (Minneapolis: Fortress, 2007).

Riesen, Richard Allan, *Criticism and Faith in Late Victorian Scotland: A. B. Davidson, William Robertson Smith and George Adam Smith* (New York and London: Lanham, 1985).

Roberts, David, *Jerusalem and the Holy Land Rediscovered: The Prints of David Roberts (1796–1864)*, contrib. by W. D. Davies, Eric M. Meyers and S. Walker Schroth, Foreword by M. P. Mezzatesta (Durham, NC: Duke University Museum of Art, 1996).

Roe, Glenn H., 'Contre Taine et Renan: Charles Péguy and the metaphysics of modern history', *French Forum* xxxiv/2 (2009), pp.17–37.

Rogers, Mary Eliza, *Domestic Life in Palestine* (London: Belle and Daldy, 1862).

Ruiz, Jean-Pierre. 'Good fences and good neighbors? Biblical scholars and theologians', *Journal of Hispanic/Latino Theology* 14 (May 2007), online at http://www.latinotheology.org/2007/fences_neighbors.

Sagarra, Eda, *A Social History of Germany 1648–1914* (London: Methuen, 1977).

Said, Edward W., *Culture and Imperialism* (New York: Vintage 1993).

—— *Orientalism* (New York: Random House, 1978).

—— *Beginnings: Intention and Method* (New York: Columbia University Press, 1975).

Schama, Simon, *Landscape and Memory* (London: HarperCollins, 1995).

Scheffler, Eben, 'Ernest Renan's Jesus: An appraisal', *Neotestamentica* 33 (1999), pp.179–97.

Scheuer, Helmut, *Biographie: Studien zur Funktion und zum Wandel einer literarischen Gattung vom 18. Jahrhundert bis zur Gegenwart* (Stuttgart: Metzlersche Verlagsbuchhandlung, 1979).

Schläger, J., 'Biography: Cult as culture', in J. Batchelor (ed.), *The Art of Literary Biography* (Oxford: Carendon, 1995), pp.57–71.

Schleiermacher, Friedrich, 'Rede am Geburtstage Friedrich des Grossen am 24sten Januar 1817 in der Akademie der Wissenschaften' in Friedrich Schleiermacher, *Akademievorträge*, ed. by Martin Rössler, KGA i/11 (Berlin: de Gruyter, 2002), pp.241–50.

—— 'Über den Geschichtsunterricht', KGA i/1, (Berlin: de Gruyter, 1998), pp.489–97.

—— *Vorlesungen über die Lehre vom Staat*, ed. by W. Jaeschke, KGA ii/8 (Berlin: de Gruyter, 1998).

—— *Friedrich Schleiermacher – eine Briefauswahl*, ed. by J. Rachold (Frankfurt: Peter Lang, 1995).

—— *On Religion: Addresses in Response to its Cultured Critics*, trans. and intro. by T. N. Tice (Richmond: John Knox, 1969).

—— *Christmas Eve*, trans. T. N. Tice (Richmond: John Knox, 1967).

—— *Der Christliche Glaube* i–ii, 2nd edn, ed. by M. Redeker (Berlin: de Gruyter, 1960; *The Christian Faith*, trans. and ed. by H. R. Mackintosh and J. S. Stewart (Edinburgh: T. and T. Clark, 1928).

—— 'Über den Begriff des großen Mannes, Am 24 Januar 1826', in Friedrich Schleiermacher, *Werke. Auswahl in vier Bänden* Band I (Leipzig: Eckhardt, 1910), pp.520–31.

—— *Das Leben Jesu*, ed. by K. A. Rütenik, Sämmtliche Werke, i/6 (Berlin: Georg Reimer, 1864); *The Life of Jesus*, ed. by J. C. Verheyden, (Philadelphia: Fortress, 1975; Repr. Mifflintown: Sigler, 1997).

Schmidt, Jochen, *Die Geschichte des Genie-Gedankens in der deutschen Literatur, Philosophie und Politik 1750–1945, Von der Romantik bis zum Ende des Dritten Reichs*, II (Heidelberg: Winter, 2004).

Schmitz, H. J., *Frühkatholizismus bei Adolf von Harnack, Rudolph Sohm und Ernst Käsemann* (Düsseldorf: Patmos, 1977).

Schölch, Alexander, *Palestine in Transformation: Studies in Social, Economic and Political Development*, trans by W. C. Young and M. C. Garrity (Washington: Institute for Palestine Studies, 1993).

Schor, Nathan, *Napoleon in the Holy Land* (London: Greenhill Books, 1999).

Schröder, Markus, *Die kritische Identität des neuzeitlichen Christentums*, Beiträge zur historischen Theologie (Tübingen: Mohr, 1996).

Schwartz, Barry, *Abraham Lincoln and the Forge of National Memory* (Chicago: University of Chicago Press, 2000).

Schweitzer, Albert, *The Kingdom of God and Primitive Christianity*, ed. by U. Neuenschwander (London: Adam and Charles Black, 1968).

———— *The Mystery of the Kingdom of God* (New York: Dood, Mead and Co., 1914).

———— *Von Reimarus zu Wrede: Eine Geschichte der Leben Jesu Forschung* (Tübingen: Mohr/Siebeck, 1906; 2nd edn *Geschichte der Leben Jesu Forschung*, 1913).

———— *The Quest of the Historical Jesus*, 1st complete edn, trans. of 2nd German edn, ed. by John Bowden (Minneapolis: Fortress, 2001).

Scott, Walter, *Letters on Demonology and Witchcraft*, 2nd edn (London: Routledge, 1885).

Seeley, John Robert, *Ecce Homo: A Survey of the Life and Work of Jesus Christ* (London: Macmillan, 1865).

Shaffer, Elinor S., 'Shaping Victorian biography', in France and St Clair (eds): *Mapping Lives*, pp.115–24.

Sheldon, Charles, *In His Steps: What would Jesus do?* (New York: Grosset and Dunlop, 1896).

Siker, Jeffrey S., 'Historizing a racialized Jesus: Case studies in the "Black Christ", the "Mestizo Christ", and white critique', *Biblical Interpretation* 15 (2007), pp.26–53.

Silberman, N. A., 'Nationalism and archaeology', in Eric M. Meyers (ed.), *Oxford Encyclopaedia of Archaeology in the Near East*, IV (New York: Oxford University Press, 1997).

Simms, Brendan, *The Struggle for Mastery in Germany, 1779–1850* (London: Macmillan, 1998).

Sluga, Glenda, 'Masculinities, nations and the New World Order', in Dudink et al. (eds): *Masculinities in Politics and War*, pp.238–56.

Smith, George Adam, *Jeremiah: Being the Baird Lecture for 1922* (London: Hodder and Stoughton, 1923).

———— *Atlas to The Historical Geography* (London: Hodder and Stoughton, 1915).

———— *Jerusalem: The Topography, Economics and History from the Earliest Times to A.D. 70* (London: Hodder and Stoughton, 1907–8).

—— *The Forgiveness of Sins and Other Sermons* (London: Hodder and Stoughton, 1904).

—— *Modern Criticism and the Preaching of the Old Testament* (London: Hodder and Stoughton, 1901).

—— *The Historical Geography of the Holy Land* (London: Hodder and Stoughton, 1st edn 1894; 16th edn 1910).

—— *Christianity and Social Life: A Course of Lectures* (Edinburgh: Macniven and Wallace, 1885).

Smith, J. Z., 'Religion, religions, religious', in M. C. Taylor (ed.), *Critical Terms for Religious Studies* (Chicago: Chicago University Press, 1998), pp.269–84.

—— *To Take Place: Toward Theory in Ritual* (Chicago: Chicago University Press, 1987).

Smith, Lilian Adam, *George Adam Smith: A Personal Memoir and Family Chronicle* (London: Hodder and Stoughton, 1943).

Sobrino, Jon, *Jesus in Latin America* (Maryknoll, NY: Orbis, 1987).

Stanley, A. P., 'Introduction' to W. Morrison (ed.), *The Recovery of Jerusalem: A Narrative of Exploration and Discovery in the City and the Holy Land* (London: Bentley, 1871).

—— *Sinai and Palestine in Connection with Their History*, new edn (New York: Armstrong, 1885).

Stinton, Diane B., *Jesus of Africa: Voices of Contemporary African Christology* (Maryknoll, NY: Orbis, 2004).

Strauss, David Friedrich, *In Defense of My Life of Jesus Against the Hegelians*, trans., ed. and with an intro. by Marilyn Chapin Massey (Hamden, CT: Archon Books, 1983).

—— *The Old Faith and the New*, 3rd English edn, trans. by Mathilde Blind (London: Asher and Co., 1874).

—— *Krieg Und Friede: Zwei Briefe an Ernst [sic]Renan, Nebst dessen Antwort auf den Ersten* (Leipzig: Hirzel, 1870).

—— *Christus des Glaubens und der Jesus der Geschichte: Eine Kritik des Schleiermacher'schen Leben Jesu* (Berlin: F. Duncker, 1865); *The Christ of Faith and the Jesus of History: A Critique of Schleiermacher's Life of Jesus*, trans. and with intro. by Leander E. Keck (Philadelphia: Fortress, 1977).

—— *Das Leben Jesu für das deutsche Volk bearbeitet* (Leipzig: Brochaus, 1864); *A New Life of Jesus*, authorized translation, 2 vols (London: Williams and Norgate, 1865); and *The Life of Jesus: For the People*, 2 vols, 2nd edn (London: Williams and Norgate, 1879).

——— *Die christliche Glaubenslehre in ihrer geschichtlichen Entwicklung und im Kampfe mit der modernen Wissenschaft* (Tübingen: C. F. Osiander, 1840–1).

——— *Das Leben Jesu kritisch bearbeitet* (Tübingen: Osiander, 1835); *The Life of Jesus, Critically Examined*, trans. from the 4th German edn by George Eliot (London: Swan Sonnenschein, 1st edn 1846; new edn 1898).

Sugirtharajah, R. S. (ed.), *Asian Faces of Jesus* (London: SCM, 1993).

Taylor, Charles, *Modern Social Imaginaries* (Durham and London: Duke University Press, 2004).

Thomson, William M., *The Land and the Book; or, Biblical Illustrations Drawn from the Manners and Customs, the Scenes and the Scenery of the Holy Land*, 2 vols (London: T. Nelson and Sons, 1859).

Tosh, John, 'Hegemonic masculinity and the history of gender', in Dudink et al. (eds), *Masculinities in Politics and War*, pp.41–60.

——— *A Man's Place: Masculinities and the Middle-Class Home in Victorian England* (New Haven and London: Yale University Press, 1999).

Tridgell, Susan, *Understanding Our Selves: The Dangerous Art of Biography* (Frankfurt: Peter Lang, 2004).

Vaage, Leif E., 'Beyond nationalism: "Jesus the Holy Anarchist"? The Cynic Jesus as eternal recurrence of the repressed', in Moxnes et al. (eds), *Jesus Beyond Nationalism*, pp.79–95.

Vial, Theodore, 'Schleiermacher and the state', in J. Mariña (ed.) *Cambridge Companion to Friedrich Schleiermacher*, pp.269–86.

Walker, P. J., '"I live not yet I for Christ liveth in me": Men and masculinities in the Salvation Army, 1865–90', in M. Roper and J. Tosh (eds), *Manful Assertions: Masculinities in Britain since 1800* (London and New York: Routledge, 1991), pp.92–112.

Walton, Stephen J., *Skaff deg eit liv! Om Biografi* (Oslo: Samlaget, 2009).

Warman, H. W., *Ernest Renan: A Critical Biography* (London: Athlone Press, 1964).

Weikart, Richard, 'The origins of social Darwinism in Germany, 1859–1895', *Journal of the History of Ideas* 54 (1993), pp.469–88.

White, Hayden, *Metahistory: The Historical Imagination in Nineteenth-Century Europe* (Baltimore: Hopkins University Press, 1973).

Whitelam, Keith W., *The Invention of Israel: The Silencing of Palestinian History* (London: Routledge, 1996).

Whitney, W. D., 'On the so-called science of religion', *Princeton Review* 57 (1881), pp.429–52.

Wilken, Robert L., *The Land Called Holy: Palestine in Christian History and Thought* (New Haven: Yale University Press, 1992).

Wilton, A. and R. Upstone (eds), *The Age of Rossetti, Byrne-Jones and Watts: Symbolism in Britain 1860–1900* (London: Tate Gallery, 1997).

Winkler, H. A., *Germany: The Long Road West*, vol. 1, 1789–1933, trans. by A. J. Sager (New York: Oxford University Press, 2006).

Winter, Thomas, *Making Men, Making Class: The YMCA and Workingmen, 1877–1920* (Chicago and London: Chicago University Press, 2002).

Wolfes, Matthias, 'Sichtweisen: Schleiermachers politische Theorie zwischen dem autoritären Nationalstaatsethos der Befreiungskriegszeit und dem deliberativen Konzept einer bürgerlichen Öffentlichkeit', in Arndt et al.: *Christentum – Staat – Kultur*, pp.375–93.

—— *Öffentlichkeit und Bürgergesellschaft: Friedrich Schleiermacher's politische Wirksamkeit*, 2 vols, Arbeiten zur Kirchengeschichte xviii/1–2 (Berlin: de Gruyter, 2004).

Wright, T. R., 'The letter and the spirit: Deconstructing Renan's *Life of Jesus* and the assumptions of modernity', *Religion and Literature* 26 (1994), pp.55–74.

Yothers, Brian, *The Romance of the Holy Land in American Travel Writing 1790–1876* (Aldershot: Ashgate, 2007).

Index of Modern Authors

Index of Subjects